Security Engineering for Cloud Computing:

Approaches and Tools

David G. Rosado
University of Castilla-La Mancha, Spain

Daniel Mellado
Rey Juan Carlos University, Spain

Eduardo Fernandez-Medina
University of Castilla-La Mancha, Spain

Mario Piattini
University of Castilla-La Mancha, Spain

Information Science
REFERENCE

Managing Director:	Lindsay Johnston
Editorial Director:	Joel Gamon
Book Production Manager:	Jennifer Romanchak
Publishing Systems Analyst:	Adrienne Freeland
Development Editor:	Myla Merkel
Assistant Acquisitions Editor:	Kayla Wolfe
Typesetter:	Deanna Jo Zombro
Cover Design:	Nick Newcomer

Published in the United States of America by
Information Science Reference (an imprint of IGI Global)
701 E. Chocolate Avenue
Hershey PA 17033
Tel: 717-533-8845
Fax: 717-533-8661
E-mail: cust@igi-global.com
Web site: http://www.igi-global.com

Library of Congress Cataloging-in-Publication Data

Security engineering for cloud computing : approaches and tools / David G. Rosado, Daniel Mellado, Eduardo Fernandez-Medina, and Mario Piattini, editors.
       pages cm
  Includes bibliographical references and index.
  Summary: "This book provides a theoretical and academic description of Cloud security issues, methods, tools and trends for developing secure software for Cloud services and applications"-- Provided by publisher.
  ISBN 978-1-4666-2125-1 (hardcover) -- ISBN 978-1-4666-2127-5 (print & perpetual access) -- ISBN (invalid) 978-1-4666-2126-8 (ebook) 1. Cloud computing--Security measures. 2. Computer security. 3. Data protection. 4. Computer networks--Security measures. I. Rosado, David G., 1977-
  QA76.585.S44 2013
  005.8--dc23
                        2012025271

British Cataloguing in Publication Data
A Cataloguing in Publication record for this book is available from the British Library.

All work contributed to this book is new, previously-unpublished material. The views expressed in this book are those of the authors, but not necessarily of the publisher.

Table of Contents

Section 1
Cloud Architecture and Patterns

Section 2
Risks and Vulnerabilities in Cloud Computing

Section 3
Hardware Security and Secure Storage and Policy Management in Cloud

Detailed Table of Contents

Section 1
Cloud Architecture and Patterns

>   *Antonio Muñoz, University of Málaga, Spain*
>   *Antonio Maña, University of Málaga, Spain*
>   *Javier González, University of Málaga, Spain*

In this chapter, the authors provide an overview of the importance of the monitoring of security properties in cloud computing scenarios. They then present an approach based on monitoring security properties in cloud systems based on a diagnosis framework that supports the specification and monitoring of properties expressed in Event Calculus (EC) as rules as the basis.

>   *Thijs Baars, Utrecht University, The Netherlands*
>   *Marco Spruit, Utrecht University, The Netherlands*

This chapter outlines the Secure Cloud Architecture (SeCA) model on the basis of data classifications, which defines a properly secured cloud architecture by testing the cloud environment on eight attributes. The SeCA model is developed using a literature review and a Delphi study with seventeen experts, consisting of three rounds.

>   *Keiko Hashizume, Florida Atlantic University, USA*
>   *Nobukazu Yoshioka, National Institute of Informatics, Japan*
>   *Eduardo B. Fernandez, Florida Atlantic University, USA*

This chapter describes some attacks in the form of misuse patterns, where a misuse pattern describes how an attack is performed from the point of view of the attacker. Specially, the authors describe three misuse patterns: Resource Usage Monitoring Inference, Malicious Virtual Machine Creation, and Malicious Virtual Machine Migration Process.

Section 2
Risks and Vulnerabilities in Cloud Computing

Chapter 4

Belén Cruz Zapata, University of Murcia, Spain
José Luis Fernández Alemán, University of Murcia, Spain

The purpose of this chapter is to provide an analysis of the most common vulnerabilities in recent years, focusing on those vulnerabilities specific to cloud computing. These specific vulnerabilities need to be identified in order to avoid them by providing prevention mechanisms, and the following questions have therefore been posed: What kinds of vulnerabilities are increasing? Has any kind of vulnerability been reduced in recent years? What is the evolution of their severity?

Chapter 5

Miguel Torrealba S., Simón Bolívar University, Venezuela
Mireya Morales P., Simón Bolívar University, Venezuela
José M. Campos, Simón Bolívar University, Venezuela
Marina Meza S., Simón Bolívar University, Venezuela

This chapter proposes a software prototype called 2thecloud, programmed in HTML and PHP under free software guidelines, whose main objective is to allow end users to be aware of imminent cloud dangers. To do this, the user must undergo a metacognitive process of basic risk analysis, which suggested result would be to what cloud the object should go.

Chapter 6

Shareeful Islam, University of East London, UK
Haralambos Mouratidis, University of East London, UK
Edgar R. Weippl, Secure Business Austria, Austria

In this chapter, the authors propose a goal-driven risk management modeling (GSRM) framework, to assess and manage risks, which supports analysis from the early stages of the cloud-based systems development. The approach explicitly identifies the goals that the system must fulfill, and the potential risk factors that obstruct the goals, so that suitable control actions can be identified to control such risks.

Chapter 7

Kashif Kifayat, Liverpool John Moores University, UK
Thar Baker Shamsa, Manchester Metropolitan University, UK
Michael Mackay, Liverpool John Moores University, UK
Madjid Merabti, Liverpool John Moores University, UK
Qi Shi, Liverpool John Moores University, UK

This chapter reviews the potential vulnerabilities of Cloud-based architectures and uses this as the foundation to define a set of requirements for reassessing risk management in Cloud Computing.

Section 3
Hardware Security and Secure Storage and Policy Management in Cloud

Chapter 8

Wassim Itani, American University of Beirut, Lebanon
Ayman Kayssi, American University of Beirut, Lebanon
Ali Chehab, American University of Beirut, Lebanon

In this chapter, the authors present a set of hardware-based security mechanisms for ensuring the privacy, integrity, and legal compliance of customer data as it is stored and processed in the cloud. The presented security system leverages the tamper-proof capabilities of cryptographic coprocessors to establish a secure execution domain in the computing cloud that is physically and logically protected from unauthorized access.

Chapter 9

Jacques Jorda, Institut de Recherche en Informatique de Toulouse, Université Paul Sabatier, France
Abdelaziz M'zoughi, Institut de Recherche en Informatique de Toulouse, Université Paul Sabatier, France

Data storage appears as a central component of the problematic associated with the move of processes and resources in the cloud. Whether it is a simple storage externalization for backup purposes, use of hosted software services or virtualization in a third-party provider of the company computing infrastructure, data security is crucial. This security declines according to three axes: data availability, integrity, and confidentiality.

Chapter 10

Hassan Takabi, University of Pittsburgh, USA
James B. D. Joshi, University of Pittsburgh, USA

In this chapter, the authors discuss access control systems and policy management in cloud computing environments. The cloud computing environments may not allow use of a single access control system, single policy language, or single management tool for the various cloud services that it offers.

Foreword

Cloud Computing is a model which enables the ubiquitous, convenient, on-demand network access to a shared pool of configurable computing resources (e.g., networks, servers, storage, applications, and services) that can be rapidly provisioned and released with minimal management effort or service provider interaction.

Although the adoption of Cloud computing brings many benefits, security is considered to be a significant barrier to this adoption. Organizations and individuals are often concerned about how security, privacy, and integrity can be maintained in this new environment. The security engineering that is applied to Cloud computing is therefore a fundamental aspect if a systematic, disciplined, secure approach to the development, operation, and maintenance of software is to be obtained. The security engineering that is focused on migration approaches of legacy systems is also a fundamental aspect in the adoption of Cloud computing by organizations and companies who additionally wish to migrate the security aspects of their existing applications and systems.

There are numerous security challenges in Cloud Computing that must be researched and studied, such as access control and user authentication, regulatory compliance, legal issues, data safety, data separation and data segregation, business continuity, recovery, lack of control, lack of visibility, lack of manageability, loss of governance, compliance risk, isolation failure, data protection, management interfaces and access configuration, and integration with internal security. This book covers many of the challenges related to the security of Cloud computing which have been written by internationally recognized leaders in this field, and the importance of and need for research into security for Cloud computing is evident in each chapter.

The first section of the book deals with security architectures, the security aspects and properties to be considered in these cloud architectures, and misuse patterns for Cloud environments.

The second section takes a look at existing risks and vulnerabilities in Cloud Computing, and at various risk analysis and management approaches for this kind of systems.

The third section of the book is focused, on the one hand, on hardware security and secure storage and, on the other, on policy management in the Cloud.

This book is therefore recommended for practitioners and researchers working in Cloud computing security. The various topics presented in this book open a wide range of possibilities from a researcher's point of view, with numerous references and attractive proposals. The readers can discover the state–of–the-art and importance of security in Cloud computing and understand what the main vulnerabilities, attacks, and risks are in order to propose security solutions, tools, mechanisms, services or standards with which to solve and avoid these issues. This book can also help its readers to make decisions about which security aspects, requirements, services, or mechanisms should be taken into account if they wish to migrate their applications or systems to the Cloud or develop them in Cloud development platforms.

Rajkumar Buyya
The University of Melbourne, Australia

Rajkumar Buyya *is Director of the Cloud Computing and Distributed Systems Laboratory in the Department of Computing and Information Systems at the University of Melbourne, Australia. His research objective is to innovate and advance the field of Internet-based distributed computing, software engineering, grid and cloud computing, and its e-science and e-business applications with distinction. His research interests also include network-based computer architecture and operating systems, parallel and distributed computing systems (cluster, grid, cloud, and peer-to-peer systems), utility computing, and internet-scale service-oriented software engineering. He earned his PhD from Monash University, his Master of Engineering from Bangalore University, and his Bachelor of Engineering from University of Mysore, all in Computer Science and Engineering.*

Preface

Cloud Engineering is a multidisciplinary method which is focused on Cloud services and encompasses contributions from diverse areas such as software engineering and security engineering. The incorporation of security into engineering processes, and the application of security engineering ensure that Cloud systems have been analyzed, designed, built, tested, deployed, and developed in the most reliable, correct, robust, and secure manner.

The need to investigate and propose security solutions for Cloud Computing is therefore justified in order to ensure and improve the quality and security of all services, applications, tools, and models based on Cloud computing. This requires the analysis and in-depth study of how security in software engineering can be used and managed for Cloud Computing. The development and modelling of security from the first phases of the development of Cloud systems makes is possible to obtain more robust and secure Cloud systems.

CLOUD COMPUTING

The global presence of the Internet and the introduction of the wireless networking and mobile devices that always feature in Internet connectivity have raised user expectations and their demands for services from the Internet. However, the architectures required by service providers to enable Web 2.0 have created an IT service that is differentiated by its resilience, scalability, reusability, interoperability, security, and open platform development. This has effectively become the backbone of Cloud Computing and is considered by a number of vendors and services to be an operating system layer of its own (CPNI, Centre for the Protection of National Infrastructure 2010). Cloud Computing appears as both a computational model or paradigm and a distribution architecture, and its principal objective is to provide secure, quick, convenient data storage, and net computing services, with all computing resources being visualized as services and delivered via the Internet (Zhao, Liu, et al. 2009; Zhang, Zhang, et al. 2010). The Cloud enhances collaboration, agility, scaling, and availability, the ability to scale to fluctuations according to demand and accelerate development work, and provides the potential for cost reduction through optimized and efficient computing (Cloud Security Alliance 2009; Marinos and Briscoe 2009; CPNI, Centre for the Protection of National Infrastructure 2010; Khalid 2010).

The importance of Cloud Computing is increasing, and it is receiving growing attention in the scientific community. A study by Gartner (Gartner 2011) considers Cloud Computing to be one of the top 10 most important technologies, with a better prospect in 2013 and successive years for companies and organizations.

Cloud Computing combines a number of computing concepts and technologies such as SOA, Web 2.0, virtualization, and other technologies that rely on the Internet, thus providing common business applications online through Web browsers to satisfy users' computing needs, while the software and data are stored on the servers (Marinos and Briscoe 2009). These technologies have allowed Cloud customer organizations to achieve an improved utilization and efficiency of their service providers' infrastructure and, greater flexibility when scaling IT services up and down. In some respects, Cloud Computing represents the maturing of these technologies and is a marketing term with which to represent this maturity and the Cloud services provided (CPNI. Centre for the Protection of National Infrastructure 2010). There is commercial pressure on businesses to adopt Cloud Computing models. However, customers need to ensure that their Cloud services are driven by their own business needs rather than by providers' interests, which will be driven by short-term revenues and sales targets and long-term market share aspirations (CPNI. Centre for the Protection of National Infrastructure 2010; Rittinghouse and Ransome 2010).

NIST (NIST 2009) defines Cloud Computing as a model with which to enable convenient, on-demand network access to a shared pool of configurable computing resources (eg, networks, servers, storage, applications, and services) that can be rapidly provisioned and released with minimal management effort or service provider interaction. The essential characteristics are (NIST 2009; CPNI. Centre for the Protection of National Infrastructure 2010):

- **On-demand self-service:** A consumer can unilaterally provision computing capabilities, such as server time and network storage, as needed, and automatically without requiring human interaction with each service provider.
- **Broad network access:** Capabilities are available over the network and are accessed through standard mechanisms that promote use through heterogeneous thin or thick client platforms (e.g., mobile phones, tablets, laptops, and workstations).
- **Resource pooling:** The provider's computing resources are pooled to serve multiple consumers using a multi-tenant model, with different physical and virtual resources that are dynamically assigned and reassigned according to consumer demand. There is a sense of location independence in that the customer generally has no control over or knowledge of the exact location of the resources provided but may be able to specify location at a higher level of abstraction (e.g., country, state, or data centre). Examples of resources include storage, processing, memory, and network bandwidth.
- **Rapid elasticity:** Capabilities can be elastically provisioned and released, in some cases automatically, in order to scale rapidly outward and inward commensurate with demand. To the consumer, the capabilities available for provisioning often appear to be unlimited and can be appropriated in any quantity at any time.
- **Measured service:** Cloud systems automatically control and optimize resource use by leveraging a metering capability at some level of abstraction appropriate to the type of service (e.g., storage, processing, bandwidth, and active user accounts). Resource usage can be monitored, controlled, and reported, providing transparency for both the provider and consumer of the service utilized.
- **Pay per use:** Capabilities are charged using a metered, fee-for-service, or advertising based billing model to promote optimization of resource use. Examples are: measuring the storage, bandwidth, and computing resources consumed, and charging for the number of active user accounts per month. Clouds within an organization accrue costs between business units and may or may not use actual currency.

TYPES OF CLOUD MODELS

This Cloud model promotes availability and is composed of three service models (NIST 2009; Zhang, Cheng et al. 2010; Subashini and Kavitha 2011):

- **Cloud Software as a Service (SaaS):** The capability provided to the consumer is to use the provider's applications running on a Cloud infrastructure. The applications are accessible from various client devices through a thin client interface such as a Web browser (e.g., Web-based email). SaaS refers to providing on demand applications over the Internet.
- **Cloud Platform as a Service (PaaS):** The capability provided to the consumer is to deploy on the Cloud infrastructure consumer-created or acquired applications created using programming languages and tools supported by the provider. PaaS refers to providing platform layer resources, including operating system support and software development frameworks that can be used to build higher-level services.
- **Cloud Infrastructure as a Service (IaaS):** The capability provided to the consumer is to provision processing, storage, networks, and other fundamental computing resources where the consumer is able to deploy and run arbitrary software, which can include operating systems and applications. IaaS refers to on-demand provisioning of infrastructural resources, usually in terms of Virtual Machines (VMs).

There are three types of cloud deployment models available. However, there are is another type of cloud deployment model known as Community Cloud which is also being used in some instances (NIST 2009):

- **Private Cloud:** The Cloud infrastructure is operated solely for an organization. It may be managed by the organization or a third party and may exist on or off the premises.
- **Community Cloud:** The Cloud infrastructure is shared by several organizations and supports a specific community that has shared concerns (e.g., mission, security requirements, policy, and compliance considerations). It may be managed by the organizations or a third party and may exist on or off the premises.
- **Public Cloud:** The Cloud infrastructure is made available to the general public or a large industry group and is owned by an organization selling Cloud services.
- **Hybrid Cloud:** The Cloud infrastructure is a composition of two or more clouds (private, community, or public) that remain unique entities but are bound together by standardized or proprietary technology that enables data and application portability (e.g., cloud bursting for load-balancing between clouds).

SECURITY IN CLOUD COMPUTING

Although there are many benefits involved in adopting Cloud Computing, there are also some significant barriers to its adoption. One of the most significant barriers is security, followed by issues regarding compliance, privacy, and legal matters (KPMG 2010). Since Cloud Computing represents a relatively new computing model, there is a great deal of uncertainty as to how security at all levels (e.g., network, host, application, and data levels) can be achieved. This uncertainty has consistently led information executives to state that security is their number one concern as regards Cloud Computing (Mather, Kumaraswamy et al. 2009).

Security is the main obstacle for many organizations in their move to the Cloud, and is related to risk areas such as external data storage, dependency on the "public" internet, lack of control, multi-tenancy, and integration with internal security. Compared to traditional technologies, the Cloud has many specific features, such as the fact that it is large-scale, and that resources belonging to Cloud providers are completely distributed, heterogeneous and totally virtualized. Traditional security mechanisms such as identity validation authentication and authorization are no longer suitable for the Cloud (Li and Ping 2009). Security controls in Cloud Computing are, for the most part, no different to security controls in any other IT environment. However, the Cloud service models employed, the operational models, and the technologies used to enable Cloud services signify that Cloud Computing may present an organization with different risks than those associated with traditional IT solutions. Unfortunately, integrating security into these solutions is often perceived as making them more rigid (Cloud Security Alliance 2009).

The ENISA report (ENISA 2009) highlights the benefits that some small and medium size companies can attain with Cloud Computing. A smaller, cost-constrained organization may find that a Cloud deployment allows it to take advantage of large-scale infrastructure security measures that it could not otherwise afford. Some of the possible advantages include DDOS (distributed denial of service) protection, forensic image support, logging infrastructure, timely patch and update support, scaling resilience, and perimeter protection (firewalls, intrusion detection, and prevention services).

The adoption of Cloud Computing has been increasing for some time, and the maturity of the market is steadily growing not only in volume, choice, and functionality, but also in terms of the suppliers' ability to answer the complex security, regulatory and compliance questions that security oversight functions are now asking. This growth has, in part, been driven by the continued view that Cloud services will deliver cost savings and increased flexibility (Wilson 2011).

SECURITY BENEFITS IN CLOUD COMPUTING

Although there is a significant benefit to leveraging Cloud Computing, security concerns have led organizations to hesitate to move their critical resources to the Cloud (Rittinghouse and Ransome 2010). With the Cloud model, users lose control over their physical security owing to the fact that they are sharing computing resources with other companies (with the Public Cloud) and moreover, if they should decide to move the storage services provided by one Cloud vendor's services to another, these storage services may be incompatible with another vendor's services. Moreover, data backup are critical aspects with which to facilitate recovery in the case of disaster, but this also implies security concerns (Subashini and Kavitha 2011). Another concern is related to the immature use of mashup technology (combinations of Web services), which is fundamental to Cloud applications, and will inevitably cause unwitting security vulnerabilities in these applications. It is recommendable that the development tool of choice should have a security model embedded in it to guide developers during the development phase and to restrict users only to their authorized data when the system is deployed in production (Rittinghouse and Ransome 2010; Subashini and Kavitha 2011).

Others needs that organizations and customers require from Cloud providers are that they provide log data in real-time, and that they permit the government policy to be changed in response to both the opportunity and the threats that Cloud Computing brings. This will probably focus on the off-shoring of personal data and the protection of privacy, whether the data is being controlled by a third party or is off-shored to another country. Enterprises are often required to prove that their security compliance accords with regulations, standards, and auditing practices, regardless of the location of the systems in which the data resides. Standards regulate how information security management is being implemented, managed, and conducted. Issues related to virtualization are also important for enterprises and organizations because virtualization efficiencies in the Cloud require virtual machines from multiple organizations to be co-located in the same physical resources, and the dynamic and fluid nature of virtual machines will therefore make it difficult to maintain the consistency of security and ensure the auditability of records (Onwubiko 2010; Rittinghouse and Ransome 2010).

In the rush to take advantage of the benefits of Cloud Computing, not least of which is significant cost savings, many corporations are probably rushing into Cloud Computing without a serious consideration of the security implications. In order to overcome customer concerns regarding application and data security, vendors must address these issues head-on. There is a strong apprehension about insider breaches, along with vulnerabilities in the applications and the systems' availability that could lead to a loss of sensitive data and money. Such challenges may dissuade enterprises from adopting applications within the Cloud (Subashini and Kavitha 2011). The focus is not therefore upon the portability of applications, but on preserving or enhancing the security functionality provided by the legacy application and achieving a successful application migration (Cloud Security Alliance 2009).

The Cloud providers and vendors have advanced in this direction by improving the security aspects and solutions which are offered to those customers who wish to move their applications and data to the Cloud, thus making it a very attractive paradigm owing to its perceived economic and operational benefits. Cloud Computing offers a set of security benefits for Cloud applications but a cause of concern is how enterprises can migrate their security requirements in such a way that they will fit with the Cloud security solutions, and how the security of their applications and data will be maintained and managed.

Within this attractive set of benefits we can find the security benefits that are offered by the Cloud providers to those of their customers who choose to move their applications to the Cloud (ENISA 2009; Velte, Toby J. Velte et al. 2010; Jansen and Grance 2011). Of the most popular security benefits in Cloud Computing, we can define the following:

- **Security and the benefits of scale:** put simply, all kinds of security measures are cheaper when implemented on a larger scale.
- **Security as a market differentiator:** security is a priority concern for many Cloud customers; many of them will make buying choices on the basis of the reputation for confidentiality, integrity and resilience of, and the security services offered by a provider.
- **Standardised interfaces for managed security services:** large Cloud providers can offer a standardised, open interface with which to manage security services providers. This creates a more open and readily available market for security services.
- **Rapid, smart scaling of resources:** the ability of the Cloud provider to dynamically reallocate resources for filtering, traffic shaping, authentication, encryption, et cetera, to defensive measures (e.g., against DDoS attacks) has obvious advantages for resilience.

In addition to these benefits, the Cloud also has other benefits such as more timely and effective and efficient updates and defaults; there are some good security traits that come with the centralization of data; Cloud providers have the opportunity to permit their staff to specialize in security, privacy and other areas of great interest and concern to the organization; the structure of Cloud Computing platforms is typically more uniform than that of most traditional computing centres; greater uniformity and homogeneity facilitate platform hardening and enable better automation of security management activities such as configuration control, vulnerability testing, security audits, and security patching of platform components resource availability; backup and recovery; redundancy and disaster recovery capabilities are built into Cloud Computing environments and on-demand resource capacity can be used for better resilience when confronting increased service demands or distributed denial of service attacks, and for quicker recovery from serious incidents; the architecture of a Cloud solution extends to the client at the service endpoint, and is used to access hosted applications; data maintained and processed in the cloud are not such a great risk to an organization with a mobile workforce as that data being dispersed on portable computers or removable media out in the field, where the theft and loss of devices routinely occur.

AIMS OF THIS BOOK

This book attempts to provide a general knowledge base on a wide range of issues related to security in software engineering oriented towards Cloud systems, in order to show the existing problems and challenges, to show what initiatives are being carried out, to propose security approaches and any aspect of security that might be of interest to both academia and the research world, and business and social environments.

This book aims to provide a theoretical and academic description of Cloud security issues, methods, methodologies, models, architectures, designs, tools, services, techniques, challenges, and trends for developing secure software for Cloud infrastructures, platforms, services, or applications.

The book covers the following topics:

- An in-depth review of the most common vulnerabilities and attacks confronted by Cloud Computing.
- Approaches based on Security in Cloud Architectures and Misuse patterns.
- Techniques for the monitoring of security properties in Cloud Computing scenarios, analysis models of risk analyses, and goal-driven risk management.
- Hardware-based security mechanisms and data availability, integrity and confidentiality techniques for a virtualization middleware.
- Access control systems and Policy management in Cloud Computing environments.

Target Audience

The proposed book could serve as a reference for:

- CEOs and CIOs
- Security managers
- Systems specialists and architects

- Security developers
- Information security professionals
- Computer Science students.

ORGANIZATION OF THIS BOOK

This book is divided into three sections and ten chapters. Each section addresses a state-of-the-art topic concerning Security in Cloud Computing, and are as follows: *Cloud Architecture and Patterns, Risks and vulnerabilities in Cloud Computing,* and *Hardware Security, Secure Storage, and Policy Management in Cloud.*

Section 1: Cloud Architecture and Patterns

Chapter 1: *Dynamic Security Properties Monitoring Architecture for Cloud Computing*
In this chapter the authors provide an overview of the importance of the monitoring of security properties in Cloud Computing scenarios. They also present an approach based on the monitoring of security properties in Cloud systems, which is based on a diagnosis framework that supports the specification and monitoring of properties expressed in Event Calculus (EC) as rules as the basis. The provision of diagnosis information is based on the generation of alternative explanations for the events that are involved in the violations of rules. This approach is based on Virtualization Architectures, which have several threats that have been identified in the instrumentation of Virtualized Environments.

Chapter 2: *The SeCA model: Ins and Outs of a Secure Cloud Architecture*
This chapter outlines the Secure Cloud Architecture (SeCA) model on the basis of data classifications, which defines a properly secure Cloud architecture by testing the Cloud environment as regards eight attributes. The SeCA model is developed by using a literature review and a Delphi study with seventeen experts, consisting of three rounds. The authors integrate the CI3A, an extension on the CIA-triad, to create a basic framework with which to test the classification inputted. The data classification is then tested on regional, geo-spatial, delivery, deployment, governance & compliance, and network and premise attributes. After this testing has been executed, a specification for a secure Cloud architecture is outputted. The SeCA model is detailed with two example cases concerning the usage of the model in practice.

Chapter 3: *Three Misuse Patterns for Cloud Computing*
The purpose of this chapter is to describe certain attacks in the form of misuse patterns, where a misuse pattern describes how an attack is performed from the point of view of the attacker. The authors describe three misuse patterns in particular: Resource Usage Monitoring Inference, Malicious Virtual Machine Creation, and Malicious Virtual Machine Migration Process.

Section 2: Risks and Vulnerabilities in Cloud Computing

Chapter 4: *Security Risks in Cloud Computing: An Analysis of the Main Vulnerabilities*
The recent and continuous appearance of vulnerabilities in software systems makes security a vital issue if these systems are to succeed. The purpose of this chapter is to provide an analysis of the most common vulnerabilities in recent years, focusing on those vulnerabilities which are specific

to Cloud Computing. These specific vulnerabilities need to be identified in order to avoid them by providing prevention mechanisms, and the following questions have therefore been posed: What kinds of vulnerabilities are increasing? Has any kind of vulnerability been reduced in recent years? What is the evolution of their severity?

Chapter 5: *A Software Tool to Support Risks Analysis about what Should or Shouldn't go to the Cloud*
This chapter proposes a software prototype called *2thecloud*, programmed in HTML and PHP under free software guidelines, whose main objective is to allow end users to be aware of imminent dangers in the Cloud. To do this, the user must undergo a metacognitive process of basic risk analysis, whose suggested result would be to which cloud the object should go. It is supposed that the user can use this tool to develop a risk analysis capability, such that it is the user who makes the final decision concerning the selection of the cloud model (public, private, hybrid and Community) in which the object will be placed. The authors finally propose four alternatives in risk analysis calculation, which are plausibly adapted to *2thecloud*.

Chapter 6: *A Goal-Driven Risk Management Approach to Support Security and Privacy Analysis of Cloud-Based Systems*
In this chapter, the authors propose a goal-driven risk management modeling (GSRM) framework, with which to assess and manage risks, that supports analysis from the early stages of Cloud-based systems development. The approach explicitly identifies the goals that the system must fulfill, and the potential risk factors that obstruct the goals, so that suitable control actions can be identified to control such risks. The authors provide an illustrative example of the application of the proposed approach in an industrial case study in which a Cloud service is deployed to share data amongst project partners.

Chapter 7: *Real Time Risk Management in Cloud Computation*
This chapter reviews the potential vulnerabilities of Cloud-based architectures and uses this as the foundation to define a set of requirements for reassessing risk management in Cloud Computing. In order to fulfill these requirements, the authors propose a new scheme for the real-time assessment and auditing of risk in Cloud-based applications and explore this with the use case of a triage application.

Section 3. Hardware Security and Secure Storage and Policy Management in Cloud

Chapter 8: *Hardware-based Security for Ensuring Data Privacy in the Cloud*
The purpose of this chapter is to present a set of hardware-based security mechanisms with which to ensure the privacy, integrity, and legal compliance of customer data as it is stored and processed in the Cloud. The security system presented leverages the tamper-proof capabilities of cryptographic coprocessors to establish a secure execution domain in the Cloud computing that is physically and logically protected from unauthorized access. The main design goal is to maximize users' control in managing the various aspects related to the privacy of sensitive data by implementing user-configurable software protection and data privacy categorization mechanisms.

Chapter 9: *Securing Cloud Storage*
Data storage appears as a central component of the problem associated with moving processes and resources in the Cloud. Whether it is a simple storage externalization for backup purposes, the use of hosted software services, or virtualization in a third-party provider of the company computing

infrastructure, data security is crucial. This security declines according to three axes: data availability, integrity, and confidentiality. Numerous techniques targeting these three issues exist, but none presents the combined guarantees that would allow a practical implementation. In this chapter, the authors present a solution for the integration of these techniques into a virtualization middleware. A definition of the quality of service allows the specification of the nature of the security to be implemented with a seamless access.

Chapter 10: *Policy Management in Cloud: Challenges and Approaches*

In this chapter, the authors discuss access control systems and policy management in Cloud Computing environments. Cloud computing environments may not permit the use of a single access control system, single policy language, or single management tool for the various Cloud services that they offer. Access control policies may be composed in incompatible ways as a result of the diverse policy languages that are maintained separately by every Cloud provider. Heterogeneity and the distribution of these policies create problems in managing access policy rules for a Cloud environment. In this chapter, the authors discuss the challenges of policy management and introduce a Cloud based policy management framework that is designed to give users a unified control point with which to manage access policies in order to control access to their resources, no matter where they are stored.

David G. Rosado
University of Castilla-La Mancha, Spain

Daniel Mellado
Rey Juan Carlos University, Spain

Eduardo Fernández-Medina
University of Castilla – La Mancha, Spain

Mario Piattini
University of Castilla – La Mancha, Spain

REFERENCES

Cloud Security Alliance. (2009). *Security guidance for critical areas of focus in cloud computing* V2.1.

CPNI, Centre for the Protection of National Infrastructure. (2010). *Information security briefing 01/2010.* Cloud Computing.

ENISA. (2009). *Cloud computing: Benefits, risks and recommendations for information security. D. C. a. G.* Hogben, European Network and Information Security Agency.

Gartner. (2011). *Gartner identifies the top 10 strategic technologies for 2012.*

Jansen, W., & Grance, T. (2011). *Guidelines on security and privacy in public cloud computing.* NIST Special Publication 800-144.

Khalid, A. (2010). Cloud computing: Applying issues in small business. *International Conference on Signal Acquisition and Processing*, (pp. 278-281).

KPMG. (2010). *From hype to future*. KPMG's 2010 Cloud Computing Survey.

Li, W., & Ping, L. (2009). *Trust model to enhance security and interoperability of cloud environment*. 1st International Conference on Cloud Computing (CloudCom), Beijing, China.

Marinos, A., & Briscoe, G. (2009). *Community cloud computing*. 1st International Conference on Cloud Computing (CloudCom), Beijing, China.

Mather, T., & Kumaraswamy, S. (2009). *Cloud security and privacy*. O'Reilly Media, Inc.

Mell, P., & Grance, T. (2009). *The NIST definition of cloud computing*. National Institute of Standards and Technology.

Onwubiko, C. (2010). Security issues to cloud computing. In Antonopoulos, N., & Gillam, L. (Eds.), *Cloud computing: Principles, systems and applications*. Springer Verlag. doi:10.1007/978-1-84996-241-4_16

Rittinghouse, J. W., & Ransome, J. F. (Eds.). (2010). *Cloud computing implementation, management, and security*. CRC Press.

Subashini, S., & Kavitha, V. (2011). A survey on security issues in service delivery models of cloud computing. *Journal of Network and Computer Applications, 34*(1), 1–11. doi:10.1016/j.jnca.2010.07.006

Velte, A. T., Toby, P. D., & Velte, J. (2010). *Cloud computing: A practical approach*. McGraw-Hill.

Wilson, P. (2011). *Positive perspectives on cloud security* (pp. 1-5). Information Security Technical Report.

Zhang, Q., & Cheng, L. (2010). Cloud computing: State-of-the-art and research challenges. *Journal of Internet Services and Applications, 1*, 7–18. doi:10.1007/s13174-010-0007-6

Zhang, S., Zhang, S., et al. (2010). *Cloud computing research and development trend*. Second International Conference on Future Networks, Sanya, Hainan, China.

Zhao, G., Liu, J., et al. (2009). *Cloud computing: A statistics aspect of users*. 1st International Conference on Cloud Computing (CloudCom), Beijing, China.

Section 1
Cloud Architecture and Patterns

Chapter 1
Dynamic Security Properties Monitoring Architecture for Cloud Computing

Antonio Muñoz
University of Málaga, Spain

Antonio Maña
University of Málaga, Spain

Javier González
University of Málaga, Spain

ABSTRACT

In this chapter, the authors provide an overview of the importance of the monitoring of security properties in cloud computing scenarios. They then present an approach based on monitoring security properties in cloud systems based on a diagnosis framework that supports the specification and monitoring of properties expressed in Event Calculus (EC) as rules as the basis. The provision of diagnosis information is based on the generation of alternative explanations for the events that are involved in the violations of rules. This approach is based on Virtualization Architectures that presents several threats identified in the instrumentation of Virtualized Environments. The monitoring model presented in this chapter focuses on runtime supervision of applications, allowing the detection of problems in the operation of individual instances of applications and supporting the automated reconfiguration of these applications. This infrastructure has been recently designed as part of the PASSIVE project. To the best of the authors' knowledge, there is not any other infrastructure providing the same features as the one presented in this chapter. For this reason, not much directly related previous work is found in the literature.

DOI: 10.4018/978-1-4666-2125-1.ch001

INTRODUCTION

Previous chapters show a wide range of issues related to security in software engineering oriented to cloud systems, which shows the existing problems and challenges. Monitoring security properties of software systems at runtime is widely accepted as a measure of increased resilience to security attacks. Along this chapter we present an approach based on monitoring security properties in cloud systems. A diagnosis framework that supports the specification and monitoring of properties expressed in Event Calculus (EC) (Shanahan, 1999) as rules is the basis. Then the provision of diagnosis information is based on the generation of alternative explanations for the events that are involved in the violations of rules.

The emergence of highly distributed systems operating in Virtualized Environments poses significant challenges for system security and dependability (S&D) and makes it necessary to develop mechanisms supporting the dynamic monitoring and evolution of applications running on it. In these settings, seamless and dynamic evolution of software becomes a central element for ensuring the security and dependability of systems by maintaining applications up to date and ensuring that they are used correctly. This problem increases in Virtualized Environments in which sets of applications run over several virtualized environments that in turn run in parallel over the same physical layer. The term virtualization is being used inflationary to describe various different technologies. In its most general meaning, virtualization stands for an abstraction of resources that provides a logical rather than an actual physical incarnation of those resources. A deep study about the different varieties of virtualization is out of the scope of this chapter, a further work of it can be found in (Hartig et al., 2008).

The approach presented in this chapter is based on Virtualization Architectures. These architectures presents several threats have been identified in the instrumentation of Virtualized Environments. Some of them are performed through the x86 interface. Malicious guest operating systems may attack the Virtual Machine Monitor (VMM) by exploiting any security breach of the x86 interface. As VMMs cannot attack themselves since they are not directly communicated, alternatively, a malicious VMM would need to attack any other component that is shared by different VMMs, for instance a device driver. But as the communication channel between the driver and different VMMs is separated, an attack to the driver can be avoided by simply shutting this communication point. Other types of attacks are related with device drivers. Any driver that performs Direct Memory Access (DMA) has access to the entire memory of the system, and therefore could handle completely the guest. By using an Input/Output Memory Management Unit (IOMMU) the hypervisor restricts DMA transfers to its own memory avoiding this situation. Attacks to device drivers may also be performed remotely through a network card, but due to the nature of the NOVA architecture, this would only compromise the driver.

The monitoring model presented in this chapter focuses on runtime supervision of applications, allowing the detection of problems in the operation of individual instances of applications and supporting the automated reconfiguration of these applications. However, in order to enhance trust in applications, it is necessary to analyse their behaviour when used in different Virtualized environments. A high-level dynamic analysis can detect situations that are not possible with static or local dynamic analysis, such as problems in the implementations, in the models describing them or even problems caused by the interaction of different solutions. The results of this analysis provide a basis for taking actions that can support the evolution of applications in response to the identified problems.

This infrastructure has been recently designed as part of the PASSIVE project. To the best of our knowledge, there is not any other infrastructure providing the same features as the one we present in this paper. For this reason, not much directly related previous work is found in the literature. Thus, this section gives an account of some partially related approaches.

Software evolution is related to the changes that need to be introduced on a software system following its release for operational use. This evolution may happen because (i) the system needs to adapt to new contexts, (ii) some requirements have changed or (ii) new errors, attacks or vulnerabilities have been found. Surveys have shown that, for many projects, software maintenance and evolution consumes the majority of the overall software life-cycle costs, and there are indications that these costs are proportionally increasing. The detection of violations from expected properties has been proposed as the initial point of maintenance and evolution activities in software development (Chowdhury & Meyers, 1993). Work on maintenance architectures is of narrow scope and obsolete (Sellink & Verhoef, 1999). Maintenance technologies (Verhoef, 2000; van den Brand, Sellink & Verhoef, 1999) tend to ignore the very first phase of this activity, which is error detection. In fact, detection of a malfunction with the objective of facilitating evolution is not supported at all.

In our monitoring system, the absence of a signal after the elapse of a given signalling period can be detected by specifying a monitoring rule, requiring that the time between two consecutive signals from the same device should not exceed the given period. Detecting, however, the occurrence of a violation of this rule is not in itself sufficient for establishing the reasons why some device has failed to send the expected signals. In such cases, a further search for possible causes of the violation could be useful for deciding how to react to the violation.

The aim of the PASSIVE monitoring framework is to analyse problems detected in the operation of applications from a high-level point of view in order to support automated reaction and evolution of applications operating in Virtualized

environments. In achieving this goal, we have designed PASSIVE dynamic security monitoring and enforcement model. As shown in Figure 1, this infrastructure is composed by: Local Application Surveillance (LAS), Intra Platform Surveillance (IPS) and Global Application Surveillance (GAS). The IPS collects information related to violations of monitoring rules in the context of different virtualized environments in order to analyze them and come up with the expected reactions to be performed by the monitoring administrators. Usually, these reactions are materialized by means of changes in the virtualized environment configuration.

Our goal is to provide new capabilities to the Virtual Environment (VE) increasing its security and reliability. The key point of this approach is an architecture based on the PASSIVE Monitoring infrastructure including a three dimension monitoring mechanism. This mechanism has to be able to provide ease of identification of origin of errors, capturing precise and specific information about attacks, errors and malfunctioning, lowering the time required to identify and fix errors, provides an early detection, an increased protection of the VE code during the monitoring process and the increased ability to assess the integrity and compliance of the VE after.

This chapter presents two main approaches the framework and the language, which are independent but they complement each other because of the proper functionality of the proposed framework did required to be highly performance and the new language is specially tailored for this purpose.

BACKGROUND

The purpose of this section is first to give an overview of the notions of security properties from the perspective of software engineering and provide the readers with the technical background on security and dependability dynamic verification or runtime monitoring. Secondly, we present

Figure 1. Dynamic security monitoring architecture (overview)

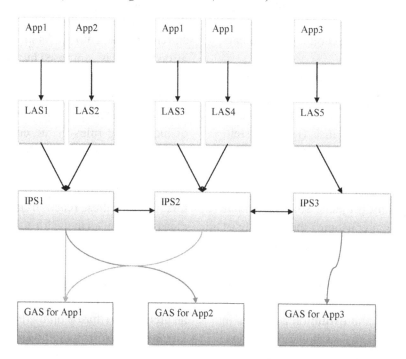

a short state of the art on abductive reasoning as technique for generating explanations.

The work presented in this chapter is part of the PASSIVE project. PASSIVE, in a nutshell, is an improved model of security for virtualized systems that tries to specifically solve the problems with the delivery of large applications in e-Government. Since the main concern that raises the shared-resource nature of virtualization technologies is the conflict with data confidentiality, this new security model will ensure: An adequate separation of concerns (e.g. policing, judiciary); That threats from co-hosted OS s can be detected and dealt with and; That public trust in application providers can be maintained even when the underlying host or any other hosted guests change.

To achieve these aims, PASSIVE offers: A policy-based Security architecture, to allow security provisions to be easily specified, and efficiently addressed; Fully virtualized resource access, with fine-grained control over device access, running on an ultra-lightweight Virtual Machine Manager and; A lightweight, dynamic

system for authentication of hosts and applications in a virtualized environment. PASSIVE lowers the barriers to adoption of virtualized hosting by government users, so that they may achieve the considerable gains in energy efficiency, reduced capital expenditure and flexibility offered by virtualization.

As for monitoring inside PASSIVE, it performs the role of observing the VM specific events and matching them to given event-sequence rules written inside monitoring specifications made in a new event-sequence language (EventSteer). Such monitoring specifications are specially tailored to ensure that specific security policies are being enforced. This is, if it is detected that the system is not working exactly as a policy intended, the monitoring will then give any relevant and specific data to the policy decision point, which will choose what the proper reaction to the problem is. Although it could also be technologically possible and very interesting to monitor events from applications running inside the VMs, that is out of the scope of the project.

In a perfect world applications and security mechanisms are correctly designed to fulfill the user needs and flawlessly implemented. Obviously monitoring in such case makes no sense, but it is different in the real world. Actually the design of applications and security mechanisms is based on wrong assumptions, oversimplified facts, vague and incomplete requirements, etc. which are then poorly implemented. In this setting, monitoring does not only make sense but becomes essential in order to achieve high levels of assurance. The role of monitoring is essentially to complement the security elements included in a system (in the wider sense: HW, OS, platform/middleware, applications...), establishing assumptions about the security of the system (e.g. whether we can assume that the different VMs running in a platform are isolated), and finding the right balance between safe and efficient but limited monitoring and powerful but slow and potentially harmful monitoring.

Traditional monitoring schemes check actual behaviour against expected execution model. Also expected execution models can be expressed as rules or policies, but when properly used in a distributed environment, it can actually help discovering unexpected interactions and flaws in the models

Since we focus on security properties from the software engineering perspective a first discussion about security requirements from relevant bibliography (Desai, 2003; Firesmith, 2003; Stickel, 1998) is essential. Security requirements cover issues related to, integrity, confidentiality, availability, non-repudiation, authentication, authorization and privacy. A complete revision in this topic includes some approaches related with dependability properties, Avizienis et al. (2000). Avizienis defined dependability as "the ability of a (computer) system to avoid failures that are more frequent or more sever, and outage durations that are longer, than is acceptable to the user(s)" and "deliver service that can be justifiably trusted". We notice that its notion of service

corresponds to the system behaviour as viewed by the user. Nevertheless there are cases such as Aspect Oriented Programming (Kiczales et al., 2001) and Monitoring Oriented Programming (Chen & Rosu, 2003) in which a monitor is generated automatically and the code is instrumented. Monitor is inserted into the code to be monitored. In the most cases, the formal specification of the requirements of the requirements that are to be dynamically verified is based on Linear Temporal Logic (LTL) (Pnueli, 1977) and variations of it including past and future time LTL (ptLTL and ftLTL respectively). In the context of monitoring oriented programming (MoP), any monitoring formalism can be added to the system. ptLTL, ftLTL and extended regular expressions (ERE), which can express patterns in strings in a compact way (Sen & Rosu, 2003), have been used to formalise properties to be monitored (Chen & Rosu, 2003). Havelund et al. (2001a; 2001b; 2003) have developed several algorithms, which are relative to temporal logic generation and monitoring. For instance, they propose algorithms for past time logic generation by using dynamic programming (Havelung & Rosu, 2002). Other logic/languages used for formalising properties are EAGLE and HAWK (D'Amorim & Havelund, 2001). EAGLE is a rule-based language, which essentially extends the μ-calculus with data parameterization and past time logic. According to the concept of Design by Contract (DBC) technique, introduced by Meyer (2000) as a built-in feature of the Eiffel programming language, specifications of pre-conditions and post-conditions can be associated with a class in the form of assertions and invariants and subsequently be compiled into runtime checks. The Monitoring and Checking (MaC) framework (Lee et al., 1999) is based on a logic that combines a form of past time LTL an models real-time via explicit clock variables. Mahbub and Spanoudakis (2004) have developed a framework for monitoring the behaviour of service centric systems which expresses the requirements to be verified against this behaviour in event calculus (1999). In this framework, event calculus is used to specify formulas describing behavioural and quality properties of service centric systems, which are either extracted automatically from the coordination process of such systems (this process is expressed in WS-BPEL) or are provided by the user. In the area of component based programming Barnett and Schulte (2001) have proposed a framework that uses executable interface specifications and a monitor to check for behavioural equivalence between a component and its interface specification. In this framework, there is no need for recompiling, re-linking, or any sort of invasive instrumentation at all, due to the fact that a proxy module is used for event emission. Robinson (2002) has proposed a framework for requirements monitoring based on code instrumentation in which the high-level requirements to be monitored are expressed in KAOS. KAOS (1993) is a framework for goal oriented requirements specification which is based on temporal logic.

This infrastructure has been designed as part of the PASSIVE project. Software evolution is related to the changes that need to be introduced on a software system following its release for operational use. This evolution may happen because (i) the system needs to adapt to new contexts, (ii) some requirements have changed or (ii) new errors, attacks or vulnerabilities have been found. Surveys have shown that, for many projects, software maintenance and evolution consumes the majority of the overall software life-cycle costs, and there are indications that these costs are proportionally increasing. The detection of violations from expected properties has been proposed as the initial point of maintenance and evolution activities in software development (Chowdhury & Meyers, 1993). Work on maintenance architectures is of narrow scope and obsolete (Sellink & Verhoef, 1999). Maintenance technologies (Verhoef, 2000; van den Brand, Sellink, & Verhoef, 1999) tend to ignore the very first phase of this activity, which is error detection. In fact, detection of a malfunction

with the objective of facilitating evolution is not supported at all.

Furthermore, as in any form of dynamic software deployment, trust in the applications that are available and can be deployed through the framework is a fundamental prerequisite. Despite the recognition of the importance and necessity of trust in human interactions and exchanges and, as a consequence, the recent increase of the volume of the literature on this topic (e.g. Corritore et al., 2003; Josang, 2007; McKnight & Chervany 1996; Resnick et al., 2000), trust is currently poorly assessed for the purposes of dynamic deployment of software. More specifically, none of these strands of work addresses effectively some important aspects of software service trust, most notably the need to assess it for dynamically composed and deployed software services, as in the case of the applications, and ground it not only on subjective opinions but also on dynamically acquired information about the behaviour and quality of a software service in diverse deployment contexts. Furthermore, each trust assessment should be accompanied by an evaluation of its accuracy and risk (Spanoudakis, 2007).

Current monitoring architectures are not well-suited for future highly distributed scenarios as cloud computing presents, indeed many security open issues in cloud computing are described in (Ko, Jeon, & Morales, 2011; Ormandy, 2007; Richter et al., 2011). Additionally existing monitoring languages are based on logical formalisms, therefore most of them are designed for expressivity, but not for the creation of highly complex specifications. Moreover, they do not help producing sound specifications. Finally, most of the time they do not consider at all the privacy aspects of the monitored system. Likewise, current monitoring languages are not designed for highly efficient implementations, thus monitoring often has a high cost in terms of efficiency, which in the end makes it unpractical. A monitoring architecture should be especially tailored to operate in future highly distributed scenarios, such as clouds, taking advantage of the characteristics of these scenarios. Monitoring languages should be designed for producing highly efficient implementations and for producing complex, but sound monitoring specifications. Additionally monitoring architectures and languages should be designed to highlight and take into account privacy aspects of the monitored systems

MAIN FOCUS OF THE CHAPTER

Problems in the Monitoring of Security Properties: Analysis and Correlation

Monitoring security properties during the operation of software systems is widely accepted as a measure of runtime verification that increases system resilience to dependability failures and security attacks. Proposed models of PASSIVE monitoring advocate the need for this form of system verification and the development of a monitoring framework that supports it. It should be noted, however, that whilst monitoring is able to detect violations of S&D properties at runtime, it cannot always provide the necessary information for understanding the reasons that underpin the violation of an S&D property and for making decisions of what would be an appropriate reaction to said violation.

Furthermore, it is often necessary to try to predict the possibility of violation using information on the current state of a system rather than wait until all the information that would enable a definite decision about the violation becomes available. This is because an accurate early prediction can widen the scope of possible reactions to the violation or even provide scope for taking pre-emptive action that prevents the violation.

Our goal is to provide new capabilities to the Virtual Environment (VE) increasing its security and reliability. The key point of this approach is an architecture based on the Monitoring infrastructure including a three-dimensional monitoring mechanism. A first version of this mechanism was

used in the Serenity EU project (Serrano et al., 2009; SERENITY, n.d.) to monitor the execution of Ambient Intelligent applications.

These are some of the objectives in detail:

- Ease of identification of the origin of errors (thanks to the LAS, IPS and GAS components, which are able to monitor each application separately or as a whole).
- Capturing precise and specific information on attacks, errors and malfunctioning
- Lowering the time required to identify and fix errors (a good set of monitoring rules helps with error identification before it further propagates in the application and becomes harder to track)
- Early detection (the monitor gives the capability to inform the developer of an unexpected behaviour right after the first case happens)
- Increased protection of the VE code during the monitoring process (by creating and using custom system monitoring rules).
- Increased ability to assess the integrity and compliance of the VE after monitoring (by being able to check at any time the current state of monitoring rules).

Monitoring security and dependability properties during the operation of software systems is widely accepted as a measure of runtime verification that increases system resilience to dependability failures and security attacks. Our monitoring model advocates the need for this form of system verification and has developed a monitoring framework, to support the monitoring of these properties during the operation of a system. It should be noted, however, that whilst monitoring is able to detect violations of S&D properties at runtime, it cannot always provide information that is necessary for understanding the reasons that underpin the violation of an S&D property and making decisions about what would be an appropriate reaction to it.

In our monitoring system, the absence of a signal after the elapse of a given signalling period can be detected by specifying a monitoring rule, requiring that the time between two consecutive signals from the same device should not exceed the given period. Detecting, however, the occurrence of a violation of this rule is not in itself sufficient for establishing the reasons why a device has failed to send the expected signals. In such cases, a further search for possible causes of the violation could be useful for deciding how to react to the violation.

As an example, consider that the violation might have been caused because the device involved malfunctions and has stopped sending signals after some point in time; the device involved is no longer present in the area covered by the server; some of the signals sent by the device have been lost in the communication channel between the device and the server; and the signal that was used to determine the start of the last period of checking was sent by an external agent (attacker) who managed to fake the identity of the device (i.e., an attacker).

Although the preceding list of possible causes is not exhaustive, it demonstrates that a decision about what would be an appropriate reaction to the violation depends on the reason(s) that have caused it and, therefore, the selection of the appropriate responding action cannot be made solely on the basis of knowledge about the violation but requires additional diagnostic information. The diagnosis mechanism of PASSIVE is invoked after the detection of a violation of a monitoring rule in order to find possible explanations of the reasons underpinning the occurrence of the events involved in the violation of the rule and assess their genuineness.

This mechanism produces diagnostic information through a process of four stages described in the following. In the generation stage, the diagnosis mechanism generates all the possible explanations of the events, which are involved in the violation. These explanations are generated using adductive reasoning based on assumptions about the behaviour of the components of the system. Application vendors provide these assumptions. In the effect identification stage, the diagnosis mechanism derives the possible consequences (effects) of the potential explanations that were identified in the previous stage. The consequences are generated from the abducted explanations and system assumptions using deductive reasoning. In the plausibility assessment stage, the diagnosis mechanism checks the expected effects of explanations against the event log to see if there are events that match them or, equivalently, the existence of further supportive evidence for the explanation. In the diagnosis generation stage, the diagnosis mechanism produces an overall diagnosis for the violation including belief measures in the genuineness of the events involved in the violation and the most plausible explanations that have been identified for these events (if any).

To deal with potential problems caused by the interaction between different VEs, a second monitoring mechanism is in charge of monitoring at the level of one particular VE. The Intra Platform Surveillance (IPS) component serves this purpose by analysing data from different VMs running on the same machine. The Intra Platform Surveillance component collects information related to the violations of monitoring rules, analyses it, and sends results to the Global Application Surveillance (GAS) component. The results sent depend on certain rules, so the administrator can choose what information is meant to be sent and what is meant to be kept as confidential.

To support monitoring of specific software pieces and detecting problems with non-compliant implementations (as well as problems in the modeling) the GAS components perform vertical analysis. They analyze data from different machines referred to the same software (application). Such GAS components receive information from several IPS components and perform a new analysis on it. Thus, the GAS components have a global view of what is the behaviour of the software in different Virtualized Environments from different machines, and thus is able to deduce proper conclusions. The existence of GAS components benefits both users of the applications and applications developers.

Solutions and Recommendations: System Behaviour Enforcement

In this section the dynamic security monitoring and enforcement model is described. As shown in figure 1, this infrastructure has three new components, namely the Local Application Surveillance (LAS), the Intra Platform Surveillance (IPS) and the Global Application Surveillance (GAS).

While other systems are usually analyzed with static and/or local methods, in a nutshell, we propose an approach that provides a solution based on a monitoring model focused on the runtime supervision on several levels: Single application instances (done by the Local Application Surveillance or LAS), a set of different applications running inside a same platform (done by the Intra Platform Surveillance or IPS), and all the instances of the same application across several platforms (done by the Global Application Surveillance or GAS).

The rationale is that in order to enhance application trust, it becomes necessary to analyze their behaviour not only as an isolated unit, but as a member of a full ecosystem living under several different virtualized environments. By making use of those three different levels acting together it is possible to build a monitor able to detect situations not possible with either of these working alone. This means that the analysis of these three levels in unison provides far more information than the sum of each one of them separated ever would, thus allowing the detection of problems not only on the implementation, but on the models describing in them or even problems caused by the interaction of different solutions.

Local Application Surveillance (LAS)

They monitor application instances (so there is one LAS per application instance) and it is the component that most closely resembles the current monitoring systems. Their job is to check if the application violates any of its established monitoring rules (the rules that express properties that need to be satisfied at runtime) and is used to detect unexpected behaviours, implementation flaws and underpin the trustworthiness of such an application.

The output of the monitoring analysis is then sent to the assigned IPS for further analysis. It is important to take into account that the integration of a LAS into a PASSIVE virtualized environment does not affect the operation of the virtualized environment itself. The purpose of the LAS is just to provide more information to the LAS administrator about the operation of applications. Using this information the LAS administrator can modify the application or virtualized environment configuration in order to adapt the system behaviour. The subcomponents are:

- **LAS Event Receiver:** Receives the application events and routes them to the analyser.
- **LAS Analyzer:** With the arriving events, it proceeds to evaluate if any of the monitoring rules from the rules databank got violated. The analysis results are expressed in terms of the LAS analyser rule violations, which express abnormal situations.
- **LAS Rules Databank:** Stores the set of the application monitoring rules. This component is managed by the GUI subcomponent.
- **LAS GUI:** A graphical user interface that communicates the LAS administrator with the LAS component. It has these main functionalities: It displays the analysis results from the analyser, manages the monitoring rules in the Databank, and inspects the contents of the Event Receiver.

Intra Platform Surveillance (IPS)

To deal with potential problems caused by the interaction between different VEs, a second monitoring mechanism is in charge of monitoring at the level of one particular VE. The Intra Platform Surveillance (IPS) component serves this purpose by analysing data from different VMs running on the same machine. The Intra Platform Surveillance component collects information related to the violations of monitoring rules, analyses it, and sends the results to the Global Application Surveillance (GAS) component. The results sent depend on certain rules, so the administrator can choose what information is meant to be sent and what is meant to be kept as confidential.

Specifically, there's one IPS per VM and they are interconnected with other IPS components of the same virtualized environment. They are responsible for analyzing the result of the LAS analyzers from the same VM, looking for security risks that might arise whenever the different VMs interact as well as whenever different applications from the same VM interact. Selected results of the monitoring analysis are then sent to the different GAS components (assuming such a GAS is available) for further analysis.

Likewise, the integration of an IPS into a PASSIVE virtualized environment does not affect the operation of the virtualized environment itself. The purpose of the IPS is just to provide more information to the IPS administrator about the operation of applications. Using this information the IPS administrator can modify the application or virtualized environment configuration in order to adapt the system behavior. The subcomponents are:

- **IPS Event Receiver:** Receives the external events and routes them to the analyzer.
- **LAS Analysis Result Reader:** Reads the result of the analysis performed by the different LAS components running on the same VM.

- **IPS Analyzer:** With the LAS Analysis results, it proceeds to evaluate whether any of the rules from the rules databank have been violated. The analysis results are expressed in terms of IPS analyzer rule violations, which express abnormal situations.
- **IPS Rules Databank:** Stores the set of the intra platform monitoring rules. This component is managed by the GUI subcomponent.
- **IPS GUI:** A graphical user interface that communicates the IPS administrator with the LAS component, with these main functionalities; it displays the analysis results from the analyser, manages the monitoring rules in the Databank, and inspects the contents of the LAS Analysis Result Reader.

Global Application Surveillance (GAS)

To support monitoring of specific software pieces and detecting problems with non-compliant implementations (as well as problems in the modelling) the GAS components perform vertical analysis. They analyze data from different machines referred to the same software (application). Such GAS components receive information from several IPS components and perform a new analysis on it. Thus, the GAS components have a global view of what is the behaviour of the software in different virtualized environments from different machines, and thus is able to deduce proper conclusions. The existence of GAS components benefits both users of the applications and applications developers.

This level is optional and there's one GAS per application (not instance). Also they might reside well outside the virtualized environment if necessary. Their task is a secondary form of analysis of the result of the IPS analyzers from all VMs in all virtualized environments in order to be able to detect application global design flaws, making it an invaluable resource for the developers of such applications. The subcomponents are:

Figure 2. Monitoring high level architecture

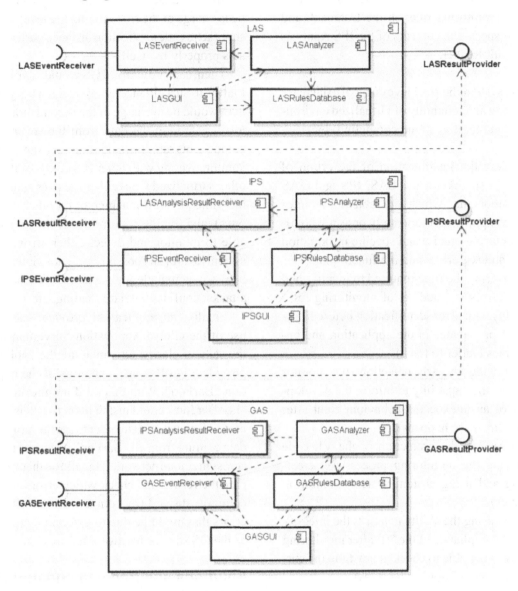

- **GAS Event Receiver:** Receives the external events and routes them to the analyzer.
- **IPS Analysis Result Reader:** Reads the result of the analysis performed by the different IPS components located globally.
- **GAS Analyzer:** With the IPS Analysis results, it proceeds to evaluate whether any of the rules from the rules databank have been violated. The results of the analysis are expressed in terms of GAS analyser

rule violations, which express abnormal situations.

- **GAS Rules Databank:** Stores the set of the intra platform monitoring rules. This component is managed by the GUI subcomponent.
- **GAS GUI:** A graphical user interface that communicates the GAS administrator with the GAS component. It has these main functionalities. It displays the analy-

sis results from the analyser, it manages the monitoring rules in the Databank and it inspects the contents of the IPS Analysis Result Reader.

All these systems help achieve our goal to increase the security and reliability of virtualized environments (and therefore cloud computing) by:

- Easing the identification of the origin of errors (thanks to the LAS, IPS and GAS components, which are able to monitor each application separately or as a whole).
- Capturing precise and specific information on attacks, errors and malfunctioning.
- Lowering the time required to identify and fix errors (a good set of monitoring rules helps with error identification before it further propagates in the application and becomes harder to track).
- Allowing an early detection (the monitor gives the capability to inform the developer of an unexpected behaviour right after the first case happens).
- Increasing the protection of the VE code during the monitoring process (by creating and using custom system monitoring rules).
- Increasing the ability to assess the integrity and compliance of the VE after monitoring (by being able to check at any time the current state of monitoring rules).

Framework Usage Example

This section gives an example scenario of the architecture presented in the previous section. Thus, let us suppose a cloud computing infrastructure composed of multiple physical machines, each one running one or more virtualized OSs, and each virtualized OS capable of running several different applications from several different clients.

First of all, for each single application instance we would have a Local Application Surveillance component attached to it. This component would be in charge of the first monitoring level, making sure each single application instance performs and acts properly by itself.

Then, each virtualized OS would have an Intra Platform Surveillance component. This component would be in charge of the second monitoring level, gathering the data from the several LAS components running inside that very same OS and communicating with other IPS components from other virtualized OSs (either the ones running on the same physical machine or on other different ones), and, by their joint efforts, they would be able to monitor and detect either errors on the system level or any possibly malicious interactions between such single applications (be it coordinated attacks, confidential data stealing, etc.).

Finally, an application provider can make use of the Global Application Surveillance. For the sake of clarity, let's imagine the application provider "FooBar Inc.", creators of the application "BarFoo". With this third monitoring level, "FooBar Inc." could install in one of their servers the GAS component in order to get the monitoring data coming from all "BarFoo" instances running across the cloud network. This allows them to compare the results and check which errors are more common, discard (by comparison and statistics) errors that might be due to external factors such as the OS state or hardware failures, etc.

Solutions and Recommendations: Monitoring Specifications and its Language

Traditional monitoring schemes check actual behaviour against an expected execution model (which can be expressed as rules or policies), but, when properly used in a distributed environment, its potential capability can be substantially increased, such as helping in the discovery of unexpected interactions or model flaws.

Nevertheless, nowadays current monitoring architectures are not well-suited for (future and ever more so present) highly distributed scenarios such as Cloud Computing. Moreover, they do not take advantage of the special characteristics these scenarios provided, precisely due the fact to they are not especially tailored to these scenarios.

Any monitoring system is based on a set of well-defined behaviour policies, also known as monitoring rules. In our particular monitoring system such rules are part of the monitoring specifications, which are written in a new language called EventSteer.

EventSteer is an extended event-sequence language (namely, a language that allows the user to create rules based on an expected or unexpected flow of events). Like Event Calculus (Hartig et al., 2008) it uses two basic concepts for representing the properties of systems that change over time; events and fluents. Whilst an event is defined as something that occurs at a specific moment in time and has instantaneous duration, a fluent is a condition that has different values in different moments in time. It is also extended because it does not only allow for specifying event sequences but also the possible consequences of failing to validate such sequences in an standard imperative programming syntax (Java in our case, but could be any other).

The main rationale behind the creation of a new language is based on three key points. The first one is that while EC provides an elegant mathematical way to formulate specifications, sometimes they are complex to understand at first sight. The second one is that the free mixing of time and events is difficult to compile, interpret and debug due to the lack of a certain fixed sequence to try to follow. The third and last one is that this very same lack of a fixed sequence in time makes it extremely complex to devise an optimal way to evaluate these rules at runtime.

Because of all this, one of the initial design goals of EventSteer was to overcome the limitations and drawbacks of current EC-based approaches. In particular we focused on the one hand on facilitating the expression of time (by avoid-

ing mixing of time and event processing, and by providing a clear distinction between the settings of a time variable (i.e. assigning a value to the variable) and the use of it (i.e. using the assigned value in the evaluation of an expression)). On the other hand, we also focused on expressing time in a past to future fixed sequence that facilitates the creation and optimization of the implementation of those rule checkers (in particular by using Finite State Machines (FSMs).

Due to the size constraints of this chapter a full description of the language becomes an impossible task. Nevertheless a description of the basic elements that are the basis for the rationale of the project has been included. The basic elements are:

Variables

In EventSteer, variables (also known as fluents in EC) can have different values in different moments in time (as their name indicates). They have names for identification purposes and can be of one of several types (Boolean, integer or double). Variables are set to specific values in the initialization section as well as in the consequences of monitoring rules as will be described in the Consequences section. Likewise, variables can be used in guards as part of event expressions by using them inside a Boolean expression that establishes when a given event can be accepted or not.

Time

Our notion of time is based on Linear Temporal Logic (LTL) (Serrano et al., 2009). LTL is a modal temporal logic with modalities referring to time that allows the definition of expressions about the future such as the fact that a condition will become true in the future, that it will be true until something happens, etc.

Opposed to other temporal logics such as Computation tree logic (CTL) or Alternating Time Epistemic Logic (ATEL), which allow the expression of different possible paths into the future, LTL can only express conditions on one path (i.e. it implicitly quantifies universally over paths), hence the name linear. This is a limitation when expressing the behaviour of software or hardware elements, especially for verifying safety or liveliness properties using model checkers. However, for the purposes of monitoring, the only path that we need to analyze is the actual execution. Moreover, as we will show, in our language different rules can represent overlapping paths, and there are several constructs to facilitate the expression of complex rules. Therefore, the limitation of representing one path in a rule does not constitute a problem for us. For this reason, it is possible to represent all monitoring rules using LTL.

Following the standard EC approach described in (Hartig et al., 2008) the time type is considered to have discrete values and consists of a set of ordered time points that can be mapped to the set of non-negative integers. However, as has already been mentioned, the treatment of time has been carefully considered in EventSteer and there are two main aspects to highlight about it: on the one hand, time treatment is detached from event treatment, and on the other hand there is a clear distinction between the setting of time variables and the use of these variables once they have been instantiated.

Here is the treatment of time in EventSteer in more detail:

- Time variables and deadlines are linked to event expressions. They are enclosed in braces after them as follows: eventExpression {timeVariable}. The semantics of this construct is that timeVariable is set to the actual time when the eventExpression is verified.
- Time variables are used in timeExpressions and can be part of time ranges. Its syntax is timeVariable (+ timeConstant). The optional integer constant is expressed in msecs.

- Time ranges, used in deadlines, take the form [(minTimeExpression)..(maxTimeExpression)]. Note that if the optional minTimeExpression is not written it means the min time range is zero.
- Also if the optional maxTimeExpression is not written it means the max time range is infinite.

Events

Events are the central element of any monitoring language. Events represent the connection between the monitor and the monitored system. For the sake of the current discussion and throughout the chapter we will consider that events are instantaneous situations that indicate some relevant change in the monitored system. In this framework, we consider three kinds of events; namely external, virtual and special events.

- **External events:** External events are externally-generated events which are triggered at certain arbitrary points by some external code. Examples of external events might be access to a file, the beginning of a password request, the acceptance of said password, or even a certain button being pressed. In our framework we concentrate on events that are relevant for the security of the system, but the EventSeer language is of course independent of this. External events are expressed in our language by directly using the event name and its attributes as parameters if applicable. This is, eventName(attrib1, attrib2, …).
- **Virtual events:** Virtual events are monitoring-oriented, internally-triggered events we use in order to keep control of the system state. Note here that by system state we really mean the monitoring machine state or whatever underlying implementation might be using the language. These kinds of events are user-defined internal

events. These events are sent inside the consequence code, thanks to an special method named SendVirtualEvent(evName, evParameters…).

- **Special events:** Special events are event predicates with special meanings. They are:
  - **true:** An event that is completed instantly, i.e., as soon as it is needed.
  - **false:** An event that is never completed and fails the completion of the event expression instantly.

Sequences

Sequences are the way to relate events in time. They define a series of temporally ordered event expressions and are done thanks to the sequence operators "," and "->". Other available operators are the complement """ operator, the any "|" operator, the all "+" operator and the except if "!" operator.

A short explanation of each of those operators follows:

- **","** **Witnessed sequence:** It defines what previous event expressions need to be completed in order to advance the sequence. This, like most other operators, is "open", meaning that no any other events can arrive in between without making the sequence fail.
- **"->"** **Rule expected sequence:** It works like the witnessed sequence operator, with the only difference that after it is used if the sequence fails the rule will become violated and will trigger its consequence.
- **"|"** **Any:** This operator is used to define an event expression constituted by several alternative sequences. That is, as long as one of all the event expressions is verified the combined event expression is considered to be verified.
- **"+"** **All (in any order):** This operator defines a sequence that is verified when all the event expressions that it contains are verified

regardless of the order in which such event expressions happen.

- **"'"** **Complement:** This operator is used to express the set of events that are not to be considered in a certain context.
- **"!"** **Except if:** This operator is used to express the set of events that are not to be witnessed in a certain context.

Reactions

Reactions allow the monitoring machine to react to certain event expressions by making changes to the internal monitoring machine state (variables / fluents, sending other kinds of virtual events etc.). In EventSteer reactions are stated as rules without a "->" operator. For instance, there could be a reaction to increase an nLoginAttempts integer variable each time an event informing of a failed login attempt happened.

Consequences

Consequences are the actions that must be triggered when a rule is violated and can have a direct effect on the monitored system or its internals. Examples of consequences can be restarting the system, halting it, suggesting actions to a higher controller or changing some system parameter, as well as changing variables, etc.

Real Life Example

While it has not been possible to provide enough information on the language grammar in such a short chapter, here a solution to a given real life case, is presented, which, with a bit of intuition on the reader's part, might prove to be useful for a basic understanding of the language.

Let us suppose a computer system. It will have the following requirements:

- When a user fails to login 3 times in a row, a login error screen must appear. If for some reason it does not then the system will be halted.

- Users can only transfer data if they are logged in and such a transfer can only take 20 seconds at most to complete.

FUTURE RESEARCH DIRECTIONS

On the on hand the validation of both the framework and the language are ongoing work, as part of the current EU project PASSIVE. Meanwhile nowadays we are not able to provide validation data due to the PASSIVE project requirements, it will be deeply tested and validated through an e-Government scenario included as proof of the concept of the project.

It is being targeted the automated reaction of the system according to the analysis resulting from the monitoring subsystem. Another interesting strand of research currently being initiated is the identification of the changes that must be applied to a component when a problem is detected. We are working on studying the feasibility of using instead of a first order temporal logic language based on Event Calculus a High order temporal logic although it is more complex; or even an intermediate step as the Event Calculus and the Alternating Time Epistemic Logic (ATEL).

CONCLUSION

Currently, the results of the analysis performed by the monitoring subsystem are reflected in the system behaviour by means of changes carried out by a human administrator. This chapter presents an infrastructure for monitoring systems deployed in Virtualized Environments. This infrastructure adds two monitoring layers on top of a virtualized monitoring model in order to provide support for evolution of applications.

REFERENCES

Avizienis, A., Larpie, J. C., & Randell, B. (2000). *Fundamental concepts of dependability*. In Information Survavility Workshop.

Barnett, M., & Schulte, W. (2001). Spying on components: A runtime verification technique. In *Proceedings of OOPSLA 2001 Workshop on Specification and Verification of Component Based Systems,* Tampa, FL, USA.

Chen, F., & Rosu, G. (2003). Towards monitoring-oriented programming: A paradigm combining specification and implementation. *Electronic Notes in Theoretical Computer Science, 89*(2).

Chowdhury, A., & Meyers, S. (1993). *Facilitating software maintenance by automated detection of constraint violations*. Tech. Rep. CS-93-37 Brown Univ.

Corritore, L. (2003). On-line trust: Concepts, evolving themes, a model. *International Journal of Human-Computer Studies, 58*(6), 737–758. doi:10.1016/S1071-5819(03)00041-7

D'Amorim, M., & Havelund, K. (2005). Event-based runtime verification of Java programs. In *Proceedings of the Third International Workshop on Dynamic Analysis*, St. Louis, Missourim, May 17 -17, 2005), WODA '05 (pp. 1-7). New York, NY: ACM Press.

Dardenne, A., van Lamsweerde, A., & Fickas, S. (1993). Goal-directed requirements acquisition. *Science of Computer Programming, 20*, 3–50. doi:10.1016/0167-6423(93)90021-G

Desai, N. (2003). *Intrusion prevention systems: The next step in the evolution of IDS*. Security-Focus. Retrieved from http://www.securityfocus.com/infocus/1670

Firesmith, D. (2003). Engineering security requirements. *Journal of Object Technology*, *2*(1), 53–68. Retrieved from http://www.jot.fm/issues/issue_2003_01/column6 doi:10.5381/jot.2003.2.1.c6

Härtig, H., Roitzsch, M., Lackorzynski, A., Döbel, B., & Böttcher, A. (2008). *L4 – Virtualization and beyond*. Korean Information Science Society Review.

Havelund, K., & Rosu, G. (2001A). Monitoring Java programs with Java PathExplorer. In *Proceedings of the 1st International Workshop on Runtime Verification (RV'01)*, (pp. 97-114).

Havelund, K., & Rosu, G. (2001B). Monitoring programs using rewriting. In *Proceedings of International Conference on Automated Software Engineering (ASE'01)*, (pp. 135-143). Coronado Island, CA: Institute of Electrical and Electronics Engineers.

Havelung, K., & Rosu, G. (2002). Sinthezising monitors for safety properties. In *Tools and Algorithms for Constructrion and Analysis of Systems (TACAS'02), LNCS 2280*, (pp. 342-356). Springer.

Jøsang, A. (2007). Trust and reputation systems. In *Foundations of Security Analysis and Design IV, FOSAD 2006/2007 Tutorial Lectures, LNCS 4677*. Springer.

Kiczales, G., Hilsdale, E., Hugunin, J., Kersten, M., Palm, J., & Griswold, W. G. (2001). An overview of AspectJ. In *Proceedings of the 15th European Conference on Object-Oriented Programming*, (pp. 327-353). Springer-Verlag.

Ko, S. Y., Jeon, K., & Morales, R. (2011). The HybrEx model for confidentiality and privacy in cloud computing. *Proceedings of the 2011 conference on Hot topics in cloud computing*, Portland, OR. Retrieved from http://www.usenix.org/event/hotcloud11/tech/final_files/Ko.pdf

Lee, I., Kannan, S., Kim, K., Sokolsky, O., & Viswanahtan, M. (1999). Runtime assurance based on formal specifications. In *Proceedings of the International Conference on Parallel and Distributed Processing Techniques and Applications*.

Mahbub, K., & Spanoudakis, G. (2004). A framework for requirements monitoring of service based systems. In *Proceedings of the 2nd Internatonal Conference on Service Oriented Computing*, NY, USA

McKnight, D. H., & Chervany, N. L. (1996). *The meanings of trust*. Technical Report MISRC Working Paper Series 96-04, University of Minnesota.

Meyer, B. (2000). *Object-oriented software construction* (2nd ed.). Upper Saddle River, NJ: Prenctice Hall.

Ormandy, T. (2007). An empirical study into the security exposure to host of hostile virtualized environments. *Proceedings of CanSecWest Applied Security Conference*, Vancouver, Canada. doi:10.1.1.105.6943

Pnueli, A. (1977). The temporal logic of programs. In *Proceedings of the 18th IEEE Symposium on Foundations of Computer Science*, (pp. 46-77).

Resnick, P. (2000). Reputation systems. *Communications of the ACM*, *43*(12), 45–48. doi:10.1145/355112.355122

Richter, W., Ammons, G., Harkes, J., Goode, A., Bila, N., de Lara, E., et al. (2011). Privacy-sensitive VM retrospection. *Proceedings of the 2011 Conference on Hot Topics in Cloud Computing* (pp. 1-6). Portland, OR. Retrieved from http://www.usenix.org/events/hotcloud11/tech/final_files/Richter.pdf

Robinson, W. (2002). Monitoring software requiements unsing intrumentation code. In *Proceedings of the Hawaii International Conference on Systems Sciences*.

Sellink, A., & Verhoef, C. (1999). An architecture for automated software maintenance. In *Proceedings of the 7th Intl. Workshop on Program Comprehension.*

Sen, K., & Rosu, G. (2003). Generating optimal monitors for extended regular expressions. In *Proceedings of the 3ʳᵈ International Workshop on Runtime Verification* (RV'03), (pp. 162-181).

SERENITY. (n.d.). *System engineering for security and dependability.* SERENITY, EU-funded project. Retrieved from http://www.serenity-project.org/

Serrano, D., Ruiz, J. F., Armenteros, A., Gallego-Nicasio, B., Muñoz, A., & Maña, A. (2009). *Development of applications based on security patterns.* Second International Conference on Dependability (DEPEND2009): IEEE Computer Society.

Shanahan, M. (1999). The event calculus explained. In *Artificial Intelligence Today, LNAI 1600*, (pp. 409-430).

Shanahan, M. (1999). The event calculus planner. *The Journal of Logic Programming, 44*, 207–239. doi:10.1016/S0743-1066(99)00077-1

Spanoudakis, G. (2007). Dynamic trust assessment of software services. *Proceedings of 2nd International Workshop on Service Oriented Software Engineering.*

Stickel, M. (1998). A Prolog-like inference system for computing minimun-cost abductive explanaitions in natural-language interpretation. In *International Computer Science Conference*, Hong Kong, (pp. 343-350).

van den Brand, M. G. J., Sellink, M. P. A., & Verhoef, C. (1999). Control flow normalization for COBOL/CICS legacy system. In *Proceedings of the 2nd Euromicro Conference on Maintenance and Reengineering.*

Verhoef, C. (2000). Towards automated modification of legacy assets. *Annals of Software Engineering, 9*(1-4), 315–336. doi:10.1023/A:1018941228255

Chapter 2
The SeCA Model

Thijs Baars
Utrecht University, The Netherlands

Marco Spruit
Utrecht University, The Netherlands

ABSTRACT

Security issues are paramount when considering adoption of any cloud technology. This chapter outlines the Secure Cloud Architecture (SeCA) model on the basis of data classifications, which defines a properly secure cloud architecture by testing the cloud environment on eight attributes. The SeCA model is developed using a literature review and a Delphi study with seventeen experts, consisting of three rounds. The authors integrate the CI3A —an extension on the CIA-triad— to create a basic framework for testing the classification inputed. The data classification is then tested on regional, geo-spatial, delivery, deployment, governance & compliance, network, and premise attributes. After this testing has been executed, a specification for a secure cloud architecture is outputted. The SeCA model is detailed with two example cases on the usage of the model in practice.

INTRODUCTION

According to both commercial reports as academic research, security issues are paramount when adoption of cloud solutions are being considered (Foster, Zhao, Raicu, & Lu, 2008; Ghinste, 2010; Mowbray & Pearson, 2009). However, no clear model exists to determine security issues and solutions.

Better yet, there is much debate which security threats and risks are applicable to computer networks, end-users or are actually cloud specific (Chen, Paxson, & Katz, 2010:4). They state that "arguably many of the incidents described as 'cloud security' in fact just reflect traditional web application and data-hosting problems [..] such as phishing, downtime, data loss, password weaknesses, and compromised hosts running botnets.". Moreover, they hold that most cloud security issues aren't new, but do need new implementations to provide the level of security wanted.

DOI: 10.4018/978-1-4666-2125-1.ch002

Therefore this chapter will provide an overview of the security issues and describe the Secure Cloud Architecture (SeCA) model to determine the security issues one might expect in a certain cloud environment and what solutions might be used to secure those issues. This framework will be developed by answering the following question:

Can the Cloud be a safe alternative for the storage and execution of organizational confidential data?

This model was developed in three steps. First, a literature review has been conducted. Second a delphi study was conducted to identify the perceived security issues by experts in the field. Third, the model was verified by the same experts in the last round of the delphi study.

By reading the overall themes in security, followed by cloud specific topics, an overview has been created that is used as the starting point in the development of the SeCA model.

A delphi study has been considered to be the best method for research in this chapter, as it provides the researchers with a qualitative data set which would allow to create and verify the model. It also allows the experts to see answers and be able to respond to these answers in upcoming rounds (Dalkey & Helmer, 1963). The first answer in question two is not per se answered by the same expert as answer one in question one, creating double-blind survey results. This way, a consensus can be reached on the various topics discussed in the delphi study. The delphi method was executed consisting of three rounds of surveys with qualitative questions. Three rounds were chosen instead of two, which is more common (Skulmoski, Hartman, & Krahn, 2007), so that a first round could be used to obtain general information on the topic, not specifically regarding to the model to be developed, while still having enough rounds to reach a consensus. The first round consisted of open questions where the experts were questioned on their experience with security and the cloud, issues and concerns

regarding security in the cloud. These questions gave a wide result set that strengthened the results of the literature research earlier performed. Seventeen respondents answered all the questions in the survey in all three rounds, a rate of 65%. See Table 1 for an overview.

This model has been verified by an expert panel. The experts were selected on the basis of their function, publications and knowledge of security, the cloud or a combination thereof. This group of experts, 26 in total, comes from organizations within the business to consumer, business to business, business to government industries and governmental organizations. They were interviewed using the Delphi tool developed at the Wharton Business School (Wharton Business School, 2005).

The burn chart (Table 2) shows the amount of consensus reached in the study, per topic addressed. White cells represent no questions in that topic were asked in that round; grey consensus was reached; chequered pattern a consensus in part was reached; black no consensus reached.

As one can see, not all topics reached consensus. This was due to the fact that in the expert selection business knowledge or technical knowledge on some topics were not taken into account. For example, the field of encryption is a very technical field that can be hard to fully understand and apply. Although some answers were very useful, other answers were dismissed in the same round as unfeasible, simpleminded or simply not true. This meant that the experience or knowledge between the experts varied too greatly to reach consensus. Subsequent research was done through literature review on the applicable topics.

BACKGROUND

The Cloud thus far has attracted a lot of attention, this section tries to provide a concise overview of key research and models previously developed.

Table 1. The experts (filtered on those that did all three rounds) in the Delphi study

#	Position/function	Organization type	Cloud	Non-cloud	Security
1	Consultant	Enterprise integrator	X	X	
2	Director	IT consultancy		X	X
3	Security consultant/architect	IT security firm		X	X
4	Researcher	American University,	X	X	X
5	Enterprise Architect	Enterprise transportation		X	
6	Sr. manager	Large accounting firm	X	X	X
7	Security advisor	Transportation firm		X	X
8	IT Architect	IT consultancy	X	X	
9	Manager	Security solutions	X		X
10	Security manager	Utilities		X	X
11	Consultant	IT consultancy	X	X	
12	Security manager	Government		X	X
13	Security manager	Healthcare products		X	X
14	Manager	IT consultancy		X	X
15	Consultant	Enterprise integrator		X	X
16	Security manager	Utilities		X	X
17	IT auditor	Accounting	X	X	X

The Jericho Forum (2009) has previously modeled the cloud in order to help users understand the different facets of the cloud and support a secure use of cloud technologies. It does however not account for the complexities seen in cloud security. Siebenhaar, Tsai, Lampe, & Steinmetz (2011) describe a holistic model for analyzing and modeling security aspects of cloud-based systems, Almorsy, Grundy, & Ibrahim (2011) provide a collaboration based framework for determining security management. The presented SeCA model in this research differs from the previously mentioned as it focuses on security measures within the architecture of the cloud determined by data classifications.

Subashini & Kavitha, (2011) discuss a survey concerning security issues in specific delivery models of the cloud. Although the encompassing research should lead to a model, that model is still under development. Benson, Sahu, Akella,

Table 2. Burn chart of the consensus reached in the Delphi study

Topic	Round1	Round2	Round3	Consensus	Comments
Security issues					All issues are accounted for in the model
Locationlessness					Location is a new issue and thoroughly discussed.
Trust issues					Outsourcing/insourcing/cloud differences are in discord
Encryption					Different knowledge levels; study done through literature.
Feasibility					Not a technical/security issue. Topic abandoned.
Model					Model validated and approved by the experts.
Auditing					Issues reached consensus; added to the CI3A.

& Shaikh (2010) discussed security issues from a cloud provider's support division perspective by looking at SLA structures. They report the most commonly found problems in IaaS architectures and offer three practical solutions. None of these are technical security solutions. Kaliski Jr & Pauley (2010) discuss risk assessment of the cloud, stating that "[t]he very characteristics that make cloud computing attractive also tend to make it hard to assess" (p.2). Richter et al. (2011) discuss VM retrospection, a method for inspecting previous VM states in order to perform forensics, debugging, troubleshooting and so forth. Christodorescu, Sailer, Schales, Sgandurra, & Zamboni (2009) discuss methods of securing Clouds at the Virtual Machine (VM) level. They provide a short overview of known VM issues and solutions, and then propose their system which protects VMs in a cloud against malware and rootkits using a white/blacklist method. Wang, Wang, Li, Ren, & Lou (2009) discuss the necessity of a Third Party Actor (TPA) to assure security standards and to provide transparency in the security controls. Jensen, Schwenk, Gruschka, & Iacono (2009) describe technical security issues related to cloud, using the Amazon EC² cloud as a case. Although all issues discussed are related to the cloud, all them were already apparent before the coming of the cloud, some just have found new grounds to be relevant again. Vigfusson & Chockler (2010) discuss in "Clouds at Crossroads: Research Perspectives" research topics in the cloud, including privacy related issues. Discussing the trust problems that arise with the complex models of some cloud environments, it provides a few solutions to suggestions that might be very feasible.

The research presented in this chapter overlaps with current research in that it provides an insight in cloud security, introducing and explaining it, but it also expands the current research with proposed solutions to solve cloud security issues at the managerial level not discussed so far. The current research explains either very technical details on protecting the cloud, where the mere

describes arbitrary issues that are not specific to the cloud, or gives overviews of the cloud where security issues are touched lightly, this research will focus on the security issues in depth that come with the cloud in a more practical sense. We specify cloud specific issues and general security issues that have found new terrain in the cloud environment. To conclude, this research provides users with a model that navigates them through the security checkpoints in cloud environment, outputting an architecture specific for their data classification.

RISKS AND THREATS IN THE CLOUD

This section describes the main overview of the security issues, risks and threats in the cloud, which are all part of the SeCA model which is presented on page 11. First, the CI3A is described, followed by all the attributes in the SeCA model: regional, geo-spatial, delivery model, deployment model, governance & compliance, network and premise.

CIA Triad (CI3A)

Because of the complexities the cloud presents as dictated by a majority of the participants of the delphi study, the *de facto* CIA triad (*e.g.* Avizienis, Laprie, Randell, Landwehr (2004)), which is used for testing the confidentiality, integrity and availability in systems, data flows and so forth, was found to be too constrained. For that reason, we developed the CI3A as an extension of the CIA triad, comprising of confidentiality, integrity, availability, accountability and auditability. See Figure 1. The proposed model utilizes CI3A to assure the right level of security is maintained within the environment. This section will describe the CI3A, following separate sections on locationlessness and trust chains.

Confidentiality is reached by proper authentication/authorization controls and encryption

Figure 1. The CI3A visualized

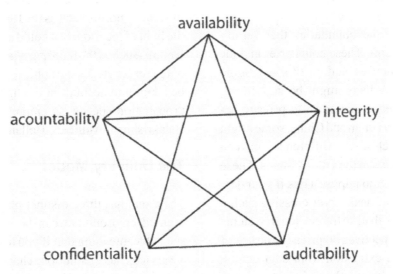

methods such as secured computing and two-factor encryption. Preventing data leakage is a central part within the confidentiality strategy. The choice of distribution and delivery model influences the level of confidentiality and the methods needed to assure confidentiality.

Integrity assures only authorized actors have access to certain data and that data gets distributed to only authorized persons. Within that distribution, any editing or changes within the data should only be made by the right persons. Governance and Compliance influence the integrity of the data; a fully compliant environment is more likely to assure integrity. As with Confidentiality, the chosen delivery and distribution model influences the level of integrity.

Availability comprises of measures to prevent unauthorized actors from deleting and moving data, or accessing those files, minimizing downtime of the environment. These measures could be a HA infrastructure, strong authentication servers, disaster recovery or external hosted service such as CloudPolice (Popa, Yu, Ko, Ratnasamy, & Stoica, 2010). Availability plays a big role within the cloud environment, as servers can be hosted anywhere in the world, at multiple loca-

tions. Although an advantage in the eyes of HA and disaster recovery; latency, desynchronization and vulnerabilities in the transceiver links can pose threats. Also, ownership of data is a part of availability. Availability is linked to regional, geo-spatial, network, premise and to the delivery and distribution models.

Accountability defines the measures taken to assure that no actor can make actions without a record. This is needed for forensics and governance. The measures needed to assure accountability greatly depend on the delivery model, but also on the distribution model and compliance in general. (Chen Wang & Zhou, 2010) have found accountability of paramount importance in the cloud, proposing a method for transferring accountability onto an external host in order to perform accountability in a multitenant platform.

Auditability, the ability of the environment to be audited, is directly related to governance and compliancy. Without a decent grade of auditability, compliance cannot be achieved. Auditability is influenced by the delivery and distribution model, as with the geo-spatial and geographic boundaries.

The Regional Attribute

Regional describe the boundaries that signify separate legal systems. These boundaries include cities, states, countries and territories. Some changes in legal systems might be significant, such as the difference in respect to privacy between the European Union and China; some might be incremental such as the difference between county and state laws in the United States. These differences however do impose a risk if your data gets placed on a physical server crossing such a boundary. Next to that, different legal systems have different perspectives on privacy, the use of subpoenas on data extraction from datacenters. As one expert commented: "bringing privacy information out of the European Union can be [a] violation of local or European law". This would mean that keeping in compliance with laws, be it local, national or international, will become more difficult without knowledge of the physical location of the data store and computing unit. Peterson & Gondree (2011) provide an elaborate view on the importance of data location awareness from an American perspective.

The Geo-Spatial Attribute

With geo-spatial risks, the distance of objects "relating to the relative position [..] on the earth's surface" (Collins English Dictionary, 2009) is meant, in this case the distance between servers, but also the location of each server. This can be of importance in the case of disaster recovery, but also with regards to physical security as presented in security norms such as the ISO 2700x series. In the light of location, one could also consider other features such as the building type, the accessibility of the server etc. Geographic location should also be taken into account in the light of latency and propagation speeds, as emphasized by Tiwana, Balakrishnan, Aguilera, Ballani, & Mao (2010).

The Delivery Model

The cloud has three distinct platforms on which a cloud environment can be offered. They are stackable, meaning that if you have a Software as a Service (SaaS) solution, chances are that your provider manages a Platform as a Service (PaaS), but takes services from an Infrastructure as a Service (IaaS) provider. See also Figure 2. This, however, does not mean that every SaaS solution is running as the top of a stack of cloud platforms. A SaaS solution can run on a traditional hardware stack with no further cloud environment attached.

Trust is a major issue in any relation, be it personal or professional. Although this is trivial, cloud computing can create trust chains, in which the end user is not always aware which other links are present in his chain of trust. This pertains especially towards delivery models. With IaaS, the tenant is in direct contact with the owner of the infrastructure (in some cases there might be a reseller in between) who can have outsourced duties associated with the maintenance of the physical systems. In a SaaS model, one is not aware if the SaaS provider also owns the platform,

Figure 2. Trust chains in cloud architectures

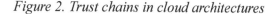
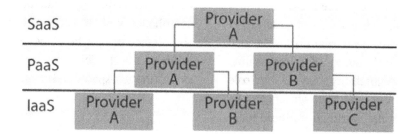

or the infrastructure. This means that there might be a variety of different actors working on the cloud, whom all might be able to access the data that is being used in the SaaS in some way or another. Actors whom the tenant initially didn't trust have now become a part of his organizational network. This might result in actions that are a threat to the data. Although doing business is about making relations and trust, yet not insurmountable, they are a risk factor.

The Deployment Model

The cloud comes in four different deployment models, these are private, public, hybrid and community/Partner clouds. The difference between these four models is the openness of the cloud to its tenants.

In a private cloud, the cloud infrastructure is operated for just one organization. This does not mean that it has to be managed by that organization. The management of the private cloud can be done by a third party, and the cloud itself can be physically located on the premises of that organization, or can be hosted somewhere else (sometimes called a virtual private cloud.) The cloud can exist behind a firewall of the organization, and thus only accessible within its private network, but can also be hosted off-premise on dedicated hardware (thus no multitenancy with other organizations). These are all factors that influence the security risks. The main difference between a mainframe or internal traditional datacenter and a private cloud is that there is a virtualization layer that can be used to host SaaS applications, rapid deployment and other benefits of cloud computing. Even though private clouds conventionally lack the flexibility of their public equivalents, a model has been proposed to allocate public cloud space for private clouds, giving it the full flexibility as public clouds with the added security of private clouds (Ko, Jeon, & Morales, 2011).

In a community cloud, a community or group of organizations share the same cloud infrastructure. These communities have shared concerns, such as a mission, goal and/or policy. The cloud can be managed by one of the organizations within the community or by a third party, and may exist on or off premise (Mulholland, Pyke, & Fingar, 2010).

In a Public Cloud, the cloud is open for use to a large group of tenants, which do not need to know each other. The cloud is a ran by a cloud service provider. An example can be a majority of offerings from Force.com and Google's Gmail to VPS.net, Rackspace cloud hosting and other public services, free or on a subscription basis. Typically these are off premise, out of the organizational network.

A Hybrid Cloud is a composition, or hybrid if you will, of two or more clouds of the types mentioned above. They are unique entities, but tied together with APIs to enable the exchange of data and applications. Due to the nature of the different clouds the hybrid consists of, it can be deployed both on and of premise, and be fully, partly or not behind the firewall of the organization.

Governance and Compliance

Executing governance and compliance is according to our experts is a much debated issue. Because governance and compliance greatly depend on the infrastructure of the system and the above mentioned boundary issues, this topic is much under the discretion of the chosen cloud environment.

Depending on the chosen delivery model, compliance can be completely out of hand. A SaaS application depends on their vendors for governance and compliance. For PaaS it is partly the same, any compliance and governance within the software and how it handles data is on the part of the developer. The governance of the infrastructure and platform on which the application relies is in the hands of the provider. As with SaaS, negotiations need to take place with the provider in order to secure compliance. For IaaS, most of the governance and compliance lays in the hands of the tenant. The IaaS provider has to take care of the compliance to standards such as SAS-70, but many issues like privacy, data encryption and authentication are the responsibility of the tenant.

Concerning deployment models, compliance and governance in a public cloud can be difficult, as you are limited to your VM instance, whereas in a private cloud your negotiation position will be stronger as there are no other tenants to take into account. In a partner cloud, one can imagine that governance and compliance is a shared goal.

Concerning boundaries, the major aspect is the geographic location of the servers. The easiest option is of course in the same region as the organization resides, most knowledge of laws and executing governance/assuring compliance will be readily available. Auditing will not be an issue, as you can identify an auditing partner with whom you can easily communicate. That being said, the hardest option is obviously a cloud environment dispersed over the globe. Although disaster recovery wise there will be no issue complying to the toughest guidelines, getting audited and governance worldwide will be tougher. Although experts in the survey were wary of the fact that it could be done, in a personal interview with an Chief Information Security Officer of a large utilities company, it was made clear that a global audit is unprecedented.

Network

Network indicates the boundary of an organizational computer network. This is an important factor, as some information is not wanted outside the corporate network, such as trade secrets. Keeping a cloud environment within the boundaries of the network can be reached by keeping it on premise and thus physically in the network, or it can be reached by creating a VPN connection (as elaborated by Wood, Gerber, Ramakrishnan, Shenoy and Van der Merwe (2009)) or a VLAN (in case of internal networks, or in public as described by Hao, Lakshman, Mukherjee and Song (2010)) in order to keep the information within the network.

Because some configurations stretch the extension of the enterprise network, additional risks are incurred due to this stretch, as some of our experts mentioned in the survey. This stretch in the network is also noticeable in the added amount of actors which have to be trusted. The cloud provider will probably have access to your network, or the possibility to illegally gain so.

An added risk is the uncertainty of the WAN infrastructure at the providers side. Connecting with the cloud provider might create vulnerabilities that could threaten the corporate network. Next to that, multitenancy might also be considered within the range of network boundaries. Although multitenancy should never be a threat to the virtual machine, in that it shouldn't have the possibility of other tenants to enter your VM, it has been proven that a vulnerability on the OS level could provide access to other VMs. Ristenpart, Tromer, Shacham and Savage (2009) describe ways to discover where nodes are hosted on Amazon's EC2 cloud, following with a discussion how to place a co-resident on that physical server in order to able to reach the hardware a selected node is on. By then compromising the system, the selected node might be entered. This is a risk that has to be considered, how small it seems to be (see (Asadoorian, 2007; Mehta & Smith, 2007; Ormandy, 2007) for an overview).

On or Off Premise

Organizational premises play a role in the physical location of the cloud environment. One can either wise choose to have the hardware reside on or off organizational premises. For high security purposes keeping the hardware on premise, and thus fully in one's control, might provide a benefit; personnel can be screened, there's extended access control to the datacenter and forensics. This extends the discussion on the geographic location of the server, presenting a trade off in security between on-premise servers versus geospatial choices.

ENCRYPTION IN THE CLOUD

Encryption plays a vital role within the cloud environment. It is affected by all but the geo-spatial attributes in the SeCA model and affects the regional, delivery and deployment model. Although encryption is a broad topic that has been covered in many papers, theses and books, there are some aspects that are specifically related to the cloud. VPN tunnels, together with SSH can provide secure access to the cloud environment. Two-factor can be very helpful for the cloud environment. Many institutions are using hardware key-tokens or SMS gateways in order to provide the second form of authentication apart from keying in a password. Authentication servers using protocols as RADIUS in combination with LDAP, Kerberos or Active Directory can handle all access requests in a proven manner as they are no different from any LAN/WAN setup at a traditional environment. The author therefore believes that in terms of access control, authentication and authorization, no cloud specific issues are at hand.

Apart from the aforementioned, an encryption method specifically pertaining to the cloud is secure computing. Secure computing offers a solution to issues that arise when multiple systems have to use secure information in transactions and computations, in essence described by Yao's (1982) Millionaires' problem. This research has been extended by Goldreich (2000), who researched the problem with multiple actors called Secure Multi-party Computations (SMCs). Recent research involves SMC geometry, researching transactions of polygons on convex hulls. See (Wang, Luo, & Huang, 2008) for an overview.

It is known that any multi-party computational problem can be solved using the generic technique of Yao (Yao, 1982). To overcome the overhead with Yoa's Millionaires' problem, and thus SMC, it seems that algorithms designed to compute a special task need to be written (Feigenbaum, Pinkas, Ryger, & Saint Jean, 2004; Goldreich, 2000). Using encryption methods such as homo-morphic encryption and public key encryption, several algorithms have shown to be applicable to the cloud (Das & Srinathan, 2007; Hu & Xu, 2009; Troncoso-Pastoriza & Pérez-González, 2010) and have proven to provide the security needed for the cloud within test situations approaching real life cloud environments.

These methods of secure computing would allow the creation of a chain of trust that is secure, even though not all parties within the chain know each other nor trust each other. This could overcome any trust issues that might be in the field of cloud environments. Together with the enhanced and proven techniques of authentication and authorization already available, encryption can make the cloud a very secure architecture.

Apart from the above mentioned, Mowbray & Pearson (2009) have developed a privacy manager that can obfuscate data in effort to protect it from malicious providers.

Table 3 shows how encryption affects and is affected by the choice of certain attributes in the model. For example, when analyzing the attribute Compliance in the model the encryption attribute is also influenced, as some standards and classifications define levels of encryption needed. Defining the attribute Encryption influences the CI3A on all but availability as the means of encryption can assure the confidentiality, integrity, accountability and auditability of an architecture.

THE SeCA MODEL

Resulting from the research conducted, we can summarize that the cloud can be secure, as long as its policies and SLAs are correctly in place and enforced. The different factors and risks involving cloud computing make it difficult to pinpoint to one secure cloud. In fact that is impossible, due to the diversity of cloud architectures and the data that is being stored on it. To circumvent this problem, the SeCA model has been designed.

Table 3. Encryption and how it is affected or affects the other attributes in the SeCA model

SeCA attribute	Confidentiality	Integrity	Availability	Accountability	Auditability
Regional	X			X	X
Geo-spatial			X		
Compliance	X	X			X
Delivery model	X	X	X		X
Deployment model	X	X	X	X	X
Encryption	X	X		X	X
Network	X		X	X	
Premises	X	X	X		

This model has been validated in the final round of the delphi study.

The model described below, the SeCA Model, gives an abstract overview of all the characteristics of the cloud. Figure 3 depicts the SeCA model. It defines a secure cloud architecture for a specific data classification.

The model outputs guidelines for the cloud environment and to which specification a cloud solution should adhere. The model can be used in two directions, from left to right (forward direction), or from right to left (backward direction). The following section describes how one can use this model in both directions. It is assumed that there are data classifications defined within the organization.

The organization in this example is trying to identify whether their standard office suite can be replaced by a cloud offering. They have identified two cloud service providers that offer office suites, one by the ACME corporation and one by WEC, Inc. They are analyzed in in Table 5. We will refer to this matrix in both sections. It depicts a matrix which describes the values of the attributes in the SeCA model for both cloud solutions.

To keep this example brief, we will only discuss a fictional data classification named "private". This classification is shown in Table 4. This classification can be created by using the template shown (template 1.) The template allows for one to map an existing data classification to the SeCA model, providing a clear overview of the attributes and their values. The final classification as shown in Table 4 shows the SeCA attributes and the corresponding values. It is already mapped to the SeCA model. One can imagine that the classification before mapping does not literally mention the attributes, nor talk about deployment and delivery

Figure 3. The SeCA Model

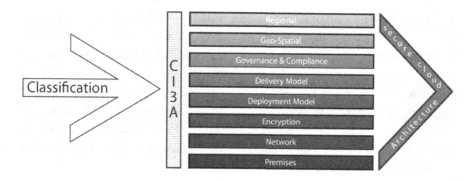

Template 1. SeCA data classification template

SeCA Data classification Template		Date: _____
Classification Name/ identification: _____	Expert's Name:_____	
Regional:		
Geo-spatial:		
Governance & Compliance:		
Delivery Model:	o IaaS o PaaS o SaaS	
Deployment model:	o Private o Partner/Community o Public oHybrid	
Encryption:		
Network:	o Within o Outside o Any	
Premises:	o On premise o Off premise o Any	

models. Some attributes, like encryption, might be already present in the classification before being mapped to the SeCA model.

Forward Direction

When the model is used with a forward direction, the assessor at the organization inputs a data classification. From this data classification a set of rules is created to which the cloud architecture should adhere. A set of outer-boundaries if you will. These are shown in Table 4.

Once this is done, a list of cloud providers/ solutions who can adhere to the results from the assessment is created. This can be done manually or by using proposed services such as CloudCMP (A. Li, Yang, Kandula, & Zhang, 2010). Ulti-

Table 4. Results from the cloud analysis

Classification: Private	Secure Cloud Architecture specification
Attribute	**Value**
Regional	Cloud environment physically within the same region as the organization.
Geo-spatial	A HA architecture is preferred, at least one backup location in a different building on separate power net.
Governance/compliance	No need to adhere to specific standards. Annual audit is required to assure proper protection.
Delivery model	Any
Deployment model	Any
Encryption	A proper authentication and authorization system should be in place for any actions. Alignment with the LDAP server in place is preferred.
Network	Any
Premises	Any

Figure 4. The position of the SeCA model of transitioning data into the cloud in a forward direction (simplified)

mately, a cloud provider is selected, arrangements are made and the data can be placed in the cloud.

The flow chart in Figure 4 shows where this assessment ordinarily should take place.

It can occur that each classification has a different output from the assessment. (it is actually most likely to do so.) In that case several options are open. For each classification a different list of cloud providers is made in order to find and select the right cloud provider who can provide the cloud architecture needed. These can be combined in Hybrid Clouds. One can also decide that for certain classifications it is simply not feasible to transfer that data into the cloud and thus stay with the solutions already in place.

The model does not provide the intelligence which classifications could be hosted at the same cloud architectures. It is for the assessor to decide which cloud architectures that are the result from the assessments can be merged.

This classification will normally be created by a security officer in the organization. He can use the SeCA Model to describe the values for the attributes in the model. On this basis the lower and upper bound values for the architecture are drafted. One can then look at the services that fit within these bounds and deem them safe enough, or not, for the data that'll be used with that service.

Backward Direction

A different way of using the model, the so-called backward direction, is to select the services one is interested in. By investigating the properties of the service and its underlying architecture a matrix can be created. This matrix, shown in Table 5 with two fictional office services, can then be

mapped to a data classification, shown in Table 4, specified by the organization. As we can see from the examples given, the Office Suite service from the ACME Corporation cannot be used for data classified as "private", as the classification clearly states that an "Annual audit is required to assure proper protection." In the Matrix, it states that in the column of the CI3A→auditability: "unclear".

This method can be easier if one wants to know if a certain cloud solution could security-wise work within the organization.

As one can see, different cloud solutions have different attribute values. It is for this reason that this direction can be preferred as it provides a great overview of the services that are being considered. Even if no effort has been put into mapping the classifications to the SeCA model, one can already get a hunch on the solution, how the architecture is setup and where the data is located.

Figure 5 provides a simplified flowchart of the backward direction. The differences with the forward direction (Figure 4) are clear: one starts with listing the cloud solutions instead of doing that at a later stage, after which the solutions are mapped to data classifications. Therefore, this method provides an early overview of which solutions fit with which data classification.

FUTURE RESEARCH DIRECTIONS

Further research can be conducted in the legal field. This was out of scope of this research, but the legal issues surrounding auditing, SLAs and NDAs are of paramount importance for the security in the cloud. SLAs especially, are of profound importance as they describe what measures a

Table 5. Service matrix

Supplier	Service	Deployment Model	Delivery Model	Location		
				jurisdiction	premise	Network
WEC	Office Suite	Public	SaaS	Safe harbor, World wide	Off	Outside
ACME	Office Suite	Public	SaaS	USA	Off	Outside, inside through VPN access

Security				
backup	location	A&A	Encryption	Certification
Synchronization, mirroring and disaster recovery	Worldwide (no particulars known)	LDAP, proprietary user/pass authentication	SSL, TLS. No storage encryption	SAS 70-II, SOX, PCI-DSS, Safe Harbor
Disaster recovery Location in the EU, Mirroring within the USA.	USA	AD setup, custom two-factor auth.	256bit SSL, TLS	ISO 27001, safe harbor, SAS 70-II.

CI3A				
confidentiality	Integrity	accountability	auditability	availability
No dedicated hardware possible	SSL, third-party apps	Full logging, data always belongs to the end user, 3rd party apps	Global internal audits, no specifics available	99.9% uptime, scheduled downtime
Possible to get dedicated hardware	SSL only	End user is responsible	unclear	99.99% uptime

cloud provider should undertake for the security of the cloud. This paper unfortunately has not had the possibility to explore the provider side of the cloud environment much.

Related to this is auditing in international/ worldwide clouds. Auditing certifications, governance and compliance to legal systems in these environments means that auditing firms, datacenter owner, providers and application owner all need to work together in order to get successful audit. In international and worldwide clouds these relations might become very complex, not to mention that multiple audit firms/offices have to work together. The issues raised with datacenters situated in different legal regions, such as China and the United States, are worth more research. Auditing plays also here a major role.

A pressing issue not discussed, but worth the research are third party appliances that are currently installed in traditional datacenters. These appliances cannot be directly converted to the cloud, as the cloud does not offer any place for such appliances. It seems that at the moment of writing many of these appliances are converted to the cloud by their developers. It is nonetheless interesting to see what impact these appliances

Figure 5. The position of the SeCA model of transitioning data into the cloud in a backward direction (simplified)

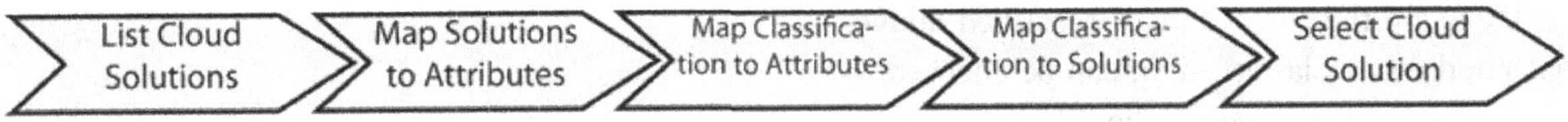

List Cloud Solutions → Map Solutions to Attributes → Map Classification to Attributes → Map Classification to Solutions → Select Cloud Solution

have on the adoption of the cloud. On that note, (Krautheim, 2009) has developed an infrastructure called PVI for the cloud that automates provisions depending on security settings. It would be interesting to see how the SeCA model can be connected to the presented PVI.

Although some cloud providers are certified, the impact of that certification on the real security of the services the provider offers is not always known. SAS70 for example does not offer any concrete security, it only offers a framework for auditing internal controls. The cloud provider will need to list its internal controls for any user to see what has been audited. It might be interesting to see how cloud providers use that information, what they do with it and whether the certifications really add up to extra level of security that is said it adds.

A case study should be conducted putting the model to practice, validating it in the work field. The validation so far has been merely theoretical by the experts in the Delphi study.

CONCLUSION

Defining something as secure depends on many factors. Depending on the sort of data, the classification of that data and taking that wholly into perspective of the cloud environment, it can be said that the cloud is secure in certain situations. Depending on the outcomes of investigations, there should always be a cloud architecture that fits one's security needs. Better yet, the cloud can provide additional layers of security by utilizing virtualization, elasticity and HA architectures. Even though the additional layer of virtualization on the system might provide additional hazards, looking at the scarcity of exploitations in this layer one can rationally say that the virtualization layer adds more protection than threats.

By using the SeCA model described above, each and every classification can be checked to see how a cloud architecture should be designed in order to meet the security standards needed. It will, however, depend on the cloud provider whether it can deliver the architecture that is needed.

For the upmost secure classifications, a private cloud, hosted on premise, within the network, with mirroring on a different physical location (branch office) utilizing the needed encryption methods will provide a very secure architecture whilst maintaining some of the flexibility the cloud has to offer.

For every architecture counts that data location awareness is essential. Without the full knowledge of where the data resides and is processed, issues will arise in all actors of the CI3A. Data location awareness will also provide the means for compliance, legally and to security standards. These standards are being adopted by all major vendors, including Amazon, Google and Microsoft, with smaller ones following. This facilitates full compliance to the de facto security and auditing standards such as SAS 70, ISO 27000 series, PCI and COBIT. It depends, once again, on the configuration of the cloud architecture and where applicable the willingness of cloud provider to allow for audits. If the selected cloud architecture features datacenters in widely spread different parts of the world, auditing might be more complicated. This of course also applies to the compliance to legal systems (privacy, intellectual property and auditing regulations) which can vary between jurisdictions. It is because of these implications that so-called locationless clouds are not preferable. They have an opaque layer that hides the user from vital knowledge in order to gain assurance from the CI3A.

The model presented covers the complexity of the cloud and gives implementers, decision makers and IT professionals a hands-on tool for deciding whether and which cloud solution to use for their data.

REFERENCES

Almorsy, M., Grundy, J., & Ibrahim, A. S. (2011). Collaboration-based cloud computing security management framework. *2011 IEEE International Conference on Cloud Computing (CLOUD),* (pp. 364–371). Washington, DC: IEEE. Retrieved from http://ieeexplore.ieee.org/xpls/abs_all.jsp?arnumber=6008731

Asadoorian, P. (2007). Escaping from the virtualization cave. *PaulDotCom.* Retrieved July 12, 2011, from http://www.pauldotcom.com/2007/07/31/escaping_from_the_virtualizati.html

Avizienis, A., Laprie, J., Randell, B., & Landwehr, C. (2004). Basic concepts and taxonomy of dependable and secure computing. *IEEE Transactions on Dependable and Secure Computing, 1*(1), 11–33. doi:10.1109/TDSC.2004.2

Benson, T., Sahu, S., Akella, A., & Shaikh, A. (2010). A first look at problems in the cloud. *Proceedings of the 2nd USENIX Conference on Hot Topics in Cloud Computing* (pp. 1-7). Boston, MA: USENIX Association. doi:10.1.1.150.2883

Chen, Y., Paxson, V., & Katz, R. H. (2010). *What's new about cloud computing security.* University of California, Berkeley Report No. UCB/EECS-2010-5 January (Vol. 20). Berkeley, CA. Retrieved from http://www.eecs.berkeley.edu/Pubs/TechRpts/2010/EECS-2010-5.pdf

Christodorescu, M., Sailer, R., Schales, D. L., Sgandurra, D., & Zamboni, D. (2009). Cloud security is not (just) virtualization security. *Proceedings of the 2009 ACM Workshop on Cloud Computing Security - CCSW '09* (p. 97). New York, NY: ACM Press. doi:10.1145/1655008.1655022

Dalkey, N., & Helmer, O. (1963). An experimental application of the DELPHI method to the use of experts. *Management Science, 9*(3), 458-467. JSTOR. doi:10.1287/mnsc.9.3.458

Das, A. S., & Srinathan, K. (2007). Privacy preserving cooperative clustering service. *15th International Conference on Advanced Computing and Communications (ADCOM 2007)* (pp. 435-440). Guwahati, India: IEEE. doi:10.1109/ADCOM.2007.52

Feigenbaum, J., Pinkas, B., Ryger, R. S., & Saint Jean, F. (2004). Secure computation of surveys. *EU Workshop on Secure* (pp. 1-6). Retrieved from http://citeseerx.ist.psu.edu/viewdoc/download?doi=10.1.1.100.3258&rep=rep1&type=pdf

Forum, J. (2009). *Cloud cube model: Selecting cloud formations for secure collaboration.* Retrieved from http://www.opengroup.org/jericho/cloud_cube_model_v1.0.pdf

Foster, I., Zhao, Y., Raicu, I., & Lu, S. (2008). *Cloud computing and grid computing 360-degree compared. 2008 Grid Computing Environments Workshop* (pp. 1–10). Austin, TX: IEEE.

Ghinste, B. V. (2010). Gartner: Private cloud computing plans from conference polls. *MSDN Blogs.* Retrieved June 27, 2011, from http://blogs.msdn.com/b/architectsrule/archive/2010/05/07/gartner-private-cloud-computing-plans-from-conference-polls.aspx

Goldreich, O. (2000). *Secure multi-party computation.* Working Draft.

Hao, F., Lakshman, T., Mukherjee, S., & Song, H. (2010). Secure cloud computing with a virtualized network infrastructure. *Proceedings of the 2nd USENIX Conference on Hot Topics in Cloud Computing* (pp. 16–16). Boston, MA: USENIX Association. doi:10.1234/12345678

Hu, H., & Xu, J. (2009). Non-exposure location anonymity. *2009 IEEE 25th International Conference on Data Engineering* (pp. 1120-1131). Shanghai, China: IEEE. doi:10.1109/ICDE.2009.106

Jensen, M., Schwenk, J., Gruschka, N., & Iacono, L. L. (2009). On technical security issues in cloud computing. *2009 IEEE International Conference on Cloud Computing* (pp. 109-116). Bangalore, India: IEEE. doi:10.1109/CLOUD.2009.60

Kaliski, B. S., Jr., & Pauley, W. (2010). Toward risk assessment as a service in cloud environments. *Proceedings of the 2nd USENIX Conference on Hot Topics in Cloud Computing* (pp. 13–13). Boston, MA: USENIX Association. Retrieved from http://portal.acm.org/citation.cfm?id=1863116

Ko, S. Y., Jeon, K., & Morales, R. (2011). The HybrEx model for confidentiality and privacy in cloud computing. *Proceedings of the 2011 Conference on Hot Topics in Cloud Computing*. Portland, OR. Retrieved from http://www.usenix.org/event/hotcloud11/tech/final_files/Ko.pdf

Krautheim, F. J. (2009). Private virtual infrastructure for cloud computing. *Proceedings of the 2009 Conference on Hot Topics in Cloud Computing* (pp. 5–5). San Diego, CA: USENIX Association. Retrieved from http://portal.acm.org/citation.cfm?id=1855538

Li, A., Yang, X., Kandula, S., & Zhang, M. (2010). CloudCmp: shopping for a cloud made easy. *Proceedings of the 2nd USENIX Conference on Hot Topics in Cloud Computing* (pp. 5–5). Boston, MA: USENIX Association. Retrieved from http://portal.acm.org/citation.cfm?id=1863108

Mehta, N., & Smith, R. (2007). *VMWare DHCP server remote code execution vulnerabilities*. IBM Internal Security Systems. Retrieved July 12, 2011, from http://www.iss.net/threats/275.html

Mowbray, M., & Pearson, S. (2009). A client-based privacy manager for cloud computing. *Proceedings of the Fourth International ICST Conference on COMmunication System softWAre and middleWAre - COMSWARE '09* (p. 1). Dublin, Ireland: ACM Press. doi:10.1145/1621890.1621897

Mulholland, A., Pyke, J., & Fingar, P. (2010). *Enterprise cloud computing*. Tampa, FL: Meghan-Kiffer Press.

Ormandy, T. (2007). An empirical study into the security exposure to host of hostile virtualized environments. *Proceedings of CanSecWest Applied Security Conference*, Vancouver, Canada. doi:10.1.1.105.6943

Peterson, Z., & Gondree, M. (2011). A position paper on data sovereignty: The importance of geolocating data in the cloud. *Proceedings of the 2011 Conference on Hot Topics in Cloud Computing*. Portland, OR. Retrieved from http://www.usenix.org/event/hotcloud11/tech/final_files/Peterson.pdf

Popa, L., Yu, M., Ko, S. Y., Ratnasamy, S., & Stoica, I. (2010). CloudPolice: Taking access control out of the network. *Proceedings of the Ninth ACM SIGCOMM Workshop on Hot Topics in Networks* (p. 7). Monterey, CA: ACM. Retrieved from http://portal.acm.org/citation.cfm?id=1868454

Richter, W., Ammons, G., Harkes, J., Goode, A., Bila, N., de Lara, E., et al. (2011). Privacy-sensitive VM retrospection. *Proceedings of the 2011 Conference on Hot Topics in Cloud Computing* (pp. 1-6). Portland, OR. Retrieved from http://www.usenix.org/events/hotcloud11/tech/final_files/Richter.pdf

Ristenpart, T., Tromer, E., Shacham, H., & Savage, S. (2009). Hey, you, get off of my cloud: Exploring information leakage in third-party compute clouds. *Proceedings of the 16th ACM Conference on Computer and Communications Security* (pp. 199–212). Chicago, IL: ACM. doi:10.1.1.150.681

School, W. B. (2005). Delphi decision aid. Retrieved October 5, 2010, from http://armstrong.wharton.upenn.edu/delphi2/

Siebenhaar, M., Tsai, H. Y., Lampe, U., & Steinmetz, R. (2011). Analyzing and modeling security aspects of cloud-based systems. *GI/ITG KuVS Fachgespräch "Sicherheit für Cloud Computing"*, (April). Retrieved from ftp://ftp.kom.e-technik. tu-darmstadt.de/papers/STLS11.pdf

Skulmoski, G. J., Hartman, F. T., & Krahn, J. (2007). The Delphi method for graduate research. *Journal of Information Technology Education, 6*, 1-21. doi:10.1.1.151.8144

Subashini, S., & Kavitha, V. (2011). A survey on security issues in service delivery models of cloud computing. *Journal of Network and Computer Applications, 34*(1), 1-11. Elsevier. doi:10.1016/j. jnca.2010.07.006

Tiwana, B., Balakrishnan, M., Aguilera, M. K., Ballani, H., & Mao, Z. M. (2010). Location, location, location! Modeling data proximity in the cloud. *Proceedings of the Ninth ACM SIGCOMM Workshop on Hot Topics in Networks* (p. 15). Monterey, CA: ACM. doi:10.1145/1868447.1868462

Troncoso-Pastoriza, J. R., & Pérez-González, F. (2010). CryptoDSPs for cloud privacy. *Workshop on Cloud Information System Engineering (CISE'10)* (pp. 1-12). Hong Kong, China. doi:10.1.1.185.429

Vigfusson, Y., & Chockler, G. (2010). Clouds at the crossroads. *Crossroads, 16*(3), 10–13. doi:10.1145/1734160.1734165

Wang, C., & Zhou, Y. (2010). A collaborative monitoring mechanism for making a multitenant platform accountable. *Proceedings of the 2nd USENIX Conference on Hot Topics in Cloud Computing* (pp. 18-25). Boston, MA: ACM. Retrieved from http://www.usenix.org/event/hotcloud10/tech/full_papers/WangC.pdf

Wang, Q. Luo, Y., & Huang, L. (2008). Privacy-preserving protocols for finding the convex hulls. *2008 Third International Conference on Availability, Reliability and Security*, (070412043), 727-732. IEEE. doi:10.1109/ARES.2008.11

Wang, Q. Wang, C., Li, J., Ren, K., & Lou, W. (2009). Enabling public verifiability and data dynamics for storage security in cloud computing. In M. Backes & P. Ning (Eds.), *LNCS, Vol. 5789, ESORICS 2009* (pp. 355-370). Berlin, Germany: Springer. doi:doi:10.1007/978-3-642-04444-1

Wood, T., Gerber, A., Ramakrishnan, K., Shenoy, P., & Van der Merwe, J. (2009). The case for enterprise-ready virtual private clouds. *Proceedings of the 2009 Conference on Hot Topics in Cloud Computing* (pp. 4–9). Monterey, CA: USENIX Association. Retrieved from http://portal.acm.org/citation.cfm?id=1855537

Yao, A. C. (1982). Protocols for secure computations. *23rd Annual Symposium on Foundations of Computer Science* (pp. 160-164). Chicago, IL: IEEE. doi:10.1109/SFCS.1982.38

KEY TERMS AND DEFINITIONS

CI3A: An extension of the traditional CIA triad which models confidentiality, integrity, availability, accountability and auditability aspects.

Cloud Computing: A disruptive delivery model which turns the internet into a storage and computing power provider.

Secure Cloud Architecture (SeCA): The SeCA model which helps determine the security issues one can expect in a certain cloud environment based on data classification through regional, geo-spatial, delivery, deployment, governance & compliance, network, and premise attributes.

Chapter 3
Three Misuse Patterns for Cloud Computing

Keiko Hashizume
Florida Atlantic University, USA

Nobukazu Yoshioka
National Institute of Informatics, Japan

Eduardo B. Fernandez
Florida Atlantic University, USA

ABSTRACT

Cloud computing is a new computing model that allows providers to deliver services on demand by means of virtualization. One of the main concerns in cloud computing is security. In particular, the authors describe some attacks in the form of misuse patterns, where a misuse pattern describes how an attack is performed from the point of view of the attacker. Specially, they describe three misuse patterns: Resource Usage Monitoring Inference, Malicious Virtual Machine Creation, and Malicious Virtual Machine Migration Process.

INTRODUCTION

The Internet has been developing quickly during the last decade. The cost of storage is increasing as well as the cost of the power consumed by the hardware (Zhang, Zhang, Chen, & Huo, 2010). Thus, organizations need new solutions. Cloud computing is a new paradigm that improves the utilization of resources and decreases the power consumption of hardware. Cloud computing allows users to have access to resources, software,

and information using any device that has access to the Internet. The users consume these resources and pay only for the resources they use.

Virtualization is a key feature for cloud computing (Gurav & Shaikh, 2010), which offers a potentially secure, reliable, scalable, shared, and manageable environment. Virtualization allows many virtual machines to run on a single physical machine. Virtual machines are created and supervised by the Virtual Machine Monitor that is a software layer that mediates between the software and the hardware. Virtualization permits users to create, copy, share, migrate, and roll back virtual

DOI: 10.4018/978-1-4666-2125-1.ch003

machines, which creates tremendous benefits for users (Garfinkel & Rosenblum, 2005). However, it also comes with new security problems. Cloud providers must undertake a substantial effort to secure their systems in order to minimize the threats that result from communication, monitoring, modification, migration, mobility and denial of service. In this work, we examine how virtualization gives raise to some security issues.

In order to design a secure system, we first need to understand possible threats to our system. Several methods have been developed to identify threats, e.g. (Braz, Fernandez, & VanHilst, 2008). Once identified, we need to describe how these threats are realized to accomplish a misuse according to the goals of the attacker. A misuse pattern describes how a misuse is performed from the point of view of the attacker (E. B. Fernandez, Yoshioka, & Washizaki, 2009). It defines the environment where the attack is performed, countermeasures to stop it, and it provides forensic information in order to trace the attack once it happens. Misuse patterns are useful for developers because once they determine that a possible attack can happen in the environment, a corresponding misuse pattern will indicate what security mechanisms are needed as countermeasures. Also, misuse patterns can be very useful for forensic examiners to determine how an attack is performed, and where they can find useful evidence information after the attack is done. An important value of misuse patterns is that they describe the components of the system where the attack is performed using class diagrams and sequence diagrams, relating the attack to specific system units.

We present in this work three examples of misuse patterns that describe some threats found in cloud computing environments. One of the vulnerabilities that is inherent in cloud computing is the co-location of virtual machines, where an attacker's virtual machine tries to reside in the same server of the victim's virtual machine with purposes of misuse, such as information inference based on resource usage (leakage of information). Moreover, sharing virtual machine images is one of the new threats that cloud computing is facing. Virtual machine images are prepackaged software templates that are used to instantiate virtual machines. Thus, these images have a significant effect on the overall security of the cloud (Wei, Zhang, Ammons, Bala, & Ning, 2009). Cloud providers offer a repository service where providers and users can store their images. Users can either create their own image, or they can use any image stored in the repository. An attacker who creates a valid account can create an image containing malicious code such as a Trojan horse. If another customer uses this image, the virtual machine that he creates will be infected with the hidden malware, which can then perform a variety of misuses. Furthermore, the contents of virtual machines such as the kernel, applications, and data being used by these applications can be compromised during live migration.

Section 2 presents background information. In Section 3, we present three misuse patterns for cloud computing including Resource Usage Monitoring Inference, Malicious Virtual Machine Creation, and Malicious Virtual Machine Migration Process. In Section 4, we present some discussion, and in Section 5 we offer some conclusions and possible future work.

BACKGROUND

Template for Misuse Patterns

This section describes each part of the template for misuse patterns.

Name

The name of the pattern should correspond to the generic name given to the specific type of attack in standard attack repositories such as CERT (Carnegie Mellon University).

Intent or Thumbnail Description

A short description of the intended purpose of the pattern (what problem it solves for an attacker).

Context

The context describes the generic environment including the conditions under which the attack may occur. This may include minimal defenses present in the system as well as typical vulnerabilities of the system. The context can be specified using a deployment diagram of the relevant portions of the system as well as sequence or collaboration diagrams that show the normal use of the system. A class diagram may show the relevant system structure. We can list specific preconditions for an attack to happen.

Problem

From an attacker's perspective, the problem is how to find a way to attack the system. An additional problem occurs whenever a system is protected by some defense mechanisms. The **forces** indicate what factors may be required in order to accomplish the attack and in what way; for example, which vulnerabilities can be exploited. Also, which factors may obstruct or delay accomplishing the attack.

Solution

This section describes the solution of the hacker's problem, i.e., how the attack can reach its objectives and the expected results of the attack. UML class diagrams show the system under attack. Sequence or collaboration diagrams show the exchange of messages needed to accomplish the attack. State or activity diagrams may add further detail.

Affected System Components (Where to Look for Evidence) (Targets)

This is a new section compared to standard security patterns. The misuse pattern should not be a comprehensive representation of all components and relationships involved in an attack. Rather, the pattern should represent all components that are important to prevent the attack and are essential to the forensic examination. This can be represented by a class diagram that is a subset or superset of the class diagram of the context.

Known Uses

Specific incidents where this attack occurred are preferred but for new vulnerabilities, where an attack has not yet occurred, specific contexts where the potential attack may occur are enough.

Consequences

Discusses the benefits and drawbacks of a misuse pattern from the attacker's viewpoint. Is the effort and cost of the attack commensurate with the results obtained? This is an evaluation that must be made by the attacker when deciding to perform the attack; the designers should evaluate their assets using some risk analysis approach. The enumeration includes good and bad aspects and should match the forces.

Countermeasures and Forensics

This section describes the security measures necessary in order to stop, mitigate, or trace this type of attack. This implies an enumeration of which security patterns are effective against this attack. From a forensic viewpoint, it describes what information can be obtained at each stage tracing back the attack and what can be deduced from this data in order to identify this specific attack. Finally, it may indicate what additional information should be collected at the involved units to improve forensic analysis.

Related Patterns

Discusses other misuse patterns with different objectives but performed in a similar way or with similar objectives but performed in a different way.

MISUSE PATTERNS FOR CLOUD COMPUTING

Resource Usage Monitoring Inference in Cloud Computing

Intent

Cloud systems allow many virtual machines to share the same physical infrastructure. An attacker's virtual machine may be placed in the same hardware as the victim's virtual machine to obtain some information such as estimate traffic rates or detect cache activity spikes. Also, the attacker may request many resources, so others customers that are sharing the same resources cannot have them available when needed (Denial of Service).

Context

In Infrastructure as a Service (IaaS) in clouds, physical infrastructure is shared by multiple virtual machines. IaaS is accessible through the Internet, and it provides a computer infrastructure that consists of physical storage and processing capabilities. A Virtual Machine Monitor (VMM) creates virtual machines and provides isolation between them.

Problem

To perform some types of misuse it is necessary to have a virtual machine co-located with the target's virtual machine in the same physical structure (availability zone). How to assign a machine to be located in the same hardware as the victim's virtual machine? Once the attacker's virtual machine is placed on the same hardware as the victim's virtual machine, how the attacker can deduce information by monitoring the victim's behavior?

The attack can be performed by taking advantage of the following vulnerabilities:

- Any person can open an account and create a VM.
- Knowing when a VM is running helps the attacker by informing him when the victim is running.
- The attacker should be able to receive unlimited resources as needed.
- Any resource that is shared by different virtual machines can become a channel that will provide some information that can be useful to infer something about any co-located virtual machine.

Solution

When the user requests a virtual machine, he specifies a region and may either choose an availability zone or is assigned one on his behalf. Also, the user specifies a VM instance type that indicates a combination of computational power, memory and persistent storage. The VMM creates a virtual machine that is assigned to a particular server located in the region specified by the user.

Like any other customers, an attacker can simply request to rent an infrastructure, and he can run and control virtual machines in the cloud. The attacker can successfully locate his virtual machine in the same hardware as the victim, and then learn some information by monitoring some channels. For example, In Amazon's EC2 and other clouds, it is more likely that an availability zone corresponds to a certain range of IP addresses (Ristenpart, Tromer, Shacham, & Savage, 2009). Knowing the IP address of the victim, the attacker can determine the location of the VM and create

Figure 1. Class diagram for virtualization in cloud computing

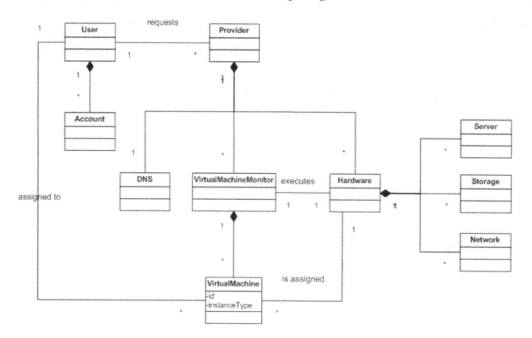

his VM in the same zone. The attacker can observe the behavior of the victim, such as traffic rate or cache activity and deduce some information. Also, after being able to be located in the same hardware, the attacker can request for more resources to the provider making the provider run out of resources (a Denial of Service attack).

In order for the attacker to determine the victim's IP address, systems such as EC2 map public IP addresses to private IP addresses through their DNS services. As a result, the attacker can make DNS queries in EC2 in order to find the required internal IP addresses. In (Ristenpart, et al., 2009), they conducted a survey of public servers on EC2 and they identified four distinct IP address prefixes. Then, they performed a TCP either to port 80 or port 443. From the IP addresses that corresponded to these ports, they performed a DNS lookup using the EC2's DNS.

Structure

Figure 1 shows a class diagram for the virtual machine structure in cloud computing. A *User*

creates one or more *Accounts* in order to use the *Provider's* infrastructure. The *Provider* is composed of a Hypervisor, Hardware (server, storage and network), and *DNS* (Domain Name System). The *Virtual Machine Monitor* (VMM) creates *Virtual Machines* (VM) and assigns their instances to the users who requested them. When the instance is launched, it is assigned to a physical server and given other hardware resources. The *Virtual Machine* passes system calls to the *Virtual Machine Monitor* which executes those calls in the *Hardware*.

Dynamics

UC1: Create a Virtual Machine for a user (Figure 2)

Summary: The Provider creates a Virtual Machine for a user.

Actor: User

Precondition: The user must have an account with the Provider.

Figure 2. Sequence diagram for the use case create a virtual machine

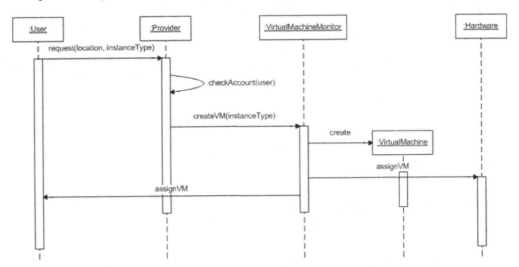

Description:

a. The User requests to the Provider to create a virtual machine. He specifies the physical location and the type of the instance.

b. The Provider checks if the user has an account and redirects the request to the Hypervisor.

c. The Virtual Machine Monitor creates an instance of the Virtual Machine and assigns it to a server and to the user.

Postcondition: A Virtual Machine is created in the specified location and assigned to a server and to the user.

UC2: Infer some of the victim's information by monitoring his resource usage (Figure 3)

Summary: An attacker's virtual machine is located in the same hardware as the victim's virtual machine.

Actor: Attacker

Precondition: The attacker must have an account and know some information about the victim such as her public IP in the cloud.

Description:

a. The Attacker requests to the Provider's DNS to map the victim's public IP address to his private IP address.

b. The Provider returns the private IP address to the Attacker.

c. The Attacker finds out victim's information such as physical location and instance type.

d. The Attacker requests to rent an infrastructure from the Provider. He specifies the physical location and the instance type which are the same as the ones obtained in step (c).

e. Do the same as the Use Case 1

f. The Attacker can now observe the resource usage and make some inference.

Postcondition: The attacker's virtual machine is created and assigned to the same hardware where the victim's virtual machine resides, and the attacker can infer some of the victim's information.

Consequences

The success of this attack implies:

- Basically, anyone who has a valid credit can request a virtual machine from a provider. For example, in Amazon's EC2, a user creates an account using his email account and a valid credit card. Thus, an

Figure 3. Sequence diagram for the use case infer some of the victim's information by monitoring his resource usage

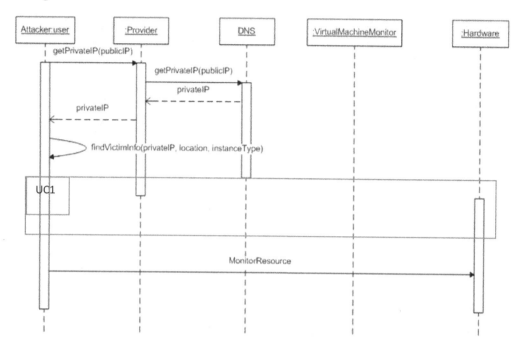

attacker can create and control virtual machines in the cloud.

- Attackers can take advantage of knowledge about the target location because the DNS provides such information. A DNS's provider can map public IP addresses to local IP addresses.

- Different physical locations are likely to correspond to different local IP addresses and the same may be true for instance types as well.

- Any physical resource that multiplexes between the attacker and the target can be a potentially useful channel: data cache, network access, CPU branch predictors and instruction cache, DRAM memory bus, CPU pipelines, scheduling of CPU cores and time slices, disk access, etc. This information could be used by a competitor to deduce an imminent product announcement, a company reorganization, or another significant institution event.

- Servers in cloud computing environments only run when needed, so an attacker can look at the status of the server and see if any virtual machine instances are running. This can make his work more efficient.

- Cloud computing offers pay as you go services where users can get more or less resources on demand. Thus, the attacker can request for more resources making other co-located users not to be able to get more computing from the cloud when needed (denial of service).

Possible sources of failure include:

- There is a possibility that an attacker's instance is not assigned to the same server as the victim's instance even when we know the location and the type of the victim's instance. That location can be composed of many servers and the same types of instances can be assigned to different servers.

- Some defenses described in the next section can stop this attack.
- In some clouds, users could request their virtual machines to be assigned on hardware that only can be occupied by virtual machines of their accounts.

Countermeasures

Resource Usage Monitoring Inference can be stopped by the following countermeasures:

- Verify the background of the user when opening an account; however, this is very hard to do and may reduce the economic incentives of the provider.
- Assign random local IP addresses to the instances, so the attacker will not associate a local IP address to a certain location or instance type.
- Control access to the DNS map.
- Control access to resource usage monitoring.
- Monitor the utilization of the infrastructure so all users get some portion of the computing in the cloud.

From the victim's perspective, cloud customers cannot monitor other customers' computations to protect themselves against timing side-channel, and the provider cannot monitor their customers' computations due to privacy concerns. However, (Aviram, Hu, Ford, & Gummadi, 2010) proposes a new approach to reduce the risk of timing channel in clouds.

From the point of view of the cloud provider, covert channel and side channel attacks cannot be detected since they rely on legitimate use of the system (Wang & Lee, 2006). However, cloud providers can mitigate these types of attacks; two possible solutions are proposed in (Wang & Lee, 2006).

Forensics

Where can we find evidence of this attack?

- Providers can keep logs of the requests made by the users.
- Providers can keep logs of the co-located virtual machines that are assigned to the same server.

Related Patterns

- The Virtual Machine Monitor (Eduardo B. Fernandez & Sorgente, 2005) provides isolation between different virtual machines that execute different operating systems.
- Resource Assignment patterns can be used for assigning servers to users.

Malicious Virtual Machine Creation

Intent

A Virtual Machine Image is a type of virtual appliance that is used to instantiate a Virtual Machine (VM). Virtual Machine Images contain initial file system state and software for the machine. An attacker may create a virtual machine image that contains malicious code so it can infect other users when they create their virtual machines. The attacker may read also confidential data from images that are publicly stored in the provider's repository.

Context

Some IaaS (Infrastructure as a Service) providers offer a VM image repository where users can retrieve images in order to initialize their VM. These VM Images can be created and published by the provider or by a client.

Figure 4. Class diagram for VM image misuse pattern

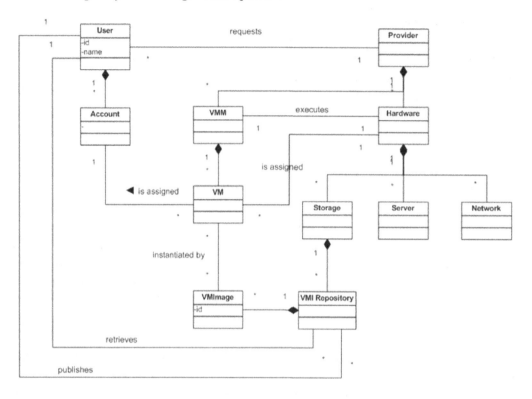

Problem

To perform some types of misuse it is necessary to be able to create and publish VM images.

The attack can be performed by taking advantage of the following vulnerabilities:

- Any person who has a valid account can create and register a VM image.
- There should be a common place where the users can share VM images.
- VM images contain prepackaged software components for an application. Thus, an attacker can create a VM image with malicious code.
- VM images contain installed and fully configured applications. The configuration may require sensitive operations such as creating username and password (Wei, et al., 2009).

Solution

When a user publishes a VM image as public, any other user of the cloud is able to use it to instantiate his VM. This VM image can contain malicious code. The Virtual Machine Monitor (VMM) will run this image in order to instantiate the user's VM. Now, the attacker can have control of the virtual machine and perform malicious activities such as infect other computers. Infected virtual machines may appear briefly, infect other virtual machines, and disappear before they can be detected (Garfinkel & Rosenblum, 2005).

Structure

Figure 4 shows a class diagram for the repository for VM images in cloud computing. A Virtual Machine (VM) is an isolated software container that has a CPU, RAM, hard disk, and network controllers. It requires the installation of operat-

Figure 5. Sequence diagram for the use case publish a malicious VM image

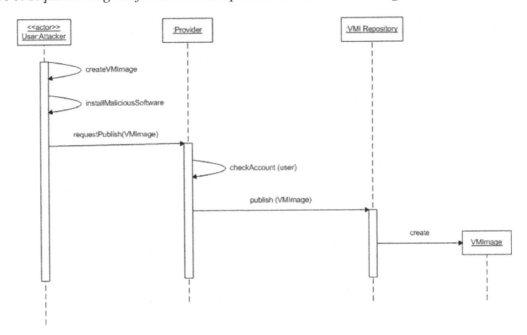

ing system and applications. A Virtual Machine Image (VMImage) is a pre-installed operating system and application stack. A User retrieves a VMImage from the Provider's Repository. These images can be created and published by other users or by the provider. The Provider is composed of a Hypervisor and Hardware (server, storage and network). The Virtual Machine Monitor (VMM) creates VMs by instantiating a VMImage, and it assigns their instances to the users who requested them. When the instance is launched, it is assigned to a physical server and given other hardware resources. The VM passes system calls to the VMM which executes those calls in the Hardware.

Dynamics

UC1: Publish a Malicious Virtual Machine Image (Figure 5)

Summary: The Attacker publishes a Virtual Machine Image that contains malicious code.
Actor: Attacker

Precondition: The Attacker must have an account with the Provider.
Description:
a. The Attacker creates a VM Image.
b. The Attacker installs malicious software within the VM image.
c. The Attacker requests to the Provider to upload the VM Image.
d. The Provider checks if the attacker (legal user) has an account.
e. The Provider uploads the VM Image into the repository.
f. The Provider sends an acknowledgement to the attacker.
Postcondition: A VM Image is created and placed into the Provider's repository, so any other user can use it and get infected.

UC2: Launch a VM using an infected VM Image (Figure 6)

Summary: A user launches a VM using an infected VM Image.

Figure 6. Sequence diagram for the use case launch a VM using a malicious VM image

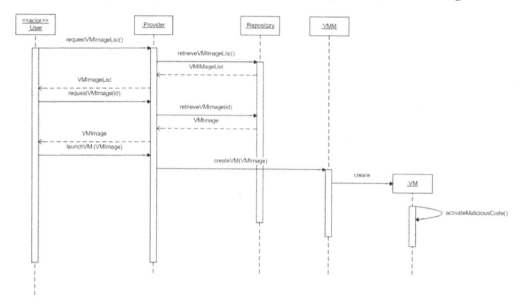

Actor: User

Precondition: The user must have an account, and the attacker has published her VM Image into the **Provider's repository.** Also, the user should choose the VM Image created by the attacker.

Description:

a. The User request to the Provider to retrieve a VM Image.

b. The Provider checks if the user has a valid account.

c. If the user is valid, the Provider sends the list of VM Images.

d. The User chooses the VM Image, and he requests to launch a VM to the Provider.

e. The Provider forwards the request to the VMM that will create the VM.

f. Once the VM is launched, it executes the malicious code.

Postcondition: The user's VM is infected and it may infect other VMs.

Consequences

Some of the benefits of the misuse pattern are the following:

- An attacker can open an account using a valid credit card and register malicious VM images into the provider's repository.

- VM Images contain all the software dependencies needed to run the Trojan horse, so the attacker does not need to worry whether the victims' software stacks satisfies the Trojan horse's dependencies (Wei, et al., 2009).

- An attacker can get control of the infected virtual machines and obtain some confidential information.

- Repositories that contain malicious VM images can be a way to distribute malware.

- Infected virtual machines may infect other virtual machines. For example, an attacker may create a malicious VM image in order to infect other machines creating a collection of infected machines, Botnet (Corporation, 2009).

Possible sources of failure include:

- There is a possibility that the users choose to create their own VM images instead of using a public VM Image.

- Since VM images are dormant artifacts that reside in the repository, they are not harmful if they are not executed.
- Users can only retrieve images that are from certified owners.

Countermeasures

Malicious VM Images can be stopped by the following countermeasures:

- (Wei, et al., 2009) proposed an image management system that control access to images, tracks the origin of images, and provides image filters and scanners that detect and repair security violations.
- Verify the background of the user when opening an account; however, this is very hard to do.
- Users can only retrieve images from certified owners.
- Use an Intrusion Detection System (IDS) to identify malicious activities such as in (Vieira, Schulter, Westphall, & Westphall, 2010).

Forensics

Where can we find evidence of this attack?

- Providers can keep logs of the users that publish/retrieve VM Images.
- We can audit a suspicious VM Image.

Malicious Virtual Machine Migration Process

Intent

The attacker tries to provoke leakage of sensitive information or modify the virtual machine (VM) content while it is in transit. An attacker can also compromise the migration module in the VMM and overwhelm the victim machine by transferring many VMs.

Context

Cloud environments mostly rely on virtualization. The virtual machine monitor (VMM) provides the foundation for virtualization management. Some VMM such as Xen (Barham et al., 2003) and VMware (VMware) have adopted live virtual machine migration in order to transfer a VM from one server to another one. Live migration of virtual machines is a process in which a virtual machine is transferred from one VMM to another one. Virtual machine migration creates new opportunities for cloud computing environments such as high availability, hardware maintenance, fault tolerance, and load balancing.

Problem

To perform some types of misuse it is necessary to be able to monitor and intercept the transfer of a VM from one server to another.

The attack can be performed by taking advantage of the following vulnerabilities:

- The migration process involves transferring the VM content across a network that can be insecure such as the Internet.
- The VM may be transferred in clear text. Thus, its information can be captured or modified by an attacker.
- The module that handles migration operations can be compromised.
- A VM can be transferred to an insecure host.
- The content of the transferred VM may have malicious code

Solution

When a VM is transferred from one server to another, an attacker can monitor the network and obtain some confidential information or manipulate the VM content while it is in transit. Also, the attacker can compromise the VMM and gain full control of the migration process. A compromised VMM can initiate migration of several VMs to the target victim causing disruptions or denial of service (DoS), or it can transfer a VM to the attacker's machine.

Structure

Figure 7 shows a class diagram for VM Migration Process. The *CloudManager* is an interface for the person who manages the *VMMs*. A *Virtual Machine Monitor (VMM)* creates and manages *Virtual Machines (VMs)*. A *VM* is a software implementation of a machine that executes programs. Its kernel operations are performed by calls to the VMM. VMMs assign instances of the Virtual Machine to a physical server, which

includes other *Hardware* resources. The *VMM* manages the migration process of a *VM* from one server (VMM) to another. The *Attacker* listens to the network in order to obtain some confidential information or to modify the content. Also, the *Attacker* can compromise the VMM, so he can gain control of the migration process.

Dynamics

UC1: Virtual Machine Migration (Figure 8)

Summary: A VM is transferred from one VMM to another one.
Actor: Cloud Manager
Precondition:
Description:
  a.   The CloudManager starts the migration process.

Figure 7. Class diagram for VM migration process

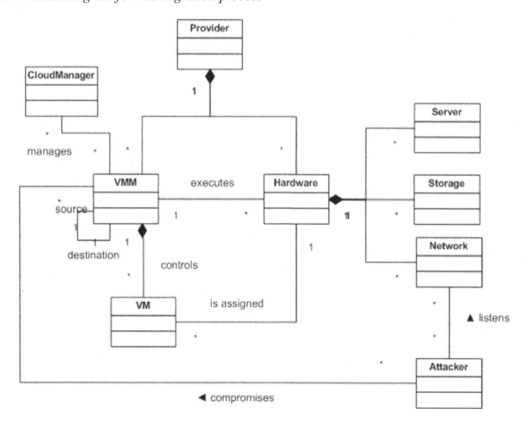

Figure 8. Sequence diagram for the use case virtual machine migration

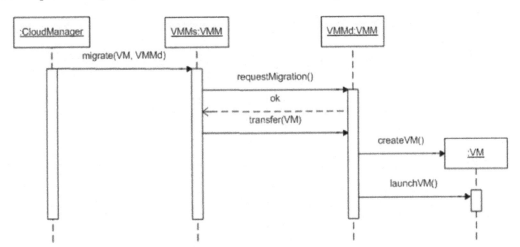

b. The source VMM requests VM migration to the destination VMM.

c. The destination VMM accepts the request.

d. The source VMM transfers the VM to the target machine.

e. The target VMM creates and starts the new VM.

Postcondition: The VM has been transferred to the destination machine. The migatred VM has been created and started.

UC2: Perform a denial of service attack (Figure 9)

Summary: A large number of VMs are transferred from a compromised VMM to the victim VMM.

Actor: Attacker

Precondition: The source VMM (VMMc) has been compromised and the attacker has gained control of the migration module.

Description:

a. The Attacker starts the migration process.

b. The compromised VMM requests VM migration to the victim VMM (VMMv).

c. The destination VMM accepts the request.

d. The compromised VMM starts transferring several VMs.

e. The victim VMM receives the VMs and starts the new VMs.

Postcondition: The attacker has overwhelmed the victim machine by migrating a large number of VMs to the destination machine.

UC3: Man-in-the-middle attack during VM migration process (Figure 10)

Summary: An attacker listens to the network during a migration process to obtain some confidential data.

Actor: Attacker, CloudManager

Precondition: The Attacker has impersonated both the source and the destination VMM.

Description:

a. The attacker starts monitoring the network traffic.

b. The CloudManager starts the migration process.

c. The source VMM requests VM migration to the destination VMM.

d. The source VMM starts transferring the VM to the destination VMM.

Figure 9. Sequence diagram for the use case perform a DoS attack

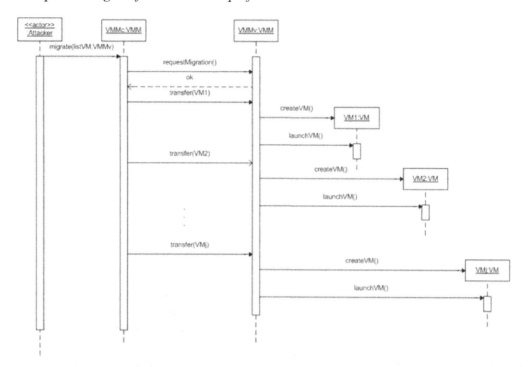

e. The attacker captures the traffic being transmitted.

f. The attacker modifies the VM.

g. The destination VMM receives the VM and starts the new VM.

Postcondition: The attacker captured and modified the VM.

Consequences

Some benefits of the misuse pattern are the following:

- The attacker can intercept the VM and obtain some confidential information, or he can modify the content of the VM while it is crossing the network.

- After the attacker compromises a VMM, he may send a large number of VMs to a victim's machine, causing disruptions or denial of service.

- A compromised VMM can transfer the victim's VM to the attacker's machine, gaining full control of the VM.

- A transferred VM may contain malicious code that can infect other VMs that are under the control of the target VMM.

Possible sources of failure include:

- When the attacker eavesdrops on the communication channel, he may not get all the necessary data.

- Some defenses described in the next section can stop this attack.

Countermeasures

Insecure VM Migration can be stopped by the following countermeasures:

- (Santos, Gummadi, & Rodrigues, 2009) proposes a Trusted Cloud Computing

Figure 10. Sequence diagram for the use case man-in-the-middle attack during VM migration process

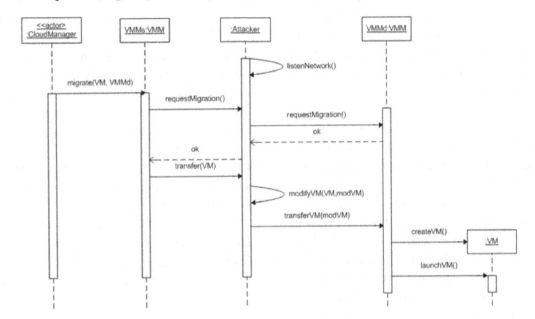

Platform (TCCP) that provides confidential execution of guest virtual machines. It provides secure VM launch and migration operations.

- (Fengzhe, Yijian, Huihong, Haibo, & Binyu, 2008) proposes a secure migration system that provides VM live migration capabilities under the condition that a VMM-protected system is present and active.
- The connection between the source and the destination VMMs should be authenticated and encrypted during the migration process.
- Isolate VM migration traffic to prevent eavesdropping attacks.

Forensics

Where can we find evidence of this attack?

- The provider can keep logs of the VMs that are transferred from one machine to another. Also, it can store information about the source and destination VMMs.

Related Patterns

- The Virtual Machine Monitor provides isolation between different virtual machines that execute different operating systems.

DISCUSSION

Designers need to understand the possible threats before designing secure systems. Our misuse patterns show that clouds are also vulnerable to attacks targeting some of its features such as shared virtual machine images, virtual machine live migration, and isolation. Identifying only threats is not enough; we need to understand how an attack is performed. These misuse patterns can help designers to understand how an attack is performed and what components of the system were used and compromised during an attack. Misuse patterns follow a template that contain different sections: context that describes the environment that the attack is performed, problem that includes forces which describes the vulnerabilities of the system, solution that depicts the components of the system using a class diagram and how an attack is performed using sequence diagrams. Also, misuse patterns describe the consequences which discuss the benefits and drawbacks of the misuse pattern from the attacker's point of view, countermeasures that enumerates security mechanisms which can be applied to mitigate the threat, and forensics that indicate how to trace an attack once it happens or where to search for forensic data.. It is possible to build a relatively complete catalog of misuse patterns for cloud computing. Having such a catalog we can analyze a specific cloud architecture and evaluate its degree of resistance to these misuses. The architecture (existing or under construction) must have a way to prevent or at least mitigate all the misuses that apply to it. When potential cloud customers buy cloud services they negotiate a Service Level Agreement (SLA) with the provider. This SLA could indicate what misuses the provider is explicitly able to control. Many providers do not want to show their security architectures; showing their list of misuse patterns would give them a way to prove a degree of resistance to misuses without having to show their security details.

CONCLUSION AND FUTURE WORK

Cloud computing is a new concept that may present some benefits for its users; however, it also raises some security problems which may slow down its use. We have presented some cloud computing threats as misuse patterns which describe in a systematic way how a misuse is performed from the attacker point of view. Virtualization, a key component for clouds, enables clouds to improve the utilization of physical resources by sharing resources by different users. Sharing resources among different virtual machines gives some opportunities to an attacker to monitor confidential information.

Also, virtual machines can be transferred from one server to another. Migration process uses a network such as the Internet to transport virtual machines; thus, attackers can exploit this vulnerability by listening to the network in order to obtain some confidential data. Also, sharing virtual machine images, virtual appliances that contain pre packaged software used to initialize the virtual machine, raises security concerns. Virtual machine images may contain malicious code that can be propagated once a user executes one of these malicious images.

We will continue developing misuse patterns for cloud environments in order to create a catalog of threats. We will also extend existing security pattern catalogs to include new patterns as defenses.

REFERENCES

Aviram, A., Hu, S., Ford, B., & Gummadi, R. (2010). Determinating timing channels in compute clouds. *Proceedings of the 2010 ACM Workshop on Cloud Computing Security Workshop*, Chicago, Illinois, USA.

Barham, P., Dragovic, B., Fraser, K., Hand, S., Harris, T., Ho, A., et al. (2003). Xen and the art of virtualization. *Proceedings of the nineteenth ACM symposium on Operating systems principles*, Bolton Landing, NY, USA.

Braz, F. A., Fernandez, E. B., & VanHilst, M. (2008, September). Eliciting security requirements through misuse activities. *Proceedings of the 2nd Int. Workshop on Secure Systems Methodologies using Patterns (SPattern '08)- in conjunction with the 4th International Conference on Trust, Privacy & Security in Digital Busines(TrustBus '08)* (pp. 328-333). Turin, Italy.

Fengzhe, Z., Yijian, H., Huihong, W., Haibo, C., & Binyu, Z. (2008, October). PALM: Security preserving VM live migration for systems with VMM-enforced protection. *Third Asia-Pacific Trusted Infrastructure Technologies Conference, APTC '08* (pp. 9-18).

Fernandez, E. B., & Sorgente, T. (2005, August). A pattern language for secure operating system architectures. *Proceedings of the 5th Latin American Conference on Pattern Languages of Programs* (pp. 68-88). Campos do Jordao, Brazil.

Fernandez, E. B., Yoshioka, N., & Washizaki, H. (2009, March). Modeling misuse patterns. *Proceedings of the 4th International Workshop on Dependability Aspects of Data Warehousing and Mining Applications* (DAWAM 2009), *in conjunction with the 4th International Conference on Availability, Reliability, and Security* (ARES 2009) (pp. 566-571). Fukuoka, Japan.

Garfinkel, T., & Rosenblum, M. (2005). When *virtual is harder than real: Security challenges in virtual machine based computing environments. Proceedings of the 10th conference on Hot Topics in Operating Systems,* Santa Fe, NM.

Gurav, U., & Shaikh, R. (2010). Virtualization: A key feature of cloud computing. *Proceedings of the International Conference and Workshop on Emerging Trends in Technology* (pp. 227-229). Mumbai, Maharashtra, India.

Intel Corporation. (2009). The dark cloud: Understanding and defending against botnets and stealthy malware. *Intel Technology Journal, 13*(02). Retrieved from http://www.intel.com/technology/itj/2009/v13i2/ITJ9.2.9-Cloud.htm

Ristenpart, T., Tromer, E., Shacham, H., & Savage, S. (2009). Hey, you, get off of my cloud: Exploring information leakage in third-party compute clouds. *Proceedings of the 16th ACM Conference on Computer and Communications Security* (pp. 199-212). Chicago, Illinois, USA.

Santos, N., Gummadi, K. P., & Rodrigues, R. (2009). Towards trusted cloud computing *Proceedings of the 2009 Conference on Hot Topics in Cloud Computing.* San Diego, CA: USENIX Association.

Vieira, K., Schulter, A., Westphall, C. B., & Westphall, C. M. (2010). Intrusion detection for grid and cloud computing. *IT Professional,* 38–43. doi:10.1109/MITP.2009.89

VMware. (n.d.). *VMware vMotion – Migrate virtual machine with zero downtime.* Retrieved from http://www.vmware.com/products/vmotion/

Wang, Z., & Lee, R. B. (2006). Covert and side channels due to processor architecture. *Proceedings of the 22nd Annual Computer Security Applications Conference.*

Wei, J., Zhang, X., Ammons, G., Bala, V., & Ning, P. (2009). Managing security of virtual machine images in a cloud environment. *Proceedings of the 2009 ACM Workshop on Cloud Computing Security* (pp. 91-96).

Zhang, S., Zhang, S., Chen, X., & Huo, X. (2010). Cloud computing research and development trend. *Second International Conference on Future Networks* (pp. 93-97). Sanya, Hainan, China.

Section 2
Risks and Vulnerabilities in Cloud Computing

Chapter 4
Security Risks in Cloud Computing:
An Analysis of the Main Vulnerabilities

Belén Cruz Zapata
University of Murcia, Spain

José Luis Fernández Alemán
University of Murcia, Spain

ABSTRACT

Any software system is exposed to potential attack. The recent and continuous appearance of vulnerabilities in software systems makes security a vital issue if these systems are to succeed. The detection of potential vulnerabilities thus signifies that a set of policies can be established to minimize their impact. This therefore implies identifying the risks and data to be protected, and the design of an action plan with which to manage incidents and recovery. The purpose of this chapter is to provide an analysis of the most common vulnerabilities in recent years, focusing on those vulnerabilities which are specific to cloud computing. These specific vulnerabilities need to be identified in order to avoid them by providing prevention mechanisms, and the following questions have therefore been posed: What kinds of vulnerabilities are increasing? Has any kind of vulnerability been reduced in recent years? What is the evolution of their severity?

INTRODUCTION

Many cloud applications are currently widely and successfully used (i.e. Google App Engine, Amazon's Computer Cloud Amazon Web Service and Microsoft Azure Service Platform). Although cloud computing is a growing technology, no

key player leads this revolution. The cloud saves money and has the backing of many large software vendors (Lillard, Garrison, Schiller, & Steele, 2010). However, one of the main reasons for the slowing down in the growth of cloud computing is that of security (Subashini & Kavitha, 2011). A few examples of this are two real incidents which occurred in 2009. One of them is Salesforce.com which suffered an outage that locked more than

DOI: 10.4018/978-1-4666-2125-1.ch004

900,000 subscribers out of crucial cloud computing applications and data needed to transact business with customers (Ferguson, 2009). Another example is the smart phone known as "Sidekick" with which users (over 800,000) temporarily lost personal data which was accessed as a cloud service. The outage lasted almost two weeks, and some losses might have been permanent (Cellan-Jones, 2009).

Data protection and data privacy are extremely important, and in a cloud computing infrastructure the detection of potential vulnerabilities is therefore of paramount importance. A cloud computing model may have the same kind of vulnerabilities that are detected in conventional computing models, while other vulnerabilities are intrinsic to the technology used by cloud computing. From a cloud customer perspective, the consequences and ultimate cost of a security attack is exactly the same, regardless of whether it has occurred within a cloud or a conventional IT infrastructure. For a cloud service provider, however, the perspective is somewhat different. If a vulnerability is prevalent in state-of-the-art cloud offerings, then it must be regarded as cloud-specific.

Being aware of these vulnerabilities is the best mechanism for prevention. The Law of Vulnerabilities 2.0 (Wolfgang Kandek, CTO & Qualys, Inc., 2009) states that "80% of vulnerability exploits are now available within single digit days after the vulnerability's public release". The cloud provider is responsible for providing secure cloud instances, which should ensure users privacy, maintain data integrity and guarantee that information and information processing is available to clients upon demand. It is therefore important to identify those vulnerabilities that are specific to cloud computing. Since risks cannot be completely eliminated, they need to be lowered to acceptable levels.

In order to better understand the singularities of cloud computing vulnerabilities, a set of essential characteristics should be considered:

- **On-demand self-service:** A user can provide services automatically without requiring human interaction with the service provider.
- **Broad network access:** Services are available via the network through standard mechanisms.
- **Resource pooling:** Resources are pooled to serve multiple consumers, and are dynamically assigned and reassigned according to consumer demand.
- **Rapid elasticity:** Resources can be rapidly and elastically provided in order to quickly scale out and scale in.
- **Measured Service:** Resource usage can be monitored, controlled, and reported.

If a clear idea of concepts such as vulnerability, threat or risk is to be obtained, then it is first necessary to describe these terms. A threat is a potential cause of an unwanted impact on a system or organization (ISO 13335-1). Threats fall into two categories, known as vulnerabilities and exposures. According to MITRE's CVE Terminology (MITRE, 2011), vulnerability is a mistake in software that can be directly used by a hacker to gain access to a system or network. It is therefore a state in a computing system (or set of systems) which: (1) allows an attacker to execute commands as another user; (2) allows an attacker to access data that is contrary to the specified access restrictions for that data; (3) allows an attacker to pose as another entity; (4) allows an attacker to conduct a denial of service.

An exposure, meanwhile, is defined by MITRE's CVE Terminology as a system configuration issue or a mistake in software that allows access to information or capabilities that can be used by a hacker as a stepping-stone into a system or network: (1) it allows an attacker to conduct information gathering activities; (2) it allows an attacker to hide activities; (3) it includes a capability that behaves as expected, but can be easily compromised; (4) it is a primary point of entry that an attacker may attempt to use to gain access to the system or data; (5) it is considered a problem according to a particular reasonable security policy.

The last term is the idea of risk. The ISO 31000 definition of risk is: the effect of uncertainty upon objectives where an effect is a deviation from the expected, positive or negative. ISO 31000 notes that risk can be regarded in terms of: (1) the likelihood of an event occurring; (2) the impact (or consequence) of the event if it occurs. ISO 27005 similarly states that a risk is a combination of the consequences that would follow on from the occurrence of an unwanted event and the likelihood of the occurrence of the event.

This chapter focuses on vulnerabilities which may imply a risk for cloud computing. Other standards with which to define a vulnerability also exist, such as ISO 27005 which defines a vulnerability as a weakness of an asset or group of assets that can be exploited by one or more threats where an asset is anything that may be of value to the organization, its business operations and their continuity, including information resources that support the organization's mission. ISO RFC 2828 defines it as a flaw or weakness in a system's design, implementation, or operation and management that could be exploited to violate the system's security policy.

The purpose of this chapter is to provide an analysis of the most common vulnerabilities to appear in recent years, focusing on those vulnerabilities that are specific to cloud computing. Examples of vulnerabilities include injection vulnerabilities, weak authentication schemes and vulnerabilities resulting from Web applications, such as cross-site scripting, cross-site request forgery, insecure direct object references or insecure cryptographic storage. Current Web applications have many inherent vulnerabilities; in fact, in 2008, over 63% of all documented vulnerabilities were for Web applications (Huynh & Miller, 2010).

This objective has been accomplished by extracting and studying data from the National Vulnerability Database (NVD) created by NIST (National Institute of Standards and Technology). In the last five years, more than 5629 vulnerabilities have been identified by NIST. For instance, SQL injection vulnerability was the most frequent type in 2008, but two years on from then, SQL injection had dropped by around 50%. Moreover, in the last two years, the percentage of high severity vulnerabilities has slightly decreased by 5% with regard to less severe vulnerabilities.

Firstly, the background to this chapter is introduced, and in the next section, the analysis, which is divided into four subsections, is presented. The first of these subsections concerns the vulnerabilities classification framework, while the next two correspond with each of the terms defining a risk that are exposed above (likelihood and impact). The last subsection concerns solutions and recommendations. The final sections deal with our future research and conclusions. References, additional reading and key terms are then presented.

BACKGROUND

Several vulnerability databases can be found in literature. Some of these are: Bugtraq (Security Focus), OSVDB, the National (U.S.) Vulnerability Database (NIST), US-CERT Vulnerability Notes (CERT); Internet Security Systems—X-Force Database (IBM); CERIAS Vulnerability Database, Secunia Vulnerability Database, Vupen Vulnerability Database and the LWN security vulnerabilities database.

Moreover, some organizations such as Symantec regularly produce reports providing information and trends with regard to vulnerability evolution thanks to their antivirus products. Strengths and weaknesses can be found in each of these vulnerability databases, and they offer the means to report and provide feedback about vulnerability. Each vulnerability database includes the general characteristics of the vulnerabilities stored in them: identifier, name, description, product affected, disclosure date. Data such as impact, advisory, CVE cross-reference and severity also appear.

Frei, May, Fiedler, and Plattner (2006) conducted a comprehensive study of more than 14,326 vulnerabilities from several vulnerability databases. The gap between exploit and patch availability after disclosure, and the increasing number of the zero-day exploits was quantified. A data analysis to examine the distributions of the exploit and patch availability by means of distribution functions, such as Pareto and Weibull was provided, thus laying the foundation for further analysis and risk management. Vache (2009) characterized the vulnerability life cycle and the exploit appearance in a qualitative manner. The author used the OSVDB data collected to determine a Beta distribution fitted with the vulnerability disclosure, the vulnerability patch disclosure and the exploit creation.

Arora, Krishnan, Telang, and Yang (2004) studied the impact of vulnerability disclosure and patch availability on attack processes. A data set composed of 308 vulnerabilities was used. The authors proposed an economical model which provides the evolution of the number of expected attacks per host and per day. Alhazmi, Woo, and Malaiya (2006) investigated the applicability of their vulnerability discovery model to certain operating systems and Web server vulnerabilities classified in eight categories and three severity levels. Seixas, Fonseca, Vieira, and Madeira (2009) analyzed 11 open source Web applications with 60 vulnerabilities written with strong typed languages (Java, C# and VB.NET), focusing on security vulnerabilities. For this analysis, the authors concluded that applications written with strong typed languages seem to have a smaller number of reported vulnerabilities. They also showed that the most frequent fault types that caused vulnerabilities were: "Missing function call" in XSS and "Missing if construct plus statements plus else before statements" in SQL Injection.

The results from an investigation showed that implementation vulnerabilities dominate in Web applications (Huynh & Miller, 2010). The most frequently vulnerabilities registered in the 20 open source applications studied were XSS (55%), SQL Injection (30%), Code Injection (6%) and others (9%). Proprietary systems had a similar distribution of vulnerability types. Vulnerability information was extracted from the OSVDB and Bugtraq databases, and covered the period from January 1, 2002 to May 31, 2007.

OSVDB covers around 73,275 vulnerabilities and some statistical information is shown on its main Web site. This information includes the number of vulnerabilities disclosed by type and by quarter from the years 2004 to 2011. Those types taken into account are XSS, SQL Injection, CSRF, File Inclusion, DoS and Overflow. The year with the greatest number of vulnerabilities was 2006, in which File Inclusion and XSS were the types that reached that maximum level.

Surveys concerning secure cloud computing or proposals for secure cloud computing models are readily available, but very little literature has been published on cloud computing vulnerabilities. Of those works which have been published, some study both vulnerabilities and threats and risks. Dahbur, Mohammad, and Tarakji (2011) present a study concerning known risks, vulnerabilities and threats, and the authors additionally explore specific cloud computing risks. The Cloud Security Alliance (CSA) group is responsible for a publication concerning the principal threats to cloud computing (CSA, 2010). CSA identified "Account or Service Hijacking" as a threat that is exploitable via software vulnerabilities. Subashini and Kavitha (2011) identified the main vulnerabilities which should be tested in the SaaS (Software as a Service) vendor, according to fourteen key security elements: data security, network security, data locality, data integrity, data segregation, data access, authentication, authorization, data confidentiality, Web application security, data breaches, virtualization vulnerability, availability, backup, identity management and sign-on process.

Some other papers focus on cloud specific vulnerabilities. Li, Liang, Yang, and Chen (2010) investigated different security vulnerabilities in cloud environments. Their experiments in 3 different scenarios showed that hackers can find easier means to obtain the target information if tools and the servers are in the same LAN. Feng, Chen, Ku, and Liu (2010) analyzed the integrity vulnerability existing in the current cloud storage platforms and showed the problem of repudiation. Grobauer, Walloschek, and Stöcker (2010) establish criteria to consider whether or not a particular vulnerability is specific to cloud computing. Hwang, Kulkareni and Hu (2009) assessed the vulnerability of three commercial cloud platforms: Google Cloud Platform, IBM Blue Cloud and Amazon Elastic Cloud. The authors found that all three platforms were weak in the area of security. Bugiel, Nürnberger, Pöppelmann, Sadeghi, and Schneider (2011) analyzed new vulnerabilities of the Secure Shell (SSH) protocol, which resulted from the cloud's dynamic nature and the usage model of Amazon Machine Images (AMIs). A security analysis (Somorovsky et al., 2011) of a large Public Cloud (Amazon) and a widely used Private Cloud software (Eucalyptus) revealed that username/password based client authentication may be highly vulnerable to XSS attacks, based on several highly critical vulnerabilities in the Elastic Compute Cloud's SOAP and Web interfaces.

Few studies have paid attention to the external threats that affect the financial viability and long-term availability of services hosted in the public cloud. Under the utility pricing model which governs the resource usage in the cloud model, public-facing Web content is vulnerable to the so-called Fraudulent Resource Consumption attack (Idziorek, Tannian, & Jacobson, 2011) in which attack clients purposefully request Web content in volumes that are economically unsustainable for the cloud consumer.

VULNERABILITIES ANALYSIS

Vulnerabilities can be characterized into three categories based on (Swiderski & Snyder, 2004). A vulnerability is classified as an Architecture vulnerability if it is caused by a design flaw; an Implementation vulnerability is caused by an insecure coding practice; and a Configuration vulnerability is caused by an incorrect configuration of the application. All of these categories are included in the classification framework.

Classification Framework

The data used in the analysis has been extracted from the National Vulnerability Database (NVD). NVD is the U.S. government repository of standards based vulnerability management data which are represented using the Security Content Automation Protocol (SCAP). This data enables the automation of vulnerability management, security measurement, and compliance.

NVD was chosen from all the possible databases because it is one of those that is most frequently referenced in literature. It offers an advanced search with a large number of different fields for the purpose of filtering, and data can be extracted in XML format. NVD and OSVDB databases rival each other in these characteristics, but NVD includes a statistics generator which is very similar to the advanced search, and simply shows the result as a summary.

Vulnerabilities present a set of features which should be specified and explained. These features are the basic criteria needed to carry out the objective of this chapter. The most important characteristics are: (1) Category; (2) Vendor; (3) Product; (4) Published Date Range; (5) Last Modified Date Range and (6) Severity, Low, Medium, and High.

With regard to category, the different categories considered are based on the Common Weakness Enumeration Specification (CWE), which is currently maintained by the MITRE Corporation with support from the National Cyber Security Division (DHS). CWE provides a common language of discourse for discussing, finding and dealing with the causes of software security vulnerabilities as they are found in code, design, or system architecture. Each individual CWE represents a single vulnerability type.

All individual CWEs are held within a hierarchical structure that allows for multiple levels of abstraction. Higher levels of the hierarchy provide a broad overview of a vulnerability type and can have many child CWEs associated with them. Deeper levels provide a finer granularity and usually have fewer or no child CWEs.

Figure 1 represents a portion of the CWE structure, in which the dark boxes represent the CWEs used by NVD. Table 1 shows a list of the set of weaknesses dealt with in the following analysis.

Vulnerabilities Statistical Analysis

In this section, a statistical analysis is conducted in order to quantitatively evaluate cloud computing security from the perspective of vulnerabilities.

Vulnerabilities referring to weaknesses enumerated previously have been analyzed year by year from 1988 to 2011. Figure 2 shows a graph representing the total number of vulnerabilities with no category considerations.

The first vulnerability was published in 1988. Hardly any vulnerabilities were published between 1988 and 1996, with only 75 vulnerabilities being registered in 1996. In 1997 and 1998 the number of vulnerabilities increased to around 250, with 252 vulnerabilities appearing in 1997. This number increased between 1999 and 2006, to around 6,000. However, in 2007 the number ceased to increase, and the number of vulnerabilities has slowly been reduced since then, it being 4,639 in 2010.

According to these results, three phases are clearly identified in the evolution of the number of vulnerabilities:

1. 1988-1998. Minimum number of vulnerabilities.
   ○ Average: 22 vulnerabilities.

Figure 1. Portion of CWE hierarchy

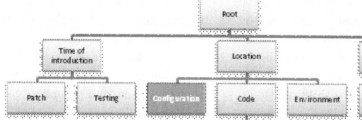

Table 1. Vulnerabilities categories

Name	CWE-ID	Description
Authentication Issues	CWE-287	When an actor claims to have a provided his/her identity, the software does not prove, or insufficiently proves, that the claim is correct.
Credentials Management	CWE-255	Failure to properly create, store, transmit or protect passwords and other credentials.
Permissions, Privileges, and Access Control	CWE-264	Failure to enforce permissions or other access restrictions for resources, or a privilege management problem.
Buffer Errors	CWE-119	The software performs operations on a memory buffer, but it can read from or write to a memory location that is outside the intended boundary of the buffer.
Cross-Site Request Forgery (CSRF)	CWE-352	The Web application does not, or cannot, sufficiently verify whether a well-formed, valid, consistent request was intentionally provided by the user who submitted the request.
Cross-Site Scripting (XSS)	CWE-79	The software does not neutralize user-controllable input before it is placed in output that is used as a Web page that is served to other users.
Cryptographic Issues	CWE-310	An insecure algorithm or the inappropriate use of one, an incorrect implementation of an algorithm that reduces security or the lack of encryption.
Path Traversal	CWE-22	The software uses external input to construct a pathname that is intended to identify a file or directory that is located beneath a restricted parent directory, but the software does not neutralize special elements within the pathname, which may cause the pathname to resolve a location that is outside the restricted directory.
Code Injection	CWE-94	The software constructs all or part of a code segment using externally-influenced input from an upstream component, but it does not neutralize, or incorrectly neutralizes, special elements that could modify the syntax or behavior of the intended code segment.
Format String Vulnerability	CWE-134	The software uses externally-controlled format strings in printf-style functions, which can lead to buffer overflows or data representation problems.
Configuration	CWE-16	Weaknesses in this category are typically introduced during the configuration of the software.
Information Leak / Disclosure	CWE-200	An information exposure is the intentional or unintentional disclosure of information to an actor that is not explicitly authorized to have access to that information.
Input Validation	CWE-20	The product does not validate, or incorrectly validates, input that may affect the control flow or data flow of a program. This overlaps other categories such as XSS, Numeric Errors, and SQL Injection.
Numeric Errors	CWE-189	Integer overflow, truncation, underflow, and other errors that may occur when handling numbers.
OS Command Injections	CWE-78	The software constructs all or part of an OS command using externally-influenced input from an upstream component, but it does not neutralize, or incorrectly neutralizes, special elements that could modify the intended OS command when it is sent to a downstream component.
Race Conditions	CWE-362	The program contains a code sequence that can run concurrently with other code, and the code sequence requires temporary, exclusive access to a shared resource, but a timing window exists in which the shared resource can be modified by another code sequence that is operating concurrently.
Resource Management Errors	CWE-399	The software allows attackers to consume excess resources, such as memory exhaustion from memory leaks, CPU consumption from infinite loops, disk space consumption, etc.
SQL Injection	CWE-89	The software constructs all or part of an SQL command using externally-influenced input from an upstream component, but it does not neutralize, or incorrectly neutralizes, special elements that could modify the intended SQL command when it is sent to a downstream component.
Link Following	CWE-59	The software attempts to access a file based on the filename, but it does not properly prevent that filename from identifying a link or shortcut that resolves an unintended resource.
Other	No Mapping	Weakness types from CWE which are not covered by previous ones.
Not in CWE	No Mapping	The weakness type is not covered in the version of CWE that was used for mapping.
Insufficient Information	No Mapping	There is insufficient information about the issue to classify it.
Design Error	No Mapping	Where no errors exist in the implementation or configuration of a system, but the initial design causes a vulnerability to exist.

Figure 2. Number of vulnerabilities per year

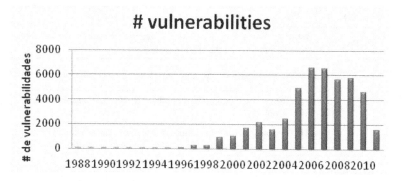

- ◦ % of total: 1.5%.
2. 1999-2004. Medium number of vulnerabilities.
   - ◦ Average: 1,520 vulnerabilities.
   - ◦ % of total: 21%.
3. 2005-2010. High number of vulnerabilities.
   - ◦ Average: 5,629 vulnerabilities.
   - ◦ % of total: 74%.

Despite the growth of security policies in software systems, the number of vulnerabilities is greater in recent years than in past years. The factor responsible for this is the complexity of the software systems. Software systems are more and more complex, and points of attack consequently emerge.

The following step is to compare number of vulnerabilities according to their category. Upon examining the NIST Database, it was observed that not all registered vulnerabilities have been assigned to a category. None of the vulnerabilities that appeared in the first years have been classified. From 1994 to 2006 only a few vulnerabilities have a category, the highest percentage being 18% (2003). Years can therefore be distinguished by:

1. 1988-2006. Minimum percentage of classification.
   - ◦ Average: 4%.
2. 2007. Medium percentage of classification.
   - ◦ Average: 40%.

3. 2008-2010. High percentage of classification.
   - ◦ Average: 100%.

In most years, viewing vulnerability data according to their category is not actually representative, and at this moment it is only possible to consider the years 2008, 2009, 2010 and 2011. As an example, in the year 2000 there were around 1,020 vulnerabilities, but only 16 of them were classified (1.57%).

Figure 3 shows the number of vulnerabilities in the last four years (2007, 2008, 2009 and 2010) which are the most reliable years, as is explained above. The size of the balloon represents the number of vulnerabilities in that year for that category.

The evolution over the years does not provide much information about the different categories since all of them follow the same pattern. The important information extracted is that of those categories which show a higher number of vulnerabilities: SQL Injection (over 2,900 vulnerabilities, 13%); XSS (over 2,800 vulnerabilities, 12.5%); and Buffer errors (over 2,600 vulnerabilities 11.6%). Owing to the nature of cloud computing applications, according to Web Services, SQL Injection and XSS are those categories which directly affect cloud computing. The vulnerability category Buffer Errors is relatively uncommon within this domain because these vulnerabilities are usually found in languages such as C.

Figure 3. Number of vulnerabilities per year and category

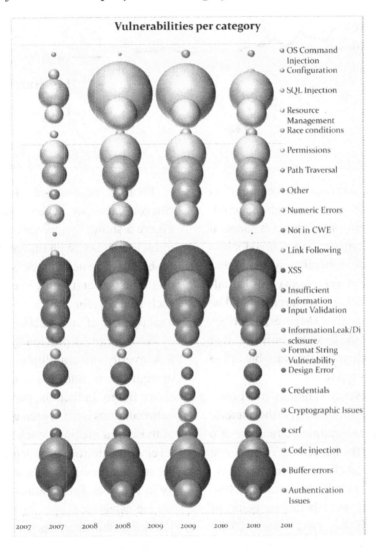

Another important feature analyzed is that of severity. Severity is a relative value which depends on the elements taken into account in each database. Some of these elements are usually: the impact of the vulnerability, the preconditions required to exploit it, the number of systems at risk or the ease with which it can be exploited. NVD supports the Common Vulnerability Scoring System (CVSS) version 2 standard. The Common Vulnerability Scoring System (CVSS) provides an open framework with which to communicate the characteristics and impacts of IT vulnerabilities. Its quantitative model ensures repeatable accurate measurement while enabling users to see the underlying vulnerability characteristics that were used to generate the scores.

A CVSS score is calculated through the definition of certain metrics. These metrics are separated into three categories: Base Score Metrics, Environmental Score Metrics and Temporal Score Metrics. The first category describes inherent characteristics of the vulnerability, and includes two subcategories: Exploitability Metrics (attack complexity or level of authentication needed) and Impact Metrics (confidentiality, integrity and availability impacts). The second category,

Figure 4. % Vulnerabilities by severity

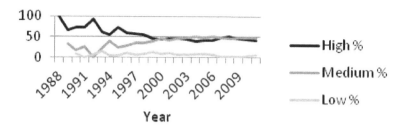

Environmental Score Metrics, describes the effect of a vulnerability within an organizational environment and includes two subcategories: General Modifiers (organization specific potential for loss and the percentage of vulnerable systems) and Impact Subscore Modifiers (system confidentiality, integrity and availability requirements). The last category, Temporal Score Metrics, describes elements related to those vulnerabilities that change over time, such as the fix available or the availability of exploit types.

NVD provides severity rankings of "Low," "Medium," and "High" in addition to the numeric CVSS scores, but these qualitative rankings are simply mapped from the numeric CVSS scores: 1. Vulnerabilities are labelled as being of "Low" severity if they have a CVSS base score of 0.0-3.9. 2. Vulnerabilities are labelled as being of "Medium" severity if they have a base CVSS score of 4.0-6.9. 3. Vulnerabilities are labelled as being of "High" severity if they have a CVSS base score of 7.0-10.0.

As Figure 4 shows, low severity vulnerabilities are not very common, and the majority of them are medium or high severity vulnerabilities. Before the year 2000, the percentage of high severity vulnerabilities was always greater than the percentage of medium severity vulnerabilities. Since the year 2000, the number of vulnerabilities belonging to these two severity levels is very similar, and their percentages have become closer and closer over the years.

Finally, the number of vulnerabilities per category and per severity has been analysed. Figure 5 shows the percentage of vulnerabilities in each category, with one column for each level of severity. The percentage is obtained by the sum of all the vulnerabilities in each category and in each severity for all the years, divided by the total number of vulnerabilities in that category.

As mentioned previously, the percentage of low severity vulnerabilities is lower than medium or high levels, and this is also reflected in the above figure. In fact, the percentage of low level vulnerabilities is never greater than the percentage of those of a medium level. This number of low level vulnerabilities is only greater than the number of vulnerabilities with a high level of severity in the XSS, Information Leak and Link Following categories.

Most of the categories have a predominant level of high or medium severity, but there are some categories in which the difference between them is very noticeable. The CSRF and XSS categories show a high percentage of vulnerabilities with a medium level of severity. Although XSS is one of the most frequent vulnerabilities, as shown previously, almost all of them have a medium level of severity. The other two categories with a marked gap between the percentages are OS Command Injection and SQL Injection. A large number of vulnerabilities in these categories have high level severity. Since SQL Injection is the category with most vulnerabilities, and since these vulnerabilities also have a high level of severity, then a close

Figure 5. % Vulnerabilities by category and severity

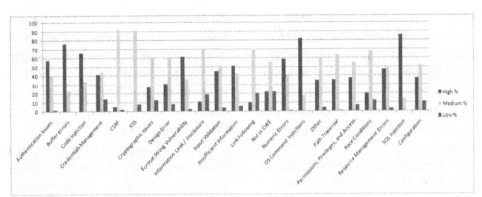

watch should be kept on this category in cloud computing. Another category which is very similar to the aforementioned one is Buffer errors, which shows a high percentage of high level severity vulnerabilities. However, this category is not so important in cloud computing. Note that related vulnerabilities show similar percentages, as seen above: CSRF with XSS; and OS Command Injection with SQL Injection.

Security Impact

Those security risks that should be considered in the cloud are no different to the security risks in a conventional IT environment. One of the security risks is Data Security. Since data is stored in public servers and, in some cases, is only logically separated from other companies' data, it is necessary to ensure that this data is being properly segregated and even encrypted. It is also necessary to ensure that the auditing and monitoring of this data is in place and cannot be overridden, or that it is encrypted while it resides in the servers. Another security risk is Physical Security. It is important to keep the physical servers secure so that only authorized staff have the ability to access them and this access can be tracked. A third risk is Application Security: the cloud provider should have a suite of testing and acceptance procedures since the applications are not behind a traditional

firewall. The cloud environment should be secured through the production of a virtual firewall among the virtual machines, in addition to suitable firewall policies. If the application being hosted is the organization's own custom application, it is necessary to conduct the same level of testing applied by the provider in that application. One last security risk is Identity Management; if there is an unplaced identity management solution within the company, there is a need to integrate the cloud infrastructure into the solution in order to control the access to the applications and data.

A risk impact may affect the access, confidentiality, availability, infrastructure or integrity. With regard to access, data must be secured to ensure that only authenticated users are allowed authorized access.

Confidentiality can be achieved by adopting robust encryption schemes. Nevertheless, cloud computing schema may be a shared physical server, so vendors should ensure that each separate customer's data remains segregated so that no data bleeding occurs across virtual servers. One key in cloud computing is the offering of 100% availability to the customer. Cloud vendors need to understand the risks arising from those who can launch a number of sophisticated denials of service attacks. With regard to infrastructure, the underlying cloud infrastructure and environment must be designed and implemented in order to ensure that they are flexible and scalable. Procedures executed in scaling the environment are managed without customer input and may change the services the customer requires. Finally, any information in cloud infrastructures must maintain its integrity if it is to be of value to the customer. The provider should ensure that all precautions are taken to guarantee that data does not become corrupt or altered.

The most common vulnerabilities are those denominated as SQL Injection, XSS and Buffer errors, and their impact should therefore be studied. XSS affects access control, confidentiality, integrity and availability. Some of its impacts are:

- The execution of unauthorized code or commands.
- Application data reading.
- Protection mechanism bypassing.

SQL Injection threatens access control, confidentiality and integrity. Its impacts are:

- Application data reading and editing.
- Protection mechanism bypassing.

If a Buffer Error occurs, integrity, confidentiality and availability will be affected. Some of its impacts are:

- The execution of unauthorized code or commands.
- Memory reading or editing.
- Denial-of-service by exit, restart, resource consumption (CPU or memory).

SOLUTIONS AND RECOMMENDATIONS

Cloud computing is an on-demand self-service which is available over the network through standard mechanisms. Most traditional security measures for Web sites can therefore be used. Security architecture is the first step towards ensuring security in a cloud computing service. The design of a security architecture begins with the onset of the requirements modeling. A secure architecture refers to the principal supports: protecting data confidentiality, data integrity and data accessing to appropriate users.

A second step should be a threat modeling, which determines the correct control and the production of effective counter-measures. There are various methods with which to carry out this modeling: Microsoft Thread Modeling Web Applications, AS/NZS 4360, CVSS or Octave.

One solution for data protection is an audit to reconstruct the succession of events that caused a specific problem. A further audit objective is that of non repudiation, which requires an electronic signature. The first function is known as an audit trail. An audit trail is a sequence of steps supported by proof documenting the real processing of a transaction flow through an organization, a process or a system, tracing data to their source. The main areas that are commonly overlooked are input validation and sanitization, error checking, error handling and session management. When validating that a service is secure, the auditor needs to investigate more than just the basic system controls. The aim should be to ensure that the implementation has been accomplished in order to ensure a complete mediation of the application. The auditor should verify that the presentation, application and persistent tiers are being used correctly. Some vulnerability assessment tools that are recommended are: Nessus, NMAP, Nikto, WebInspect, ScanDo, NStealth, or AppScan.

Nessus is the world-leader in active scanners, featuring high-speed discovery, configuration auditing, asset profiling, sensitive data discovery and vulnerability analysis of the user security posture. Nessus scanners can be distributed throughout physically separate networks. Nessus is constantly updated, with more than 20,000 plugins. Nessus uses Common Vulnerabilities and Exposures (CVE) as its standard.

NMAP (Network Mapper) is a free and open source utility for network exploration or security auditing. It can be used to perform vulnerability assessments, network inventories, the management of service upgrade schedules, and the monitoring of host or service uptime. Nikto is an open source Web server scanner which is used to carry out tests on Web servers for multiple items, including over 6,400 potentially dangerous files/CGIs, checks for outdated versions of over 1,200 servers, and version specific problems on over 270 servers. Scan items and plugins can be automatically updated. Nikto uses the OSVDB vulnerability database.

SPI Dynamics' WebInspect application security assessment tool is a powerful Web application scanner which is used to identify vulnerabilities within the Web application layer and to check that a Web server is configured properly, thus attempting common Web attacks such as parameter injection, cross-site scripting and listing traversal. ScanDo is a Web application scanner which offers a structured, three-stage process for application risk assessment: (1) it explores the entire Web application environment and registers its structure and contents; (2) it mimics actual hacking methods to identify and uncover the details of any point that is susceptible to attack; (3) it outputs all scan results into reports that show how to eliminate vulnerabilities.

N-Stealth is a Web server security-auditing tool that scans for over 30,000 vulnerabilities. N-Stealth is actively maintained and can audit both local and remote Web servers. AppScan is an IBM program which conducts a black box software testing technique, consisting of finding implementation bugs using malformed/semi-malformed data injection in an automated fashion. This kind of application is called a Fuzzer.

Architectures and virtualization techniques have been proposed to guarantee security in cloud resources. A new advanced architecture (ACPS) is provided for cloud protection (Lombardi & Pietro, 2011), which can monitor both guest and middleware integrity and protect them from most kinds of attack while remaining fully transparent. In (Li et al., 2011), the key security challenges faced by contemporary green cloud computing environments are analyzed to propose a virtualization security assurance architecture.

The first consideration is that virtual machines can be moved around according to demands and priorities. Security in virtualization includes keeping the virtual and physical network traffic separate through use of VLANs, implementing firewall systems to monitor and inspect traffic between the virtual machine host servers and setting up antivirus within the guest machines, although session virtualization makes any virus cleanup much easier.

Various tools exist for debugging and analysis in virtualization based systems. These tools examine anomalies in the system and study kernel malware. Some examples are K-Tracer, PoKeR and AfetrSight. These are based on the execution of a virtual machine monitor known as a hypervisor. Examples are Xen or VMware. In addition, Wang and Jiang (2010) have developed a new software, HyperSafe, to secure hypervisors against attacks, reasoning that actual hypervisors still have a large and complex code base. Hyper-Safe uses a non-bypassable memory lockdown to avoid the introduction of new code by anyone other than the hypervisor administrator. It also uses a restricted pointer indexing to characterize a hypervisor's normal behavior and prevent any derivation from it.

FUTURE RESEARCH DIRECTIONS

Cloud computing is a growing technology, and several future research directions which must be studied consequently exist. One direction is to analyze other information sources, such as

OSVDB, since this is one of the most important vulnerabilities databases. Other vulnerability features could also be investigated in this database. The most interesting features would be vulnerability disclosure, vulnerability patch disclosure and exploit creation dates. These dates could be used to create a model with which to establish the relationship between them through the use of a neural network.

Furthermore, a balanced combination of both static and dynamic analysis will be needed to ensure the quality of cloud computing systems. Testing will be a key activity in the evolution and development of cloud computing. The new tools should allow testers to design tests for the specific characteristics of cloud computing, thus covering features such as performance, virtualization, system issues and even usability. If all these goals are to be achieved, then the research into testing must continue to develop new techniques and practices.

CONCLUSION

Cloud environments are scalable, expandable and virtualized, thus making security more complex. In this paper, the importance of knowing the most common vulnerabilities has been exposed. Attackers can exploit weaknesses in the data security model to gain unauthorized access to data in the cloud via vulnerabilities such as: XSS, CSRF, Access Control, OS Command Injections, SQL Injection and Configuration. The data segregation in a multi-tenant deployment can be threatened by application vulnerabilities such as SQL Injection and Input Validation. Cryptographic and Configuration Issues are vulnerabilities which can be exploited to violate the security of the data backup and cloud recovery services. Authentication Issues, Credential Management, Permissions, Privileges, and Access Control are vulnerabilities which should be tested to ensure availability in the cloud. Moreover, Authentication and Configuration Issues can be also exploited in order to take over user accounts and compromise sensitive data when the identity management is federated. In general, since Web applications and SaaS are tightly coupled in providing services to the cloud users, most of the vulnerabilities of Web applications should also be considered in the cloud.

The results of the statistical analysis show that some kinds of vulnerabilities are more common than others, these being SQL Injection and XSS vulnerabilities (about 26% of vulnerabilities belong to one of these categories). Moreover, it is important to observe their associated severity, and that most of them have a medium or high severity level, particularly SQL Injection and OS Command Injection whose severity is high in 80% of cases. Authentication Issues and Code Injection have a severity of 58% and 66% in cases of high severity, which also leads a significant risk for the security in the cloud.

The percentage of classified vulnerabilities extracted from the selected database is very small in the years before 2007 (around 4%). This fact has caused a limitation when attempting to answer some initial questions. However, in the last three years, the number of SQL Injection and XSS vulnerabilities has dropped slightly. A clear trend is not apparent in the remaining vulnerabilities, signifying that in the near future it will be more and more important to establish secure mechanisms with which to avoid exploits. With regards to severity, in the last three years the percentage of vulnerabilities with high severity has decreased, whereas the percentage of vulnerabilities with medium severity has slightly increased.

Note that cloud computing requires migration from server-attached storage to network-based distributed storage. The storage of security will therefore become a key issue in the cloud based infrastructure, and further studies should thus be tackled on that inter-communication security which includes data security and network security.

REFERENCES

Alhazmi, O. H., Woo, S. W., & Malaiya, Y. K. (2006). Security vulnerability categories in major software systems. In *Proceedings of the Third IASTED International Conference on Communication, Network, and Information Security* (pp. 138-143). Cambridge, MA: IASTED/ACTA Press.

Arora, A., Krishnan, R., Telang, R., & Yang, Y. (2004). *Impact of vulnerability disclosure and patch availability - An empirical analysis*. Third Workshop on the Economics of Information Security.

Bugiel, S., Nürnberger, S., Pöppelmann, T., Sadeghi, A. R., & Schneider, T. (2011). AmazonIA: When elasticity snaps back. In *Proceedings of the 18th ACM Conference on Computer and Communications Security*, (pp 389-400). New York, NY: ACM.

Cellan-Jones, R. (2009). The sidekick cloud disaster. *BBC News*. Retrieved January 14, 2012, from http://www.bbc.co.uk/blogs/technology/2009/10/the_sidekick_cloud_disaster.html

Cloud Security Alliance. (2010). *Top threats to cloud computing* v1.0. Retrieved January 14, 2012, from https://cloudsecurityalliance.org/topthreats/csathreats.v1.0.pdf

Dahbur, K., Mohammad, B., & Tarakji, A. B. (2011). A survey of risks, threats and vulnerabilities in cloud computing. In *Proceedings of the 2011 International Conference on Intelligent Semantic Web-Services and Applications* (pp. 12:1-12:6). New York, NY: ACM.

Feng, J., Chen, Y., Ku, W. S., & Liu, P. (2010). Analysis of integrity vulnerabilities and a non-repudiation protocol for cloud data storage platforms. In *39th International Conference on Parallel Processing Workshops* (pp. 251-258). Washington, DC: IEEE Computer Society.

Ferguson, T. (2009). Salesforce.com outage hits thousands of businesses. *CNET News*. Retrieved January 14, 2012, from http://news.cnet.com/8301-1001_3-10136540-92.html

Frei, S., May, M., Fiedler, U., & Plattner, B. (2006). Large-scale vulnerability analysis. In *Proceedings of the 2006 SIGCOMM Workshop on Large-Scale Attack Defense* (pp. 131-138). New York, NY, USA: ACM.

Grobauer, B., Walloschek, T., & Stöcker, E. (2011). Understanding cloud computing vulnerabilities. *IEEE Security & Privacy*, *9*(2), 50–57. doi:10.1109/MSP.2010.115

Huynh, T., & Miller, J. (2010). An empirical investigation into open source web applications' implementation vulnerabilities. *Empirical Software Engineering*, *15*(5), 556–576. doi:10.1007/s10664-010-9131-y

Hwang, K., Kulkareni, S., & Hu, Y. (2009). Cloud security with virtualized defense and reputation-based trust management. In *Eighth IEEE International Conference on Dependable, Autonomic and Secure Computing* (pp. 717-722). Washington, DC: IEEE Computer Society.

Idziorek, J., Tannian, M., & Jacobson, D. (2011). Detecting fraudulent use of cloud resources. In *Proceedings of the 3rd ACM Workshop on Cloud Computing Security Workshop* (pp. 61-72). New York, NY: ACM.

Li, H. C., Liang, P. H., Yang, J. M., & Chen, S. J. (2010). Analysis on cloud-based security vulnerability assessment. In *International Conference on E-Business Engineering* (pp. 490-494). Washington, DC: IEEE Computer Society.

Li, J., Li, B., Wo, T., Hu, C., Huai, J., Liu, L., & Lam, K. P. (2012). CyberGuarder: A virtualization security assurance architecture for green cloud computing. *Future Generation Computer Systems*, *28*(2), 379–390. doi:10.1016/j.future.2011.04.012

Lillard, T. V., Garrison, C. P., Schiller, C. A., & Steele, J. (2010). The future of cloud computing. In *Digital Forensics for Network, Internet, and Cloud Computing* (pp. 319-339). Syngress.

Lombardi, F., & Pietro, R. D. (2011). Secure virtualization for cloud computing. *Journal of Network and Computer Applications*, *34*(4), 1113–1122. doi:10.1016/j.jnca.2010.06.008

Mell, P., & Grance, T. (2011). *The NIST definition of cloud computing* (Draft). Recommendations of the National Institute of Standards and Technology. NIST Special Publication 800-145.

MITRE. (2011). *Common vulnerabilities and exposures*: *Terminology*. Retrieved January 14, 2012, from http://cve.mitre.org/about/terminology.html

Seixas, N., Fonseca, J., Vieira, M., & Madeira, H. (2009). Looking at Web security vulnerabilities from the programming language perspective: A field study. In *International Symposium on Software Reliability Engineering*, (pp. 129-135). Washington, DC: IEEE Computer Society.

Somorovsky, J., Heiderich, M., Jensen, M., Schwenk, J., Gruschka, N., & Iacono, L. L. (2011). All your clouds are belong to us: Security analysis of cloud management interfaces. In *Proceedings of the 3rd ACM Workshop on Cloud Computing Security Workshop* (pp. 3-14). New York, NY: ACM.

Subashini, S., & Kavitha, V. (2011). A survey on security issues in service delivery models of cloud computing. *Journal of Network and Computer Applications*, *34*(1), 1–11. doi:10.1016/j.jnca.2010.07.006

Swiderski, F., & Snyder, W. (2004). *Threat modeling*. Redmond, WA: Microsoft Press.

Vache, G. (2009). Vulnerability analysis for a quantitative security evaluation. In *Proceedings of the 3rd International Symposium on Empirical Software Engineering and Measurement* (pp. 526-534). Washington, DC: IEEE Computer Society.

Wang, Z., & Jiang, X. (2010). HyperSafe: A lightweight approach to provide lifetime hypervisor control-flow integrity. In *Proceedings of the 31st IEEE Symposium on Security & Privacy* (pp. 380-395). Washington, DC: IEEE Computer Society.

Wolfgang Kandek, CTO & Qualys, Inc. (2009). *The laws of vulnerabilities 2.0*. Retrieved January 14, 2012, from http://www.qualys.com/docs/Laws_2.0.pdf

ADDITIONAL READING

Abraham, L. (2011). Cloud computing: Security risks. *Alliance Global Services blog*. Retrieved January 14, 2012, from http://www.allianceglobalservices.com/blog/labraham/cloud-computing-security-risks

Cheng, Z., & Yoon, J. (2010). IT auditing to assure a secure cloud computing. In *Proceedings of the 2010 6th World Congress on Services* (pp. 253-259). Washington, DC: IEEE Computer Society.

Paquette, S., Jaeger, P. T., & Wilson, S. C. (2010). Identifying the security risks associated with governmental use of cloud computing. *Government Information Quarterly*, *27*(3), 245–253. doi:10.1016/j.giq.2010.01.002

Wyk, K. (2010). Managing the cloud's security risks. *ComputerWorld blog*. Retrieved January 14, 2012, from http://www.computerworld.com/s/article/9187319/Managing_the_cloud_s_security_risks.

Zissis, D., & Lekkas, D. (2011). Securing e-government and e-Voting with an open cloud computing architecture. *Government Information Quarterly*, 28(2), 239–251. doi:10.1016/j.giq.2010.05.010

Zissis, D., & Lekkas, D. (2012). Addressing cloud computing security issues. *Future Generation Computer Systems*, 28(3), 583–592. doi:10.1016/j.future.2010.12.006

KEY TERMS AND DEFINITIONS

Cloud Computing: A new computation model with which to access shared computing resources accessed on demand via a network.

Exposure: A mistake in software that allows access to a system or network.

Risk: The relative impact that an exploited vulnerability would have on a user's environment.

Severity Level: Score that indicates the security risk posed by the exploitation of the vulnerability and its degree of difficulty.

Threat: The likelihood or frequency of a harmful event occurring.

Vulnerability: A bug in an application, system, device, or service that could lead to a failure of confidentiality, integrity or availability.

Chapter 5
A Software Tool to Support Risks Analysis about what Should or Should Not go to the Cloud

Miguel Torrealba S.
Simón Bolívar University, Venezuela

Mireya Morales P.
Simón Bolívar University, Venezuela

José M. Campos
Simón Bolívar University, Venezuela

Marina Meza S.
Simón Bolívar University, Venezuela

ABSTRACT

This chapter proposes a software prototype called 2thecloud, programmed in HTML and PHP under free software guidelines, whose main objective is to allow end users to be aware of imminent cloud dangers. To do this, the user must undergo a metacognitive process of basic risk analysis, which suggested result would be to what cloud the object should go. Through the use of this tool is expected that he / she can develop a risk analysis capability, so that in this way he/she is the one who makes the final decision about selecting between different cloud models (public, private, hybrid, and community) where the object will be placed. An important aspect is that the user has to understand that different cloud models provide different levels of security and this will allow him/her to question safety in other settings, given that it is a work that goes beyond simply encrypting and filtering information. It also presented 2thecloud functions and a description of each step that indicate how it operates. Finally, the authors propose four alternatives in risk analysis calculation, which are plausibly adapted to 2thecloud and if they are implemented they will provide different advantages.

DOI: 10.4018/978-1-4666-2125-1.ch005

INTRODUCTION

Mr. Decker: Shouldn't we take every possible precaution?
Captain Kirk: Mr. Decker...
Mr. Spock: Captain. I suspect there's an object at the heart of that cloud.
Captain Kirk: Mr. Decker. I will not provoke an attack.

Star Trek – The Motion Picture

Cloud computing is a design, instrumentation, management and information technology paradigm, oriented to offer the use of computing resources as services normally through a pay-per-use business model. For the user, the way in which the service is offered (software, platform or infrastructure) is unknown, and he/she only has to understand that the cloud is adapted dynamically to his/her needs and that can access to it from different places. This is thought mainly considering it as a way to make business in Internet that reduces costs to the final user (Mcfredries, 2008). From the point of view on how the cloud is conformed, a technical illusion is offered to the end user that simplifies his/her activity, given that the cloud reality is recognized and operated, that it is a jumble of connections of huge information repositories and various access points to diverse devices or resources (Krutz & Vines, 2010). This constitutes an Internet field where company data and software are allocated, according to previous agreements, service level contracts (SLC) agreed by the parties involved in that business model. So, under this conception, security has a secondary role since it is thought that the cloud has to be used and then provide it with desirable security levels. This is clearly stated as follows:

Security is a major concern when entrusting an organization's critical information to geographically dispersed cloud platforms not under the direct control of that organization. (Krutz & Vines, 2010, p. 61)

Something relevant about the aforementioned is that users do not commonly think that when they make use of the cloud they are transferring part of the control they posses. That is to say, cloud service providers can physically place their data without requiring approval, even in other continents latitudes. CSP can decide who has access to that data in order to carry out technical operations as for instance routine data backs up. Moreover, the control over some security services such as confidentiality, availability, access control, protection against duplication, time and authorization, can be shared and transferred. The fact that some of that information would be encoded do not guarantee that an illegal copy of it will be made and a brute force attack applied behind the user's knowledge, who would be believing that his/her data are still kept secret.

This means that the first critical consideration is ignored which it is relevant to pose when assuring appropriate cloud use, that is, what should or not go to the cloud?, that is because users commonly believe that the cloud is secure as they expect and that it is possible to move their data, applications or make use of any service (software, platform, hardware e infrastructure) with equal or higher confidence levels that private networks already have (Schneier, 2000). In this research we consider that such assumption is erroneous and as a result of it, in this chapter, an alternative of action is described to address this dilemma.

A software instrument called "2theCloud is presented, that adjusts to the proposed solution and was created to serve as support in the decision making process. A tool developed under a GNU free software orientation and mainly directed to users who do not have experience as security analysts. This tool is conceived to guide users in the decision-making procedure, about which information or resources can be placed or not in the cloud. Additionally, it helps the end user to understand his/her own sequence of actions towards getting a result through a metacognitive process and serves as a support mechanism, to know what basic elements should be taken into account during evaluating risks.

SECURING SERVICES AND DIGITAL RESOURCES IN THE CLOUD IS MUCH MORE THAT ENCRYPTING AND FILTERING INFORMATION

Digital insecurity has many causes; there are technical, organizational, economic, social and even human factors, sometimes catalogued as psychological, that can serve as a main element to violate the security of any system. The renowned expert in information security Bruce Schneier, proposed that *"Security is a process, not a product"* (Schneier, 2000, p. xii), but there is still the idea that using some kind of technology can guard appropriately digital and information systems. It is because of this that there is the belief that the cloud can be protected with the same technical elements that are employed by the private or corporate networks. Taking into consideration this approach, the systemic vision is ignored, putting aside particular contexts and realities, therefore it is common that controls come to be exceeded so insecurity increases. Nowadays, certain constant attacks in the form of Distributed Deny of Service (DDoS), can harm drastically the functioning of any business that depends on the network for communication or basic operations (Dunn, 2011).

This is how, most of managers and high-level executive boards that do not necessarily have factual knowledge about the complexity of information security, make decisions about what will be moved to the cloud without applying any formal criterion that indicates the risks that such action will carry out. Sometimes, they delegate such decision to any enterprise that they contract via outsourcing and which has its own conception about handling that topic. That vision unlikely includes dismissing the business model which makes use of the cloud and that can be sprinkled by a conflict of interests between the client and

the one who is doing the work. Therefore, that is not the way though, since it is all about an initial question that shall be solved by themselves, and then proceed to set up, if they really need cloud specialized consultants.

Large cloud service providers, similarly present a segmented view of security, a thing that brings about confusion among potential clients and can take to fake suppositions. They declare how much insecure is the net (Internet), but on the other hand, promote the belief that it does not affect cloud security (Girouard, 2010, n.p). The systemic vision is distorted and divided without outlining the relationships. En January 2010, David Girouard, Google's President wrote various lines on his official blog about that enterprise which illustrates the point:

This was not an assault on cloud computing. It was an attack on the technology infrastructure of major corporations in sectors as diverse as finance, technology, media, and chemical. The route the attackers used was malicious software used to infect personal computers. Any computer connected to the Internet can fall victim to such attacks. While some intellectual property on our corporate network was compromised, we believe our customer cloud-based data remains secure (Girouard, 2010, n.p).

From the quotation, we want to underline the subjective phrase "We believe…" that supports this enterprise position as an official declaration to calm down many of their clients that make use of the cloud. It should be added that there is not the only case that can serve as a reference, and the thematic about protecting the cloud is still in technological development. It is because of what has been explained that our proposal is directed to provide the strategic management simple and useful mechanisms that will help them in their initial analysis of dangers that the cloud extensive use offers. A means that allows them to comprehend the nature of risks and establish if these can be reduced to a minimum, or transferred o assumed as they appear.

This is not an easy decision since securing a cloud is a task that demands continuous analysis, design and experimentation and risk evaluation. In addition, each case has particular characteristics that should be taken into consideration in order to avoid failure of protection.

It is in this way that we can deduce that to protect the cloud and what it offers, is a task that demands the application of knowledge, schemes and procedures of security engineering parameters (Chorafas, 2011). Some of these are the established concepts and models to offer multilateral security. Compartamentation -information flow control in lateral mode and access control when sharing data between adjacent compartments- (Anderson, 2008), constitute security approximation to consider as feasible alternative, in the face of the simple proposal of using the cloud and encrypting messages in the network.

If a user would be able to make a risk analysis, he/she could make a the first decision with better knowledge when questioning him/herself: ¿is it worth to use the public cloud?, if it is an affirmative answer, he would think about asking for assistance, in this way, he/she would evaluate which service providers for that cloud would be appropriate. Additionally, in his case, the net service provider is different from the cloud one, he/she would repeat the question of which is the most suitable. There are other important aspects that are more difficult for a user to notice; such as cloud provider technical personnel in charge of handling data, applications or services, that is to say, the persons who perform roles as computers, networks, information and communication services administrators.

There are other important aspects that are more difficult for a user to notice; such as cloud provider technical personnel in charge of handling data, applications or services, that is to say, the persons who play roles as computers, networks, information and communication administrators,

as well as their honesty and expertise. The support functions of these roles are designated technical management and it should be considered that the ones performing those roles could be transformed in potential threats (USD-C, 2010) if only there is some kind of working distress situations in the company, or if they are blackmailed by client's competitors in order to get classified information as well as industrial secrets. Even worse, if one of those specialized employees quitted the job and is employed by a competitor, the company could make him/her reveal information that was once confidential. The only way to stop all this is having contracts with specific clauses protecting clients, eventhough the employee leaves the cloud service provider, and such scenarios could not be scorned.

If there would be some kind of legal conflict, which is the most advangeous geographical location? At this point, it is worth to point out that laws vary in each nation and that international law does not necessarily cover all the problems that could show up. In addition, not all companies have resources and power to start a legal international action against some well established providers that operate at the global market. To answer some of the above questions for a variety of situations requires viewing the possible dangers that each case carry with them, that is, to run a risk analysis. It can be qualitative and basic, but should be complete and adjusted to existing threats.

In this chapter, we propose a software tool to bring about user's awareness of the cloud; that he can make a first assessment of these scenarios and their imminent dangers. So his/her first decision should be supported by a risk analysis to show him/her alternatives to be chosen, the first being whether or not to use the public cloud. Additionally, we propose the use of a computerized tool which allows the user to select between different cloud models. In turn, each of these clouds operates differently in setting where they set forth their actions and also process digital resources and services in different ways. These are independent and isolated among them. It is also assumed, that the control over technical management and legal authority to operate those clouds widely, is what allows offering various alternatives for diverse security levels. That is, security lies in the process of adapting the cloud in any technical instance, to provide the desired protection, and this means that the technical control and command of the cloud should lay on the end user hands; he/she will have more options for protection. This might result in opposition to some advantages that the cloud offers to end users as for example the black box functioning in its structure. Therefore, the cloud type model is assigned and/or used depending on security needs.

From the involved actors' point of view, cloud safety can be modeled by: cloud services providers; network access providers, the parliaments which make laws that regulate corporate business technologies, and end users. The software tool described in this paper focuses on improving the end user's ability to analyze risks hoping that his/her decisions will be more accurate. A less confident user could make it more difficult to be used as a cloud attacking vector. Moreover, as actors increase their security levels, they will be better prepared to coordinate preventive, reactive and even forensics group actions.

Insecurity in the cloud is a dynamic environment, this means, what it is reliable today, tomorrow will not be, and for each case a risk analysis will be required for each moment. This is something that all the ones involved should apply. It is then a deduction that securing the cloud requires much more work that only encoding and filtering information.

DIFFERENT MODELS OF CLOUDS PROVIDE DIFFERENT LEVELS OF SECURITY

In a special NIST publication 800.145, Mell & Grance (2011) established the following definitions for clouds deployment models:

- **Private cloud:** It is the one whose cloud infrastructure is only operated for an organization. It may be managed by the organization or a third party and may exist on premise or off premise.
- **Community cloud:** The cloud infrastructure is shared by several organizations and supports a specific community that has shared concerns (e.g., mission, security requirements, policy, and compliance considerations). It may be managed by the organizations or a third party and may exist on premise or off premise.
- **Public cloud:** The cloud infrastructure made available to the public or a large industry group and owned by an organization selling cloud services.
- **Hybrid cloud:** The cloud infrastructure is a composition of two or more clouds (private, community, or public) that remain unique entities but are bound together by standardized or proprietary technology that enables data and application portability (e.g., cloud bursting for load balancing between clouds).

Figure 1. Model forInvolved actors in cloud insecurity

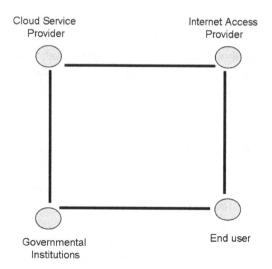

In this chapter, technical management and control are considered critical in order to minimize cloud insecurity, this is because there are many elements involve in doing such task like trust, personnel, tools, products and other means. So it is assumed that different cloud models have different security levels. According to the client's needs, the type of cloud model will be selected, for this technical management and control of the cloud should be in his/her hands, since it allows providing more resources to protect it. For many years, this control loss has been perceived as a lost of governability and catalogued as risk in the cloud (ENISA, 2009). For that reason, the public cloud is considered to be the most insecure and the private as less insecure, so the vision to go to the cloud consists of placing the objects in a public cloud, while not going to the cloud implies to avoid uploading sensible objects unless a private cloud is used. In this way, cloud benefits can be employed and includes security as a determinant element when selecting which cloud model will be taken.

It is necessary to warn that this approach does not indicates that the cloud own nature already warranties a higher level of protection, this is, that they have more characteristics and facilities to secure any resource (hardware, software or information), so the decision about which cloud model to use is the first step to minimize risks.

2THECLOUD: A SOFTWARE TOOL THAT SUPPORTS THE ANALYSYS FOR CHOSING THE CLOUD TO USE

Nowadays, it is common to see that the ICT managerial board makes a traditional decision about using or not the cloud. In that sense, it is usually thought about the public cloud as the principal alternative, this is due to the existence of commercial providers which already have a significant knowledge and expertise and also offer multiple services. It is perceived as one of the most expensive, complex and slow alternatives to develop a private, community or hybrid cloud since security is subordinated to a choice criterion and election is simplified in a binary mode.

As an alternative to the aforementioned issue, a software tool was designed in order to support decision-making about which cloud(s) to use and acts as a guide to make the user reflect carefully about his final choice or decision. A preliminary system version called "2theCloud" was developed in HTML® and PHP®, according to GNU® free software guidelines. This prototype can be reached from a code repository in the following link: http://sourceforge.net/projects/tothecloud/

2theCloud operates according to a simple model of risk analysis (Wheeler, 2011, p.7), which is substantially supported on provided information in order to process each organization characteristics. So it is assumed as a premise that the user's value judgement when entering data is determinant, since he/she is the one who knows his/her working context and reality which would give a specific result. The user is the one who have the complete system view for each object that should be considered; a vision that is difficult to mechanize all its way. Because of that, he/she is the protagonist during the process of analysis, since this tool should be implemented in a reliable environment and requires the provision of detailed information of what should go or not to the cloud. The degree of granularity of this information will be established by the end user and while more information is entered accuracy will be better in the results.

Additionally, the use of this tool seeks to motivate the user's conscience about how he/she carries out a risk analysis, that is to say, the second purpose of this software tool is to encourage the end user to understand the risk analysis process, without giving complicated terminology o difficult procedures. Using the pedagogic approach "teaching to do", we are betting for each individual's own capacity to analyse risks, that he/she applies in his/her daily life without realizing it.

To achieve this, a set of questions based on objects and factual cases is provided about what should go or not to the cloud. As a helping aid, a group of options are supplied for selection, such as: threats, time periods and predetermined contexts, but the possibility of adding new elements and relevant to his/her reality is left open. 2theCloud restrictions have been reduced and only applied when there is a logical contradiction in the information, for instance, to qualify any highly secret datum as public.

2theCloud main design guidelines are:

1. Risk analysis metacognition should be generated.
2. If there are judgement discrepancies between tool valuation and the user, the latter will prevail.
3. Simplicity in design.
4. Functions and calculations should be reduced to a minimum in order to facilitate user's adaptation to the software tool and can make the most of it, the advantage of using open source software.

5. The tool will supply a collection of files with the compiled data, so that the end user can examine or alter them in order to study the results.
6. It is incorporated the use of an expert judgement as an option as a way to establish the probability that a specific threat will be fulfilled.
7. It is not recommended to incorporate a data base system manager to reduce insecurity code problems cause by the software of that system manager.

Figure 2 shows a 2theCloud screen. In this display, it is presented a way to fill in data items for end users.

2THECLOUD: A SET OF REDUCED FUNCTIONS

The logic model of the software tool has seven basic functions: owner, category, process, procedure, risk, concrete and impact. These are used in

Figure 2. 2theCloud opening screen for entering data

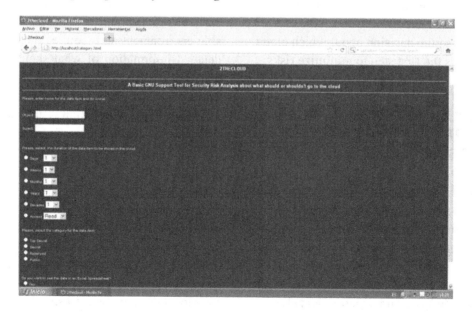

Table 1. Object category and impact level matrix that determines the type of cloud to be used

Category	High Impact	Medium Impact	Low Impact
Highly Secret	private cloud	private cloud	community cloud
Secret	private cloud	community cloud	communiy-cloud
Reserved	community cloud	hybrid cloud	hybrid cloud
Public	hybrid cloud	hybrid cloud	public cloud

sequence and allow establishing two values, the object category and the damage impact, which are entered in a matrix that informs to which type of cloud the object should be assigned. Table 1 shows the matrix to be used for each object or asset that will be protected. From it, the type of

cloud can be established and the system links the processed object to the one suggested. The major result of "2theCloud" is the lists for cloud types that contain a collection of objects that belong to each one.

To establish these values for objects, a procedure has been drawn following the steps shown in Table 2 where the logic conception of each function is described, as well as its purposes and some important associated observations.

2THECLOUD GENERAL PROCESS

In general, 2the cloud operates in stages. The first stage compiles basic data of the relevant objects to be placed in the cloud and then determines the category for each one of them. Categorization

Table 2. 2theCloud system logic functions

Function	Description	Observations
Subject = **Owner** (object)	This indicates who is the owner of the object	The objects are determined to migrate to the cloud The system user assigns the owner's relationship
Type = **Category** (object, subject, length, permissions)	This points out which is the security classification that a subject has for an object	The owner of each object is who enters the data. An object can be categorized in a slightly different way with diverse subjects. Some restrictions are applied, for example, an object cannot be confidential for a user and public for another.
Boolean = **Process** (process, object)	This establishes if a process can operate on an object	This restricts organizational processes that can access or operate on an object.
Boolean = **Procedure** (object, subject, process)	This determines if a subject can make use of a process to operate on an object	This reduces the subjects that can employ a process to operate on an object. This requires verification to establish coherence with the previous function.
Level of Danger = **Risk** (object, threat, duration, context)	This indicates how much danger there is for a threat will prevail on an object, during a specified time and under a certain context	This establishes high, medium and low risk levels. It is presented a large list of threats for the user to select from.
Probability of Occurrence = **Concrete** (object, threat, context, user probability, expert probability)	This points out how much probable is that a threat on an object and under certain context, can be materialized as an attack	This supports the subjective probability of a user, but it can optionally introduce the probability based on an expert judgment and in this way, the average of both is calculated. The output of this function permits to discard attacks with a probability lower tan 33, 3%.
Degree of lost = **Impact** (object, attack, duration, context)	This estimates the degree of damage that will generate the occurrence of an attack on an object, during a certain period of time and under a determined context	The user assigns values between 0 & 100. The system calculates the median for the degree of lost (impact) to subsequently categorize it as a low, medium or high impact. When the median is lower than 33,33 is low, medium is from 33,33 to 66,67 and high is higher than 66,67

Figure 3. 2theCloud first stage flow chart

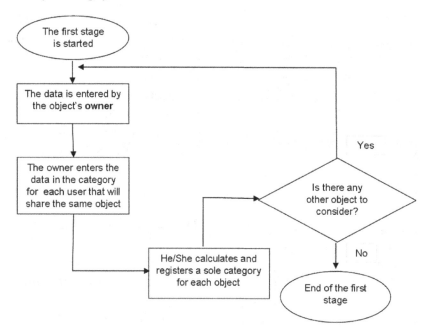

allows associating to an object a security label such as: highly secret, secret, reserved and public. This label is one of the entries when the matrix in table 1 is applied. Figure 3, shows the flow chart for this stage.

The main idea of this stage is to take the user to enumerate from a perspective centred in insecurity the fundamental elements that will be placed in the cloud. This list of objects can be constituted by information in various formats, applications, or data bases. It can also include hardware elements that offered by the cloud as infrastructure. When closing this stage, 2theCloud delivers files which contain the data supplied and has taken the user not to think of migrating to cloud as a sole entity moving process an electronic platform, software applications and personal data. On the contrary, it has made him/her to consider each object individually with certain characteristics that have to do with security evaluation.

The second stage is mostly about which operations and who are to be permitted to treat each analyzed object. Figure 4 shows the flow chart for this stage.

The second stage has as principal purpose to make the user reflect and consider the authorized methods to operate over an object and those persons that will employ each of them. The function "process" guides the user in identifying not only allowed processes but also the ones that will be denied. In this way, the user starts recognizing those actions that are not expected to happen. In a similar way the function "procedure" makes something alike since it incorporates subjects and this implies defining coherent restrictions for them based on procedures and permissions established in the previous stage in the function "category". This stage also provides files with collected information so that the user can examine and perform the variations that he/she considers necessary.

The third stage is aimed to make the user concentrate on reflecting about valuable objects insecurity that he/she thinks will be placed in the cloud, this will result in the estimation of a damage degree that will be caused if an attack compromises the security of those objects. Figure 5 illustrates the algorithm for this stage.

Figure 4. 2theCloud Second Stage flow chart

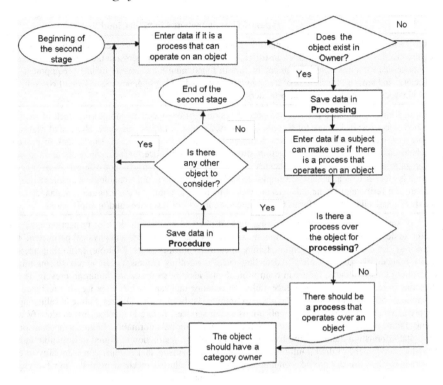

In this stage, it is important to point out that the task begins with a wide list of threats (see Table 3), which as the processing of supplied data progresses, it starts reducing as a result of the probabilities average that are entered in the "concrete" function (ruling out threats with probabilities lesser than 33,3%). On the other hand, the algorithm takes the user to make the analysis from a general perspective adjusting it to his/her reality. In this way, the function "risk" induces him/her to ponder all possible threats, and therefore it is necessary to visualize contexts and variations

Figure 5. 2theCloud third stage flow chart

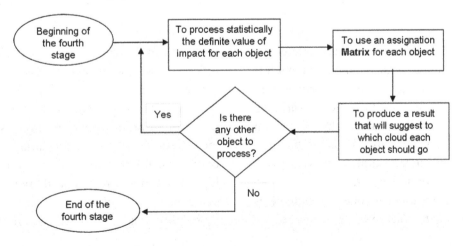

Table 3. 2theCloud threats categorization

Label	Types of Threats Included in "2theCloud"
Organizational	Insufficient budget, lack of decision making, Lack of back up from high level management, no responsible entity or require profiles in organization chart, insufficient personnel, untrained personnel, bad treatment to users or clients, lack of functioning for a quick answer equipment, lack of functioning for a security incidents equipment, lack of training for associates and branch offices, lack of trained employees, lack of contingency plans, lack of continuity or recovery business plans, existence of non reliable providers.
Procedural	Lack of formal established policies and procedures, lack of engagements monitoring, lack of monitoring for security reached objectives, lack of use for security indicators, absence of failures response, absence of trial scenarios for reliable employees, lack of physical parameters definitions, absence of auditing at all levels, lack of preventive maintenance mechanisms, lack of practice for dangerous situations, lack of practice for intrusion penetration in infrastructure and/or organizational systems, absence of schemes for classifying information, absence of mechanisms to guarantee that information is processed by an authorized employee, lack of methods to avoid technological obsolescence, lack of methods to prepare and verify appropriate data backup, lack of methods to reduce Social Engineering dangers, absence of methods for sharing tasks linked to platforms technological security of host services and/or applications.
Technical	Lack of surveillance and digital monitoring, lack of physical protections, lack of protection against natural disasters, failure to define digital protection dominions, failure of controls in virtual and physical perimeters, failure in operating intrusions' detection and /or prevention, failure to correctly identify users, failure in controlling access goods, failure in maintaining digital parches, failure in detecting and/or controlling Trojans, failure in recognising time bombs, failure in controlling forgery attacks, failure in controlling digital identity theft attacks, failure in preventing malware, failure in detecting in real time malware presence, failure in isolating malware, failure in processing malware forensic, failure in examining Software vulnerabilities, failure in examining Hardware vulnerabilities, failure in validating inappropriate data supply entrance to the operation of applications and/or services, failure in mechanisms to identify valuable digital elements, failure in mechanisms to recognise undue alteration of digital information, failure in mechanisms to reduce filtering of digital information, failure in mechanisms to reduce undue destruction of digital information, failure in mechanisms to reduce the forgery of digital information, failure in mechanisms that provide confidentiality to digital information, failure in mechanisms that provide communications privacy, failure in mechanisms that combat services negation, failure in mechanisms that stop communications hijacking, failure in mechanisms to check new applications and/or services security, failure in mechanisms which provide plenty resources to virtually instrument any system, failure in mechanisms to verify security resulting from digital systems fusion, failure in verifying security in the development process of new applications and/or services, failure in testing the available security when incorporating new technologies, lack of security evaluations over the forgery of users interfaces when interacting with digital systems, failure in evaluating security for integration procedures of computer systems with portable and/or mobile devices, failure in verifying virtual platforms security in case of power cuts.
Corporate Culture and/or Human Factor	Scarce responsibilities assignation, not reliable personnel, ill-humoured personnel, personnel getting trained for a professional profile that the company cannot pay for adequately, personnel that promotes dependence and/or individualism, lack of knowledge in Ethics application in corporate work, lack of methods for identifying considerable financial growth in goods and/or reliable personnel properties, inexistence of support plans and/or financing for employees and/or workers economic growth, inexistence of enough expertise to work in virtual platforms, lack of coordination for operating technical formalities in platforms provided by a host.
Legal setting	Lack of laws and/or jurisprudence that regulate the area, untrained police system to carry out any investigation, unprepared judicial system to sustain any case, interests' conflicts between the legal setting and level service agreements.

in specific periods of time. These last parameters are initially provided as an enumeration, but it is left open the possibility for the user to adapt them to his/her particular situation. Some variation elements can result from valuing the same threat over the same object. Thus, as wider the output of this function, a more complete analysis is carried out about current dangers.

The fact that the user has gone thorough stages 1 and 2 can help him/her to recognize more eas-

ily what can go wrong. The user begins his/her reflection process evaluating the risk for each threat over an object, thinking about duration and context. His/her valuation is a qualitative one over an ordinal scale of three levels: high, medium or low; there are not cutting edge points over a quantitative level to categorize what is high, medium or low, and in addition to this, risk components are not considered separately: the probability that a threat will be effectively accomplished (concrete function) and the impact or degree of lost (impact function).

After that, the function "concrete" makes the user to start reflecting about which is the probability (percentage form) that the threats previously considered, are estimated to effectively happen. In this function, it is provided the option to introduce as well, the evaluation of an external expert. The idea is to strengthen the estimation using at least two points of view, given that the user is who can better judge elements such as an annoyed employee willing to sabotage an operation, and the consultant expert can establish feasible possibilities that a potential technical attack, could be "Clickjacking" over any object. In this way, there is a data grouping that in real circumstances is difficult to gather, but that can surely threat the security of what will be taken to the cloud. Table 3, details the types of threats and its corresponding labels.

In this example, the user is given the task to identify all threats. He/she can recognize these dangers since they are linked to the infrastructure where he/she has operated his/her informatics systems. Therefore, he/she should be capable of identifying them and also evaluate the possibility that these could really happen. If a user learns to run a simple qualitative risk analysis, he/she could later repeat such process en some other context, the cloud he/she selected for example. In other words, it is hoped that the user will be capable of asking him/herself if the threats present in his/her context can be also applied to the service provider infrastructure that will offer the cloud operational platform. It is then relevant to check the security measures that the contracting provider will incorporate and in this way, he/she can establish criteria and make comparisons to decide which the one that best suits him/her is.

It is also important to note that "2theCloud" also serves as a mechanism to show the user that threats to digital information in the cloud, are much more than just think about malware and hackers. At the time, the user makes use of the tool and it indicates that there are numerous cat-egorizations for dangers; he can see the magnitude and the existing taxonomies in this field. Table 3, describes categories such as a range of threats that can emerge for each of the items identified therein. If the user develops the ability to recognize the perils that will be most helpful for providers because he/she would not have to wait for the provider to recognize the greatness of what is happening and therefore the responsibilities and obligations of each actor can easily understand as it is shown in Figure 1. So he may think that each vendor implements his own risk analysis, and can ask about results and methods. It is assumed that he/she could select his/her cloud provider or the access to it, not only by reciving propaganda, but for what he/she really finds out about in each case.

In a similar way, he/she could understand better the importance of contracts and legislations. The service contract would not only be considered by each company legal departments, but also by technicians and managers who could ask basic questions such as: what if this goes wrong?, What can be done if such problem happens?, could we recover if such a failure happens, and what would be the provider's answer if such a mistake comes to be, could the government limit my business or transactions if I work with a company that does noy comply with the current regulations?

In order to continue the data processing flow, the user should interact with the "impact" function. It was generated to make the user focuses to estimate the damage that can be caused by an attack, those which he/she considered possible to happen (the interface only allows to evaluate threats that are above 33,33% to be fulfilled). Hence, the idea is to assign a numbered value in a 0 to 100 scale, which reflects the level of damage that can be produced. The 100 value is interpreted as complete damage to the organization or total loss of property, according to the user's concerns. The last activity in this stage is to carry out an easy statistic analysis that will generate an impact unique value for each object. The median calculation of lost levels (Impact) is a fundamental part of this procedure, since it is the appropriate summary measure for this quantitative variable. This measure will divide en two equal parts an ordered group of data, being more convenient than the arithmetic mean when there are extreme or atypical values (too high or low values in relation to most of them), this means that applying this measure aims to avoid an incorrect summary of impact levels when possible atypical values are present. From this measure value the level of impact will be established in this way, above 66,67% is high, medium if it is between 33,33% y 66,67% or low if it is under 33,33%, this classification is based on a priori uniform interval partition. The terciles division is suitable to generate categories when the historical records begin to be produced. This stage records all the data as files that the user can subsequently process or alter as he/she wants to experiment.

The fourth stage is simple; it is about using the assignation matrix that was presented in Figure 2, to establish which cloud should be the object linked to. This task is carried out for each of the categorized objects and it is represented as an algorithm in Figure 6.

The sequence of these stages is designed to allow any 2theCloud user and with no expertise in the area could go deeply in the risk analysis process in a simple manner. This is a different option, not like the traditional one, which is going to the cloud and then be worried about its security. What we want is to make the user understand that there is an alternative that gives priority to security and this has to do with deciding what to move to the cloud or not. All this is because risks will vary depending on what is going to be move or use there and also that different clouds provide various protection levels. A means to approach this perspective is to determine the risk that is capable of tolerating for each valuable object that is thought to be migrated, and then decide to what type of cloud will be entrusted.

2 THE CLOUD STEP BY STEP

The complexity and length of a risk analysis for information or value assets that anyone wants to carry out, for instance, for all those objects that he/she would like to migrate or/and use in the cloud, can result overhelming. Therefore, it is simplified and divided into steps that would allow the analyst to focus on an activity at each stage of the analysis. Additionally, the qualitative approach is chosen because it reduces difficulties in understanding the process. Another important aspect of how to do the analysis is applied for each of the assets to be assured. The reiterative nature of the process may then lead the user to recognize a pattern in the work done, and even seeing how it can be improved or adapted to his/her needs. The possibilities are also open for exploration and experimentation. Because the tool is open source, it could be altered in way final results are given of what should or should not go to a paryticular type of cloud, allowing the user to enter items that were initially left out.

Other thing that is crucial to point out is that if the user achieves knowledge of how to make a basic risk analysis in a methodical way, he/she can do it in different situations and opportunities. He/she can even require more information from cloud providers and Internet access providers in order to make more robust decisions. Table 4 outlines how "2theCloud" operates:

USER'S METACOGNITIVE PROCESS THROUGHOUT 2THECLOUD

What has been previously described represents the development of a user's metacognitive process which is executed through the combination of two features, the user's interaction with *2thecloud*, a tool that provides a series of propositional screens and the user's knowledge and handling of contextual information related to his/her business

Figure 6. 2theCloud fourth stage flow chart

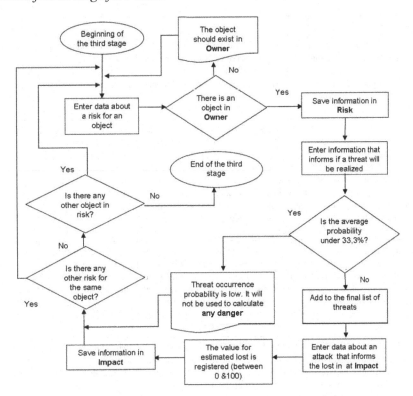

position in a company. In order to understand this process, firstly it is important to explain in brief what is understood by metacognition and the cognitive processes involved and secondly, the description of the interwoven nature of the user's metacognitive process.

When talking about metacognition, the first thing that we should bear in mind is that it has to do with *cognition (knowledge)* that is the mental faculty or process by which knowledge is acquired through perception, reasoning, and intuition; this is generally learning. Accordingly, a cognitive process is the way of using knowledge determined by knowledge and it consists of a range of mental processes of using knowledge, which can be summarized as follows; a.- *information gathering*: persons and organizations dynamically engage in searching valuable information based on their knowledge; b.- *sense-making*: after acquiring significant information, they combine

their existing knowledge with the information in order to make sense of it; c.- *choice*: this takes places when people develop alternative courses of action that satisfies their goals using knowledge; d.- *commitment*: this is when people and organizations commit themselves to the selected course of action. (Kagono, 2006)

Naglieri (2011) summarized this when referring to the term *cognitive process* as a recognized, neuropsychological identified ability that supplies the means by which an individual functions in this world. They are associated and underlie all mental and physical activity, because when applying cognitive processes humans beings get hold of varied types of knowledge and skills.

Related to the aforementioned is metacognition, which has been studied and researched since the 70's and it is defined by various authors in the following ways:

Table 4. How 2theCloud works

Step	Description	Activity center
1	This is the first action that the user is faced to. In this case, he must identify the objects that will be placed in the cloud. He/she will also run a mental process to break up or separate objects and then will perform an association process that allow him/her to assign a responsible person who will own the selected object.	It is intended to make the user understand that any risk analysis must begin by recognizing what you want to protect. In addition, goods and valuable assets must be classified by certain criteria in order to organize them, is for example financial cost, the owner, geographic location, etc..
2	In this step, a classification process of previous information is carried out; since the main focus is to see the information as main asset, information confidentiality is the criterion to be used, therefore a kind of categorizatiform is expressed through the following elements: top secret, secret, restricted and public. This is essential as it will define who have access to that information and under what restrictions. A critical consideration is that decisions are assigned to time limits (days, weeks, months, years and centuries) in this stage, allowing dynamic provision. Over time, an object categorization can change as well as its permissions to to be processed.	It is hoped that the user understands that if he/she considers the information that will be stored in the cloud as a principal asset, its categorization should be based upon information secrecy. Meanwhile this estimation is temporary and reflects the dynamism of information value.
	Processes herein are selected to operate on the object. In this step the user also makes a simple selection process, such a process would be to use the email to send information. This step is also a true or false option that allows him/her to certify whether a process is associated or not to the object. It is important that he/she will learn to identify the processes involved over an object; because the way to break objects security rules is by improperly execute processes that empower processing.	It is desired that the user will be aware of what are the mechanisms used to process goods. It is desired that he/she identifies those being valid and the ones that should not be used because they would result against information security
4	In this step it is desirable to determine whether a subject can use a valid procedure to treat a shared specific object. Therefore, a list of processes associated with the object is displyed and select the user who will carry out the procedure. It is also included a true or false option, that checks whether the user is authorized or not to use a process. The selection made must correspond with the true or false option in the process. Each procedure must meet the organization security policy. As seen in the example from Step 3, the procedure associated to sending an e-mail could be that, according to the assigned categorization, the information should be encrypted to be transferred.	It is an imperative to direct the user's thoughts towards the importance of sharing goods and process them in different ways.
5	It is in this step is where the user starts his/her risk analysis in a local context but within his/her organization. A threat categorization with inherent dangers for each of them is presented, from it he/she may consider whether it is a risk for each of the objects he/she will like to protect. It is also important to include the context, as a threat can materialize given a particular situation but in other conditions nothing would ever happen. He/she also asks about the value associated to danger, which is categorized as high, medium and low.	It is hoped that the user after thinking about what He/she wants to protect and how he/she will use the object, and it will be shared, he/she must be able to recognize faults in the treatment of what is protected and whether these can become a potential threat. In other words, he/she should now focus his/her analysis on the dangers that can come over valuable goods.
6	Continuing with the sensibilization process, in this step, the user is expected to consider the probability that a threat will materialize as an attack on an object during a period of time and under a certain context. The idea is that users estimate this probability according to his/her knowledge and can also look for help from an expert insecurity that according to his/her expertise would indicate the probability of an attack, this datum is optional. As in the previous step these data are supported within the local context of the organization.	The user is asked to set his/her attention on the probability that recognized threats will materialize in attacks.
7	This step consists in estimating loss or damage degree that would generate an attack on an object for a certain period of time and under a certain context. Loss value is estimated within a range between 0 and 100. Similarly within the local context in the organization.	Here the user focuses on the degree of damage or negative impact that could occur if an attack takes place.

Metacognition, narrowly defined, concerns people's cognitions and feelings about their cognitive states and cognitive processes. However, the term metacognition has been also used more broadly to refer to cognitions about cognition in general, as well as self-regulation processes that take cognitive processes as their object (Koriat, 2004, p.261)

If metacognition is conceived as (knowledge of) a set of self-instructions for regulating task performance, then cognition is the vehicle of those self-instructions. These cognitive activities in turn are subject to metacognition, for instance, to ongoing monitoring and evaluation processes. (Veenman, Van Hout-Wolters, & Afflerbach, 2006, p. 6)

Taking into consideration each of the definitions and trying to construct our own conceptualization, it is relevant to point out that metacognition is cognition directed at monitoring and controlling the process of cognition, that is to say, it is the conscious regulation and rearrangement of how people think when confronting complex problems which involve new and original solutions. Metacognition can be then said to be thinking about thinking.

In this respect, Pressley, (2000) emphasized that in effect; metacognition draws on cognition. This researcher explained that it is very difficult to have an acceptable metacognitive knowledge of one's competencies in a domain without substantial (cognitive) domain-specific knowledge, such as knowledge about relevant concepts and theories in a domain, about intrinsic difficulties of a domain, and about what is irrelevant.

The central idea developed in the above paragraph has to do with the emergence of the user's significant domain – specific knowledge and handling of contextual information related to his/her business position in a company, this is essential when interacting with the tool 2thecloud, given that it turns out to be an interactive and thoughtful

process as the user demonstrates his capacity to employ knowledge and expertise in order to make decisions on what type of information should go or not to a particular cloud. This interaction shows that each time people think on what they know, they consider their thought processes, or look for additional information, in that way, they are demonstrating their capacity for metacognition.

In relation to this, Beran et al. (2010) explained that metacognition is closely associated to key aspects of mind, including cognitive control, self-awareness, and consciousness and that is why, it is broadly recognized as one of human beings' most sophisticated cognitive capacities, and also their capability of metacognitive processing.

That is to say, metacognition becomes the conscious regulation and rearrangement of how people think when facing complex problems that require new solutions by monitoring and controlling their cognitive processes.

As it was mentioned before, 2thecloud makes the user monitor and control his/her cognitive processes being engaged in interaction with the propositional screens, hence he/she feels involved in a communication process with the system and the system with him/her, that is to say, it becomes an interwoven process of learning for the user. This is what we called the user's interwoven metacognitive process.

The user's interwoven metacognitive process can be described as follows; the user employs high level cognitive processes such as analysis, selection and classification to create a significant strategy that develops metacognition when he/she relates his/her previous knowledge with the system and at the same time there happen to appear other linked processes like planning, supervising, and evaluating which objects should go or not to a particular cloud. This means that the user thinks about how a risk analysis is carried out and that also has to do with the way 2thecloud was designed because it was built up following a human centred approach.

STATISTICS AND DATA FILES GENERATED BY 2THECLOUD

Each processing stage records data as text or Microsoft Excel® files which are at the user's disposable to be examined and altered if he/she thinks is necessary. This characteristic gives the user the opportunity to replant the whole processing system and study results variations. In this way, he/she has the chance to check how determining are certain critic values, as for example, the probabilities that have been supplied in a subjective mode.

Additionally, the spreadsheet application gives the possibility to use some statistics functions (calculating time average, calculating the modal value for all qualitative results, the median, or the average of threats that can be fulfilled, among others) and graphic facilities that are part of this type of systems, in order to make other types of calculations that the software does not originally posses.

The user can develop new functions or altering the behaviour of how these formerly operate in 2theCloud, without having to modify its open source code. The alternative that the user thanks to the simplicity of the software structure can change some system programs offers an extension of that idea, in order to gain a higher degree of automation. This advantage is important if there is the possibility of wanting to do risks analysis over other scenarios, which are not necessarily linked to the cloud.

On the other hand, the statistical processing of common data has been simplified to such a degree that only central tendency measures are used such as the mean and the median for subjective probabilities assigned by users and experts or for values o lost (from 0 to 100) in case threats are materialized as attacks. These measures constitute the resources used by 2theCloud.

WHAT IS OFFERED BY 2THECLOUD

The system was conceived taking into account the premise that every human being, in practice, knows how to make risks analyses (Schneier, 2009). What he/she does in his/her daily life is decision making in every case, although he/she can not express it mathematically or in another sophisticated form. That is the fact we explore by offering a guidance tool of step by step analysis, which shows some instances of how the analysis is carried out. There lays the possibility to learn about how the process takes places and how to improve it. A different alternative provided is also about how to use the cloud. The traditional scheme of employing the public cloud resources depends on the security he/she is thinking about or what he/she will put in the cloud or use from it. An orientation is given to make use of other cloud models and outstood the importance of making a decision based on the characteristics and relevance of each object to the user in relation to his/her business position.

Another important aspect is that users are unaware that security normally involves elements as varied as the procedures within organizations and that the failure of properly conducting a process may bring a potential threat or an imminent attack. Nor are they aware that every individual has a responsibility within the organization, therefore they can carry out actions associated to inappropriate behavior or forbidden operations that are far away from established norms weakening the organization security. Another element to consider is that they have very little technical knowledge about malicious programs because they generally relate any abnormal behavior of their computers with viruses. In this regard, an important contribution for the user's learning process using the tool is that the user recognized that there is a threats categorization, which involves a range of malware whose functionalities vary and differ from those of the viruses. Although, in this categorization, elements such as corporate culture, procedural and legal organization are included, the organization is the one responsible to train its staff about proper use of procedures by a good education policy and not only the use of 2thecloud. This will help users be aware of their responsibilities and to do an appropriate handling of procedures, thereby minimizing risks that may affect safety.

Finally, 2theCloud tries to call attention over the approach (conscience) that securing digital information and all resources that can be used to protect it, is much more that using encrypted protocols, antivirus, firewalls, intrusion detection or prevention systems or others helpful means common to this area. The presence of an initial categorized list of possible threats brings on to consider non traditional areas however they are of crucial importance for security. If the user understands this and realizes the basics of his/her risk analysis process, it has been reached an alternate behavioural way from that of the classic view, let's go to the go and then let's think about how to protect what we have in it.

2THECLOUD RISKS ANALYSIS ATERNATIVES

Eventhough 2thecloud does a risk analysis as explained in the previous section, it is possible to alter the mode by modifying the source code itself, specifically in the risk analysis module to include objects in the cloud. Here are four possible schemes for calculating risk that can be adapted for this software.

A PRIORI AND CALCULATED RISK APPROACH

This scheme performs a priori qualitative risk evaluation and subsequently the quantitative evaluation of its two components (probability that a threat is realized and its impact). In that way, the program establishes a classification for risk level and the type of cloud where the object should go.

In the first phase of this analysis, the user begins a reflection process evaluating the risk to select threats over objects, considering duration and context. This valuation is ordinal qualitative in three levels: high, mediun or low, and the user does not go deep in risk components. The program calculates the mode of a priori different risks, and the central function of this scheme is:

Level of Danger = Risk (object, threat, duration, context)
Example:

Let's suppose that the sequence is available for threats assessment in different contexts and duration.

Medium = **Risk** (report1, virus, 1 month, normal state)
Low = **Risk** (report1, virus, a week, auditing)
Low = **Risk** report1, virus, a week, emergency)
High = **Risk** (report1, ilegal copy, 1 year, normal state)
Low = **Risk** (report1, alter, 1 year, normal state)
Low = **Risk** (report1, alter, 1 year, auditing)
Medium = **Risk** (report1, erase, 1 decade, normal status)

The user a priori risk in this example is low, since it is the most repeated, and this value corresponds to the mode. This risk is used to compare the risk value that is calculated using specific functions and impact.

From the concrete function the list of threats is shown again to assign the user's subjective probability and the one for a consulted expert. Probabilities are placed in percentage form without the % symbol; and if the expert also assigns an estimation, that will be averaged with the user´s probability.

Probability = **Concrete** (object, threat, context)

In this option, the program will calculate the probabilities median (or average probability medians if an expert valuation is included). This probability is then classified into low probability (less than 33.33%), medium (between 33.33% and 66.67%) or high (greater than 66.67%)

Example:
50% = **Concrete** (report1, virus, normal state)
31% = **Concrete** (report1, alter, normal state)
75% = **Concrete** (report1, alter, normal state)
25% = **Concrete** (report1, illegal copy, normal state)
11% = **Concrete** (report1, erase, 1 month, normal state)

The program calculates the median directly and it would be done according to the following algorithm:

1. Percentage probabilities are ordered from lowest to highest: 11, 25, 31, 50, 75
2. The median is the value allocated in $(n+1)/2$ this means $(5+1)/2 =3$ and in that position is 31. This is interpreted that 50% of the probabilistic threats evaluations is less than a 31%.

Then it is clasiffied in high, medium or low probability according to the rule mentioned before.

As the median = 31 is less than 33, 33 so the probability is classifies as **low**.

In this second phase of risk analysis, the user makes a quantitative assessment and re-considers the threats evaluated qualitatively for the object in the risk function, but he/she does not think what high, medium or low is, he/she only assigns values between zero and 100.

This time, the categorization is made by the program into high, medium or low. Here the risk is broken into two parts: the concrte function and impact function. The final result is contrasted with

a priori risk function, which is the starting point for the user's risk analysis. If there is a historical record of different assessments, the percentiles calculation can help getting other limits to determine what is low, medium or high.

In the impact function, values between 0 and 100 are assigned to threats evaluated in the concrete function and the program calculates the median for degrees of loss, in order to classify into low impact (less than 33.33), medium (between 33, 33 and 66,67) or high (higher than 66.67).

Loss = **Impact** (object, attack, duration, context)

The user is only responsible for evaluating the degree of loss that would be generated by an attack.

Example:
12 = **Impact** (report1, virus, 1 year, normal state)
20 = **Impact** (report1, virus, 1 year, audit)
43 = **Impact** (report1, virus, 1 year, emergencia)
5 = **Impact** (report1, alter, 1 year, normal state)
10 = **Impact** (report1, illegal copying, 1 year, normal state)
3 = **Impact** (report1, erase, 1 month, normal state)

The median of the sorted values 3, 5, 10, 12, 20, 43 is calculated by the following rule:

If n is even, the median is the average of the two central values (that is, values that are in $n / 2$ and $(n / 2) +1$ position, in this case $(10 +12) / 2$ implies that the median is equal to the median 11. Because the impact median is less than 33.33 then the impact will be classified as **low**.

The user evaluates again quantitatively the threats to objects, under certain contexts and durations but this time considering the degree of loss if a particular attack is realized. For this second risk component, the program calculates the median for all impact assessments and categorizes them into low, medium, or high impact and subsequently values the risk qualitatively according to the following matrix:

Calculated Risk Function

The program classifies risk according to the probability that an attack is realized and its impact.

If we suppose that:

Probability that a threat is realized = Low
Impact if the attack is realized = Low

According to Table 5, this will indicate that the risk is low and fits the a priori risk used in the example. Although, the simple a priori analysis run by the users agreed with the step by step analysis considering risk components (concrete function and impact), the user employs his/her cognitive processing during the evaluation when comparing these two strategies. Finally, he/she reaches a conclusion about the type of cloud where the object should go.

The program output generated for each object includes the type of cloud it should go, the level of calculated risk and the level of a priori risk. If it was indicated in the object categorization public category and low calculated risk as low, then, the object can go to a public cloud, in spite that the data will be in third hands and there will be service provider dependence.

Private clouds are the best choice for enterprises that need high protection for data, since the client is the one that controls applications and determines the proper use. The company is the owner of the infrastructure and can authorize users. If the enterprise can not create a private cloud, the risk is high, the right decision would be to avoid taking confidential data to the cloud.

Other alternative consists in classifying the risk in 5 levels: very low, low, medium, high, and very high, this would imply a change in the risk matrix since the probability that a threat is realized and its impact would also adopt the 5 level risk scale. A priori uniform intervals would have a 20% range to take this classification. Subsequently, if the user keeps a record of his/her evaluations, then they could be ordered usings percentils.

The level of estimated risk (R_i) can be also calculated as the percentage probability that a threat is realized (P_i) by the impact (I_i) divided between 100, that is to say:

$$R_i = P_i*I_i/100$$

The sum of all $R_{i\,S}$ divided between the total evaluated risks would represent the average risk (however, la median is still the main alternative, because it is not affected by very low or very high values), afetrwards they would be classified in 2, 3, 4 ro 5 levels.

Example:
Threat 1 ($A_1 = 50\%$; $I_1 = 50$) → $R_1 = 25$
Threat 2 ($A_2 = 80\%$; $I_1 = 90$) → $R_2 = 72$
Threat 3 ($A_3 = 60\%$; $I_1 = 10$) → $R_3 = 6$
Threat 4 ($A_4 = 100\%$; $I_4 = 100$) → $R_4 = 100$
Threat 5 ($A_5 = 25\%$; $I_5 = 30$) → $R_1 = 7,5$

Table 5. Calculated risk matrix

	High Impact	Impact Medium	Low Impact
High Probability	high risk	high risk	medium risk
Medium Probability	high risk	medium risk	riesgo bajo
Low Probability	medium risk	low risk	low risk

Table 6. Appropriate cloud type according to object category and calculated risk level

	High Risk	Medium Risk	Low Risk
Highly Secret Category	private cloud	private cloud	community cloud
Secret Category	private cloud	community cloud	community cloud
Reserved Category	community cloud	hybrid cloud	hybrid cloud
Public Category	hybrid cloud	hybrid cloud	public cloud

Risk average = 42.1
Risk Median = 25

Threat 4 has a 100% probability and a 100 for impact, these extreme values show that threat will be realized as an attack and there will be total lost. This extreme case increases risk average, but the median is not affected. On the other hand, a 100 risk for only one threat will be enough to decide that the final risk is high, without considering the other threats average. Final risk will be used according to Table 4, or a 5 level risk table.

We are confronting settings with continuous variations that impact the security strategy in cloud computing. In these circumstances, threats are variables, as well as their probabilities and risks. Risk management and norms fulfillment are divided between the cloud computing provider, Internet provider and the client. There should be a guarantee that data are only stored in locations allowed by contracts, SLAs and norms. Any datum classified as private should be encoded in order to reduce the risk if it is going to be sent to the cloud. The mode and median supply context consideration and risk duration.

FUTURE RESEARCH DIRECTIONS

2theCloud available version in Internet is still a prototype, and has not been subjected to a security dynamic of its code, nor includes internal characteristics that allow checking the provided probabilities and estimations, in order to alert of any value deviation, this means that the intelligence level of the tool should be elevated.

Other critical aspect to point out is that an extended use of the tool is under development and it is hoped that the results show the main modifications and needs that users think should be incorporated. In the Impact function, three uniform intervals a priori are generated to determine what low, medium or high impact is. In a future version of the tool, a partition is made according to percentiles 33,33 and 66,67, this is called terciles and are calculated from historical records. This partition is going to be dynamic since increasing the use of the tool; the values for impact saved in the users' data base will modify the limit values which define impact categories high, medium and low. In this tool version, the uniform classification given is ideal due to lack of historical information. Next version of the program will generate appropriate countermeasures to mitigate each threat base on a countermeasure repository.

Future research should include a Bayesian estimation of risk given that the Bayesian conception is focused in updating the probabilistic knowledge we have about the phenomenon (a priori knowledge), using the available information. All these considerations will point out to assign validity to the conception that 2the Cloud sustains that the user can correctly do risk analyses and that he/she only requires guidance and support to accomplish the task.

Another research that should be carried out relating to 2theCloud is to validate the user's meta-cognitive process while using the tool, through different assessment protocols that would give us more insights about one of the essential principles of 2theCloud that is the user's conscience grasping of his/her learning interaction with the tool.

CONCLUSION

2TheCloud is a work in progress related to a software application that supports client's risk decision making with expertise in traditional scheme. The tool guides the end user with the purpose of reducing, avoiding, transferring or accepting the risk of what is going to be uploaded to the cloud, through a qualitative and quantitative validation associated to various threats, interrelated with time contexts and dynamics. The main idea is to avoid that the user sees all his/her assets as an indivisible unit and considers various alternatives for his/her final decision. This complex analysis emerges from the comparison of estimating basic dangers that a human mind can think of and its capability to record the information, by means of method to implement this task provided by 2thecloud. It is in that way that a learning process is promoted and the metacognition of this non traditional risk analysis allows the end user to place a variety of valuable objects in the cloud that is best suite for each of them (public, private, hybrid o community).

REFERENCES

Anderson, R. (2008). *Security engineering. A guide to building dependable distributed systems* (2nd ed.). Indianapolis, IN: Wiley Publishing, Inc.

Beran, M. J., Couchman, J., Coutinho, M., Boomer, J., & Smith, J. D. (2010). Metacognition in non-humans: Methodological and theoretical issues in uncertainty monitoring. In A. Efklides & M. Plousia (Eds.), *Trends and prospects in metacognition research* (pp. 21-35). Springer Science+Business Media, LLC 2010.

Chorafas, D. (2011). *Cloud computing strategies*. Boca Raton, FL: CRC Press.

Dunn, J. (2011). DDoS attack sends Hong Kong stock exchange back to paper. *Techworld,* Aug 2011. Retrieved September 08, 2011, from http://bit.ly/nSAb84

European Network and Information Security Agency (ENISA). (2009). *Cloud computing. Benefits, risks and recommendations for information security.* Retrieved August 4, 2011, from http://bit.ly/CLeIX

Girouard, D. (2010). *Keeping your data safe.* Official Google Enterprise Blog. Jan 2010. Retrieved August 10, 2011, from http://bit.ly/7SabbN

Kagono, T. (2006). Cognitive theories and knowledge management: A review of recent studies. In *The Annual Bulletin of Knowledge Management Society of Japan* (Eds.), *The Knowledge Forum 2005: Japanese Chi: Edge of Evolution*: N° 7. Track A-1. Knowledge Management Society of Japan. Japan.

Koriat, A. (2004). Metacognition research: An interim report. In Perfect, T., & Schwartz, B. L. (Eds.), *Applied metacognition* (pp. 261–286). Cambridge, UK: Cambridge University Press.

Krutz, R., & Vines, R. (2010). *Cloud security. A comprehensive guide to secure cloud computing* (p. 61). Indianapolis, IN: John Wiley & Sons, Inc.

Mcfredries, P. (2008). The cloud is the computer. *IEEE Spectrum,* (August): 2008. Retrieved July 24, 2011 from http://www.spectrum.ieee.org/computing/hardware/the-cloud-is-the-computer

Mell, P., & Grance, T. (2011). *The NIST definition of cloud computing* (Draft). (NIST Special Publication 800-145). Retrieved August 06, 2011, from http://1.usa.gov/eZ8PSn

Naglieri, J. A. (2011). The discrepancy/consitency approach to SLD identification using the PASS theory. In Flanagan, D. P., & Alfonso, V. C. (Eds.), *Essentials of specific learning disability identification* (pp. 147–148). Hoboken, NJ: Wiley.

Pressley, M. (2000). Development of grounded theories of complex cognitive processing: Exhaustive withing- and between study analyses of thinking-aloud data. In Schraw, G., & Impara, J. C. (Eds.), *Issues in the measurement of metacognition* (pp. 262–269). Lincoln, NE: Buros Institute of Mental Measurements.

Schneier, B. (2000). *Secrets and lies. Digital security in a networked world* (p. xii). New York, NY: John Wiley & Sons, Inc. doi:10.1108/14636690332200829

Schneier, B. (2009). *People understand risks - But do security staff understand people?* Retrieved September 1, 2011, from https://www.schneier. com/essay-282.html

Veenman, M. V. J., Van Hout-Wolters, B., & Afflerbach, P. (2006). Metacognition and learning: Conceptual and methodological considerations. *Metacognition and Learning, 1*, 3–14. doi:10.1007/s11409-006-6893-0

Wheeler, E. (2011). *Security risk management. Building an information security risk management program for the ground up.* Syngress, MA: Elsevier Inc.

ADDITIONAL READING

Arshad, J. (2009). An integrated intrusion detection and diagnosis approach for clouds. In the *Proceedings of the 39th IEEE International Conference on Dependable Systems and Networks (DSN), Student Forum.*

Bertino, E. (1998). *Security for Web services and services-oriented architecture.* Berlin, Germany: Springer-Verlag. doi:10.1007/978-3-540-87742-4

Buyya, R., Yeo, C. S., & Venugol, S. (2008). Market–oriented cloud computing: Vision, hype, and reality for delivering IT services as computing utilities. *Proceedings of the 10th IEEE International Conference on High Performance Computing and Communications* (pp. 5-13).

Chen, Y., Paxson, V., & Katz, R. H. (2010). *What's new about cloud computing security?* Technical Report UCB/EECS-2010-5, EECS Department, University of California, Berkeley.

Chow, R., et al. (2009). Controlling data in the cloud: Outsourcing computation without outsourcing control. In *Proceedings of the 2009 ACM Workshop on Cloud Computing Security,* (pp. 85-90). Retrieved July 25, 2011, from http://doi. acm.org/10.1145/1655008.1655020

Cloud Security Alliance. (2009). *Security guidance for critical areas of focus in cloud computing V2.1.* Retrieved June 10, 2011, from http://www. cloudsecurityalliance.org/csaguide.pdf

Dillon, T., Wu, C., & Chang, E. (2010). Cloud computing: Issues and challenges. *AINA, 2010 24th IEEE International Conference on Advanced Information Networking and Applications* (pp. 27-33).

Herrmann, F., & Khadraoui, D. (2007). Chapter XIV security risk management methodologies. In D. Khadraoui & F. Herrmann (Eds.), *Advances in enterprise information technology security,* (pp. 261-273). Hershey, PA: Information Science Reference.

Hutter, B. (2010). *Anticipating risks and organizing risk regulation.* New York, NY: Cambridge University Press. doi:10.1017/CBO9780511761553

Jensen, M., Schwenk, J., Gruschka, N., & Iacono, L. L. (2009). On technical security issues in cloud computing. *IEEE International Conference on Cloud Computing, CLOUD'09,* (pp. 109–116).

Kaufman, L. M. (2009). Data security in the world of cloud computing. *Security & Privacy, 7*, 61–64. doi:10.1109/MSP.2009.87

Keahey, K. (2009). Nimbus: Open source infrastructure-as-a-service cloud computing software. In *Workshop on Adapting Applications and Computing Services to Multicore and Virtualization, CERN,* Switzerland.

Krause, P., Fox, J., Judson, P., & Patel, M. (1998). Qualitative risk assessment fulfils a need. *Lecture Notes in Computer Science, 1455*, 138–156. doi:10.1007/3-540-49426-X_7

Menary, R. (2007). *Cognitive integration: Mind and cognition unbounded.* Houndmills, UK: Palgrave Macmillan.

Perfect, T., & Schwartz, B. L. (Eds.). (2004). *Applied metacognition.* Cambridge, UK: Cambridge University Press.

Pfleeger, C. (2008). *Reflections on the insider threat. Insider attack and cyber security. Beyond the hacker*, (pp. 5-15). New York, NY: Springer Science + Business Media, LLC.

Rand Europe. (2011). *The cloud: Understanding the security, privacy and trust challenges.* Technical Report. Retrieved August 17, 2011, from http://www.rand.org

Ren, K., et al. (2009). *Ensuring data storage security in cloud computing.* Retrieved June 25, 2011, from www.ece.iit.edu/~ubisec/IWQoS09.pdf

Savage, M. (2009). *Security challenges with cloud computing services.* Retrieved August 1, 2011, from http://searchsecurity.techtarget.com/news/article /0,289142,sid14_gci1368905,00.html

Senft, S., & Gallegos, F. (2009). IT governance. In (Eds), *Information technology control and audit* 3rd ed., (pp.181-201). Boca Raton, FL: CRC Press.

Simon, B., Millard, C., & Walden, I. (2010). *Contracts for clouds: Comparison and analysis of the terms and conditions of cloud computing services.* Queen Mary School of Law Legal Studies Research Paper No. 63, 2010. Retrieved 2 September, 2011, from http://papers.ssrn.com/sol3/papers. cfm? abstract_id=1662374

Stokes, J. (2009). T-Mobile and Microsoft/danger data loss is bad for the cloud. *Ars technica.*

USD-C. (2010). *Soldier faces criminal charges.* Retrieved January 13, 2012, from http://www.cbsnews.com/htdocs/pdf/ManningPreferralofCharges.pdf?tag=contentMain;contentBody

Veenman, M. V. J., Van Hout-Wolters, B., & Afflerbach, P. (2006). Metacognition and learning: Conceptual and methodological considerations. *Metacognition and Learning, 1*, 3–14. doi:10.1007/s11409-006-6893-0

Vogels, W. (2008). *A head in the clouds - The power of infrastructure as a service.* In First Workshop on Cloud Computing and in Applications (CCA'08).

Vouk, M. A. (2008). Cloud computing: Issues, research and implementations. *Journal of Computing and Information Technology, 16*(4), 235–246.

Weinhardt, C., Anandasivam, A., Blau, B., & Stößer, J. (2009). *Business models in the service world* (pp. 28–33). IEEE IT Professional, March/April.

William Voorsluys, J. B., & Buyya, R. (2011). Introduction to cloud computing. In *Cloud Computing: Principles and paradigms* (pp. 3–5). Hoboken, NJ: John Wiley & Sons, Inc. doi:10.1002/9780470940105.ch1

Yumin, Y. Y. (2009). Application of cloud computing on network security. *Science Mosaic, 7.*

KEY TERMS AND DEFINITIONS

Function: A logic instrument programmed and presented to a user through a web interface, so that it only focuses in considering a part of the same problem. Its output defines the abstraction to reach and its parameters represent variables about a phenomenon that can alter a possible produced result. An analysis or reflection conformed by a sequence of functions.

Impact: It measures the degree of lost or damage (from 0 to 100) that can occur if a threat materializes as an attack over an object.

Metacognition: It concerns people's cognitions and feelings about their cognitive states and processes, as well as referring to cognitions about cognition in general, as well as self-regulation processes that take cognitive processes as their object.

Object: valuable asset that needs to be protected. This concept is so wide that can refer to some kind of tangible thing, as network switch or data base information, or a document that contains information about a person, a working team or an organization, among others.

Risk: Estimation of the exposure degree that a source of danger prevailed over an object producing damage (lost). In our approach, the user evaluates the risk qualitatively (low, medium o high) and subsequently in a quantitative way in order to replant its components (probability that a threat materializes and the impact). This gradual approach takes the user, step by step, analyzing the risk in depth and adjusting hi/her perception.

Subjective Probability: Subjects assign this probability based upon their belief degree that a threat will occur (event), considering contexts and durations, since it is established according to knowledge, experience or simple intuition.

Threat: It is the potential source of a security incident, that can cause damages to a hosted, processed asset or that makes use of a service in cloud computing environments.

Chapter 6
A Goal–Driven Risk Management Approach to Support Security and Privacy Analysis of Cloud–Based System

Shareeful Islam
University of East London, UK

Haralambos Mouratidis
University of East London, UK

Edgar R. Weippl
Secure Business Austria, Austria

ABSTRACT

Cloud Computing is a rapidly evolving paradigm that is radically changing the way humans use their computers. Despite the many advantages, such as economic benefit, a rapid elastic resource pool, and on-demand service, the paradigm also creates challenges for both users and providers. There are issues, such as unauthorized access, loss of privacy, data replication, and regulatory violation that require adequate attention. A lack of appropriate solutions to such challenges might cause risks, which may outweigh the expected benefits of using the paradigm. In order to address the challenges and associated risks, a systematic risk management practice is necessary that guides users to analyze both benefits and risks related to cloud based systems. In this chapter the authors propose a goal-driven risk management modeling (GSRM) framework to assess and manage risks that supports analysis from the early stages of the cloud-based systems development. The approach explicitly identifies the goals that the system must fulfill and the potential risk factors that obstruct the goals so that suitable control actions can be identified to control such risks. The authors provide an illustrative example of the application of the proposed approach in an industrial case study where a cloud service is deployed to share data amongst project partners.

DOI: 10.4018/978-1-4666-2125-1.ch006

INTRODUCTION

Cloud computing is a promising business concept that allows businesses to increase IT capacity in real time without investing more in new infrastructure, personnel training, and licensing of new software. The paradigm provides flexibility both in terms of possible delivery models, i.e., Software as a Service (SaaS), Platform as a Service (PaaS), and Infrastructure as a Service (IaaS), and in terms of possible deployment models, i.e., private, community, public, and hybrid cloud. It is easier to deploy, maintain, and update software in the cloud compared to the end-user machine (Choo, 2010). As any new technology, it creates new opportunities but also introduces risks. In the case of cloud computing, many challenges are related to security, privacy, and control of data and resources. Such challenges can cause potential risks, which may outweigh the expected benefits. Attackers could steal users' intellectual property and other sensitive information that is stored, processed, and managed in the cloud. A small service failure on the provider's end, which may last only an hour, sometimes has dramatic effects on an enterprise. The failure may stop usual operation, which in turn may cause financial losses. Challenges may also arise from the cloud provider's business model. For example, providers who frequently improve their range of services in response to evolving customer demand introduce the possibility of new security bugs with every additional feature. In a worst case scenario, cloud providers might not notify their clients of security breaches. According to the IT Cloud Service User Survey (Cloud Survey, (2008), many organizations consider security concerns to be the most serious barrier to cloud adoption. While the cloud offers a number of advantages, many of the major players will be tempted to hold back until some of the risks are better understood (Viega, 2009). It is important to consider those aspects that might cause risks before users decide whether to move their systems, services, applications, and/or data

to the cloud. Understanding security and privacy risks and finding solutions to control these risks is a critical issue for the success of cloud computing paradigm (Takabi et al., 2010).

In this chapter, we propose a goal-driven risk management modeling framework to assess and manage risks related to cloud-based systems (Islam,2009;Islam & Houmb, 2011; Islam, 2011a;Islam2011c). Risks are always negations of the goals (Lamsweerde, 2009). Therefore, the concept of risk is directly related to the concept of goal. We believe identifying goals provides a focus for risk management activities, in particular in identifying, analyzing and managing risks. The approach explicitly establishes a relationship between goals that are required for successful deployment of a cloud based system and risk factors that obstruct the goals. This allows us to select the appropriate control actions in order to prevent the risks for goal fulfillment. The framework adopts goal and obstacle concepts from the KAOS goal modeling language and extends it with risk assessment and treatment (Lamsweerde, 2009). The model considers goals based on the security and privacy issues of cloud service and deployment models. A set of risk factors that obstruct the goals is identified. These risk factors, such as threats and vulnerabilities, are the main causes for the occurrence of risk events, such as loss of data or service unavailability. Like other technology, cloud computing includes generic and unique threats and risks. For example, due to the virtualization of the storage space, an attack can disrupt many users. Such threats need to be adequately analyzed. Finally, the model identifies treatment actions to prevent, reduce, and avoid the likelihood and impact of risk factors and events. In our case, the actions can be a specific list of refined requirements, security and privacy-enhanced technology, introduction of a new goal, etc., depending on the context. To support the elicitation and analysis of security and privacy requirements, we adopt the security constraints concept of Secure Tropos (Mouratidis 2004; Mouratidis

& Giorgini 2007; Mouratidis & Giorgini 2009). Secure Tropos supports the analysis of security requirements based on concepts such as actor, action, goal, and constraint and diagrams such as security-enhanced actor diagram. This allows us to analyze the requirements identified in the risk treatment actions. The proposed approach is implemented at the Secure Business Austria (SBA) research center to identify and analyze the goals and risk factors before deploying a cloud-based service for sharing data.

BACKGROUND ABOUT RISK MANAGEMENT

There are a number of risk management approaches particularly focusing on software and system engineering domain. Among all these contributions, there is a consensus that risk management commonly comprises two general phases including risk assessment and control. The theoretical foundation of putting risk management into a single framework is initially contributed to Boehm (Boehm, 1991). Boehm's risk driven spiral model was the first life cycle model to integrate risk management throughout software development life cycle through iterative manner. Karolak (karolak, 1995) proposed Software Engineering Risk Model (SERIM) framework by taking Just-In-Time (JIT) software approach. SERIM attempts to minimize the amount of risks involved, while optimizing the contingency strategies for problematic situations. The approach considers three main risk elements, i.e., technology, cost and schedule from technological and business perspectives. These elements are interconnected with 81 risk factors. The risk factors are influenced from organization, estimation, monitoring, development methodology, tools, risk culture and usability. Konito proposed the Riskit methodology (Konito, 2001), which provides a complete conceptual framework for risk management using a goal/expectation approach from the stakehold-

ers and risks which threaten the goals. Risks are ranked in terms of probability and utility loss by a specific Riskit Pareto ranking technique. There are risk management methodologies targeting the security domain. The information system security risk management (ISSRM) reference model is a security risk management approach combined three main concepts, asset-related, risk-related, risk-treatment related concepts at three different levels, i.e., asset, risk and risk treatment (Mayer et al., 2007). The concepts identify the assets which need to be protected from risk. Risk is an event that has an impact to the assets. Risk treatment is an intentional decision to treat identified risks through control and requirements to ensure the overall security. ISSRM integrates risk management from the early information system development. CORAS is another risk management framework which follows asset driven strategy and uses UML for model based risk assessment of security critical system (Stolen et al., 2002). The models are used to describe the target of assessment, documents the risk management results and as a medium for communicating among groups of stakeholders involved in a risk assessment

The approaches discussed above are important for the development of risk concepts, framework, and a systematic risk management practice, but they also demonstrate a number of limitations. The Spiral model requires intensive active involvement of project customer/user, which is difficult to attain in real on-going project situation. SERIM approach does not show when and where the risk management initiates during the development and who will be involved into the process. In Riskit, there are no clear sources specified from where the goals are originated and how the identified goals are modeled. Risks are analyzed and prioritized by deriving scenarios which is a non-trivial task when a scenario depends upon more than one probabilistic element. CORAS also supports the evaluation of alternative treatment options, but does not provide any guideline as such. In contrast, the proposed goal-driven risk management model systematically assesses risks as an obstruction of the goal from a holistic perspective (Islam, 2009; Islam & Houmb, 2010; Islam, 2011a). A clear source is given based depending on the context from where the goals and risks should originate. We follow privacy issues along with security for analyzing potential security and privacy risks. Our approach initializes risk management plan in particular defining the scope, threshold, and boundary of performing risk management activities before identifying any risks. This certainly helps to understand how risky the undertaking project is. The underlying process is precise and produces adequate artifacts for controlling security and privacy risks in cloud based system. We believe our approach improves the state of the art about a systematic risk management practice in security and privacy domain.

SECURITY AND PRIVACY ISSUES IN CLOUD COMPUTING

Security and privacy are among the most important concerns in cloud computing, as large amounts of personal and other sensitive data are managed in the cloud. Several surveys among potential cloud adopters indicate that security and privacy is the primary concern hindering its adoption (Bruening & Treacy, 2009). Therefore, it is necessary to understand and analyze the relevant security and privacy issues before adopting cloud computing into existing infrastructure. This section discusses security and privacy issues from both the provider and the customer perspectives.

Security Issues in Cloud Computing

The Cloud computing paradigm faces security challenges, such as attacks on integrity, private data leakage, malicious code execution, deployment of organizational data or services to the cloud, and many more. These concerns make it risky to transition to cloud computing or integrate it into

the existing IT infrastructure. It is necessary to consider these security issues from all potential perspective in particular from both service and deployment model.

Service Model

In IaaS, sometimes also called hardware-as-a-service (Grobauer et al, 2011), providers generally supply a set of virtual infrastructure components, such as virtual servers and storage. Users (customers) can order these components and have them running in a matter of minutes. User applications and data run on the provider's virtual machine and are stored in a virtual space. It is the provider's responsibility to ensure basic security, such as virtualization and low-level data protection capabilities. Virtualization infrastructure can be used as a launching pad for new attacks (Choo, 2010). Issues such as VM image and securing inter-host communication are critical from the provider perspective (Gellman, 2009). Users have the responsibility to ensure the security of the applications managed by them.

PaaS provides a programming environment that has a visible impact on the application architecture deployment with the exception of issues related to the underlying operating system (Gong, 2010). It is the bridge between hardware and application. Although customers are mostly responsible for protecting their own applications, providers also need to ensure that the operating system, its modules, and anything below the application layer are secured and inaccessible or that there is limited access between applications.

The main idea behind SaaS is to replace applications running on local machines and provide customers with the ability to use applications from different providers. Customers do not have control over the underlying cloud infrastructure, including network, operating system, storage, core functionality of the application, and the server itself. Security issues arise from the software that is used to manage the relevant customer information.

Providers are usually responsible for ensuring the security of the customer data.

Deployment Model

Before deploying an organization's data and processes to the cloud, it is recommended to analyze all deployment models. This is because not all cloud deployment models are appropriate for every service and may not meet specific customer expectations (Bruening & Treacy, 2009). It highly depends on the customer's requirements of the system, such as control needed over the service and importance of data stored. A private cloud is limited to a single customer. Customers generally have control over deployed applications and their own infrastructure and can request customizations to fit their needs. Due to this exclusiveness, a private cloud is considered safer than the other models. In a public cloud, security issues are more critical due to aspects such as virtualization, which arise from supporting multiple users. Security measures, such as ensuring access control, data access, and availability of individual customer resources is necessary for a secure multi-tenant environment. In case of a hybrid cloud, the resources are divided between a private and a public cloud. Therefore, security and privacy issues should be paid adequate attention, similar to a public cloud.

Privacy Issues in Cloud Environments

Like security, privacy is an important issue in cloud computing in terms of both legal compliance and trust. Customers pay more attention to the privacy issues in cloud because customer data stored in the cloud often contains sensitive information (Islam et al., 2011b). Customers have less control over this data and the overall cloud infrastructure may not be trustworthy.

Data Protection

Customer data protection is a core concern of security and privacy measures in cloud computing. Privacy is a moral and legal right of individuals. Storing data and applications that reside outside the organization's premises poses the potential risk of unauthorized access and processing of the data and application (Chen, 2010). Customers may lose control over their critical assets. Data confidentiality and privacy risks may be more critical when providers reserve the right to change their terms and conditions. Therefore, measures such as complete privacy policy, subject consent and control, unlinkability, transparency of data, data operations, and assurance of data protection are necessary.

Legal Compliance

Legal compliance is a significant challenge for cloud-based systems. Although a large number of information security and data privacy laws exist, depending on the country and location, there is no single, comprehensive legal framework in which the legal rights, liabilities, and obligations of cloud providers and cloud users are formulated (Islam et al, 2011b). Both providers and customers need to comply with existing regulatory requirements and Service Level Agreements (SLAs). On the one hand, customers may have to give their private data and important processes into the hands of personnel and out of their control. On the other hand, providers may be obliged to search the data due to national security or to comply with local jurisdiction. The law is enforced at the place the data is stored as well as the place from where data is transmitted. Therefore, it is necessary to identify and analyze issues such as legal rights and alignment of SLA with legal obligations, protection and enforcement requirements before deploying a cloud computing solution.

Figure 1. Cloud computing components

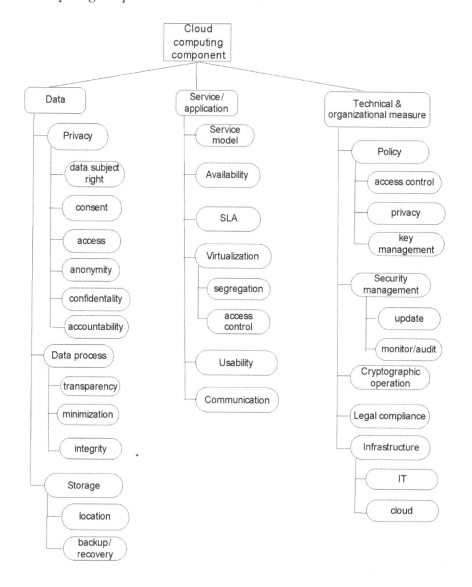

CLOUD COMPUTING COMPONENTS FOR RISK MANAGEMENT

For a systematic risk management practice, it is necessary to understand the main components of cloud computing. We consider three main components that support the deployment and service model of cloud computing. These are: data, service/application, and technical and organizational measures. Individual components consist of several elements related to that component.

Figure 1 shows the components and the elements they contain.

Data

Data is the central part of cloud computing. Cloud customers usually store their business data on the provider system; therefore, data protection within a shared environment is important. Any vulnerability of a particular service restricts user access to data within the service until the provider can control the vulnerability. In a survey, 40.5% respondents agreed that enterprises may seriously increase the risk of data leakage due to their focus toward using SaaS and cloud computing solutions (Proofpoint, 2009). Privacy is the ability to decide when, how, and to what extent our information is shared. Data privacy needs to address the issues related to the privacy protection goals, such as data subject rights, owner consent, data access, anonymity, and confidentiality and accountability of the data. All these issues are considered according to the principles of Fair Information Practice.

Data processing must ensure the transparency of the processed data. Only the minimum required data should be used for processing. The provider should inform the user how their data will be handled, and in particular, what types of security measures are used to protect the data, and how it will be handled if the data is compromised. Data integrity can be easily achieved in a stand-alone system, but as cloud computing employs multiple databases to store multiple tenants' data, ensuring transaction durability and consistency is very complex. Integrity can be even more complicated when it comes to shared resources with multiple databases. Due to virtualization, transactions cannot be guaranteed using standard methods such as HTTP. Therefore, the Application Programming Interface (API) level is used for this purpose (Subashini & Kavitha, 2011). However, API introduces additional complexities that can create security vulnerabilities in the API stack itself or in the technology responsible for handling the API calls. Therefore, secure channels and the reliability of the API-handling transaction are necessary for data integrity. In cloud computing, customer data is located in a provided storage place. The security of storage depends not only on the application responsible for storing the data but also on the operating system and other applications that run on the same platform. The physical location of the stored data is a factor as well, as it is important for the user to know where the data really resides due to privacy laws and whether

it is secured sufficiently. Backup and recovery refer to secure storage and the recovery of data in case of a failure. Data backups should be done regularly, and as an additional security measure, backed-up data should be encrypted and stored in a different location. The recovery plan should be executed in real time in the interest of the user.

Service/Application

Service/application in a cloud are used to process the customer data or to support mission-critical business functions. We consider a number of elements, such as service model, availability, SLA, virtualization, usability, and communication, as parts of this component.

Service orientation is one of the main concepts behind the business model of cloud computing. Abstraction and accessibility are two main properties of the cloud service model (Grobauer, 2011). Depending on the customer expectations, any of the three service models IaaS, PaaS, and SaaS can meet the goals. However, every model has its own features, which depend on the provider or customer to ensure security and privacy. Providers generally have the responsibility to ensure the security and privacy of the individual model, but the client is also responsible for securing their application when it is deployed into IaaS.

Virtualization supports a shared resource environment. It provides an abstract view of the underlying infrastructure to the cloud user, which reduces both the need for the cloud user to learn the details of cloud architecture and the threshold of application development. PaaS and SaaS services are usually built on top of a supporting IaaS infrastructure, so the importance of virtualization also extends to these service models. Virtualization restricts the transparency of user transactions. Software applications running on one VM should not be able to impact or influence software running on another VM. An individual VM should be unaware of the other VMs running in the environment as all actions are confined to its own address space. Using a side-channel attack, however, an attacker can instantiate new VMs of a target VM so that the new VM can potentially monitor the cache hosted on the same physical machine (Gong, 2010).

Usability is an essential issue for the successful use of an application offered by the cloud provider. The service should be easy for the users to access. Applications in cloud environments mainly offer Internet-based interfaces that should not be complex but mature enough for users to easily use the services of the application. Usability should ensure an easy to use system and hide the overall complexity from the users.

Secure communication is necessary within the application as well as from the customer to the provider. Businesses are highly dependent on Internet access to access their corporate information; therefore, loss of connectivity is a major risk for business continuity. Depending on the nature of the business, delay in real-time communication, e.g., in a 3D online game, may directly cause financial loss for the customer's business.

Technical and Organizational Measure

This component includes overall infrastructure and organizational support for cloud computing from both the user and provider perspective. The cloud provider needs to establish trust in the service offered to the customers (Chen,2010). To achieve a certain level of trust, adequate technical and organizational measures are necessary for the existing policies, security management, cryptographic operation, legal compliance and overall infrastructure. Policy refers to a set of rules to be followed by the participating entities within the cloud environment (Islam & Dong, 2008). Organizations should have a clearly defined access control, privacy, and key management policy. Access control determines how customers and providers can be identified, authenticated and authorized to access data and service. Privacy policy

is a comprehensive description of the way the information is handled, stored and used. It should truly protect customer privacy and the customer should have maximum control over the data and processing. Key management policy deals with the management of keys for the cryptographic operation. This policy provides guideline how to generate exchange, store, distribute, and replace keys. This policy should also suggest approaches to satisfying information security and data privacy laws and directives with a view to minimizing the impact of management overhead on organizational resources and efficiency. Policies should be unambiguous, understandable and agreed upon by all participating entities.

Security management refers to the management of the overall infrastructure, such as updating the security and privacy enhancing technologies, auditing, and monitoring. All threats and vulnerabilities must be addressed before they can pose a risk. Responsibility must be clearly assigned in case something goes wrong; especially as customers only have remote access to the provider infrastructure. Security management supports periodic updates and monitoring/auditing of the activities and overall infrastructure.

Legal compliance is critical for both customer and provider within the cloud computing context. Failure to comply with relevant legislation, such as data protection acts, may lead to criminal sanctions. Therefore, the customer should ensure that SLAs and other legally binding contractual arrangements with cloud service providers comply with relevant laws and legislation. Providers are liable for any violation of legal compliance or data breach, as the data resides at the provider end.

We consider two types of infrastructure, IT and cloud. IT infrastructure relates to the facilities and services common to any IT service, cloud or otherwise. The cloud infrastructure layer provides an abstraction level for basic IT resources. These resources offer services to higher layers: computational resources (usually VMEs), storage, and (network) communication. The infrastructure includes security and privacy-enhancing technologies. Cloud infrastructure should include a fault tolerance mechanism so that a backup part will instantly support a failed part. There are four possible places where faults can occur in cloud computing: provider-inner, provider-across, provider user and user-across (Grobauer, 2011). Therefore, it is necessary to address any fault arising from these places within the cloud infrastructure.

Goal-Driven Risk Management Model for Cloud Computing

Risk management requires a strategy that addresses potential security and privacy failures with a cloud computing integration. However, the task is challenging, as there is almost infinite number of possible scenarios. Without appropriate security and privacy considerations, the strategy would be likely to fail. It is particularly important to base the identification of threats and vulnerabilities on the system context and use security and privacy solutions designed for cloud environments. In our approach, we start with identifying the main goals in order to determine the risk management scope. The proposed method is based on our earlier work on goal-driven risk management models (Islam, 2009; Islam & Houmb, 2010; Islam 2011a). Risk management needs to consider all issues, in particular any threat that poses risks, from both the customer and the provider perspectives. It requires a strategy that considers possible failures, violations, and loss in the specific context of a cloud computing integration. Although most of the risks are not new, and many of the same risks exist on the platform without a cloud environment, we need to re-analyze the risks in the cloud context. Risk management helps to identify a set of requirements and control measures that can be used by the customer to monitor the provider's compliance with the services they offer.

The Approach

We present a risk management model that effectively addresses the risks which obstruct the successful deployment of cloud computing. The approach explicitly models the relationships between the goals and expectations based on the cloud computing components, the project success factor and the risk factors that obstruct these goals. Risks are then assessed and suitable control actions are selected to mitigate the risks so that the identified goals can be attained. Therefore, it is important in our approach to model the relationship between goals, obstacles and treatment. The reason for choosing a goal modeling language is that goals and risks are complementary entities (Lamsweerde, 2009). A risk is usually defined as negation of one or several goals or the non-attainment of corresponding objectives. The goal-driven approach anchors the risk management process (Islam, 2011c). It allows us to trace and rationalize the risk factors, events, and control actions to the goals. Figure 2 depicts the conceptual view of the proposed approach. The goal-risk model and associated artifacts play the main role in this approach. Goals are derived from the components, security and privacy issues, and stakeholder expectations, and are obstructed by the risks. Risks are then assessed and suitable treatment methods are identified to attain the goals. As stated above, ensuring security and privacy in cloud computing relies on many factors. The impact of these factors varies depending on the context. Our approach identifies goals based on these factors. Risks are defined as a negative consequence that directly or indirectly obstructs these goals. The goal-risk model, the security attack scenario, and the security-enhanced actor model shown in Figure 2 are the three main models of the proposed approach. A goal-risk model breaks a high-level goal down into sub-goals and creates obstruction links from the risks to the goal or goals in question. A security attack scenario establishes a link

Figure 2. Conceptual view of the proposed approach

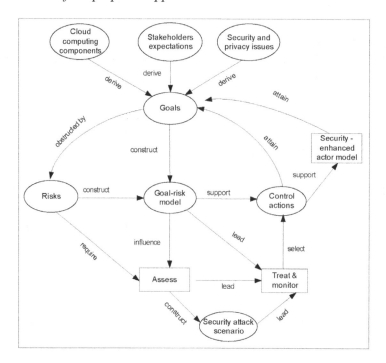

between attack intent, possible threat, resource, and secure capability. The security-enhanced actor model analyzes how the chosen control action and constraints support the attainment of the goals within a specific context.

Framework

The proposed goal-driven risk management framework is based on the KAOS goal modeling language. Our approach adopts the goal and obstacle concepts from KAOS and maps them with security and privacy issues in the cloud computing context and extends them with risk assessment and treatment. The framework consists of four layers to support the goal-driven risk management model. The advantage of a layer-based modeling framework is that it includes suitable tasks, methods and techniques for performing a specific activity on a given layer. Each layer supports iterative activities for assessing and managing security and privacy risks and produces one or multiple artifacts. These

artifacts are part of the risk specification concept and support the decision-making process during the deployment and management of cloud computing infrastructure. The framework consists of four layers of modeling structure. They are:

Goal Layer

The goal layer focuses on the factors that contribute effectively to addressing security and privacy issues for a successful cloud computing project. These goals are important as they describe what needs to be done to provide protection against the threats and vulnerabilities. Therefore, goals in our proposed approach consider several dimensions of the cloud computing components, stakeholder expectations, and security and privacy issues. They are project specific and focus on the economic benefits of cloud computing, provider expectation, project success criteria and boundaries, customer satisfaction, provider reputation, successful delivery of the service and deployment model, and security and privacy goals. Goal satisfaction requires cooperation between the system agents. These agents are the project stakeholders, security and privacy-enhancing technologies, tools, and infrastructure. The main activity of this layer is to identify and model the goals. However, before goal specification, the project stakeholders should agree on a concrete risk management plan; in particular, the risk management scope, underlying processes, risk threshold, and resources. Goal modeling supports the refinement of coarsely grained higher level goals to finely grained lower level goals through AND or OR refinement. In GSRM, the latter are referred to as sub-goals. Each sub-goal contributes to its parent goal. A graphical representation of the goal refinement is the core part of the goal model. Some goal types, such as soft goals, are suitable for the goal-driven risk management context as there are generally multiple ways of meeting such a goal. The same sub-goal that relates to a specific development component also contributes to the satisfaction of other development components. These sub-goals are important for the project and require extra care for their fulfillment. Therefore, if required, the goals are prioritized according to their importance to the project success.

Obstacle Layer

Obstacles are the main factors that reduce the ability to achieve one or several goals. We treat risk factors as obstacles that directly or indirectly lead to goal negation and create problems in the project. These risk factors are the threats and vulnerabilities within the system context. Vulnerability is defined as a weakness or flaw, in terms of security and privacy that exists from a resource, an actor and/or a goal. A threat is an attack or incident within a specific context that exploits vulnerability. Obstacles are the opposites of the goals (i.e., undesirable categories that are linked to the goals). Therefore, the obstacle categories should be aligned with and derived from the goal

categories and the situation should be modeled to show how several obstacles violate the identified goals. The obstacle layer enhances goal clarity. It identifies the potential threats and vulnerabilities and formulates the obstruction to the goal satisfaction. Like the goal model, the obstacle model refines obstacles to provide a complete overview of the threats and vulnerabilities that exist in the project. The main focus is to identify as many risk factors as possible so that corresponding control actions can be selected at an early stage. The obstacle layer supports the risk identification activities and categorizes the risk factors by cloud computing components. One risk or obstacle can be relevant to more than one goal. It is important to express this in the risk obstacle layer, as it is crucial information when considering effective treatment options. It is generally more effective to counter risk factors that affect more than one goal. The main tasks of this layer are risk factor identification, categorization, and modeling. However, the risks identified by this layer are not sufficient to determine the required control actions because risk factors first need to be quantified to determine their severity. Therefore, the identified obstacles are analyzed further in the assessment layer.

Assessment Layer

The assessment layer analyzes the risk events as a consequence of one or several risk factors to the goal. Risk quantification is an important first step in assessing the risk. However, this task is non-trivial due to the inherently subjective nature of the risks. This layer annotates each individual risk event in detail. Risk events are the potential consequence of the risk factors. Furthermore, it also establishes a causal relationship model between risk factors and risk events. This layer focuses on the severity the risk events' effect on the goal. For high-priority goals, obstacle identification and refinement should be extensive. Each risk event is characterized by two properties: likelihood and impact (Islam, 2011c). Likelihood specifies the possibility of a risk event occurrence and is modeled as a property of the risk event. The impact quantifies the negative consequence caused by the risk event to one or several goals. The same risk factor may lead to more than one risk event and the same risk event can obstruct more than one goal (Islam & Houmb, 2010). A goal can also be obstructed by multiple obstacles related to risk events and associated factors. This representation allows us to model situations where an event is influenced by more than one risk factor and impacts on one or several goals. An obstruction link is established from the risk event to the specific goal that it obstructs. This supports the construction of a goal-risk model by refining risk factors to risk events and their combined obstruction of the goals. The process of obstacle refinement mirrors goal refinement. The benefit of obstacle refinement is that we do not need to analyze every individual risk factor separately. In a real project situation this is important, in particular when budget and time are limited.

Treatment Layer

The final layer focuses on the control actions to counter the risks so that goals can be properly attained. Once the goals, risk factors and risk events have been identified and analyzed by the goal, obstacle and assessment layers, the final task is to implement suitable and cost-effective countermeasures. Therefore, the aim of this layer is to control risks as early as possible before the cloud technology is deployed into the existing infrastructure. This layer is also responsible for monitoring the risk status throughout the life cycle of the deployment. However, initial considerations focus on the risk events and associated factors that negatively affect several goals, i.e., high-priority risks. Generally, there is more than one countermeasure to the obstacles, but this layer should select the most cost-effective one for risk mitigation. Appropriate security and privacy-enhancing technologies for the given context must

be chosen. This layer includes two different links: a contribution link from the control action to the goal that it fulfills, and an obstruction link from the control action to the specific obstacle that it obstructs. The treatment layer allows modeling, reasoning and tracing the adopted control action for risk mitigation and goal satisfaction. It also includes a responsibility link from the control action to an agent, so that a specific active agent will be responsible for implementing the control action required to mitigate the risks. Once the selected risk control action is implemented, we need to monitor the risk status until it has been completely mitigated. The risk status changes in the course of the process. Control actions may not effectively reduce the risks and new risks may be identified. Therefore, the treatment layer continues to monitor risks throughout the development and communicates with the stakeholders about the risk status by risk status report.

Figure 3 shows framework of GSRM. GSRM uses the same graphical notations for goals (parallelogram) and obstacles (reverse parallelogram) as the KAOS model. At the top is the goal layer, which refines the goals into sub-goals through AND and OR refinement. The two middle layers collectively represent the software development risks as obstacles that directly obstruct the goals and create problems for the development. At the bottom is the treatment layer, which initially contains goals in terms of prevention, reduction and avoidance of risks and assigns responsibilities to the agents who implement the selected control actions to obstruct the obstacles.

Goal-Driven Risk Management Process

The process contains five activities that define the major area of concern for goal-driven risk management (Islam, 2011c). The activity describes all the tasks necessary for the creation of the risk specification artifact type. Each task produces an expected output based on the input. If required,

Figure 3. Goal-driven risk management framework

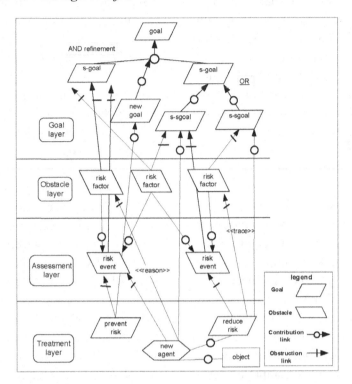

each task includes steps that define a concrete method for constructing the selected output as artifact. Artifacts are the deliverables that are produced, modified and used by a sequence of tasks as part of the risk specification. Artifacts include content that reflects on the concept of a specific domain, precisely defining the elements used and their relationships for specific description techniques. This section provides a brief overview of the activities involved in this method of risk management.

Activity 1: Initialize Goal-Driven Risk Management

This first activity formally approves the execution of the goal-driven risk management activities at an early stage of the project. Therefore, this activity requires the active involvement of the management and the project manager to emphasize the importance of risk management in early develop-

ment. It contains two tasks, which are responsible for creating the risk management plan. The first task is to determine the riskiness, i.e., inherent challenges, of the project. This task decides how risky the project is in terms of economic benefit, deployment, user satisfaction, security, privacy, and other critical factors. This makes it easier to decide at a high level whether it is worth incorporating the cloud computing technology into the existing infrastructure or updating the existing provider. Three levels of project riskiness are possible: high, medium and low. Once the project challenges are identified, the next task is to plan risk management. It focuses on several parameters that require confirmation from the project manager and main project stakeholders, such as risk management scope, generic risk events and associated thresholds, schedule and resources, risk treatment and monitoring strategy. It would be effective, at this stage, to define and agree on the risk management scope and to assign responsibilities, authority and a schedule for risk management. The scope should also define objectives along with the boundaries for risk management, in particular which risks can be ruled out in the running project. Once the plan has been agreed upon, the remaining risk management activities continue for the project. A complete risk management plan is the main artifact concept from this activity.

Activity 2: Identify and Model Goals

This activity identifies and models the goals by focusing on the cloud computing components, stakeholder expectations, and security and privacy issues. It consists of two tasks: identify and categorize the goals, and model the goals. If necessary, the identified goals are refined or revised so that they reflect the stakeholder expectations, project success factors, project scope, and business goals. Once the goals have been identified, they are categorized based on the cloud computing components. We also need to delimit the number of goals that are relevant to the project and to the risk management scope. The goals need to link up with each other in order to specify their contribution to addressing the security and privacy challenges. Occasionally some of the identified goals are too abstract, which makes it hard to understand their specific significance. Therefore, initial goals can be refined to provide more concrete meaning in terms of their contribution to the project success. In goal modeling, AND or OR refinement can be used, depending on the context. An AND refinement means higher level goals can only be satisfied by satisfying all lower level sub-goals. An OR refinement means higher level goals can be satisfied by satisfying any of the sub-goals. Sub-goals are complementary for AND refinement and alternative for OR refinement. The model supports a contribution link from a sub-goal that contributes to the parent goal. Finally, the activity constructs a detailed goal specification document that triggers the risk assessment and management activities. The specification provides a precise description of every individual goal that should be addressed for risk management.

Activity 3: Identify and Model Obstacles

This activity identifies a list of risk factors that obstruct the identified goals and models them as goal obstruction links. Obstacle identification considers the vulnerability and threats that influence any potential risks in cloud computing. We follow the cloud computing component hierarchy to identify and categorize the risk factors. The threats related to security and privacy can be complex and context-specific. This activity models the related risk factors as main causes for the potential risk events. It is necessary to identify as many likely obstacles as possible from the data, service, and organizational context so that the project team can be aware of the problems early on. We use state-of-the-art methods to identify the vulnerabilities and threats in cloud computing and analyze them based on the specific system context. The identified risk factors are modeled as goal negations through an obstruction link from risk factor to the goal. The goal-risk model is an extension of the goal model that adds obstruction links from obstacles to goals. It comprises two different links: a contribution link from sub-goals to goals and from risk factors to risk events, and an obstruction link from risk factors and risk events to goals. This allows the visual representation of the goals and risk factors. The model also shows those critical sub-goals and risk factors that require more attention than the others. This information is critical at any stage of the project.

Activity 4: Assess Risk

This activity quantifies individual risk by estimating the risk level and priority. Risk estimation prioritizes the risks so that appropriate treatment actions can be planned and implemented. Each risk is estimated through two properties: likelihood and severity of impact. However, identifying risk event likelihood is a challenging task due to the subjective nature of the risks. Risk is very context-specific and risk values from one context may not be suitable in another. Moreover, there is lack of historical data on which likelihood estimation could rely. The probability of an individual event becomes purely subjective when there is no true value (Houmb, 2007). In such a case, the focus is placed on the observable values, based on observation, individual belief or focusing on the states of the cloud components.

Our approach considers expert opinion, project context and goals for estimating the likelihood and severity of a risk event. Project context plays an important role in this task. For instance, a customer who is concerned mainly with the economic benefit of using cloud computing would have a different risk estimation strategy than a customer who focuses more on the quality of the service or compliance with the relevant legislation due to the deployment of a cloud environment. We summarized threats/vulnerabilities as risk factors and risk events, shown in Table 1, based on the results of our literature review. However, this summary only provides a guideline for this task and, in particular, helps to formulate the risk factors and associated events for the project context. Once the risk events have been estimated,

Table 1. List of threats/vulnerabilities and associated risk events applicable in cloud based system context

Component	Vulnerabilities/threats	Risks
Data	Unavailability of data Lack of data segregation Lack of validation check Provider misuse of data Unauthorized access Linkability of data due to dynamic service interaction and data exchange Virtual machine replication Insecure storage Data recovery vulnerability Hardware failure	Data leakage Data replication Data deletion Poor data availability Loss of integrity
Service/ application	Session riding/hijacking Lack of data leak prevention due to virtual machine replication Unexpected side channels/covert channel Lack of transparency Injection of malicious code into the application Access control weakness Breach of SAL, DDOS Virtual machine escape and template image Insufficient authorization check Error in provider and user communication, e.g., network congestion, request time out, busy	Poor service availability Poor SLA Difficult to access application
Technical/ Org. measures	Poor configuration Insufficient monitoring facilities Inability to respond to audit findings Launching dynamic attack points, hosting malicious data Insecure or obsolete cryptography Unsafe user behavior Poor management procedures Unclear privacy policy/terms Lack of control to ensure compliance Lack of integration of the legacy system with the cloud application Poor physical control Poor optimization of using computing resources	Regulatory violation Loss of trust Loss of privacy Data leak Lack of infrastructure Cross-tenant unauthorized access Poor data availability Poor service availability

the risks are prioritized. Several risks can have the same priority, so the same rank value may be assigned to more than one risk. At the end of the risk assessment activity, the risk details artifact is compiled. This artifact document provides details on the concept of risk for security and privacy issues in cloud computing.

Activity 5: Treat and Monitor Risk

This is the final activity is to controls the risk as early as possible and monitors the effectiveness of the implemented control actions. It also identifies any new risks in later phases of the project. This activity identifies the possible countermeasures and selects the most appropriate ones to mitigate the risk. It consists of three tasks. The first task, plan risk treatment, mainly determines the possible control actions that are relevant to controlling the risk event and selects the most appropriate ones so that the control action can be implemented immediately. The selection of the suitable control actions mostly depends on the possible counter-measures identified and the overall risk control strategy. There are five different strategies that can be followed to select the appropriate control actions for the prioritized risks: risk avoidance, no control action, risk prevention, risk reduction, and risk retention (Barry, 1991; Charette,1999). Once the possible countermeasures are identified, we need to select the most suitable one to control a risk. Every treatment action requires evaluating the cost, agent availability, project goals, project riskiness and risk management scope for its imple-mentation. We define those as evaluation criteria for selecting the appropriate control action. A project always has to have trade-offs among the goals to select the appropriate countermeasure. However, this trade-off also depends on the goals the project emphasizes. Once the control action has been selected, the next task is to assign the agent to implement the control action. Agents are the active components within software de-velopment that perform a specific role for goal

satisfaction. Risk treatment actions generate one or several tasks, and agents are responsible for performing the tasks so that the control actions are implemented. The risks generally evolve over time, during the course of development, use and maintenance of the product. Furthermore, new risks can also emerge. Continuous monitoring is essential and effective for analyzing the changes in risks in the software project. This is initiated once the identified risks have been analyzed and selected control actions implemented.

ILLUSTRATIVE EXAMPLE

To demonstrate the applicability of the proposed goal-driven risk management model in cloud computing, we employ the proposed approach in a real-world application at Secure Business Austria (SBA). SBA is an IT security research institute in Vienna (SBA, 2011). The organiza-tion has a large amount of research collaboration with academic and industry partners focusing on various domains of IT security. Therefore, SBA needs to share data among the partners in a proj-ect. Collaborative work environments are quickly moving into the cloud environment for effective document exchange support. Specialized services such as Google Docs or general-purpose file sharing services (Dropbox, 2011) are commonly used to support data sharing in collaborate work. Dropbox, for instance, offers corporate accounts where users can share a common file repository and access rights can be defined centrally.

The research center SBA planned to use tools such as Dropbox to share non-sensitive docu-ments with partner companies and to collaborate on ongoing research. Before making this cloud-based service a part of normal business processes, the management decided to identify the possible benefits and risks for deploying Dropbox into the existing infrastructure. This investigation was important for SBA for making the decision of deploying cloud technology for projects with other partners. Therefore, our proposed goal-driven risk management model was deployed to assess and manage the risks of using Dropbox to share data. We followed the goal-driven risk management process step by step to perform risk management activities for the purpose.

Activity 1: Initialize Goal-Driven Risk Management

The management formed a team consisting of one key researcher and two research employees to assess the Dropbox project before deploying the cloud service. The team was also responsible for performing the risk management activities. Several challenges were identified for the project: security and privacy of the data stored in Dropbox, convincing other project partners to use Dropbox, availability of data, and backup. However, the team agreed that there is no direct development, deployment and maintenance cost for deploying Dropbox, and the costs could be included if the SBA management decided to purchase the add-ons such as large shared quotas for a team and centralized admin. Therefore, the economic benefit was certainly larger than the challenges. The project was considered a medium to low-risk project regarding the issues related to the data component of cloud computing. The risk management scope was defined to identify security and privacy vulnerabilities, threats, and risks relating to data sharing in Dropbox. Risks related to the infrastructure, maintenance, and issues related to the project partners were not considered in this project.

Activity 2: Identify and Model Goals

The team first identified several goals that could be achieved by the project by following the cloud computing components given in the previous section: improving collaboration, simple deployment procedures, user satisfaction, availability of data and service, confidentiality of data. The

goal of improving collaboration can certainly be achieved by using Dropbox in the sense that project partners have direct access to current research draft documents and that their employees can be better integrated into projects while working at different geographic locations. Deployment was expected to be fairly easy as most researchers would use Dropbox on their private computers; simple server-based processes would ensure that a copy of the Dropbox files would be made to one file server, and thus all files would also be included in the standard backup cycles. Therefore, a simple deployment procedure is connected to the usability of the application. User satisfaction was expected to rise, since this had been actually requested by the users to allow them to access files on many different devices and from remote locations. Confidentiality of data help to ensure the security and privacy of the files stored in Dropbox. Note that the purpose of SBA is to only store data and to share it with other partners, therefore, integrity is not relevant in this context. These goals are linked with each other and combine both technical and non-technical issues for the project. Improving collaboration is considered the goal with the highest priority. This is a rather high-level goal, and other identified goals were considered as its sub-goals. The goal model is shown in the upper part of Figure 5 where the top goal "improving collaboration" is refined into sub-goals, illustrating that sub-goals contribute to achieving the parent goal.

Activity 3: Identify and Model Obstacles

The risk management team identified several threats as risk factors that might obstruct the goals, in particular reducing the expected economic benefit. The risk factors were identified for the cloud computing components. Most of the threats concerned the data and application. Data security is one of the main problems in this context. Furthermore, web applications and

Figure 4. Security attack scenario for data leakage

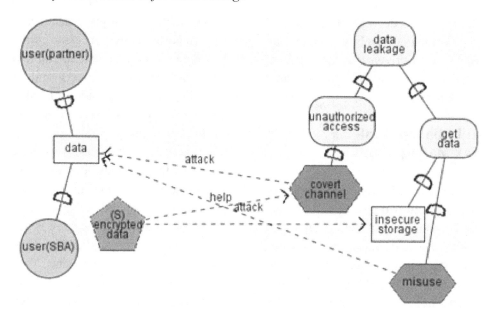

services as well as virtualization have inherent threats for the cloud context. Several threats were identified, such as insecure storage, unauthorized access, data recovery vulnerabilities, and insufficient authorization check, which obstruct the confidentiality and availability of data. For the files that we considered storing online, confidentiality is of medium importance. There are other factors concerning confidentiality and availability of data, such as Dropbox insiders being able to access the files, and – more importantly – the threat of a Trojan stealing information on low-bandwidth covert channels. Since files are identified by hash values of 4MB chunks, stealing the hash values (on a low-bandwidth channel) is sufficient to later be able to retrieve the entire file directly from the Dropbox server. (Mulazzani et al., 2011) found that this attack requires the attacker to be able to execute code and to have access to the victim's file system, e.g., by using malware. The complexity of the application deployment can directly obstruct the usability of the application. Some other risk factors were identified in the area of technical and organizational measures, such as poor configuration and unsafe user behavior.

Activity 4: Assess Risks

Once the risk factors are identified, the next activity is to determine the potential risk events that can be caused by the risk factors. Based on the project context, three risk events are identified that are mainly related to data. These risk events are: data leakage, poor backup and recovery, lack of privacy protection. Data leakage is a common problem in cloud environments, as the probability of unauthorized access occurring is much higher compared to the traditional systems. There are also some risk factors specific to Dropbox, such as the low-bandwidth covert channel attack, which is more frequent in cloud. These two factors have a strong impact on the probability of data leakage. Figure 4 shows the security attack scenario for data leakage considering three main risk factors covert channel, insecure storage, and misuse. As stated previously, we use Secure Tropos notation to model the attack in order to analyze the risk.

Figure 5. Partial goal-risk model

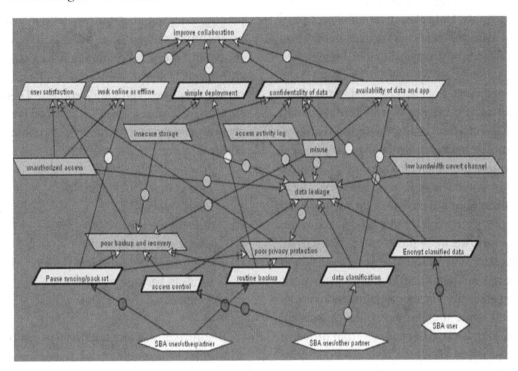

Here, encrypted data is shown as a control action, which helps to protect the risk factors. Figure 5 shows the contribution link from the risk factors to the risk events and the obstruction link from the risk events to the goals.

Data backup and recovery is also a major problem as there is no backup option in this cloud service. In Dropbox, a local copy of user data is stored on a user system and a history of changes can be kept on the Dropbox servers. This feature for paid customers is called *'pack-rat'*. Without pack-rat there might be a possibility of poor backup and recovery. Privacy is important for users, as they might not like the feeling that someone can watch all their activities. Whenever a file is saved, a copy is synced to the Dropbox servers and there is an event list that displays who edited which file at which time (Ciriani,2010). Using this timeline in combination with the changes stored between each version, it is possible to reconstruct precisely what actions were executed by the user. Therefore, user privacy

protection is not adequate in this context. Risk factors such as insecure storage, unsafe user behavior such as poor passwords, insufficient authorization checks, and the complexity of using Dropbox have an impact on the occurrence of risk events such as data leakage, poor data availability, and poor backup and recovery.

Activity 5: Treat and Monitor Risk

Finally, risk treatment actions are identified for the project context based on the level of the risk events. As the project focuses on the deployment of Dropbox into the existing SBA infrastructure, the risk management team agreed to choose a risk treatment strategy that would completely prevent or reduce risk. Data leakage is considered the highest ranked risk for the project context. The identified treatment actions focus on eliminating the main causes of this risk event. Several risk treatment actions were chosen for data leakage: data classification, store encrypted data, access control policy, strong key management, and check user credentials. Data classification is necessary so that sensitive data such as project budget and deliverables can be stored in the cloud in encrypted form only; non-sensitive data can be stored in the cloud in plain text. For encrypted data, strong key management is necessary. It was recommended that SBA develop and institute among its employees a complete access control policy for the users who will use the cloud service. Access control policy can prevent unsafe user behavior. Users should always have to provide a strong password and their user credentials must be checked when they attempt to log in. To protect the privacy, users can pause the sync process. This is an easy and effective risk mitigation method; it does, however, impact availability since no intermediate results are synced while the Dropbox client is paused. Dropbox allows users to access it from different platforms such as Windows, Linux, MacOS, and mobile devices. Therefore, deployment is platform independent. Regular backups are necessary to facilitate quick recovery in case of disasters. The use of strong encryption schemes to protect the backup data is also recommended to prevent accidental leakage of sensitive information. The team recommended having a copy of every file on the local machine; as an alternative, SBA could purchase the pack-rat feature for Dropbox. Table 2 provides a brief overview of the risk factors, events, and the treatment actions that can obstruct

the risk factors and prevent the events from happening. A partial goal-risk model is constructed by inputting values from the other activities is shown in Figure 5. We summarized a number of constraints from risk management that need to be executed before deploying Dropbox. These constraints are requirements that focus on protecting security and privacy in the system context. The constraints are:

- Encrypt classified data
- Pause syncing
- Selectively sync
- Check user credentials
- Complete access control policy
- Routing backup
- Pack-rat

Figure 6 shows the actor model to demonstrate how the security requirements are incorporated as constraints for the deployment of Dropbox. Users are intended to use a data-sharing service from the cloud provider, i.e., Dropbox, and expect the confidentiality of data that is stored in the cloud. When users upload data, the provider expects users to provide credentials before uploading any data, and users also expect that classified data is encrypted. Users should also confirm selective syncing for privacy protection. The actor model supports the analysis of the requirements identified through the risk treatment action. We

Table 2. List of risk factors, events and treatment actions

Risk factor	Risk event	Level	Treatment
Low bandwidth covert channel Unsafe user behavior Insecure storage Misuse Unauthorized access	Data leakage	Medium to High	Data classification Store encrypted confidential data Access control policy Strong key management Check user credentials
Access user activity log Misuse Unauthorized access	Poor privacy protection	Medium	Not instant sync Selectively pausing the sync
Insecure storage Unsafe user behavior Misuse	Poor backup and recovery	Medium	Routing backup to local storage Access control policy Pack-rat

Figure 6. Security-enhanced actor model

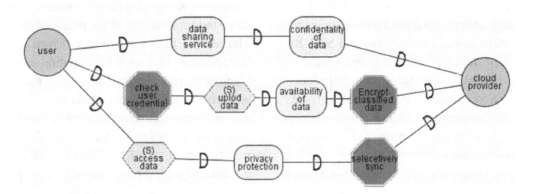

use the Secure Tropos tool SecTro to draw the security-enhanced actor model and the security attack scenario.

DISCUSSION

In this work, we propose a goal-driven approach for analyzing security and privacy risks in a cloud computing context and provide an illustrative example by deploying the risk management method in an industrial context. The process consists of five activities and each includes tasks and produces specific risk management artifacts, such as risk management plan, goal details, risk details, and goal-risk model. The approach first identifies the riskiness nature of the project based on the inherent project challenges, and ranks the project as a high, medium or low-risk project. It helps to determine the scope of risk management and to systematically incorporate the risk management activities starting in the early stages of the project. The model adopts goal and obstacle concepts from the KAOS goal modeling language and extends them with risk assessment and treatment methods. The goal-risk model is constructed using the KAOS concepts and the KAOS tool Objectiver. The approach also uses the Secure Tropos method to analyze and model the requirements and threats identified in the risk assessment and treatment activities. We also use the Secure Tropos tool

SecTro to construct the security-enhanced actor model and the security attack scenario.

We used a case study from the SBA research centre to demonstrate the applicability of the proposed goal-driven risk management framework for analyzing security and privacy issues in cloud computing. The project, by inherent nature, is medium to low risk project. As the cloud-based service will be used as part of normal business processes, the management needs to know the benefits and risks of using Dropbox. Our project scope only considers issues related to data sharing in cloud and issues related to the maintenance and project partners are out of boundary for the project context. Our approach identified three risk events: data leakage, poor privacy protection, poor backup and recovery, which obstruct goals such as improving collaboration, user satisfaction, availability of data and service, and confidentiality of data. There are several risk factors that act as causes for the risk events, i.e., low bandwidth covert channel, misuse, access to user activity log, and unauthorized access. Factors like low bandwidth cover channel, which eases stealing the hash value of the stored file, is a threat specific for the cloud context. Data leakage is considered the highest ranked risk event. Our analysis also identified several control actions to mitigate the risks, such as data classification, access control policy, user credential, and not instant sync. We also recommended SBA to purchase pack-rat feature of Dropbox for addressing poor backup and recovery.

The application of our goal-driven risk management framework has certainly assisted SBA for making their decision regarding deployment of cloud services into their existing business process. It provides a comprehensive analysis of the issues relevant for the context. Several observations are made. Identifying the project risks support an effective determination of the scope of using the risk management approach. Same risk factors may influence multiple risk events and these are the important risk factors that need immediate attention. The security attack scenario supports traceability of the attacker motivations and attacks to the system and resources. The security-enhanced actor model also supports the analysis of the requirements identified in risk treatment in the system context. The SBA management indicated that without implementation of our goal-driven risk management framework, it would be difficult to identify and address the risks which obstruct their goals. The SAB management also decided to purchase the recommended Dropbox add-ons for securing the backup and recovery.

CONCLUSION AND FURTHER RESEARCH DIRECTIONS

Cloud computing provides opportunities such as cost saving and on-demand service, while at the same time it poses risks such as data leakage and loss of control. Users can only enjoy the benefits of cloud computing if the security and privacy issues are addressed. Therefore, a systematic risk management practice is necessary to recognize and minimize threats in order to allow the successful adoption of cloud computing. A goal-driven risk management model is presented in this paper to assess and manage security and privacy risks in a cloud computing context. The model supports making timely and well-informed decisions for controlling risks during the deployment of a cloud

environment into the existing infrastructure. A case study from an industrial context is used to demonstrate the applicability of the proposed approach. The results show that the goal-driven approach is applicable to a cloud computing context to identify the risk factors that obstruct the security and privacy goals. Several goals, risk factors, risk events, and treatment actions are identified in the case study. Early identification of risk events and treatment actions helps the organization to successfully deploy a cloud service. The approach considers risk management activities from a holistic perspective by addressing both technical and non-technical issues of the cloud computing components. More case studies are necessary in order to be able to generalize the findings of using the proposed risk management method in a cloud computing context. Moreover, we are also planning to develop taxonomy of goal and risk factors for the cloud computing context, which will help the stakeholders to make an informed decision before deploying a cloud computing environment.

REFERENCES

Bannerman, P. L. (2008). Risk and risk management in software projects: A reassessment. *Journal of Systems and Software*, *81*(12), 2118–2133. doi:10.1016/j.jss.2008.03.059

Barry, B. W. (1991). Software risk management: Principles and practices. *IEEE Software*, *8*(1), 32–41. doi:10.1109/52.62930

Bruening, P. J., & Treacy, B. C. (2009). *Cloud computing: Privacy, security challenges*. Bureau of Nat'l Affairs. Retrieved from www.hunton.com

Charette, R. N. (1999). The competitive edge of risk entrepreneurs. *IT Professional*, *1*(4), 69–73. doi:10.1109/6294.781627

Chen, Y., Paxson, V., & Katz, R. H. (2010). *What's new about cloud computing security?* (Technical report UCB/EECS-2010-5). EECS Dept., University of California. Retrieved from www.eecs.berkeley.edu/Pubs/ TechRpts/2010/ EECS-2010-5.html

Choo, K. R. (2010). *Cloud computing: Challenges and future directions, Trends & issues in crime and criminal justice.* Australian Institute of Criminology, No. 400.

Ciriani, V., Vimercati, S., Foresti, S., Jajodia, S., Paraboschi, S., & Samarati, P. (2010). Combining fragmentation and encryption to protect privacy in data storage. *ACM Transactions on Information and System Security, 13*(3). doi:10.1145/1805974.1805978

Cloud Survey. (2008). *IT cloud services user survey (2008), pt. 2: Top benefits & challenges.* Retrieved from www.blogs.idc.com

Dropbox. (2011). Retrieved June 16, 2011, from https://www.dropbox.com

Gellman, R. (2009). *Privacy in the clouds: Risks to privacy and confidentiality from cloud computing.* Retrieved from http://www.worldprivacyforum. org/pdf/WPFCloud_Privacy_Report.pdf.

Gong, C., Liu, J., Zhang, Q., Chen, H., & Gong, Z. (2010). The characteristics of cloud computing. *Proceedings of the 2010 39th International Conference on Parallel Processing Workshops.* Washington, DC: IEEE Computer Society, USA.

Grobauer, B., Walloschek, T., & Stocker, E. (2011). Understanding cloud computing vulnerabilities. *IEEE Security & Privacy Magazine, 9*(2), 50–57. doi:10.1109/MSP.2010.115

Hardesty, L. (2009). *Secure computers aren't so secure.* MIT Press. Retrieved from www.physorg. com/news176107396.html

Houmb, S. H. (2007). *Decision support for choice of security solution- The aspect-oriented risk driven development (AORDD) framework.* PhD thesis, Department of Computer and Information Science, Norwegian University of Science and Technology.

Islam, S. (2009). Software development risk management model: A goal driven approach. In *Proceedings of the Doctoral Symposium for ESEC/ FSE on Doctoral Symposium*, The Netherlands.

Islam, S. (2011c). Software development risk management model – A goal-driven approach. PhD thesis, Technische Universität München, 2011. Retrieved from http://mediatum.ub.tum.de/

Islam, S., & Dong, W. (2008). Human factors in software security risk management. In *LMSA '08: Proceedings of the First International Workshop on Leadership and Management in Software Architecture*, (pp. 13–16). New York, NY: ACM.

Islam, S., & Houmb, S. H. (2010). Integrating risk management activities into requirements engineering. In *Proceedings of the 4th IEEE Research International Conference on Research Challenges in IS*, Nice, France.

Islam, S., & Houmb, S. H. (2011a). Towards a framework for offshore outsource software development risk management model. *Journal of Software, 6*(1), 38–47. doi:10.4304/jsw.6.1.38-47

Islam, S., Mouratidis, H., & Jürjens, J. (2011b). A framework to support alignment of secure software engineering with legal regulations. *Journal of Software and Systems Modelling (SoSyM) Theme Section on Non-Functional System Properties in Domain-Specific Modelling Languages, 10*(3), 369–394.

Karolak, D. (1996). *Software engineering risk management.* CA, USA: IEEE Computer Society Press.

Kontio, J. (2001). *Software engineering risk management: A Method, improvement framework and empirical evaluation.* PhD thesis, Helsinki University of Technology.

Lamsweerde, van A. (2009). *Requirements engineering: From system goals to UML models to software specifications.* Wiley.

Mayer, N., Heymans, P., & Matulevicius, R. (2007). Design of a modelling language for information system security risk management. In *Proceedings of the 1st InternationalConference on Research Challenges in Information Science* (RCIS 2007), (pp. 121–131).

Mouratidis, H. (2004). *A security oriented approach in the development of multiagent systems: Applied to the management of the health and social care needs of older people in England.* PhD thesis, University of Sheffield, U.K., 2004.

Mouratidis, H., & Giorgini, P. (2007). Security attack testing (SAT) - Testing the security of information systems at design time. *Information Systems, 32*(8), 1166–1183. doi:10.1016/j. is.2007.03.002

Mouratidis, H., & Giorgini, P. (2009). Secure Tropos: A security-oriented extension of the Tropos methodology. *International Journal of Software Engineering and Knowledge Engineering, 17*(2).

Mulazzani, M., Schrittwieser, S., Leithner, M., Huber, M., & Weippl, E. (2011). Dark clouds on the horizon: Using cloud storage as attack vector and online slack space. *Proceedings of Usenix Security.*

Proofpoint. (2009). Outbound email and data loss prevention in today's enterprise. Sunnyvale.

Roy, G. (2004). A risk management framework for software engineering practice. In *Proceedings of the 2004 Australian Software Engineering Conference*, IEEE Computer Society.

SBA. (2011). Secure Business Austria. Retrieved November 15, 2011, from http://www.sba-research.org/research/

Stolen, K., den Braber, F., Fredriksen, R., Gran, B. A., & Houmb, S. H. Stama-tiou, Y. C., & Aagedal, J. Â. (2007). Model-based risk assessment in a component-based software engineering process - Using the CORAS approach to identify security risks. In F. Barbier (Ed.), *Business component-based software engineering.* Kluwer Academic Publishers.

Subashini, S., & Kavitha, V. (2011). A survey on security issues in service delivery models of cloud computing. *Journal of Network and Computer Applications, 34*(1). doi:10.1016/j.jnca.2010.07.006

Takabi, H., Joshi, J. B. D., & Ahn, G. (2010). *Security and privacy challenges in cloud computing environments. IEEE Computer And Reliability Societies.* November/December.

Viega, J. (2009). Cloud computing and the common man. *Computer, 42*(8), 106–108. doi:10.1109/MC.2009.252

ADDITIONAL READING

Buyya, R., Shin Yeo, C., & Venugopal, S. (2008). Market-oriented cloud computing: Vision, hype, and reality for delivering IT services as computing utilities. *Proceedings of the 10th IEEE International Conference on High Performance Computing and Communications.*

Catteddu, D., & Hogben, G. (2009). *Cloud computing: Benefits, risks and recommendations for information security.* ENISA. Retrieved from www.enisa.europa.eu/

Cloud Security Alliance. (2009). *Security guidance for critical areas of focus in cloud computing V2.1.*

Hayes, B. (2008). Cloud computing. *Communications of the ACM, 51*(7), 9–11. doi:10.1145/1364782.1364786

Kaufman, L. M. (2009). Data security in the world of cloud computing. *IEEE Security & Privacy*, July/August, 61–64.

Malcolm Surgient, D. (2009). *The five defining characteristics of cloud computing*. Retrieved from www.news.zdnet.com

Mather, T., Kumaraswamy, S., & Latif, S. (2009). *Cloud security and privacy*. O'Reilly.

Sotomayor, B., Montero, R. S., Llorente, I. M., & Foster, I. (2009). Virtual infrastructure management in private and hybrid clouds. *IEEE Internet Computing, 13*(5), 14–22. doi:10.1109/MIC.2009.119

Tung, L. (2008). *Queenslanders debate cloud computing*. ZDnet. Retrieved from www. zdnet. com.au

Vaquero, L. M., Merino, L. R., Caceres, J., & Lindner, M. (2009). A break in the clouds: Towards a cloud definition. *ACM SIGCOMM Computer Communication Review, 39*(1).

Weiss, A. (2007). Computing in the clouds. *ACM Networker*, December, 16–25.

Zhou, M., Zhang, R., Xie, W., Qian, W., & Zhou, A. (2010). *Security and privacy in cloud computing: A survey*. International Conference on Semantics Knowledge and Grid, IEEE Computer Society.

KEY TERMS AND DEFINITIONS

Contribution Link: A contribution link is defined as an interface between sub-goal to the parent goal and between risk factor to the risk event. A sub-goal contributes to attain the parent goal and a risk factor responsible for the occurrence of a risk event through a contribution link.

Goal-Driven Risk Management Model: A systematic risk management method to assess and manage risks that obstruct the goals of a project. The method first identifies the riskiness of the project by considering inherent challenges of the project and contains five activities that each include multiple steps, and produces a risk specification artifact.

Goal-Risk Model: Goals are the core concept of the goal-driven risk management model. The identified goals are refined by breaking down high-level goals into lower level goals so that they can be quantified as more easily achievable goals. Obstacles are the negation of the goals and are responsible for the occurrence of any undesirable security or privacy events. A goal-risk model contains refinement links from a parent goal to one or more sub-goals, and obstruction links from obstacles to goals.

Goals: Goals are the objectives, expectations and constraints of the stakeholders and the cloud computing components, in particular considering security and privacy issues, as prescriptive statements of intents for the deployment of cloud computing. The satisfaction of these goals contributes to the overall project success.

Obstruction Link: An obstruction link is defined as an interface between goal and obstacle. A goal is obstructed by an obstacle through the obstruction link.

Risks: Risks are obstacles caused by threats and vulnerabilities as risk factors and associated events, whose combined consequences increase the chance of one or several undesirable circumstances arising that obstruct the goals and reduce the likelihood of the project success.

Secure Tropos: Secure Tropos is an extension of the Tropos methodology that adopts the i* modeling framework and uses the concepts of actors, goals, tasks, resources, and social dependencies for defining the relationship of one actor (depender) to other actors (dependees). Secure Tropos introduces security-related concepts (e.g., security constraint, secure dependency, secure goal) to the Tropos methodology, which enables developers to consider security issues throughout the development life cycle.

Security Attack Scenario: A security attack scenario is a scenario of an attack situation describing the actors of a software system and their secure capabilities as well as possible attackers and their goals, and it identifies how the secure capabilities of the system's actors prevent (if they do so) the satisfaction of the attackers' goals.

Security Constraint: A security constraint is defined in Secure Tropos as a restriction related to security issues, such as privacy or integrity, which influences the analysis and design of the system development by restricting some alternative design solutions, by conflicting with some of the requirements of the system, or by refining some of the system's objectives. Effectively, security constraints in Secure Tropos represent the initial high-level security requirements of a system.

Chapter 7
Real Time Risk Management in Cloud Computation

Kashif Kifayat
Liverpool John Moores University, UK

Michael Mackay
Liverpool John Moores University, UK

Thar Baker Shamsa
Manchester Metropolitan University, UK

Madjid Merabti
Liverpool John Moores University, UK

Qi Shi
Liverpool John Moores University, UK

ABSTRACT

The rise of Cloud Computing represents one of the most significant shifts in Information technology in the last 5 years and promises to revolutionise how we view the availability and consumption of computing storage and processing resources. However, it is well-known that along with the benefits of Cloud Computing, it also presents a number of security issues that have restricted its deployment to date. This chapter reviews the potential vulnerabilities of Cloud-based architectures and uses this as the foundation to define a set of requirements for reassessing risk management in Cloud Computing. To fulfill these requirements, the authors propose a new scheme for the real-time assessment and auditing of risk in cloud-based applications and explore this with the use case of a triage application.

INTRODUCTION

Cloud computing represents one of the most significant shifts in information technology. In cloud computing physical computer resources (storage, processing power and services, including software platforms and applications) are abstracted in the way it enables the users to work and access their information and services through multiple devices and networks. It means users can avoid the cost

on hardware, software, and services by paying a service provider only for what they use. Computing services as a utility are a promising innovation and have great potential in the future and has been raising significant levels of interest among individual users, enterprises, and governments in recent years (Kifayat, Merabti, & Shi, 2010).

The most commonly cited benefit of cloud computing is its high degree of redundancy (both at the hardware and software levels but also geographically) that cannot be matched by most localized enterprise infrastructures. This is a key

DOI: 10.4018/978-1-4666-2125-1.ch007

attribute of the cloud that enables a higher degree of service availability. Since the resources are shared between multiple services and customers, the cloud infrastructure can handle peak demand from individual customers much more effectively and at lower overall cost. Geographic redundancy also provides another key benefit from the data protection perspective. It allows the data to survive any localized failures, including power outages, natural disasters or damage to local physical facilities. In many cases, the data can be accessed remotely from anywhere in the world, even if the user-company's headquarters and data centres are temporarily unavailable (Broda et al., 2010).

Top industry analysts such as the IDC (International Data Corporation) analysis, the worldwide forecast for cloud service in 2009 was in the order of $17.4bn and the estimate for 2013 amounts to $44.2bn, with European market ranging from $971m in 2008 to $6,005m in 2013. However, Steve Ballmer (Microsoft CEO) predicted in his talk at Washington University that cloud computing will be $3.3tn bidding around the globe. This year alone the move to the cloud by many businesses has been exceptional, so much so that some cloud business has grown by over 200%. Large vendors see this as the growing model for software and services in the future so more focus by the vendors is afforded.

Users are excited by reduced capital cost opportunities, a chance to separate them from infrastructure management, and focus on core competencies. However, there are concerns about the risks of cloud computing if not properly secured, and the loss of direct control over systems for which they are, nonetheless, accountable. Recent reports by the Cloud Security Alliance (CSA), European Network and Information Security Agency (ENISA) and Community Research and Development Information Service (CORDIS) identified a variety of security challenges and potential research areas in cloud computing security such as lacking control over data, trust

establishment, ensuring integrity, confidentiality, virtualisation, access control, privacy and identity provision (Broda et al., 2010; Brunette & Mogull, 2009; Catteddu & Hogben, 2009; Jeffery & Neidecker-Kutz, 2010). Additionally, the CSA also identified some of the core security issues which we will discuss later in this chapter.

Many of these cloud security risks are not new, and can be found in the enterprises but, perhaps due to its popularity, a wave of new cyber-attacks and zero-day vulnerabilities has been found in recent years related directly to Cloud Computing. In addition, the number of attacks is now so large and their sophistication so great, that many organizations are having trouble determining which new threats and vulnerabilities pose the greatest risk and how resources should be allocated to ensure that the most probable and damaging attacks are dealt with first (TippingPoint, 2009). Therefore it is important to have well design risk management methodology to identify security risks, highlight their impacts and how to mitigate them in order to avoid loss. It is also important to handle risks with the greatest potential loss first and lower risks in descending order. In practice this process can be very difficult, and in particular balancing between risks with a high probability of occurrence but lower loss versus a risk with lower probability but high loss. In cloud computing risk management could imply in different security areas and cyber-attacks. However in this chapter we focus on web application auditing which could help us to identify the risks.

We organise the rest of this chapter as follows. Section 2 describes the security challenges in cloud computing. Section 3 presents possible cyber-attacks on cloud. Section 4 describes the security requirements of the future cloud computing. Section 5 explains risk management process whereas section 6 presents background and related work. Finally, section 7 proposes the first step towards a new real time risk assessing/auditing scheme for cloud computation based applications.

SECURITY CHALLENGES IN CLOUD COMPUTING

One of the major barriers to the deployment of cloud computing has always been the vulnerability of the infrastructure to a range of both innocent threats and malicious attacks and the risks this poses. This has proved a strong disincentive to potential users to date who are wary of placing data and services outside of their direct control and therefore under greater threat of being stolen, hijacked or shutdown. This section identifies some of the key threats to Cloud Computing and distributed systems, outlines the particular risks that they pose in this case, and discusses approaches that are attempting to neutralize them.

Possible Threats

The Cloud Security Alliance (2010) identifies the seven top threats to cloud computing as the following:

- Abuse
- Insecurity
- Malicious insiders
- Shared technology issues
- Data loss
- Service hijacking
- Risk transparency

Also, one problem with any new technology is the potential for criminals to exploit it and improve the effectiveness of their own activities. As such clouds providers with weak security and monitoring mechanisms pose a potential risk to others, both in that cloud and in the wider Internet. For this reason, it is vital that providers enforce strong customer interfaces and APIs or risk exposing themselves, their customers, and others to a range of confidentiality, integrity, availability, and accountability threats. However, arguably the greatest new threat to cloud customers is the unknowing acceptance of risk due to the provider's limited disclosure of security, configuration hardening, and monitoring procedures. These threats are addressed in this section under the following topics: Identity and Access Management, Trust, Application Security, Secure Virtualisation, and Data Confidentiality.

Identity and Access Management

The on-demand self-service characteristics of cloud computing necessitate that its customer management interfaces be publicly accessible to all cloud users. As such, this is a particular vulnerability for cloud systems as the potential that unauthorized access could occur is much higher than for traditional systems. Managing identities and access control for enterprise applications remains one of the greatest challenges facing IT today (Cloud Security Alliance, 2010) and extending an organization's Identity and Access Management (IAM) services into the cloud is an obvious prerequisite for its use. In this context, we discuss identity provisioning, authentication, federation, user profile management and support for compliance functionality as they are each essential for IAM to be properly provisioned in cloud computing.

1. **Identity Provisioning:** Enterprises typically already have mature user management processes will naturally seek to extend those processes into the cloud and this must be accommodated by the cloud provider. However, this action adds potential security risks, or at the very least significant additional complexity to the providers systems.
2. **Authentication:** Organizations deploying services in the cloud will require that all users are authenticated in a trustworthy and manageable manner. This covers a range of challenging issues such as credential management, strong authentication, delegated authentication, and managing trust which are active research areas in cloud computing.

3. **Federation:** Federated Identity Management techniques could also play a vital role in enabling organizations to authenticate users across the whole range of cloud services via an Identity Provider. Organizations considering federated identity management in the cloud should understand the tradeoffs here with respect to identity lifecycle management, authentication methods, and integrity while supporting non-repudiation.

4. **User Profile Management:** The requirements for user profiles and access control policy will vary depending on whether the user is a consumer or a member of a larger organization but will include establishing trusted profiles and policy information within the cloud service.

5. **Compliance:** Finally, it is important for customers relying on cloud services to understand how Identity Management supports compliance with internal or industry regulatory requirements.

Trust

In recent years the increasing use of sensitive information in everyday computing environments, together with the proliferation of threats, has led many technology researchers to advocate development of trusted computing (TC) systems. In 2003, the Trusted Computing Group (TCG) was formed to introduce of the concept of "roots of trust" into computer platforms.

The Trusted Computing Platform (TCP) operates through a combination of software and hardware to provide two basic but interlinked services, authenticated boot and encryption. Authenticated boot services monitor the Operating System during startup while the encryption system encompasses six core concepts as specified in the TCG specifications: Endorsement key, Secure input and output, Memory curtaining / protected execution, Sealed storage, Remote attestation and Trusted Third Party (TTP) as shown in Figure 1.

This range of techniques secures system resources; providing guarantees over the integrity of running processes, and authenticates communication endpoints for all transactions. In practice, this functionality is integrated into a specialized chip, called the Trusted Computing Module (TCM). In the context of cloud computing, trusted computing may also have a role to play in securing the underlying infrastructure and giving customers a measure of confidence that they can be trusted to host their services (Shen & Tong, 2010).

Figure 1. Overview of the components in a trusted platform module

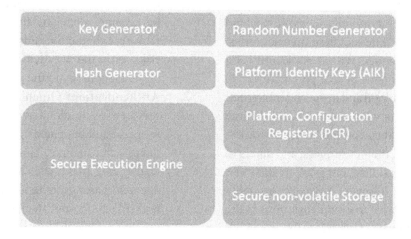

Application Security

Many of the most pressing cloud application security issues relate to the lack of control over the underlying infrastructure. For example, an organization moving its legacy applications to a cloud environment will effectively give up its control over the operating infrastructure including server configuration, access to network logs, incident response and patch management which are often vital tools used by administrators to detect, diagnose and remedy potential threats and failures. Moreover, applications are typically designed to be built and run in the context of a data center, such that the way they store and transmit data to other systems is assumed to be both trusted and secure. This is no longer necessarily the case in cloud computing and we expect that in the future, distributed security engineering must be integrated into all stages of application specification and development.

More immediately, Service-Level Agreements (SLAs) with and between cloud providers currently focus on the performance-oriented parameters of a contract, and it may be necessary to extend this in the future to establish security boundaries and provide assurances over system integrity. Ultimately however, application level security must be viewed as an end-to-end problem as not only must the customer and provider be considered, but also all the intermediate network domains, especially in the case of public clouds, which raise the potential of intermediary attacks.

Secure Virtualization

Cloud computing heavily leverages virtualization to support load balancing via the dynamic provisioning and migration of virtualised services among physical nodes which can both facilitate and inhibit system security. On a basic level for example, virtualization can be used as a security component to support monitoring of VMs, allowing easier security management of the cloud computing infrastructures. Also, through the provision and enforcement of strong management interfaces and APIs, the provider can maintain a degree of separation between virtualized services.

However, simply through sharing physical resources, virtualization opens threats that would not be applicable in privately operated data centers. For example, through attacking the cloud management interface or simply snooping active connections, a malicious user could gain unauthorized access to another users resources, and use this to attack the user services or launch further attacks elsewhere. Moreover, users of shared resources can use the characteristics of virtualization to infer or gain access to potentially sensitive information about how customers utilize the service in specific scenarios. Securing the virtualization component is therefore an essential step for organizations to protect their business and to manage risk (Lombardi & Di Pietro, 2011).

Data Confidentiality

However, perhaps the most critical vulnerability of employing cloud computing is the significant threat introduced to the privacy of personal or confidential data hosted in the cloud (Dahbur, Mohammad, & Tarakji, 2011). While the storage of user data on remote servers is by no means new, the current expansion of cloud computing warrants a further look at its potential privacy and confidentiality consequences. For example, not all types of cloud computing raise the same privacy and confidentiality risks and private clouds retain a degree of control and security by keeping data and services 'in-house'. However, since many public cloud providers do not currently enforce default data encryption, the risk of unauthorized disclosure of sensitive data may be higher and this is a major factor affecting uptake (Zhang et al., 2010).

Many techniques for ensuring confidentiality protection have already been explored here including access control, identity management, end-to-end data confidentiality and integrity assurance. However, these techniques cannot adequately ensure data confidentially since the range and types of potential attack go beyond current third-party external malicious users. This issue is expected to remain a barrier to cloud adoption for users until a flexible, robust, and scalable solution is found.

CYBER-ATTACKS ON CLOUD

Based on the threats identified in the previous section, we now explore how these risks can be exploited in the form of network-based attacks on Cloud computing platforms. Many of these attacks are among the most potent and commonly encountered in the wider Internet and are therefore by no means specific to Clouds. Moreover, effectively countering such attacks is a very active research area and no definitive solutions are currently available as the field is constantly evolving.

Side-Channel Attacks

A side channel attack refers to any attack that is based on information gathered from the physical implementation of a system, in contrast to vulnerabilities in the algorithm itself (Lawson, 2009). This is a particular problem in the context of cloud computing because multiple users share the same physical resources and, without strong separation between virtualized services, therefore have the potential to observe and infer information about sensitive services run by others. This is a derivative of the malicious insider attack and even if strong cryptographic mechanisms are implemented there is still the potential for abuse. For example, an attacker can monitor the power consumption or the Electro Magnetic (EM) emanation from a cryptographic device, and then analyse the collected data to extract the associated crypto key. Simple Power Analysis (SPA), Differential Power Analysis (DPA), Simple Electromagnetic Analysis (SEMA), and Differential Electromag-

netic Analysis (DEMA) are all examples of side channel attacks that enable extraction of a secret key from cryptographic devices in this way.

DDoS Attack

A Denial of Service (DoS) attack is any event that diminishes or eliminates a service's capacity to perform its expected function through hardware failures, software bugs, resource exhaustion, malicious broadcasting of messages, environmental conditions, or any complicated interaction between these factors (Gresty, Shi, & Merabti, 2001). While such events can occur naturally (or innocently) we focus here on organized, malicious activity aimed at an organization or service. In cloud computing, this increasingly takes the form of a distributed network attack coming from many sources (such as a botnet), hence Distributed DoS or 'DDoS'. The attack specifically attempts to overload services running on a cloud (or the connecting network links) as opposed to the cloud infrastructure itself. A famous DoS network attack is the TCP SYN flood which bombards a server with synchronise requests to overload the connection handling resources.

There are many recent examples of DDoS attacks against cloud services that one can select but perhaps the most notorious event would be the recent attacks against Amazon and PayPal organized as a response to the crackdown against WikiLeaks and subsequent arrest of its founder Julian Assange (Pras et al., 2010). Overcoming DDoS attacks is notoriously difficult due to the increasingly complex attack patterns and overwhelming rapid spike in traffic.

Flooding Attack

This is a form of Denial of Service attack that targets the actual cloud infrastructure, attempting to overload servers and therefore bring down running services. Typically, whenever a particular cloud server approaches its capacity, it transfers some of its running jobs to another server, subject to operational, geographical and legal restrictions, to offload itself and enforce load balancing. In a simple example once an attacker gains authority to make requests to the cloud, they can create bogus requests and submit these to be run on the cloud. In processing these requests, the server will first perform some preprocessing checks to verify the authenticity of the requested job and schedule it appropriately, etc. Because all requests must be checked in this manner this process will consume CPU, memory, and other resources which occupy resources on the cloud server. If this can be scaled appropriately it can potentially overload a server which causes all jobs to be offloaded, opening the potential to overload the next server in turn and flood the infrastructure. Preventing this will necessitate monitoring and attack characteristic identification mechanisms to detect attacks early and active automated filtering systems to trigger prompt remedial action to block malicious activity.

Malware-Injection Attack

Code injection is the exploitation of a vulnerability that is exposed by processing invalid data (which appears as a valid service) into a cloud service to change the course of its execution (Zunnurhain & Vrbsky, 2010). Code injection attacks can result in serious security breaches such as propagating computer worms, introduce eavesdropping, causing deadlocks or a meta-data spoofing attacks whereby an attacker can gain admin rights on a cloud server. Preventing this form of attack will involve validating the integrity of cloud services before they are started. A simple first step to this would be to modify the scheduler / hypervisor to both verify user instances before they are run and enforce monitoring services while they are running. However, effectively combatting this depends largely on the form of cloud computing being provided and the level at which it is running.

Wrapping Attack

Wrapping attacks aim to inject faked elements into a legitimate message structure such that a valid signature covers the malicious element while it is processed by the business logic in the cloud. For example, a malicious service could, unknowingly to the user, alter the amount charged on a contract after it has been approved by the customer but before it is submitted. In practice, when a user interacts with virtualised services in the cloud, the browser request may first be directed to a web server where a SOAP message is generated containing the information that will be exchanged between the browser and cloud server. In a wrapping attack the attacker gains control of the web server and interrupts translation of the SOAP message in the TLS (Transport Layer Security) layer where the message is duplicated and the faked elements are inserted before it is sent on to the cloud server where it is processed as a legitimate message. Overcoming this form of attack can be achieved by proper authentication, whole message encryption, and the establishment of proper trust with any intermediate servers.

Data Stealing Problem

This is the most common form of threat that will be faced in the cloud or elsewhere in the wider Internet whereby a user account is compromised and the data is exposed to an attacker. Typically, a cloud user account is first broken into by one the methods listed above. Once this is achieved, the attacker is free to steal, tamper with, or even destroy data held in the cloud. This is a particular problem for public clouds as these platforms are operated by a third party and thus cannot be supplemented by their own additional security measures. As such, it is critical that users can understand and rely on the security measures employed by the cloud provider. Depending on the scale and scope of the organizations involved, this might actually be more complex and sophisticated than SME or even some enterprise customers can deploy. For example, Google uses quite sophisticated security mechanisms to enhance data security within its data centers (Ghemawat, Gobioff, & Leung, 2003).

FUNDAMENTAL CLOUD SECURITY REQUIREMENTS

Due to the range of cloud services, potential users and services and application environments that we have touched on above, defining any definitive list of security requirements for cloud computing is very difficult. Based on our analysis of the most pressing threats and potential attacks in current cloud platforms, this section aims to draw this together to present a concise set of fundamental cloud security requirements that will bring much needed additional strength to today's cloud networks. These requirements can be presented as follows:

1. **Strong and verifiable internal security mechanisms:** The first fundamental requirement for cloud security is to implement and provide assurances over to the mechanisms protecting the cloud infrastructure itself from attack. This includes deploying a secure virtualization environment to isolate services and components from each other and the underlying infrastructure, providing powerful Identity and Access Management systems to limit the potential for unauthorized access, and ensure the highest 'physical' security mechanisms are employed to minimize the threat from physical attack or malicious insiders. Additionally, the cloud provider must be able to provide customers with sufficient assurances over the mechanisms employed to limit the perceived risk.

2. **Comprehensive service integrity assurance:** The second requirement is to provide the same assurances over the integrity of customer data and services running in the cloud. While the first requirement will obviously impact on the second, the provider must also ensure as far as possible that customer instances are not compromised such that information can be stolen, corrupted or destroy by unauthorized users. This will include deploying improved security mechanisms to protect the integrity of virtualized resources, such as through the increased use of encryption, and ensuring that attacks through any of the means identified above are detected as early as possible and neutralized.

3. **Enhanced network Security mechanisms:** Finally, the cloud provider must provide assurances over the security of the internal and external network infrastructure both between them and the customer and within the cloud itself. There are many examples of ongoing research into next-generation network management systems to supplement traditional firewalls and monitoring/IDS systems that will help secure a network but perhaps the most pressing concern here is to address the current vulnerability to DDoS attacks which can bring down fundamental systems. If anything, cloud computing has a natural strength here as services can be rapidly migrated or scaled in response to current network conditions (flash crowds) or, say, in response to an attack.

4. **Risk Management:** In addition, to assure customers that every effort is being made to protect them, and their data, from loss or attack, cloud providers should undertake thorough and on-going risk management to understand and mitigate potential faults as early as possible. This is addressed in the following section.

RISK MANAGEMENT

Risk management is a process to identify, assess, and mitigate risks by reducing the impact of unfortunate events. Risk management process is followed in many areas like financial markets, project management, engineering, industrial processes, public health, safety and security. However risk management methods, definitions and goals vary according to the area. The risk management process is an on-going activity that aims to continuously improve its efficiency and effectiveness. Several risk management standards have been developed including the BSI (British Standards Institute) standards, ISO (International Standard Organisation) standards, Project Management Institute and the National Institute of Science and Technology. Risk management process has some common steps which are adopted by all the standard organisations as shown in Figure 2.

Similar to all other areas risk management is important and essential requirement of cloud computing. In this chapter we, are mainly focused on the risk management process in context of secure cloud computing. Furthermore we have considered BSI standards in context of secure cloud computing (2006) as presented in coming subsections.

Figure 2. BSI risk management process model

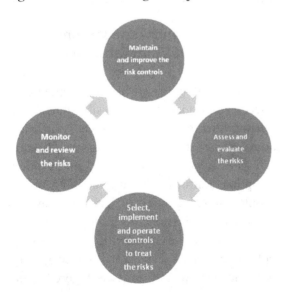

Risk Assessment Process

In cloud computing the assessment of possible security risks could be an important part of the risk management process and this must be accepted as part of business process of any enterprise. The assessment of security risks in cloud computing could follow similar process mentioned by BSI. The risk assessment includes the following actions and activities.

- Identification of assets. This is the first step in risk assessment process.
- Identification of technical, legal and business requirements that is relevant for the identified assets.
- Valuation of the identified assets, taking account of the identified technical, legal and business requirements and the impacts of a loss of confidentiality, integrity and availability.
- Identification of significant threats such and vulnerabilities (described in section 2.1) for the identified assets.
- Assessment of the likelihood of the threats and vulnerabilities to occur.
- Calculation of risk.
- Evaluation of the risks against a predefined risk scale.

Asset Identification

An asset is something valuable for the organisation, its business operations and their continuity. Therefore it is important to protect the organisation assets to ensure business continuity. The risk management solution should have the complete list of assets with their importance. In cloud computing one of the most valuable and important types of asset is information and it should be protected. Information could be in a form of databases and files. In addition, the assets like processes which store or process information, or have an impact on the security of cloud should be protected. Fur-

Figure 3. Assets in cloud computing

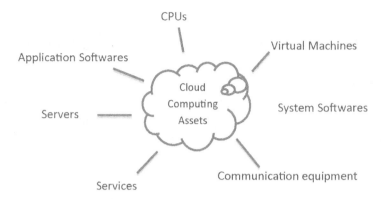

Figure 4. Threat events

thermore other assets of cloud computing include share infrastructure such as disks, CPUs, cache and etc., services, softwares (such as application software, system software development tools and utilities) and physical items (computer, communication and servers).

In order to find the right protection for identified assets, it is important to assess their value in terms of their importance to the business. One way to express asset values is to use the business impacts that unwanted incidents, such as disclosure, modification, non-availability and/or destruction, would have to the asset and the related business interests that would be directly or indirectly damaged. These incidents could, lead to loss of revenue or profit, market share, or image

and reputation, and these considerations should be reflected in the asset values.

Identification and Assessment of Threats and Vulnerabilities

After finding all the assets in cloud computing it is necessary to identify the possible threats and vulnerabilities related to these assets. A threat can cause damage to the cloud and its assets. The harm such as unauthorized disclosure, modification, corruption, destruction and unavailability or loss in could computing can occur due to cyber-attacks on the cloud infrastructure. A threat normally exploits one or more vulnerability of the systems, applications or services used or provided by cloud in order to cause the harm to assets. Figure 4 shows

Figure 5. Core vulnerabilities

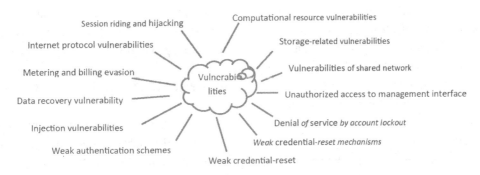

number of threat events compromising cloud and internet security (Saripalli & Walters, 2010).

Furthermore, vulnerabilities in cloud computing are security flaws associated with cloud computing (services provider and client) assets. The vulnerability in itself does not create problem, it is just a condition or set of conditions that might allow a threat to exploit and cause damage or loss to the cloud computing assets. It is also important to understand the relationship between threats and vulnerabilities. Figure 5, shows possible core vulnerabilities in cloud computing (Grobauer, Walloschek, & Stocker, 2011).

Once all possible threats and vulnerabilities are identified than it is important to assess the likelihood that they appear and cause the risks. The assessment process includes to find how easy vulnerability can be exploited by threats. The assessment of the likelihood of threats in cloud computing should take account of the following.

- **Deliberate threats:** The likelihood of deliberate threats depends on the motivation, knowledge, capacity and resources available to possible attackers, and the attractiveness of assets to sophisticated attacks.
- **Accidental threats:** The likelihood of accidental threats can be estimated using statistics and experience. The likelihood of these threats might also be related to the cloud computing or client. The likelihood

of human errors (one of the most common accidental threats) and equipment malfunction should also be estimated.

- **Historical incidents:** It is always important and useful to consider incidents that have taken place in the past, which illustrate problems in the current protective arrangements.
- **New technologies:** Technology always has new developments therefore it is important to be aware of these changes to assess the new threat situation.

Furthermore an assessment scale needs to be identified to assess threats and vulnerabilities e.g. a scale between threats or vulnerabilities could be a distinction between low likelihood, medium likelihood and high likelihood. For example, low likelihood could mean it is not likely that the threat will occur or the vulnerability is hard to exploit. Furthermore it is always recommend having a matrix which includes values for all cloud computing assets, threats and vulnerabilities with the scale values (low, medium and high likelihood).

Risk Calculation, Evaluation, and Treatment

The risk calculation is done through the combination of asset values expressing the likely impact resulting from the loss of confidentiality, integrity and/or availability. It is up to the cloud service provider to identify the risk assessment that is more suitable for their organisation and their security requirement. A risk has two contributing factors, one expressing the impact if the risk occurred, and one expressing the likelihood that the risk might occur as shown in below formula. The impact factor of the risk is based on the asset valuation. It is important to differentiate between risks for confidentiality, integrity and availability using the respective asset value as the impact value. Moreover, consider three distinct risks for each asset and sum the three values and make sure that no important information get lost.

Risk = Impact of Risk event x Probability of Occurrence

Risk can be managed through a combination of prevention and detection controls. It is always important to match these controls to the specific needs of the cloud service provider or client.

Once a risk has been assessed at service provider end or client side decision need to be made is how to treat the risk. The decision process may be influence by two important factors, the cost each time risk event happen and how frequently it is expected. This will give the warning of loss that might expect to occur, if nothing is done to mitigate the assessed risks. Information security related risks can be difficult to quantify in terms of the probability of occurrence due to, dynamic nature of threats, a new wave of cyber-attacks, the rise of zero-day vulnerabilities and the lack of publicly available statistics on frequency of occurrence. Furthermore it is require estimating the recovery cost of particular security incident occurs. The cloud service provider and client need to ensure that it achieves the right balance between achieving security and the benefits of protection.

The impact of risk can be reduced by using strong measurement against possible attacks, reducing the likelihood of vulnerabilities and detecting unwanted events. Furthermore, risk can be avoided by not conducting certain activities and adopting best practices. For example, sensitive data should not be store on third party location if sufficient protection cannot be guaranteed.

Management and Monitoring

Risk management of security events is on-going activity and security mechanisms such as security policy, antivirus, firewall and etc, should be regularly monitored and reviewed to ensure that they function correctly and effectively. The majority of security mechanisms will require maintenance and administrative support to ensure their correct and appropriate functioning e.g. the checking of log files. Moreover, the results from an original security risk assessment and management review need to be regularly reviewed for change. There are several factors that could change the originally assessed risks and any new business function could mean new or changed information assets, and any changes documented and considered in the risk assessment and management process.

ASSESSING/AUDITING A CLOUD-BASED APPLICATION

Background

Efficient and timely assessment is critical in order to respond quickly in managing and monitoring risk and responding to faults and failures in a competitive business environment. Assessing/Auditing models based on traditional methods are no longer viable to detect to modern security threats in cloud based applications, as there is a lack of agility in being able to provide up-to-date information: Runtime data is required by the user to correct faults and respond quickly to risk. Most system information arrives too late to be useful or provides too restrictive or limited a scope, giving an inaccurate or out-of date representation of the system.

A new web technology is required that allows users to make fast well-informed decisions in real time. In reality, at present there is no agile auditing model where all of the three most important attributes, necessary for runtime assessing, are in evidence:

Events: The state changes and other factors that affect the system availability.
Logs: Comprehensive information about the application and its runtime environment.
Monitoring: Should not be intrusive and must be limited to what the user reasonably needs in order to run their facility/application. Runtime monitors (Joshua, Hassen, & Tomas, 2002) are the "standard" solution for assessing the quality of running applications.

From auditing cloud computation perspective – as discussed in (Miseldine & Taleb-Bendiab, 2005) – "*a consequence of employing open introspection is that applications can be audited as they maintain the context needed for description within the system*". As such, providing a form of auditing encompasses the above stated critical properties is crucial for any cloud computation based system to increase the security and hence the quality of the entire applications.

Related Works

For the execution and monitoring of business process models, many organizations are increasingly using Business Process Management Systems to improve the efficiency of their processes and reduce costs. During the execution of the business process, workflow management systems record many types of events, such as the start and completion time of each activity, the assigned resources, and the outcome of the execution. Major Business Process Management Systems lack capabilities for transforming, accumulating and condensing audit trails of distributed business processes and using this information for monitoring and

analysis purposes to provide feedback about the performance of business processes (in particular inter-organisational business processes).

Leymann and Roller point out that audit trail data from automated business processes can quickly increase to a sizable amount (Leyman & Roller, 1997). If several organizations are involved, e.g. if processes across an integrated supply chain are to be supervised, the volume of information can quickly reach levels that negatively impact the operational performance of enterprise applications. One way to handle data intensive operations is the outsourcing of data processing to external parties. The outsourcing of process management services allows for the sharing of process information across multiple organizations. The positive economic effect of shared information in an integrated supply chain has been demonstrated in a number of studies (Lee & Whang, 2000; Li et al., 2001).

Jeng and Schiefer have developed an agent-based architecture with the aim of providing continuous, real-time analytics for business processes (Jeng, Shiefer, & Chang, 2003). For the analytical processing they introduce an agent framework that is able to detect situations and exceptions in a business environment, perform complex analytical tasks and reflect on the gap between current situations and desired management goals. McGregor and Kumaran have presented a Solution Management framework that analyzes workflow audit logs, utilizing decision support system principles and agent technologies to feedback performance measures (McGregor & Kumaran, 2002). This framework forms part of the Intelligent Workflow Monitoring System (IWMONS) meta-methodology. An extension for this framework using web services was proposed by McGregor and Schiefer, who state that current web service frameworks do not include the functionality required for web service execution performance measurement from an organizational perspective (McGregor & Schiefer, 2003). Part of this work is the extension of the Business Process Execution

Language for Web Services (BPEL4WS) with mechanisms to obtain performance information.

Zur Muehlen has developed a generic architecture for workflow-based Process Information Systems (zur Muehlen, 2004). Based on the flow of management information in an organization, he developed a cybernetic model of three distinct feedback levels for automated process regulation, operational process management, and strategic process management. Baresi and Guinea (2005) as well as Lazovik, Aiello and Papazoglou (2004) state that correctness and quality of applications in the service-oriented world, which are captured in an increasingly abstract manner, cannot be assessed with the same techniques as other software pieces. Underlying services and their providers as well as the process structure itself can be adjusted very easily which is one of the strengths of the Service Oriented Architecture (SOA) paradigm, but it has the disadvantage of a never-ending testing deficit. Therefore, particularly Baresi and Guinea propose that the validation of these systems has to be shifted to the run-time. Their goal is not to monitor process instances to gain real-time information, which can be used to assist with managerial tasks, but to detect participating services that deliver unexpected results.

Assessing/Auditing

Assessing cloud-based applications for the risk management is a new field/way of tracking the cloud-based applications' steps and/or movements and thus still in its infancy phase. In the global computing market, there are some security auditing freeware and/or shareware tools and applications focus generally on this very important subject and particularly on auditing the network and servers [IT Audit: Security beyond the checklist]. Although, auditing the network and servers is essential in getting a complete real time management of the entire system and its environment, however web-based applications in general and cloud-based application in particular are, often among the

other parts of the system, vulnerable to attacks that will not be detected by network and server security and auditing controls. This could also be more dangerous to the level that it compromises not only the application, its components, services and its data but also the network and servers.

Since this chapter is focusing on the real time audit of cloud-based computation applications, the available auditing routines (e.g. review the application development policies, design requirements, and application code) are no longer usable/viable to accomplish the above list of objectives. In addition, when auditing a web-based application at runtime, there are many aspects to consider (Leymann & Roller, 1997). Some of those aspects are immediately visible and observable like whether the page construction adheres to standards or the site is easy to navigate and so on. These aspects are easy to identify and are visible at design time. There are other aspects, however, such as the policies and procedures used to manage and monitor the application on the cloud, the methods of keeping information in the application consistent and up to date, and others that cannot be ascertained by looking at application using a browser.

The out of date unusable auditing approach and the dichotomy between visible/reachable and invisible/unreachable characteristics forces the carrying out of extensive research to create the PAA Auditing Model and its auditing generator to find out what data is required at runtime for auditing a web-based application. From the implementation perspective, the capability of the system to provide audit and/or assurance services at runtime is essential if information systems of the future are to assist the users in finding the information and services they need or solving the problems they have. Auditing based on traditional "Static" methods is no longer viable as it provides information too late to be useful. Users are becoming less willing to accept static; periodic audit information and web technology is increasing the expectations of information for decision

Figure 6. High-level PAA components

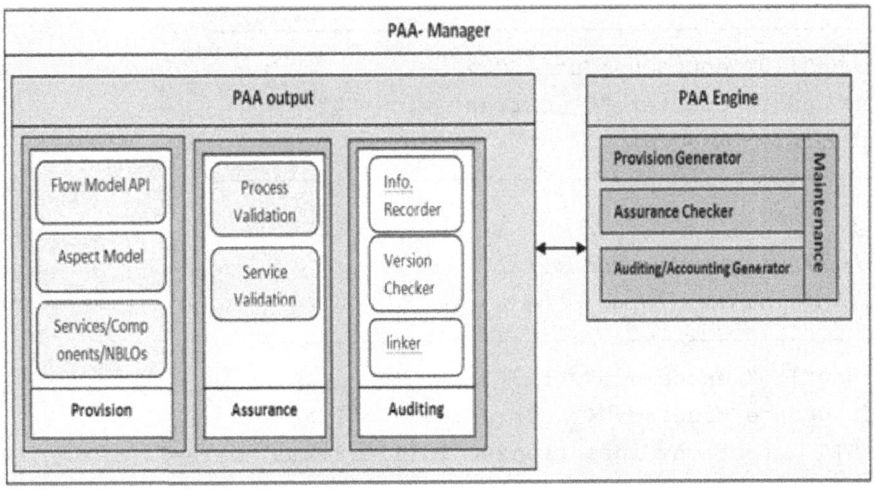

makers and other users of financial information to be available in real time.

PROPOSED ASSESSING/ AUDITING MODEL FOR CLOUD RISK MANAGEMENT

Provision, Assurance and Auditing (PAA) is proposed to overcome the traditional static audit drawbacks by using the new dynamic auditing model, which provides the necessary runtime auditing information produced by the auditing generator within the PAA engine as shown in Figure 6. Since provision and assurance models of this approach are both out of the scope of this chapter, more details about them can be found in (Baker, Taleb-Bendiab, & Al-Jumeily, 2010), however, this chapter will concentrate on the auditing model of PAA. As described by the author in (Baker, Taleb-Bendiab, & Randles, 2009), PAA allows the user to amend and modify the entire application, its behaviour and components by modifying the intention model of the application at runtime using a PAA WikiEditor, which will be described (Section 7.1). The user is able, through the intention model adaptation, to add,

remove any web services, scale up and down the cloud resources flexibly and easily at runtime, as will be explained shortly. This means that the applications created by PAA approach will be runtime dynamic/full adaptive applications. The worst scenario that might happen at runtime is the use of the WikiEditor to completely replace the entire intention model with an incompatible/ un-executable intention, which then results the application to crash.

In this case, auditing such kind of dynamic applications is particularly essential to keep track of every single step of the application modification and to prevent/avoid the abusive use of the application, intention and its editor. The auditing generator is responsible for creating a new auditing xml-based document automatically at runtime whenever intention modification has happened. The document provides all of the information the user needs at runtime to manage the cloud-based application and make an on-time decision about the application and its components. Additionally, this auditing model will be used as a real time monitoring and controlling schema that will record every step completed by the user in the application at execution time.

Sample 1. Initial auditing model code

```
--------------------------------------------------------
<?xml version="1.0" encoding="utf-8"?>
<update_info update_counter="0" current_view="0">
    </update_info>
--------------------------------------------------------
```

Sample 2. Code for the current version is 2

```
--------------------------------------------------------
<?xml version="1.0" encoding="utf-8"?>
<update_info update_counter="4" current_view="2">
<update id="1" intention="intention201083111628.xml" date="2010/08/03"
time="11:16:28" ip_address="192.168.239.1" ip_address_list="InterNetwo
rk=150.204.48.163" host_Name="cmptsham" />
<update id="2" intention="intention201083111628.xml" date="2010/08/03"
time="11:16:28" ip_address="192.168.239.1" ip_address_list="InterNetwo
rk=192.168.192.1" host_Name="cmptsham" />
<update id="3" intention="intention201083111628.xml" date="2010/08/03"
time="11:16:28" ip_address="192.168.239.1" ip_address_list="InterNetwo
rk=192.168.245.1" host_Name="cmptsham" />
<update id="4" intention="intention201083111628.xml" date="2010/08/03"
time="11:16:28" ip_address="192.168.239.1" ip_address_list="InterNetwo
rk=192.168.239.1" host_Name="cmptsham" />
</update_info>
--------------------------------------------------------
```

The auditing model is designed and created to be very easy to read and understand by the user. In the first instance, when the cloud-based application is just loaded, the model will be simply an empty xml document because neither no single adaptation has happened yet nor the user start practically using the application to record his/her movements. The only xml tag that appears in the initial document is the update_info. The updateinfo tag includes two attributes, which hold the value zero in the first appearance: the update_counter and the current_view as shown in Sample 1.

The update_counter is an automatic counter increases by one each time the end user modifies the application at runtime to save the total number of the intention adaptations that have been done or accomplished by the user. Whereas the current_view counter shows the currently loaded version of the application/intention and thus gives the user an indication of the application behaviours. In this case, all the application versions will be controlled and managed by these two attributes. For example, in the code shown in Sample 2, there are four versions of the intentions (update_counter="4") and thereby four versions of the application since each intention represents a different application that has been updated by the user. The actual current_view="2" means that the user has been using the second version (update id="2").

Sample 3. Initial values and the maximum limit

```
--------------------------------------------------------
public int updatelimit = N;   // Maximum backup intention model file for each
application.
private int counter = 0;
private int updatecounter = 0;
private int currentview = 0;
--------------------------------------------------------
```

To distinguish between the versions, the date and time of the update or creation of the application will be associated with each version. So the user will be provided with more information about the history of the creation of those models.

In addition, to help in avoiding the misuse of PAA WikiEditor to modify the application and its intention and tracking the provenance of the modification, the user's computer IP address and the computer's name were also provided here by the auditing model via (ip_address, ip_address_list, host_Name), e.g. host_Name="cmptsham". This will help to identify the source of the misuse and hence take an appropriate action against.

To accomplish the above auditing characteristics/functionalities, the Auditing_function service is used. This service is responsible initially to initiate the maximum number of the intention/application versions that can be saved in case of application adaptation has occurred. This is represented in Sample 3 as N, where N is a variable identifier that could be any number assigned by the application developer to back up/save the updated application versions.

For example, if N equal 10 then this means that ten versions of the application can be generated and saved. Now as 10 represents the maximum number of the user trials to modify the application, so if the user needs to create a new version the oldest version will be removed from the auditing model and the newest one put at the front of the queue (first in first out)..

PAA Auditing WikiEditor

Unlike the traditional wiki editors, Semantic wikis (Volkel et al., 2006) and MediaWikis (n.d.) that are distributed/located all over the web such as Wikicfp (n.d.), which deal with simple structured text files and hyperlinks, PAA Auditing WikiEditor deals with the xml-based code model. Using this tool, the user will be able to interact with and modify the auditing model xml code at runtime by changing the xml attributes' values (e.g. current_view value) to move/jump from a version of the application and load another one by pressing on the UPDATE button, see Figure 7. Back to Figure 6, the auditing linker links the current_view value, which is updated by the user using the auditing WikiEditor, to the requested version of the intention by using the version id and the date/time of the version. The requested version could be modified again and saved as a new version (Baker, Taleb-Bendiab, & Al-Jumeily, 2009). The PAA parser will read the current view value and re-load the equivalent intention version that holds that value. For example, as shown in Sample 2, if the current view value is 2, then the intention version will be intention="intention201083111628.xml".

By this, the user can move very quickly from a version to another in an unordered fashion. In this case, the Auditing WikiEditor would be the main application interface that the user interacts with directly providing a high level of flexibility and a way to state all the changes made by the

Figure 7. PAA auditing life cycle

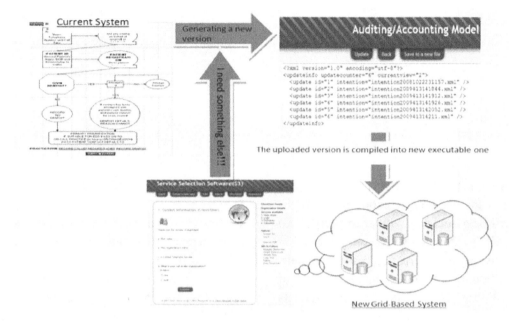

user in different versions to control and monitor the entire cloud-based application. Figure 7 shows the cloud-based application auditing life cycle. It demonstrates how after uploaded the first version of the cloud-based application, the auditing WikiEditor can be updated and uploaded again in the grid (Miseldine & Taleb-Bendiab, 2007) to produce a new web application. The full details of the design, implementation and evaluation will be described in the next sections onwards.

CASE STUDY: CLOUD-BASED CLOVE TRIAGE APPLICATION

Regardless of the broad acceptance of cloud-based solutions in different industry sectors, the healthcare sector is still in the very early stages to adopt the cloud solution due to different concerns such as patient information confidentiality and also to what level the use of cloud-based applications can improve patient care and reduce overall healthcare costs.

This was the trigger behind the design and implementation of Cloud-Based Clove Triage application using the auditing techniques stated above. The next sub-sections give a detailed overview of this case study.

Design Overview

In the healthcare sector, where the decisions can be made by the software in order to aid in the treatment and checkup of the patients, software requires a high level of assurance to ensure the correct interpretation of the tasks it is automating. In addition to this, the system needs a high level of controlling, monitoring and auditing to provide a full history of the updated decision processes and all the related information using the described PAA auditing model.

The case study investigates the improvement of a dental clove triage system used currently by Liverpool Royal Hospital. The original clove triage system combined Microsoft Word and Microsoft Excel documents to provide flow through the process of triage for patients. In this way, infor-

Figure 8. The Clove Triage application front end

mation elicited from the patient formed the basis of decisions on their perceived health. The more critical the condition (such as persistent bleeding) the higher priority the patient was given to see a dentist. Updating such a huge hospital information system will require an extensive amount of efforts, from everybody involved in using the system, to find out what, how and why should be updated and of course on top of all that is the time that the system needs to stop working for the updating and run it again after the updating and testing is finished.

Thus, the main requirement of the case study was to produce a system that could be updated at runtime by using the idea of PAA intention model through the using of PAA WikiEditor as a tool to update the system, as well as, recording all the decision processes so that it will be possible to move from one version to another and to ensure the correctness and the validity of the processes and log patient details and their eventual classification by the system whilst providing a high level of flexibility for new practices in the triage process. The new system was named Clove Triage, which is qualitatively evaluated in the next section.

Auditable Clove Triage Application

By encoding the decision processes of Clove Triage using the PAA way, a complete brand new solution was produced that read its complete tasks from the PAA intention model utilising the new created intention. To achieve the same functionality in the original implementation used by the hospital, the three important auditing attributes: events, logs and monitoring have been implemented in this application to make sure that the state changes and other factors that affected the system availability are saved and treated as well as, to provide comprehensive information about the application and its runtime environment, and for assessing the quality of running applications. On the other hand, integrating the three auditing model of PAA provides statistics that enables users (doctors) to make on-time decisions when analysing the application resources for potential risks or fraudulent processes (Baker, Taleb-Bendiab, & Randles, 2009).

Updating the system by way of intention model adaptation allows the hospital doctors and the system managers to update the decision process of the system at run time, according to the new cases

Sample 4. Auditing model code (current version is 2)

```
<?xml version="1.0" encoding="utf-8"?>
<update_info updatecounter="1" currentview="2">


        <update id="1" intention="intention201083111628.xml" date="2010/08/03"
time="11:16:28" ip_address="192.168.239.1" ip_address_list="InterNetwo
rk=150.204.48.163" host_Name="cmptsham" />

<update id="2" intention="intention201083111628.xml" date="2010/08/03"
time="11:16:28" ip_address="192.168.239.1" ip_address_list="InterNetwo
rk=192.168.192.1" host_Name="cmptsham" />

<update id="3" intention="intention201083111628.xml" date="2010/08/03"
time="11:16:28" ip_address="192.168.239.1" ip_address_list="InterNetwo
rk=192.168.245.1" host_Name="cmptsham" />

<update id="4" intention="intention201083111628.xml" date="2010/08/03"
time="11:16:28" ip_address="192.168.239.1" ip_address_list="InterNetwo
rk=192.168.239.1" host_Name="cmptsham" />
</update_info>
```

Sample 5. Initial values and the maximum limit

```
// Maximum backup intention model file for each application.
public int updatelimit = 10;
private int counter = 0;
private int updatecounter = 0;
private int currentview = 1;
```

and their treatments, without the need to go back to the programmer or the designer of the application to update and modify the decision process. It will also help the doctors and other users to re-upload the previous/old version of the application if incorrect information/treatment were added to the application. Figure 8 shows the main new Clove Triage application cloud-based interface that is created using the proposed approach.

As is evident previously in this chapter, the created auditing model will be an empty XML-based document at the beginning of the execution of the Clove Triage application. The only tag that appears in the auditing model is the updateinfo. In this case, the whole versions will be controlled and managed by using the auditing model attributes. For example, if a doctor has modified the system at runtime by adding a new disease and its treatment, the new value of the update_counter will be changed from 0 to 1 according to the change the doctor has made to the intention model of the application.

The current_view attribute shows the ID of the current version being used by the doctor at the moment. This would be used as an indicator to the actual version of the system used and parsed in case there were many different versions. For example, in the code shown in Sample 1, according to the underneath auditing information has been updated only once in the date and time shown bellow as id="1" in the all four update tags. The current_view="2" means that the user has been using the first modified intention version as the original one will be current_view="1".

To distinguish between the versions, the date and time of the creation or updating will be associated with each version by providing the user with more information about the history of the creation of those models. (Sample 4)

The main service used behind the auditing model is called the Auditing_function. This service is responsible firstly to initiate the maximum number of the intention and/or the provision versions: This is shown in Sample 5 as 10.

When ten versions are generated, and the user needs to create a new version, the oldest version will be removed from the auditing model and the newest one put at the top of the stack.

Thus, from the intention model integrity and governance perspectives, the auditing model here represents the spinal of the Clove Triage control to switch from intention version to another one and to keep track the history of the runtime modifications.

REFERENCES

Baker, T., Taleb-Bendiab, A., & Al-Jumeily, D. (2009). Process-oriented e-government application development. *UKSim 2009:11th International Conference on Computer Modelling and Simulation*, (pp. 634-639). Cambridge, UK: IEEE Computer Society. ISBN: 978-0-7695-3593-7

Baker, T., Taleb-Bendiab, A., & Al-Jumeily, D. (2010). Assurance support for full adaptive service based applications. *12th International Conference on Computer Modelling and Simulation* (UKSim), (pp. 179 – 185).

Baker, T., Taleb-Bendiab, A., & Randles, M. (2009). Auditable intention-oriented Web applications using PAA auditing/accounting paradigm. *Proceeding of the 2009 Conference on Techniques and Applications for Mobile Commerce,* (pp. 61–70).

Baresi, L., & Guinea, S. (2005). Towards dynamic monitoring of WS-BPEL processes. In *Conference on Service-Oriented Computing* (ICSOC-05), (pp. 269-282).

British Standards. (2006). Information security management systems. *British Standards, BS, 7799,* 2006.

Broda, M., Buttyan, L., Clemo, G., Kijewski, P., Merle, A., Mitrokotsa, K., & Munro, A. (2010). *Priorities for research on current and emerging network trends*. ENISA.

Brunette, G., & Mogull, R. (2009). *Security guidance for critical areas of focus in cloud computing V2.1*. Cloud Security Alliance.

Catteddu, D., & Hogben, G. (2009). *Cloud computing: Benifits, risks and recommendations for information security. European Network and Information Security Agency*. ENISA.

Cloud Security Alliance. (2010). *Guidance for identity & access management* v2.1. Retrieved from https://cloudsecurityalliance.org/guidance/csaguide-dom12-v2.10.pdf

Cloud Security Alliance. (2010). *Top threats to cloud computing*. Retrieved from http://www.cloudsecurityalliance.org/topthreats

Dahbur, K., Mohammad, B., & Tarakji, A. B. (2011). *A survey of risks, threats and vulnerabilities in cloud computing*. International Conference on Intelligent Semantic Web-Services and Applications 2011 (ISWSA '11). ACM, April 2011.

Ghemawat, S., Gobioff, H., & Leung, S. (2003). The Google file system. *19th ACM Symposium on Operating Systems Principles* (SOSP '03), Vol. 37, (pp. 29-43). ACM, October 2003.

Gresty, D. W., Shi, Q., & Merabti, M. (2001). Requirements for a general framework for response to distributed denial-of-service. *IEEE ACSAC, 2001*, 422–429.

Grobauer, B., Walloschek, T., & Stocker, E. (2011). Understanding cloud computing vulnerabilities. *IEEE Security & Privacy, 9*(2), 50–57. doi:10.1109/MSP.2010.115

Jeffery, K., & Neidecker-Kutz, B. (2010). *The future of cloud computing opportunities for European cloud computing beyond 2010*. European Commission: CORDIS: FP7.

Jeng, J.-J., Schiefer, J., & Chang, H. (2003). An agent-based architecture for analyzing business processes of real-time enterprises. *Proceedings of EDOC, 2003*, 86–97.

Joshua, L., Hassen, S., & Tomas, U. (2002). Combining monitors for run-time system verification. In Havelund, K., & Rosu, G. (Eds.), *Electronic Notes in Theoretical Computer Science, 70(4)*. Elsevier Science.

Kifayat, K., Merabti, M., & Shi, Q. (2010). Future security challenges of cloud computing. *International Journal of Multimedia Intelligence and Security, 1*(4). doi:10.1504/IJMIS.2010.039241

Lawson, N. (2009). Side-channel attacks on cryptographic software. *IEEE Security and Privacy, November/December,* 65-68.

Lazovik, A., Aiello, M., & Papazoglou, M. (2004). Associating assertions with business processes and monitoring their execution. In *Conference on Service-Oriented Computing* (ICSOC-04), (pp. 94-104). Lee, H. L., & Whang, S. (2000). Information sharing in a supply chain. *International Journal of Manufacturing Technology and Management, 1*(1), 79.

Leymann, F., & Roller, D. (1997). Workflow-based applications. *IBM Systems Journal, 36*(1), 102–123. doi:10.1147/sj.361.0102

Li, J., Shaw, M. J., Sikora, R. T., Tan, G. W., & Yang, R. (2001). *The effects of information sharing strategies on supply chain performance*. College of Commerce and Business Administration, University of Illinois, Urbana-Champaign, IL. Retrieved September 9, 2011, from http://citebm.cba.uiuc.edu/B2Bresearch/ieee_em.pdf

Lombardi, F., & Di Pietro, R. (2011). Secure virtualization for cloud computing. *Journal of Network and Computer Applications, 34*(4), 1113–1122. doi:10.1016/j.jnca.2010.06.008

McGregor, C., & Kumaran, S. (2002). An agent-based system for trading partner management in B2B e-commerce. In *Proceedings of RIDE 2002*, (p. 84).

McGregor, C., & Schiefer, J. (2003). A framework for analyzing and measuring business performance with web services. In *Proceeding of CEC 2003*, (p. 405).

MediaWiki.Org. (n.d.). Retrieved September 9, 2011, from http://www.mediawiki.org/wiki/MediaWiki

Miseldine, P., & Taleb-Bendiab, A. (2005). A programmatic approach to applying sympathetic and parasympathetic autonomic systems to software design. In H. Czap, R. Unland, C. Branki, & H. Tianfield (Eds.), Self-organisation and autonomic informatics (pp. 293-303). Amsterdam, The Netherlands: IOS Press. ISBN I-58603-577-0

Miseldine, P., & Taleb-Bendiab, A. (2007). *Neptune: Supporting semantics-based runtime software refactoring to achieved assured system autonomy*. Technical report, DASEL Technical Report 2007/07/PM01, LJMU. Retrieved September 5, 2011, from http://www.cms.livjm.ac.uk/taleb/Publications/07/TR- 2007.07.PM01.pdf

Pras, A., et al. (2010). *Attacks by anonymous WikiLeaks proponents not anonymous.* CIIT Technical Report, December 2010. Retrieved September 9, 2011, from http://www.ctit.utwente.nl/news/archive/2010/dec10/Attacks%20-anonymous.docx/

Saripalli, P., & Walters, B. (2010). *QUIRC: A quantitative impact and risk assessment framework for cloud security.* IEEE 3rd International Conference on Cloud Computing.

Shen, Z., & Tong, Q. (2010). The security of cloud computing system enabled by trusted computing technology. *2nd International Conference on Signal Processing Systems* (ICSPS), Vol. 2 (pp. 11-15). July 2010.

TippingPoint. (2009). *The top cyber security risks.*

Volkel, M., Krotzsch, M., Vrandecic, D., Haller, H., & Studer, R. (2006). Semantic Wikipedia. *Proceedings of the 15th International Conference on World Wide Web,* May 23-26, Edinburgh, Scotland, 2006.

Wiki Call for Papers. (n.d.). Retrieved March 9, 2011, from http://www.wikicfp.com/cfp/

Zhang, X., Wuwong, N., Li, H., & Zhang, X. (2010). HHH. Information security risk management framework for the cloud computing environments. *10th IEEE International Conference on Computer and Information Technology* (CIT 2010), (pp. 1328-1334). July 2010.

Zunnurhain, K., & Vrbsky, S. (2010). *Security attacks in solutions in clouds.* 2nd IEEE Conference on Cloud Computing Technology and Science (CloudCom), Poster, November 2010.

zur Muehlen, M. (2004). *Workflow-based process controlling: Foundation, design and application of workflow-driven process information systems.* Berlin, Germany: Logos.

Section 3
Hardware Security and Secure Storage and Policy Management in Cloud

Chapter 8

Hardware–Based Security for Ensuring Data Privacy in the Cloud

Wassim Itani
American University of Beirut, Lebanon

Ayman Kayssi
American University of Beirut, Lebanon

Ali Chehab
American University of Beirut, Lebanon

ABSTRACT

In this chapter, the authors present a set of hardware-based security mechanisms for ensuring the privacy, integrity, and legal compliance of customer data as it is stored and processed in the cloud. The presented security system leverages the tamper-proof capabilities of cryptographic coprocessors to establish a secure execution domain in the computing cloud that is physically and logically protected from unauthorized access. The main design goal is to maximize users' control in managing the various aspects related to the privacy of sensitive data by implementing user-configurable software protection and data privacy categorization mechanisms. Moreover, the proposed system provides a privacy feedback protocol to inform users of the different privacy operations applied on their data and to make them aware of any data leaks or risks that may jeopardize the confidentiality of their sensitive information. Providing a secure privacy feedback protocol increases the users' trust in the cloud computing services, relieves their privacy concerns, and supports a set of accountable auditing services required to achieve legal compliance and certification.

DOI: 10.4018/978-1-4666-2125-1.ch008

INTRODUCTION

Cloud computing has achieved unprecedented success and adoption in the last few years. This evolutionary computing model relies on the great advancements in virtualization technologies, commodity hardware, processor design, and most importantly Internet communication networks to provide compelling services to enterprises and individuals.

In spite of all the advantages delivered by cloud computing, several challenges are hindering the migration of customer software and data into the cloud. On top of the list is the security and privacy concerns arising from the storage and processing of sensitive data on remote machines that are not owned, or even managed by the customers themselves. With cloud computing, all the customer can see is a virtual infrastructure built on top of possibly non-trusted physical hardware or operating environments. Thus, customers' fear of sensitive data leakage, misuse, or regulatory incompliance is real and justifiable as long as cloud services are not designed with security in mind (Pearson, 2009). We believe that data privacy should be provided to cloud customers as a service with minimal additional cost. Moreover, we believe that the cloud privacy model should be configurable and user-centric. That is the cloud customer should be able to flexibly control and manage the different privacy mechanisms necessary to protect sensitive data and achieve legal compliance. Customers should be made aware through a secure privacy auditing process of all the operations carried out to secure the storage and processing of their sensitive information. This fact will become more pressing with the expansion of the cloud computing infrastructure where the need will arise for a comprehensive security model that targets the strictest privacy requirements of a wide set of cloud applications and services.

Hardware-based security protocols are believed to be the natural trend that the cloud com-

puting market will follow in the coming years to resolve the different data privacy and integrity challenges hampering the adoption of cloud computing, particularly in healthcare and financial applications. This fact is corroborated by a set of signals received from the IT industry itself:

1. The considerable advancement in physical security mechanisms and packaging technology and the assortment of secure applications that can be implemented on top of physically-secure cryptographic coprocessors.
2. The availability of a set of successful crypto coprocessor implementations meeting the strictest FIPS 140 security standards (Dyer et al., 2001).
3. The emergence of general-purpose open-source cryptographic coprocessor designs that provide competitive performance and higher functionality compared to commercial products at one to two orders of magnitude lower cost.
4. The proposed work of the Trusted Computing Group for developing a set of cloud security services and protocols based on their Trusted Platform Module (TPM) (Bajikar, 2002).

In this chapter we present, PasS (Privacy as a Service), a set of hardware-based security mechanisms for ensuring the privacy, integrity, and legal compliance of customer data as it is stored and processed in the cloud. PasS leverages the tamper-proof capabilities of cryptographic coprocessors to establish a secure execution domain in the computing cloud that is physically and logically protected from unauthorized access. The main design goal is to maximize users' control in managing the various aspects related to the privacy of sensitive data by implementing user-configurable software protection and data privacy categorization mechanisms. Moreover, the presented security system provides a privacy feedback protocol to inform users of the different privacy operations applied on their data and to make them aware of any data leaks or risks that may jeopardize the confidentiality of their sensitive information. Providing a secure privacy feedback protocol increases the users' trust in the cloud computing services, relieves their privacy concerns, and supports a set of accountable auditing services required to achieve legal compliance and certification.

The rest of the chapter is organized as follows: the next section provides a literature survey of the state of the art research in the field of data security and privacy in cloud computing. The third section describes the hardware-based components that can be utilized to solve these security challenges, mainly cryptographic coprocessors. On this front, we provide: (1) a survey of the general architecture of crypto coprocessors and a description of their tamper-proof and tamper-responding capabilities, (2) a brief description of the attack model on such devices and the security countermeasures to avoid such attacks, (3) a summary of the most influential commercial and open-source implementations, and (4) a description of a set of secure applications leveraging the tamper-proof capabilities of cryptographic coprocessors in various IT domains. This provides the reader with a practical insight into the concepts to be discussed later in the chapter and lays the ground for a better comprehension of the significance of the problem described and the effectiveness of the solution presented. After this, we move to describe the hardware-based security solution in the fourth section. This includes (1) a description of the cloud computing environment targeted and the role of each of the participating parties in this environment, (2) a detailed discussion on the system design and architecture and how it fits in the cloud computing model, and (3) a comprehensive presentation of the privacy protocols employed and their execution steps. The fifth section presents a sample proof of concept implementation of the cloud privacy system on the popular VMware cloud computing platform

(Lowe, 2009). The sixth section provides a security analysis of the privacy protocols by abstracting the data privacy and integrity mechanisms employed to secure the privacy of customer data when stored and processed in the cloud. This section serves to represent a set of blueprint guidelines for designing hardware-based security and privacy protocols for cloud computing environments. The seventh section outlines an economic feasibility study demonstrating the practicability of deploying the system in a real cloud computing environment. Conclusions are presented in the eighth section.

SURVEY OF RESEARCH IN CLOUD SECURITY AND PRIVACY

Research on data privacy in cloud computing is still in its early stages. Good reports on the topic are presented in (Gellman, 2009) which discusses the risks imposed by the adoption of cloud computing on data privacy and legal compliance, and (Cavoukian, 2008) which emphasizes on the need to develop a sound digital identity infrastructure to support tackling privacy and security concerns in computing clouds. (Pearson, 2009; Pearson & Charlesworth, 2009) present a comprehensive set of guidelines on designing privacy-aware cloud services. Pearson (2009) summarizes the privacy patterns in six recommended practices: "(1) minimizing customer personal information sent to and stored in the computing cloud; (2) protecting sensitive customer information in the cloud; (3) Maximizing user control; (4) Allowing user choice; (5) Specifying the purpose of data usage and limiting this usage solely to the specified purpose; (6) providing the customer with privacy feedback". Note that tips 2 to 6 are addressed in this chapter. The first recommendation is not addressed since we believe that it does not comply with the cloud computing spirit. We believe that the customer should be able to safely send any kind of sensitive data to the cloud and to secure it by providing user-configurable privacy enforcement mechanisms.

The work in this chapter is primarily based on the cloud privacy system presented in (Itani, Kayssi, & Chehab, 2009). This chapter provides a more elaborate and organized description on the privacy protocols and on the overall system design and extends the system model with a better economic feasibility study and a comprehensive security analysis.

It should be noted here that Homomorphic encryption techniques (Gentry, 2011; Van Dijk et al., 2010; Gentry, 2009) for allowing specific algebraic operations on encrypted data are still theoretical and lack any pragmatic implementation. A practical fully-homomorphic cryptosystem is still an open research topic (Schneier, 2009).

In (Doelitzscher, Reich, & Sulistio, 2010) the authors present the Cloud Data Security project which proposes a layered security model to aid in the design of cloud services compliant with the various governmental privacy laws. This work is presented using high level concepts and lacks the necessary technical discussion when describing the different security and privacy layers comprising the security model.

Chuang et al. (2011) present the "Effective Privacy Preserving Scheme" (EPPS) which aims at satisfying the user privacy requirements while maintaining system performance. Thus EPPS strives at achieving a tradeoff between system security and performance by tuning the strength of the encryption operations based on the sensitivity of the data sets secured. In EPPS, data privacy is achieved by encrypting data using client cryptographic keying material which facilitates a minimum reliance on the cloud provider and provides protection to data irrespective of its physical location. This work suffers from a couple of conceptual drawbacks related to the sound understanding of the privacy problem in the cloud and to the timeliness of the problem to be solved. Firstly, the system model assumes

that it is sufficient to encrypt the data to make it safe and confidential at the cloud provider side. This is true if the data needs to be merely stored and not processed in the cloud. When data needs to be processed, the encryption operations have to be reversed to operate on the plaintext data version. This leaves the data in the clear on the provider side which jeopardizes its confidentiality. The need to do computations on the cloud data is not an option or a luxury feature anymore, it is rather one of the main driving forces of the cloud computing model and should be considered when designing cloud data privacy solutions. The second comment on EPPS is that it targets an old problem that is not specific to cloud computing but to generic client/server enterprise systems. Achieving the correct balance between security and performance was extensively studied by (Itani, Kayssi, & Chehab, 2008). In this work, the authors provided a set of practical solutions to this problem by defining a policy-based security platform that encrypts data based on content and sensitivity to efficiently satisfy the user's security and performance requirements.

In (Rodrıguez-Silva et al. 2011), the authors introduce the encrypted domain processing concept which is a set of homomorphic encryption libraries capable of doing basic processing operations on encrypted data in the cloud. As stated previously, homomorphic encryption techniques are still infeasible due to their high complexity. This fact is corroborated by the sample prototype implementation presented in the paper itself which supports very basic arithmetic operations such as additions and multiplications. We believe that a practical homomorphic privacy scheme, that supports any generic processing operation in the cloud, is still out of reach.

The work in (Li, Raghunathan, & Jha, 2010) aims at providing a secure execution environment for virtual machines (VMs) running on top of untrusted management operating systems. This work targets type-I virtualization architectures such as the Xen virtualization system (Barham et al., 2003). The main concept behind this work is to reduce the Trusted Computing Base (TCB) of the virtualization system by excluding the management OS out of this TCB. This exclusion reduces the size of the trusted code and thus aids in limiting the number of attacks that can jeopardize the security of the entire execution environment. Unlike the scheme that we present in this chapter, the security model presented in (Li, Raghunathan, & Jha, 2010) is susceptible to hardware, side-channel, and direct memory access attacks.

CRYPTOGRAPHIC COPROCESSORS: ARCHITECTURE, SECURITY, IMPLEMENTATIONS, AND APPLICATIONS

Architecture

The cloud security solution we present in this chapter relies on cryptographic coprocessors (Tygar & Yee, 1993; Best, 1980) to provide secure and isolated processing containers in the computing cloud. A cryptographic coprocessor is a small hardware card that interfaces with a main computer or server, mainly through a PCI-based interface. It is a complete computing system that is supported with a processor, RAM, ROM, backup battery, non-volatile persistent storage (mainly used to securely store cryptographic data structures and keying material) and an Ethernet network card. For economical reasons, a crypto coprocessor is generally less capable in terms of processing and memory resources than the main server system it interfaces to. The main property that gives a crypto coprocessor its secure capabilities is the tamper-proof casing that encloses it and makes it resist physical attacks. A secure coprocessor tamper-resistance or tamper-responding mechanisms should reset the internal state of the coprocessor (RAM, persistent storage, processor

registers) upon detecting any suspicious physical activity on the coprocessor hardware

The only logical interface to the functionality of the coprocessor is done through a *root* highly-privileged process burned at manufacturing into the ROM of the coprocessor. This process represents a minimal operating system for the coprocessor. More on the *root* process is presented in the fourth section. The Input/output access to the cryptographic coprocessor can be either done locally via the main server system bus, or remotely via the coprocessor network card.

Security

The main axiom we consider in this chapter is that a secure coprocessor is capable of ensuring the privacy and integrity of the data it possesses in its address space. In fact, every security protocol depends on a set of assumptions, which if respected, supports the proper fulfillment of the promised security properties and mechanisms. For instance, when designing cryptographic protocols, it is usually assumed that encryption algorithms are computationally-secure in resisting cryptanalysis and that a successful brute force attack on the key space is highly expensive considering current technological and computational capabilities. Thus analogously, we believe that it may be possible to violate the physical security protections of a crypto coprocessor but this would require enormous effort and resources that are not currently possessed by attackers. Based on this, we do not associate the protocol designs we present in this chapter with any available crypto coprocessor design technology, but rather present them using a generic crypto coprocessor model that serves the physical security axiom we initially assumed. In other words, we believe that just as cryptographic algorithms can be evolved and modified to increase the cost required to break them, tamper-proof security packaging technology can be enhanced to increase the cost and effort required to breach the crypto coprocessor physical security mechanisms.

In (Anderson et al., 2006), the authors categorize the attacks on cryptographic coprocessors into four main classes:

1. **Invasive attacks:** these attacks operate by gaining direct electrical access to the internal components of the cryptographic coprocessor. For instance, the attacker may capture electrical signals from a bus line connected to the microcontroller chip of the cryptographic coprocessor by inserting a probing needle that bypasses the passivation layer of the chip.

2. **Semi-invasive:** these attacks also operate by gaining direct access to the coprocessor but without physically bypassing or damaging the passivation layer of the chip. A typical scenario is for the attack to modify the state of the transistors storing the coprocessor's protection state by ionizing them via laser beams.

3. **Local non-invasive attacks:** these attacks do not try to actively control the crypto coprocessor, but rather strives to passively monitor and analyze the device's operation to get some classified information that may be used later on for launching active attacks via standard interfaces. A popular example is the power analysis attack that measures the current drawn by the cryptographic coprocessor and links it to the processing operations executed to statistically deduce the value of the cryptographic keying material.

4. **Remote attacks:** These attacks, unlike the previous attack classes, do not require physical unsupervised access to the crypto coprocessor. Typically, remote attacks take advantage of vulnerabilities and flaws in the coprocessor Application Programming Interface (API) to gain unauthorized access, manipulate the device's operation, or cryptanalyze the implemented security protocols.

With the advancement in physical packaging sensing technologies, most modern crypto coprocessors can eliminate the first three attack classes. Remote attacks remain the weak link in the chain and diminishing them depends on following secure patterns and guidelines when engineering the coprocessor's API libraries and protocols. To defend against physical attacks crypto coprocessor designers encloses the device's chips by several layers of conductor grids that are monitored by protected circuits to inspect any shift in the electrical, mechanical, or chemical state of these conductors. Advanced tamper responding capabilities rely on a set of environmental sensing components such as temperature, pressure, radiation, humidity, and acidity sensors as well as on electrical monitoring devices that can detect suspicious changes in supply voltage, current drain, or in the coprocessor clock frequency. Due to the space limitations of this presentation, we cannot elaborate more on the different types of possible attacks and their countermeasures. The interested reader may refer to (Anderson et al., 2006; Tygar & Yee, 1993; Weingart, 1987) for an extensive discussion on this topic.

Implementations

A large amount of research work has dealt with the design and implementation of secure cryptographic coprocessors. The secure cryptographic processor concept was firstly introduced in (Best, 1980). In this paper, Best presents how crypto coprocessors can be utilized to enforce software copyright protection and prevent software piracy. Popular crypto coprocessor designs included Citadel (White et al., 1991), μABYSS (Weingart, 1987), and CProc (Theodoropoulos, Papaefstathiou, & Pnevmatikatos, 2008). The considerable advancement in physical security mechanisms and packaging technology (Weingart, 1987) and the assortment of secure applications that can be implemented on top of physically secure coprocessors was a major driving force to a prosperous commercial market. IBM was the leader on this front by providing a set of successful implementations meeting the strictest FIPS 140 security standards. FIPS 140 is a set of standard benchmarks that certifies the compliance of cryptographic modules with a variety of security requirements and specifications and measures the degree of hardware tamper resistance supported in these modules. FIPS 140 specifies four security levels, starting with the lenient first level that only specifies software cryptographic support with no physical security requirements and ending in the rigorous fourth level that requires advanced tamper detection and responding mechanisms. FIPS level 4 certifies the capability of the device to self-destruct its memory structures upon a physical compromise or a suspicious deviation in the environmental conditions under which the module operates. The most influential IBM coprocessor implementations are represented in the IBM 4758 PCI cryptographic coprocessor (Dyer et al., 2001) and the IBM 4764 PCIX cryptographic coprocessor (PCIXCC) (Arnold & Van Doorn, 2004). These crypto coprocessors provided a tamper-responding environment and a custom hardware for performing DES, TDES, AES, RSA, and SHA-1 cryptographic operations. The IBM coprocessor product family was the first to meet the FIPS level 4 security standard based on its tamper-resistance and tamper-responding mechanisms. Moreover (Gutmann, 2000) presented a general-purpose open-source cryptographic coprocessor that provides competitive performance and higher functionality compared to commercial products at one to two orders of magnitude lower cost.

Applications

Research on crypto coprocessors also targeted the implementation of a wide set of secure applications leveraging the tamper-proof capabilities of these coprocessors. Of these we can mention the Dyad project by Tygar and Yee (1993) which employed physically secure coprocessors to provide security solutions to five application categories: Integrity protection of publicly accessible workstations, tamper-proof audit logs, software copy protection, electronic currency without centralized supporting servers, and electronic contracts. Tygar and Yee extended these five coprocessor implementations with a secure postage implementation in (Yee & Tygar, 1995). Schneier and Kelsey (1997) presented a solution for remotely authenticating software outputs using a trusted cryptographic coprocessor. Their solution employed an ABYSS-based (White & Comerford, 1990) software division mechanism similar to the one presented in this chapter. The main assumption in the paper, which makes the solution feasible to implement, is that the secure part of the application running on the trusted coprocessor can determine the output of the whole software program. However, Kelsey and Schneier have not presented any software division patterns or blueprints to support this assumption. Kelsey, Schneier, and Hall (1996) used a physically trusted coprocessor to design an authenticated camera. With simple cryptographic techniques, the authenticated camera allows its users to verify the authenticity of a digital image by cryptographically binding it to a specific time and place. (Garfinkel et al., 2003) utilized cryptographic coprocessors for implementing trusted virtual machine monitors on top of untrusted operating systems. The trusted virtual machine monitor allows the partitioning of the crypto coprocessor into a set of isolated virtual machines with different security requirements and configurations. In (Bhattacharjee et al., 2006) secure coprocessors are used to protect the privacy of data mining and sharing in Anti Money Laundering (AML) and credit rating application areas. The main idea behind this research is to design lightweight data mining algorithms that can efficiently run on resource constrained coprocessors to securely isolate the mining and join operations on the data in the cryptographic coprocessor.

It is worth mentioning here that substantial research efforts had been carried out to develop tamper resistant hardware technologies for supporting data and platform integrity assurance protocols. The Trusted Computing Group led the way in this field by developing tamper-resistant TPM modules. Moreover, virtualization support has been lately developed for TPMs (Berger et al., 2006; Sadeghi, Stüble, & Winandy, 2008) allowing operating systems and applications running in virtual machines to utilize the trusted computing capabilities of these modules. Nevertheless, TPM modules are typically equipped with limited processing and memory resources which makes them suitable for mere personal integrity enforcement on single user devices. This fact renders TPMs infeasible for supporting virtualized multiuser processing in enterprise service environments as is the case in cloud computing.

A HARDWARE-BASED CLOUD PRIVACY SYSTEM

This section describes a hardware-based security solution for achieving customer data privacy, integrity, and legal compliance in the cloud. The system supports these security services on stored as well as on processed data. The section starts by presenting the system and trust models assumed in this chapter, then it describes the system design and architecture, and ends by a comprehensive discussion on the privacy protocols supported.

System and Trust Models

The system model assumed in this chapter is a typical cloud computing model with two main players:

1. A cloud provider which manages and operates a cloud infrastructure of storage and computing services.

2. A cloud customer or consumer that employs the cloud storage and computing resource facilities to remotely store and process data. The Internet is the main communication backbone for exchanging information between the cloud customer and the computing cloud.

A cloud service provider could be an individual, a business enterprise, or a governmental or federal organization. In the same sense, a cloud customer could be any of the above mentioned entities.

As stated previously, PasS provides the cloud customer with a full control on the privacy mechanisms to be applied on the cloud data. The notion of customer trust in the services published by the cloud provider is based on the degree of sensitivity of the customer's information. PasS supports three trust levels in the cloud service provider:

1. **Ultimate trust:** this level applies to insensitive data that can be safely stored and processed in the clear (without any form of encryption) on the computing cloud side. The provider is fully trusted for data storage and processing.

2. **Compliance-based trust:** This level applies to customer data that needs to be stored encrypted to support legal compliance regulations (such as the Health Insurance Portability and Accountability Act (HIPAA) (Annas, 2003) for securing medical records and patient's information and the Gramm-Leach-Bliley Act (Janger & Schwartz, 2001) for ensuring the confidentiality of financial records and banking transactions for any institution providing a financial service). In this level the customer trusts the cloud provider in storing her data encrypted using a provider-specific cryptographic key.

3. **No trust:** This level applies to highly-sensitive customer data that should be concealed from the cloud provider. This kind of sensi-

Figure 1. PasS system and interaction model

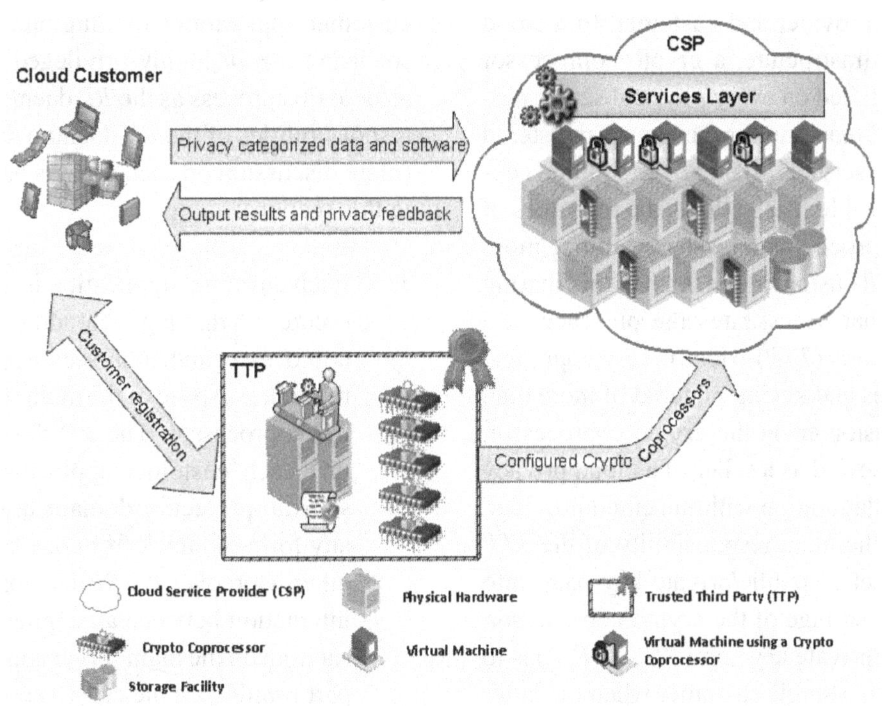

tive information should be stored encrypted using customer-trusted cryptographic keys and should be processed in isolated cryptographic containers in the cloud. These isolated containers are configured, distributed, and maintained by a third-party that is trusted by the cloud customer as well as by the cloud provider. The trusted third-party is considered the entity that sells the privacy service to cloud customers.

Figure 1 outlines the system model and sketches the interaction among the cloud customer, cloud provider, and the trusted third-party.

Note that other trust levels, such as those supported by role-based trust models, can also be considered.

Finally, it should be noted that the application of virtualization technologies in computing clouds provides relatively safer software execution environments. Hence it can be reasonably assumed that the cloud provider fully trusts the cloud customers in running their software applications on the computing resources of the cloud.

System Design

This section presents an overview of the system design and architectural components. It starts with a discussion on the methodology used to configure and distribute the crypto coprocessors, then it describes the coprocessor process structure, and finally presents the software division and data categorization mechanisms used to support the privacy of data storage and processing in the computing cloud.

Coprocessor Authoritative Configuration and Distribution

The organizational unit responsible of configuring the crypto coprocessors and distributing them to cloud providers is a third-party entity that is trusted by the cloud provider and customer. In a cloud computing infrastructure, a crypto coprocessor should be installed on every physical server running a virtual machine for customers registered in the privacy service. To make the solution economically feasible, PasS allows the resources of the crypto coprocessor to be shared among more than one cloud customer. In fact, it is this sharing mechanism that necessitates the presence of a trusted third-party (*TTP*) to load the cryptographic data structures and keying material of more than one cloud customer on the crypto coprocessor. The *TTP* is viewed as a seller of a cloud privacy service in collaboration with the cloud provider. Technically, the main responsibility of the *TTP* is to load a set of public/private key pairs into the persistent storage of the crypto coprocessor. Every public/private key pair (PU_{CID}/PR_{CID}) is to be allocated to a single customer when the latter registers with the cloud privacy service. Upon registration, the cloud customer will securely receive a copy of her public/private key pair. This can be achieved through a face-to-face transaction or through a secure electronic session.

The PU_{CID}/PR_{CID} key pair set can be remotely updated by the *TTP* even after the crypto coprocessor is installed in the computing cloud. This remote key update mechanism is very important to support the registration of new customers and the service revocation of existing customers.

In addition to loading the customer's PU_{CID}/PR_{CID} key pair, the *TTP* also loads its own private key, K_{TTP}, into the persistent storage of the crypto coprocessor. This key is needed by the *TTP* to remotely authenticate to the crypto coprocessor and to securely execute commands against it.

Coprocessor Process Structure

The ABYSS (White & Comerford, 1990) processor model is followed in structuring the processes of the cryptographic coprocessor. The main con-

cept is to logically isolate the set of protected customer applications running on the coprocessor using a *root* highly-privileged process. We refer to this process as the *RP* daemon. The main responsibilities of the *RP* daemon are as follows (more discussion on each point is presented later in this section):

1. Each customer application is divided into a secure part running in the address space of the coprocessor and a non-secure part running in the address space of the main server hosting the coprocessor. The *RP* daemon ensures that each customer application runs in a separate protection domain, thus preventing any form of attack from one process to the other. Moreover, the *RP* daemon protects the interaction between an application process running on the main server and its protected part running on the crypto coprocessor.

2. The *RP* daemon authenticates software and data entering the coprocessor address space.

3. The *RP* daemon is the only process having access to the cryptographic keying material stored in the crypto coprocessor persistent storage. Therefore, it is responsible of the encryption/decryption operations required by the privacy enforcement mechanisms.

4. The *RP* daemon authenticates remote connections from cloud customers and the *TTP*.

5. The *RP* daemon participates in a secure privacy feedback process.

Due to the central role the *RP* daemon plays in the privacy service and to support a scalable security mechanism, it is recommended to execute multiple replicas of the same *RP* daemon in the crypto coprocessor.

Software Division

In the PasS security model, the cloud customer is responsible of configuring her software applications to support the security mechanisms enforced by the privacy service. To provide an economical and performance efficient security solution, the concept of software division is adopted. Based on this concept, the cloud customer classifies the set of logical components constituting the software application as protected and unprotected. The protected classification indicates that the logical component should be executed in a protected process in the address space of the crypto coprocessor. On the other hand, the unprotected classification indicates that the logical component can be executed in a traditional process on the main server. The set of protected processes running in the crypto coprocessor and belonging to different registered customers are isolated from each other using the *RP* daemon. The *RP* daemon also coordinates the secure interaction between the protected and unprotected parts of the same software application. The protected application part should be stored encrypted (by the customer) on the provider's side. When this part is loaded into the crypto coprocessor, the *RP* process decrypts its contents and executes the resulting binary code. The classification process is implemented using the concept of privacy tags which are a set of metadata attributes, cryptographic constructs, and identification information attached to the

respective software application. The constituents of the privacy tag and the software application structure after applying the division process is sketched in Figure 2. a. The detailed semantics of the privacy tag attributes is comprehensively discussed in the "*Privacy Protocols*" subsection.

It should be noted here that it is possible to run the entire software application in the secure coprocessor without applying any software division, however this would affect the performance and economic efficiency of the application. This is due to the fact that in this case the coprocessor resources would be unnecessarily overloaded by executing code that does not require any protection. In the same sense, employing cryptographic coprocessors which are, at least, as powerful as the main server hosting them would render the solution economically infeasible. This refutes the whole concept of a coprocessor.

Data Privacy Specification

Before uploading the data to be stored and processed in the computing cloud, the cloud customer classifies this data, based on significance and sensitivity, into three privacy categories:

Figure 2. a) Customer software components after the division process; b) Data privacy categorization mechanism

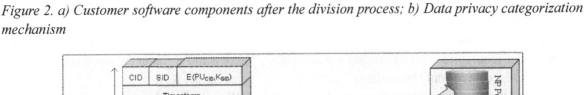

1. **No Privacy (*NP*):** Data marked with this attribute is not sensitive and hence the provider is fully trusted to store it without any form of encryption. If network security is needed, the client can send the data over a secure SSL session.

2. **Privacy with Trusted Provider (*PTP*):** Data marked with this attribute is stored encrypted by a specific provider key. In this case the provider is trusted to encrypt the data using her own cryptographic key. This attribute is crucial for compliance with regulatory policies that enforce the encrypted storage of customer data in the cloud storage facilities. To send *PTP* data to the provider, the customer is required to encrypt it over a secure SSL session to achieve network data confidentiality and integrity. The cloud provider is obligated by the contractual policy to extract the SSL secured data and store it encrypted. The encryption algorithm to be used and the ciphering key strength could be some parameters obligated by the regulatory policy or specified by the client in the privacy contract.

3. **Privacy with Non-Trusted Provider (*PNTP*):** This data category is encrypted at the customer side by a customer-specific key (K_{CID}) shared with the cryptographic coprocessor (see the "*Privacy Protocols*" subsection). This kind of data is stored encrypted on the cloud storage facility and it cannot be accessed or viewed by the cloud provider (encrypted with a customer key). The *PNTP* data can only be processed in the address space of the trusted cryptographic coprocessor which shares the customer the possession of K_{CID}.

For each data category, the cloud provider allocates a logical storage partition that we refer to as a storage pool. The storage pool name is referenced by the name of the data privacy category. Thus, *NP*, *PTP*, and *PNTP* data is stored in the *NP*, *PTP*, and *PNTP* cloud storage pools respectively.

Privacy Protocols

Data and Software Transfer Protocol

This section describes the protocol steps executed by the cloud customer to add the privacy enforcement structures to the software and data before transferring them to the computing cloud. Starting with the software privacy data structure, the customer configures the cloud software based on the format presented in Figure 2. a. The software application is composed of 3 main components: the privacy tag, the protected software part S_{SID}, and the unprotected software part S'_{SID}. The privacy tag consists of the following elements:

- **CID:** This is a unique customer identification number provided by the cloud provider upon customer registration with the cloud privacy service.

- **SID:** This is a unique software identification number provided by the customer to each of her software applications.

- $E(PU_{CID}, K_{SID})$: firstly, K_{SID} is a symmetric key generated by the cloud customer to encrypt the protected software part S_{SID}. $E(PU_{CID}, K_{SID})$ is a public-key encryption of K_{SID} by the customer's public key PU_{CID}. This encryption process ensures that no entity, other than the *RP* daemon (having access to PR_{CID}) on the crypto coprocessor, can extract K_{SID}.

- **DS:** is a digital signature on the fields of the software package. It ensures the authenticity and integrity of the package as a whole. Symbolically it is represented as follows: $DS = E(PR_{CID}, H(CID||SID||E(PU_{CID}, K_{SID})||Timestamp||Identification||S_{SID}||S'_{SID}))$.

Where H is a hash function such as SHA-1 and || is the concatenation operator.

- **Timestamp:** this field represents the time just before the digital signature is created. It is included in the digital signature to protect against replay attacks.
- **Identification:** This field includes general information about the software application such as its name, version, etc.
- $E(K_{SID}, S_{SID})$: This is the protected software part encrypted by K_{SID}.
- S'_{SID}: This is the unprotected software part. It can be safely executed on the main server in the computing cloud.

Based on the above software configuration, the customer constructs the software packages and transfers them to the computing cloud. Optionally, the network transfer can be protected by a secure SSL session.

Receiving the different software messages, the cloud provider checks their integrity and authenticity using the digital signature *DS* and stores them in the cloud storage facility.

Concerning the data transfer to the computing cloud, the customer executes the following protocol steps:

1. Classify the data according to the three privacy categories presented in the previous subsection.
2. If the privacy category is *NP* or *PTP*, then the client sends this data as is to the provider. In the case of *PTP* data, the transfer should be secured by an SSL session. This is optional in the case of *NP* data. Receiving the data, the provider stores it in the appropriate storage pool.

If the privacy category is *PNTP*, the customer executes a secure implementation of the Diffie-Hellman key management protocol with each crypto coprocessor this customer is registered with (the network addresses for accessing the crypto coprocessor are published by the cloud provider upon the coprocessor installation in the cloud). The result of the Diffie-Hellman protocol execution is a shared secret K_{CID}. Using K_{CID}, the customer encrypts the *PNTP* data and sends it to the cloud provider to be stored in the *PNTP* storage pool. Note that the shared secret K_{CID} is securely stored by the *RP* daemon in the crypto coprocessor persistent storage. The stored key entry is identified by the *CID*. To ensure the integrity of data on the network links and when stored in the cloud, Message Authentication Codes (*MACs*) using K_{CID} are applied on logically-separated data units. The selection of the logical unit is implementation-dependent. A unit could be a file, a set of related files, or any other customer-preferred integrity element.

Software Execution and Data Processing Protocol

This protocol describes the steps executed by the crypto coprocessor and the main server hosting the coprocessor to safely execute the customer cloud software. It also presents the privacy enforcement mechanisms that ensure the privacy of the customer sensitive data when processed in the computing cloud. The protocol steps are schematically presented in Figure 3 and explained as follows:

1. The main server loads the unprotected software part and sends the software package to the crypto coprocessor.
2. The *RP* daemon on the crypto coprocessor reads the software privacy tag and ensures the authenticity and integrity of the software package by verifying *DS*. Moreover, the *RP* daemon checks the validity of the timestamp and extracts the key K_{SID} by decrypting $E(PU_{CID}, K_{SID})$ with the customer's private key. Note that the customer PU_{CID}/PR_{CID} key pair was stored by the *TTP* in the processors

Figure 3. Software execution and data processing protocol steps

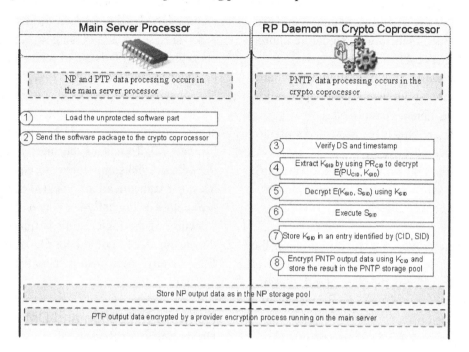

persistent storage in an entry identified by *CID*.

3. The *RP* daemon decrypts the protected software part $E(K_{SID}, S_{SID})$ using K_{SID} and executes this part within the address space of the trusted coprocessor.

4. The *RP* process stores K_{SID} in an entry identified by the (*CID*, *SID*) pair in the persistent storage of the coprocessor. This step avoids an expensive public-key decryption operation if the same software is loaded once again.

5. The unprotected part of the application can only process data with the *NP* and *PTP* privacy categories. Practically the unprotected part cannot access *PNTP* data since it does not have access to the ciphering key K_{CID} with which the data was encrypted. If the data requested belongs to the *NP* storage pool, then it is loaded immediately from the cloud central storage.

6. On the other hand, if the data belongs to the *PTP* storage pool, the provider is responsible

of decrypting the data before the application can load and process it. The main responsibility of the protected part of the application is to process sensitive customer data belonging to the *PNTP* privacy category (technically, the protected part can also process *NP* and *PTP* data in the same manner presented above). Data belonging to the *PNTP* privacy category is encrypted with the customer key K_{CID}. This key is safely stored in the persistent storage of the crypto coprocessor. To get access to the plaintext version of this data, the protected software part requests the *RP* daemon to load the data from the cloud central storage. The *RP* daemon, having access to K_{CID}, loads the encrypted data, decrypts it, checks its integrity, and presents it to the protected application part.

Output results produced by the customer software also belong to the three privacy categories *NP*, *PTP*, and *PNTP* (*PNTP* data is only produced by the protected software part). Data produced in the crypto coprocessor with the *NP* privacy category is sent by the protected application to the *RP* daemon. The latter sends it, as is, to the *NP* storage pool. *NP* data can be also produced by the unprotected software part. In this case the unprotected part is responsible of sending the data to the *NP* storage pool.

Data produced with the *PTP* privacy category in the crypto coprocessor is sent by the protected application to the *RP* daemon which in turn transfers it to a provider's encryption process running on the main server. This process encrypts the *PTP* data with a provider ciphering key and stores it in the *PTP* storage pool.

Finally, data produced with the *PNTP* privacy category is sent to the *RP* daemon which encrypts it using K_{CID} and stores it in the *PNTP* storage pool. This data category can only be produced by the protected software part running in the crypto coprocessor. Figure 2. b graphically illustrates the effect of the privacy categorization mechanism and the transfer of customer data to the cloud storage pools.

Secure VM Migration Protocol

A major goal that we strived to achieve in the PasS design is for it to support the migration of VMs between physical servers in the cloud environment. Migration refers to moving a particular VM from one physical server (source server) to another server (destination server) while the VM is in the production phase. VM migration is crucial in virtualized cloud environments to enable the cloud system to dynamically adapt to changing customer workloads. The PasS migration support is effectuated when the VM running the protected customer code is moved to a destination physical server containing a crypto coprocessor hardware module. This is due to the fact that the protected code can only be executed in the address space of a tamper-proof crypto coprocessor possessing

the necessary cryptographic keying material as described earlier in this chapter. A very important aspect of the PasS migration support is that it does not interfere with the standard VM mobility protocols that are applied at the provider site. The only PasS functional requirements to support VM migration are: (1) The migrated VM should move to a destination server containing an already installed crypto coprocessor, (2) the *RP* daemon on the source crypto coprocessor has to be informed of this migration process and fed with the address details of the destination physical server and its respective crypto coprocessor and (3) the *RP* daemon should be provided with the (*CID, SID)* pairs of the protected software components currently running on the migrated VM.

The PasS VM migration support is realized in two concurrent phases:

1. **Migration of the VM instance:** In this phase the cloud virtualization system reports to the *RP* daemon on the source crypto coprocessor that a particular VM is about to be migrated to a specified physical server. The *RP* daemon is provided with the address of the physical server and the crypto coprocessor installed on it. Moreover the *RP* daemon is supplied with the (*CID, SID*) pair of the customer software running on the VM to be migrated. At this point, the *RP* daemon executes the Security Layer migration phase which is described in the next bullet. Afterwards the VM instance migration can proceed using provider-specific migration protocols as is typically achieved in traditional cloud environments not providing the privacy service.

2. **Migration of the Security Layer:** for the destination crypto coprocessor to be capable of executing the protected customer software running on the migrated VM and processing encrypted sensitive data, it has to acquire the necessary cryptographic material from the source crypto coproces-

sor. This cryptographic material is termed as the Security Layer and is represented in the K_{SID} keys associated with the different (*CID, SID*) pairs and the K_{CID} key of every customer running protected software in the migrated VM. In this phase the Security Layer containing the cryptographic keying material is securely migrated from the source to the destination crypto coprocessor. The security layer migration process is carried out by the respective *RP* daemons on the source and destination ends. To ensure the confidentiality and integrity of the security layer during the migration process, the source *RP* daemon encrypts it using K_{TTP} and MACs the encrypted result using the same K_{TTP} key. On the destination crypto coprocessor, the *RP* daemon uses K_{TTP} to check the integrity of the encrypted Security Layer (by verifying the MAC received) and decrypt its contents. The cryptographic keying material, retrieved from the decrypted Security Layer, is installed on the destination crypto coprocessor to support the PasS privacy and integrity operations on the migrated VM. It is worth mentioning here that the PasS migration support does not induce any performance degradation on the VM migration process due to the relatively small Security Layer size compared to the VM instance size. This fact renders the migration of the Security Layer typically performed much faster than that of the VM instance by amortizing the time needed to migrate the Security Layer in the total VM migration time.

Privacy Feedback Protocol

The privacy feedback protocol is an essential component that should be considered and planned thoroughly when designing privacy-aware cloud services. The main responsibility of this protocol is to inform users of the different privacy mechanisms applied on their data and to make them aware of any data leaks or risks that may jeopardize the confidentiality of their sensitive information. Providing a secure privacy feedback protocol increases the users' trust in the cloud computing services, relieves their privacy concerns, and supports a set of accountable auditing services required to achieve legal compliance and certification.

The design of the *RP* daemon supports the operation of the privacy feedback process. This is due to the fact that the *RP* daemon represents a centralized processing entity that handles all the privacy enforcement mechanisms in the crypto coprocessor. The operation of the protocol is summarized as follows:

1. Whenever the *RP* daemon executes a privacy-related operation it creates a privacy audit record describing this operation. The type of the privacy operation and the contents of the privacy record are specified by the customer upon registration with the privacy service. Possible fields that may be included in the privacy audit record are: a description of the privacy operation, the application process performing the operation, the cryptographic key strength used in performing the encryption mechanisms, the process providing input data to the operation, the process receiving the operation output data, the privacy category of the input and output data, the number of consecutive failed signature verifications, the date and time of the operation, etc.

2. The *RP* daemon encrypts the privacy record with K_{CID} to protect its confidentiality.

3. The *RP* daemon constructs a hash chain data structure over the encrypted privacy record (Schneier and Kelsey, 1999; Itani, Kayssi, & Chehab, 2005). This is illustrated in Figure 4. In this figure, HC_i is the hash chain constructed by hashing the ith privacy record and the hash chain entry of the previous privacy record. Since HC_i includes HC_{i-1}, it

Figure 4. Confidentiality and integrity protection of the privacy audit records

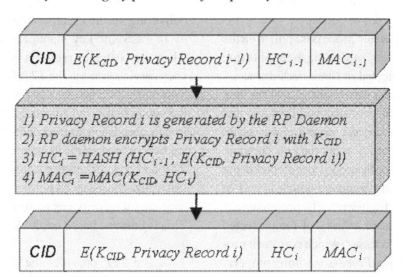

is possible to verify the integrity of all previous privacy records by only authenticating HCi. Initially, HC_{-1} is given a default value to start the hash chain. To authenticate HC_i, a MAC_i field is added to the privacy record. This field represents the MAC of HC_i using K_{CID}.

4. The *RP* daemon stores the resulting secure record on the cloud storage facility.
5. A special customer application polls the contents of the privacy audit log every predefined period of time. After verifying the integrity of the privacy records using the hash chain and the respective *MAC* value, the application decrypts the contents of the privacy records using K_{CID}. The customer can analyze the decrypted privacy records and take actions based on this analysis.

It should be noted here that since the feedback process is wholly executed in the secure cryptographic coprocessor and since K_{CID} is safely stored in the coprocessor persistent storage, the cloud provider would not be able to read the contents of the privacy audit log, or modify it without being detected. Hence, the confidentiality of the privacy records is assured and the authenticity and integrity of the hash chain are guaranteed.

SYSTEM IMPLEMENTATION

A prototype implementation of the PasS protocols is tested on a simple banking application. The prototype included, in addition to a sample implementation of the privacy protocols, an implementation of the data privacy categorization and software division mechanisms. The infrastructure used in the prototype emulates a standard cloud computing unit. The physical server used is an Intel Core 2 Duo machine running Windows Server 2008 Enterprise Edition. The two server processors run at 3.0 GHz and the system is supported with 4 GB of RAM. The virtualization layer is provided using VMware VSphere 4 (Lowe, 2009). The guest operating system runs Windows Server 2003 Enterprise Edition. To implement the functionality of the secure cryptographic coprocessor, we assume that one of the core CPUs is the physically secure coprocessor, while the other core is that of the main untrusted server. We believe that for the sake of testing the system functionality and security mechanisms, the current configuration provides a viable proof of concept.

The software division process is applied on the banking application by separating the application functions into a protected and unprotected process. The protected process carries out critical banking operations (account deposits, withdrawals, and transfers) and runs on the crypto coprocessor, while the unprotected process runs on the main server CPU. The application is developed using the C# programming language which is part of the Microsoft.Net framework. To programmatically set the processor affinity of the protected and unprotected processes (which core each process will run on), the *ProcessorAffinity* property of the *Process* class in the *System.Diagnostics* namespace is used. The experience obtained in implementing the software division mechanism makes us believe in the feasibility of developing a set of standard patterns to systematically support the division process.

SECURITY ANALYSIS

This section aims at reinforcing the design patterns presented in this chapter by abstracting the main security mechanisms and procedures employed on the cloud software and data.

Key Management in PasS

Key agreement is the process that governs the generation and distribution of cryptographic key material in a secure communication network. It is mainly required to support entity authentication and data confidentiality and integrity protocols in delivering their security services by supplying these protocols with the necessary secret key parameters. Typically, key agreement is the most complex phase in the design of any security protocol. In fact, the security of the privacy and integrity protocols mainly relies on the success

of the key management system in producing and delivering secure cryptographic keys.

In PasS, the key management process starts when the customer registers with the cloud privacy service through the *TTP*. The *TTP* allocates a unique public/private key pair (PU_{CID}/PR_{CID}) to the newly registered customer and loads this pair into the persistent storage of the crypto coprocessor before the latter is deployed in the cloud. The *TTP* and the customer are the only entities that can utilize the assigned public/private key pair in subsequent security mechanisms and procedures. This is ensured based on the following points:

1. The *TTP* provides the customer with the public/private key pair via a face-to-face transaction or through a secure electronic session. This process guarantees the secure delivery of the keys from the *TTP* to the customer.
2. The tamper-proof physical capabilities of the crypto coprocessor and the secure access control mechanisms implemented (using the RP daemon process) prevents the cloud provider, or other customer applications, from gaining access into the public/private key store on the crypto coprocessor.

As discussed earlier in this chapter, the (PU_{CID}/PR_{CID}) key pair participates in:

1. Assuring the integrity and authenticity of the customer software package when transported, processed, and stored in the cloud.
2. Securing the K_{SID} cryptographic key, used for encrypting the protected software part.
3. Generating the K_{CID} cryptographic key used to secure the sensitive customer data when transported and stored in the cloud. Moreover, K_{CID} is used to secure the privacy feedback process as described in the fourth Section.

Data Privacy and Integrity in PasS

PasS ensures the privacy and integrity of customer data through all its lifecycle stages. In the rest of this section we confine the discussion to the security mechanisms applied on sensitive customer data of the *PNTP* privacy category.

In the Transport Phase

When sensitive data is transferred from the customer to the cloud, the privacy, i.e. confidentiality, of data is achieved by encrypting it using the K_{CID} key. As stated earlier in this chapter, K_{CID} is generated via an authenticated Diffie-Hellman protocol execution. The encryption process prevents the disclosure of sensitive data contents on the network links.

The integrity of data in the transport phase is achieved by applying cryptographic MAC structures using K_{CID} on implementation-dependent logical data units.

In the Processing Phase

The processing phase is considered very important from a data privacy point of view. This is due to the fact that in this phase the data has to be decrypted and transformed from its ciphertext to its plaintext version to be processed by the software running in the cloud. To protect the privacy of data, PasS ensures that the decryption process only takes place in a physically and logically isolated execution environment represented in the tamper-proof crypto coprocessor. Sensitive data units of the *PNTP* privacy category can only be decrypted on behalf of the respective customer software inside the address space of the cryptographic coprocessor. To get access to the plaintext version of the data, the protected customer software requests the *RP* daemon to load the data from the cloud storage. The *RP* daemon is the only coprocessor process that has access to the K_{CID} key with which the customer *PNTP* data is encrypted. Hence, the *RP* daemon loads the encrypted data, decrypts it in the crypto coprocessor address space, and presents it to the protected software part of the customer application.

In the Storage Phase

The privacy and integrity of sensitive customer data when stored in the cloud is ensured using analogous constructs as in the transport phase. Storing *PNTP* data encrypted using K_{CID} ensures the privacy of data and prevents the cloud provider from accessing and reading the plaintext version of the data. The integrity of data is ensured by appending MAC constructs, created using K_{CID}, on logical storage data units.

Software Privacy and Integrity in PasS

In the Transport Phase

The protected part of the customer software package is encrypted at the client-side using the K_{SID} key. The integrity of the entire software package (protected and unprotected parts) is ensured using the *DS* digital signature created using the customer private key PR_{CID}.

In the Execution Phase

The cryptographic coprocessor tamper-proof capabilities and the access control mechanism implemented using the RP process are the main design factors leading to a secure and private software execution. The protected software part can only be executed in the crypto coprocessor since the K_{SID} key encrypting this software part is stored in the coprocessor tamper-proof storage and under the control of the central *RP* daemon. This guarantees the privacy of the customer data and applications and prevents the cloud provider from tampering with the execution of the software and the processing of the sensitive customer data.

In the Storage Phase

The same cryptographic constructs constituting the privacy tag, discussed in the fourth section, are employed to protect the privacy and integrity of the customer software, particularly the protected part of it, when stored in the cloud.

Security Aspects of the Privacy Feedback Process in PasS

The privacy feedback process is wholly executed in the secure cryptographic coprocessor and the key K_{CID} is safely stored in the coprocessor persistent storage. This ensures the confidentiality and integrity of the audit logs even if stored on the non-trusted cloud side. The encryption of the log records ensures its confidentiality by preventing the cloud provider from reading the contents of the privacy records. Moreover, the hash chain structure and its respective MAC values ensure the integrity of the privacy audit log by guaranteeing the detection of any unauthorized modification imposed on it.

ECONOMIC FEASIBILITY ANALYSIS

A brief economic study shows that commercial cryptographic coprocessors range in price from several hundreds to several thousands U.S. Dollars. The cost of the coprocessor mainly depends on the processing and memory capabilities of the coprocessor, the degree of physical security and tamper-resistance supported, the compliance of the coprocessor with FIPS standards, and the crypto functionality (hardware acceleration and cryptographic implementations) provided. We believe that the cost of the privacy solution presented can be greatly reduced based on a set of external economic factors as well as internal design choices related to the PasS protocol architecture itself. These factors are summarized in the following points:

1. The increase in demand on cryptographically secure facilities to provide practical security solutions, particularly to computing clouds, will increase the competitiveness in the crypto coprocessor commercial market and will gradually result in a higher functionality/cost ratio.

2. The technological advancements in computing and memory hardware, as well as in physical packaging mechanisms, will result in delivering cost-effective cryptographic coprocessors.

3. The emergence of open-source cryptographic processor designs will support the elimination of monopolism in the coprocessor market, and hence will lead to considerable price reductions.

4. The coprocessor sharing mechanism employed in PasS (where more than one customer shares the resources of a particular crypto coprocessor) participates in mitigating the cost of the privacy services provided and reducing the payback period of the cloud provider investment (the payback period is the length of time required for an investment to recover its cost). This sharing mechanism plays a major role in the cost-effectiveness of the security solution. To illustrate this, we will derive a general equation to calculate the payback period of the cloud provider investment in the privacy service. Without loss of generality, we calculate the payback period of a single crypto coprocessor as follows: Let C_{sp} denote the capital cost of the cryptographic coprocessor unit. C_{sp} consists of the following cost components: (1) The cost of the crypto coprocessor hardware, (2) the coprocessor configuration and distribution, (3) the coprocessor installation in the computing cloud, and (4) the operational and maintenance costs including power consumption and network bandwidth usage for carrying out remote configuration. Let R and R_{sp} represent the cost of computation

per hour on the main server processor and crypto coprocessor respectively. Let M be the ratio of R_{sp} to R ($M = R_{sp}/R$). Let L represent the average number of customers sharing the resources of the crypto coprocessor per hour. The payback period in months, PB_m, is calculated as follows:

$$PB_m = \frac{C_{sp}}{L \times M \times R \times 24 \times 30} \qquad (1)$$

Assume that C_{sp} is \$ 10,000, L is 3 users, M is 2 (the cost of 1 computing hour on the crypto coprocessor is double that on the main server processor) and R is \$ 0.52 per hour (based on the Amazon EC2 Windows standard on-demand instance rate using the Large AMI profile). Therefore, based on Equation 1, PB_m is equal to 4.45 months. This payback period is very reasonable in return of the privacy service provided. From the cloud provider's perspective, we believe that the payback period will be even shorter as the number of privacy-demanding customers increase and as the cost of the crypto coprocessor decrease with the technological advancements in packaging technology. By adopting a privacy service that relieves customers' privacy concerns and supports legal compliance, the cloud provider will attract and maintain a significant number of privacy-demanding businesses. This fact becomes more evident if we know that the main factor hindering the adoption of cloud computing, particularly in healthcare and financial applications, is the lack of privacy and compliance support in current cloud service implementations.

5. The software division mechanism implemented and the light-weighted nature of the PasS privacy protocols support a better utilization of the crypto coprocessor and avoids any unnecessary loads on its resources. This aids in reducing the resource requirements, and hence the price, of the coprocessor. It is true that the software division process adds considerable costs in restructuring legacy applications. However we believe that the reduction in the coprocessor cost resulting from this process outweighs the software partitioning cost. Moreover, we believe that the software development industry will be able to accommodate the software partitioning design model using standard patterns and blueprints which will highly reduce the software division costs. From experience in this field we witness how open and flexible is the software development industry in accepting novel software development models. The rapid success of the procedural and Object-oriented development paradigms is a good example to illustrate this point.

6. The functional requirements of the PasS design do not rely on any form of hardware cryptographic implementation or acceleration. All the cryptographic mechanisms can be implemented in software at the expense of a slight decrease in performance.

7. Cloud computing security research is giving more attention to trusted hardware security approaches to provide technical solutions for solving several data privacy and integrity issues in the computing cloud. This fact is supported by the proposed work of the Trusted Computing Group (Trusted Computing Group, 2011) for developing a set of cloud security services and protocols based on their TPM modules (Bajikar, 2002).

CONCLUSION

In this chapter we presented a set of hardware-based security mechanisms for ensuring the privacy and legal compliance of data storage and processing in cloud computing. The system relies on tamper-proof cryptographic coprocessors to establish a secure execution environment in the computing cloud that is physically and logically protected from unauthorized access. The main design goal is to maximize users' control in managing the various aspects related to the privacy of sensitive data by implementing user-configurable software protection and data privacy categorization mechanisms. Moreover, the presented security system provides a privacy feedback protocol to inform users of the different privacy operations applied on their data and to make them aware of any data leaks or risks that may jeopardize the confidentiality of their sensitive information. The chapter started by providing a literature survey of the state of the art research in the field of data privacy in cloud computing. Then a description of cryptographic coprocessors is presented. This included a survey of a cryptographic coprocessor architecture and tamper-proof capabilities, a description of the main attack categories on such devices and their countermeasures, a summary of leading crypto coprocessor implementations in the commercial and open source sectors, and a description of a set of secure applications supported by crypto coprocessors. After this, the chapter presented a comprehensive description of PasS, a hardware-based cloud security solution utilizing crypto coprocessors. On this front, the chapter shed light on the design of the privacy protocols employed, their implementation on the prominent VMware cloud computing platform, a security analysis that abstracts the privacy mechanisms used to protect the different aspects of the data processing and storage operations in the cloud and an economic feasibility study demonstrating the practicality of deploying the system in a real cloud computing environment.

REFERENCES

Anderson, R., Bond, M., Clulow, J., & Skorobogatov, S. (2006). Cryptographic processors-a survey. *Proceedings of the IEEE, 94*(2), 357–369. doi:10.1109/JPROC.2005.862423

Annas, G. J. (2003). HIPAA regulations—A new era of medical-record privacy? *The New England Journal of Medicine, 348*(15), 1486–1490. doi:10.1056/NEJMlim035027

Arnold, T. W., & Van Doorn, L. P. (2004). The IBM PCIXCC: A new cryptographic coprocessor for the IBM eServer. *IBM Journal of Research and Development, 48*(3-4), 475–487. doi:10.1147/rd.483.0475

Bajikar, S. (2002). *Trusted platform module (tpm) based security on notebook pcs-white paper*. Mobile Platforms Group, Intel Corporation (June 20, 2002).

Barham, P., Dragovic, B., Fraser, K., Hand, S., Harris, T., Ho, A., et al. (2003). Xen and the art of virtualization. *Proceedings of the Nineteenth ACM Symposium on Operating Systems Principles,* (pp. 164-177).

Berger, S., Aceres, R. C., et al. (2006). vTPM: Virtualizing the trusted platform module. In *USENIX-SS'06: Proceedings of the 15th Conference on USENIX Security Symposium*.

Best, R. M. (1980). Preventing software piracy with crypto-microprocessors. *Proceedings of IEEE Spring COMPCON, 80*, 466–469.

Bhattacharjee, B., Abe, N., Goldman, K., Zadrozny, B., Chillakuru, V. R., del Carpio, M., et al. (2006). Using secure coprocessors for privacy preserving collaborative data mining and analysis. *Proceedings of the 2nd International Workshop on Data Management on New Hardware*.

Cavoukian, A. (2008). Privacy in the clouds. *Identity in the Information Society, 1*(1), 89–108. doi:10.1007/s12394-008-0005-z

Chuang, I., Li, S. H., Huang, K. C., & Kuo, Y. H. (2011). An effective privacy protection scheme for cloud computing. *2011 13th International Conference on Advanced Communication Technology (ICACT)*, (pp. 260-265).

Doelitzscher, F., Reich, C., & Sulistio, A. (2010). Designing cloud services adhering to government privacy laws. *2010 10th IEEE International Conference on Computer and Information Technology (CIT 2010)*, (pp. 930-935).

Dyer, J. G., Lindemann, M., Perez, R., Sailer, R., Van Doorn, L., & Smith, S. W. (2001). Building the IBM 4758 secure coprocessor. *Computer*, *34*(10), 57–66. doi:10.1109/2.955100

Garfinkel, T., Pfaff, B., Chow, J., Rosenblum, M., & Boneh, D. (2003). Terra: A virtual machine-based platform for trusted computing. *ACM SIGOPS Operating Systems Review*, *37*(5), 193–206. doi:10.1145/1165389.945464

Gellman, R. (2009). *WPF REPORT: Privacy in the clouds: Risks to privacy and confidentiality from cloud computing.*

Gentry, C. (2009). Fully homomorphic encryption using ideal lattices. *Proceedings of the 41st Annual ACM Symposium on Theory of Computing,* (pp. 169-178).

Gentry, C. (2011). *Fully homomorphic encryption without bootstrapping,* Gutmann, P. (2000). An open-source cryptographic coprocessor. *Proceedings of the 9th Conference on USENIX Security Symposium,* Vol. 9, (p. 8).

Itani, W., Kayssi, A., & Chehab, A. (2005). Short paper: PATRIOT-a policy-based, multi-level security protocol for safekeeping audit logs on wireless devices. *First International Conference on Security and Privacy for Emerging Areas in Communications Networks, SecureComm 2005* (pp. 240-242).

Itani, W., Kayssi, A., & Chehab, A. (2008). Policy-based security for M-commerce networks. In Huang, W. W., Wang, Y., & Day, J. (Eds.), *Global mobile commerce: Strategies, implementation and case studies* (p. 53).

Itani, W., Kayssi, A., & Chehab, A. (2009). Privacy as a service: Privacy-aware data storage and processing in cloud computing architectures. *2009 Eighth IEEE International Conference on Dependable, Autonomic and Secure Computing,* (pp. 711-716).

Janger, E. J., & Schwartz, P. M. (2001). Gramm-Leach-Bliley Act, information privacy, and the limits of default rules. *Minnesota Law Review*, *86*, 1219.

Kelsey, J., Schneier, B., & Hall, C. (1996). An authenticated camera. *12th Annual Computer Security Applications Conference, 1996* (pp. 24-30).

Li, C., Raghunathan, A., & Jha, N. K. (2010). Secure virtual machine execution under an untrusted management OS. *2010 IEEE 3rd International Conference on Cloud Computing,* (pp. 172-179).

Lowe, S. (2009). *Mastering VMware vSphere 4.* Sybex.

Pearson, S. (2009). Taking account of privacy when designing cloud computing services. *Proceedings of the 2009 ICSE Workshop on Software Engineering Challenges of Cloud Computing,* (pp. 44-52).

Pearson, S., & Charlesworth, A. (2009). Accountability as a way forward for privacy protection in the cloud. *Proceedings of the 1ˢᵗ International Conference on Cloud Computing,* (pp. 131-144).

Rodrıguez-Silva, D., González-Castano, F., Adkinson-Orellana, L., Fernández-Cordeiro, A., Troncoso-Pastoriza, J., & González-Martınez, D. (2011). *Encrypted domain processing for cloud privacy.*

Sadeghi, A., Stüble, C., & Winandy, M. (2008). Property-based TPM virtualization. In Wu, T.-C., Lei, C.-L., Rijmen, V., & Lee, D.-T. (Eds.), *Information Security* (*Vol. 5222*, pp. 1–16). Lecture Notes in Computer Science Berlin, Germany: Springer. doi:10.1007/978-3-540-85886-7_1

Schneier, B. (2009). *Schnier on security*. Retrieved from Http://www.schneier.com/blog/archives/2009/07/homomorphic_enc.html

Schneier, B., & Kelsey, J. (1997). Remote auditing of software outputs using a trusted coprocessor. *Future Generation Computer Systems*, *13*(1), 9–18. doi:10.1016/S0167-739X(97)00004-6

Schneier, B., & Kelsey, J. (1999). Secure audit logs to support computer forensics. *ACM Transactions on Information and System Security*, *2*(2), 159–176. doi:10.1145/317087.317089

Theodoropoulos, D., Papaefstathiou, I., & Pnevmatikatos, D. (2008). *Cproc: An efficient cryptographic coprocessor*. 16th IFIP/IEEE International Conference on very Large Scale Integration.

Trusted Computing Group home page. (n.d.). Retrieved from http://www.trustedcomputinggroup.org/

Tygar, J., & Yee, B. (1993). Dyad: A system for using physically secure coprocessors. *Proceedings of the Joint Harvard-MIT Workshop on Technological Strategies for the Protection of Intellectual Property in the Network Multimedia Environment*, (p. 87).

Van Dijk, M., Gentry, C., Halevi, S., & Vaikuntanathan, V. (2010). Fully homomorphic encryption over the integers. *Advances in Cryptology–EUROCRYPT*, *2010*, 24–43.

Weingart, S. H. (1987). Physical security for the mABYSS system. *System*, *1*(2), 3.

White, S. R., & Comerford, L. (1990). ABYSS: An architecture for software protection. *IEEE Transactions on Software Engineering*, *16*(6), 619–629. doi:10.1109/32.55090

White, S. R., Weingart, S. H., Arnold, W. C., & Palmer, E. R. (1991). *Introduction to the Citadel architecture: Security in physically exposed environments*.

Yee, B., & Tygar, J. (1995). Secure coprocessors in electronic commerce applications. *Proceedings of the 1st Conference on USENIX Workshop on Electronic Commerce*, Vol. 1, (p. 14).

KEY TERMS AND DEFINITIONS

Cloud Computing: The set of technologies and tools that manages the process of software and data migration to remote computing servers.

Cloud Customer: Is the entity that employs the cloud storage and computing resource facilities to remotely store and process data.

Cloud Provider: Is the entity that manages and operates a cloud infrastructure of storage and computing services.

Cryptographic Coprocessor: A standalone computing unit that interfaces to a server. It is supported with tamper-proof casing that makes it resist physical attacks.

Cryptography: Is the science of secret writing that involves the mathematical algorithms and tools for protecting the confidentiality, integrity, authenticity, and availability of data and services.

Privacy Feedback: Is the process that informs users of the different privacy operations applied on their data to make them aware of any data leaks or risks that may jeopardize the confidentiality of their sensitive information.

Virtual Machine: Is a software program that emulates a real computer system.

Chapter 9
Securing Cloud Storage

Jacques Jorda
Institut de Recherche en Informatique de Toulouse, Université Paul Sabatier, France

Abdelaziz M'zoughi
Institut de Recherche en Informatique de Toulouse, Université Paul Sabatier, France

ABSTRACT

Data storage appears as a central component of the problematic associated with the move of processes and resources in the cloud. Whether it is a simple storage externalization for backup purposes, use of hosted software services or virtualization in a third-party provider of the company computing infrastructure, data security is crucial. This security declines according to three axes: data availability, integrity and confidentiality. Numerous techniques targeting these three issues exist, but none presents the combined guarantees that would allow a practical implementation. The authors' solution relies on the integration of these techniques to a virtualization middleware. Quality of service definition allows specifying the nature of the security to implement with a seamless access.

INTRODUCTION

Cloud storage can be used in many ways. First, it can serve as a data backup, such as Apple's iCloud service, or Dell Datasafe online storage service. Even Amazon's Simple Storage Service (also known as Amazon S3) can be used in that way. It can also be used to store used by cloud computing services: both services accessible via internet (Software as a Service (SaaS), such as those provided in the Microsoft Azure offer) and

server virtualization require cloud storage to store data or virtual filesystems disks.

This cloud storage has all the advantages of cloud computing: only what is used has to be paid, without heavy initial investment or hidden fees. It also has the same pitfalls: data security being critical, the confidence in the operator abilities to ensure this security must be complete.

In the next section, we will present the different possible security vulnerabilities relative to cloud data storage, and the way to tackle them. These vulnerabilities are classical (data leakage due to an external user) or specific to cloud computing

DOI: 10.4018/978-1-4666-2125-1.ch009

issue (data leakage due to a cloud administrator). We will see how to ensure data security in this context. Classical encryption techniques can be used in conjunction with data distribution services linked to the storage resource nature found in these environments. Track access methods can complete these security techniques to detect unauthorized accesses, including by the host infrastructure managers. We will conclude this section by showing why no global solution is available at this time.

In the following section, we will introduce the principle of storage virtualization. We will present the architecture of our storage virtualization middleware, and show how it can handle the problematic of cloud storage security. This virtualization can be implemented at the host infrastructure to provide virtual storage resources to the applications or to user virtual machines disks; it can be extended to user virtual machines to provide secure and seamless accessible backup storage volumes.

BACKGROUND

When data are moved in the cloud, the storage security is critical. Because data are no longer managed by their owner, the latter must be ensured that security is maintained. This security is defined by three main parameters: confidentiality, integrity and availability. These three parameters are used to characterize threats likely to affect the data.

Data availability is crucial. Storage provider must ensure that the data will be available independently of what could happen, by committing fast turnaround time subjected to a penalty. Providers such as Amazon with its Simple Storage Service are likely to be unavailable for several hours. When it happens, the user computing infrastructure becomes partly ineffective (when only few services are hosted by Saas solutions) or completely ineffective (when the all user server infrastructure is virtualized and hosted by the provider), leading to significant losses. To always ensure data

availability, the provider must thus implement not only redundancy solutions but also backups.

Data integrity issue relies on the guarantee sought by the user that all his externalized data are effectively present and non-altered in its provider infrastructure. Data integrity damages may results from malicious third party attacks, hosting infrastructure vulnerabilities, or conscious choice of the hosting infrastructure to delete non-accessed data to maximize its costs. This issue begins to be well studied in the literature with, for example, the use of POR (Proof Of Retreivability) and PDP (Proof of Data Possession) tools. These techniques allow detecting data integrity damage without requiring local data copy storage by the user (the aim being exactly to externalize the storage).

Data confidentiality remains one of the main concerns and the major barrier to the development of cloud services. This confidentiality is vulnerable to conventional threats (injection attacks, cross-site scripting...) but also to specific cloud computing threats (hypervisor flaws, management of the security perimeter within a company, confidence in the provider). At this level, differences can be separated according to the user infrastructure externalization degree in the provider infrastructure:

- The user uses the application server hosting (database, web services, mail servers...), these applications being accessed by the user with secured connexions. Usually, it involves a minimal user infrastructure, because some applications can not be placed in the cloud and desktop application data remain within the own user infrastructure – and therefore require, at least, both authentication and file servers. Here, data protection is complex because the application is managed by the provider.
- The user virtualizes its servers (and when necessary the desktops). Here, the all user server infrastructure is moved to the cloud and all his data are hosted on dedicated vir-

tual servers. The user can then secure his data – or at least, reinforce their access.

We will first detail the nature of threats affecting data externalized in the cloud. These threats can be either classical or specific to cloud computing. Then, we will review the solutions that currently exist to implement data confidentiality, availability and security. These solutions address one of these issues, sometime two but never the three. We will conclude with the requirements needed to address these three security issues.

Threats to Externalized Data

There are two potential types of security vulnerabilities. The first type includes classical data damages – those faced by any infrastructure administrator. The second type is linked to the cloud computing nature itself: resource sharing with a third party and management of the externalized material infrastructure.

Classical Threats to Data

Conventional threats to data apply to data stored in the cloud, independently of the selected externalization level. Indeed, the more common threats apply equally to the services provided by the cloud manager and virtualized infrastructures. The more frequent attacks involve:

- Injections
- Cross-site scripting
- Phishing

An injection attack occurs when unreliable data, being part of a command or request, are sent to an interpreter. The principle is as follows: a web application receives external data and these data are used by the application to create database requests, commands, system calls ... If the external data received are not checked before their use, a malicious third party can divert the expected external data semantic to insert additional content affecting company data security and integrity. Several types of injections can be distinguished, according to the nature of the target interpreter: SQL injection, LDAP injection, code injection, XPATH injection ... Note that this type of attack is also used by the applications during user identification and authentication processes since an application uses a database for user name/password storage.

It is clear that this type of attack allows not only a malicious third party accessing company data likely sensitive, but also that it is dangerous for the data since data commands such as modification/deletion can be executed. To be protected against such attacks, non approved data must never be given to an interpreter. This means that the variables must be either linked or analyzed prior use.

Cross-site scripting attacks are the second most important threat to data security. Rather than directly attack the data present on the server, this type of threat targets the user browser to fraudulently introduce the company website. The principle is simple: malicious data (containing a script) disguised as harmless (for example a message in a forum or a blog) are injected in a website. When these malicious data are read by the user browser, the browser will execute the script they contain and then, its author can access to the website with the identity of the real user or to the cookies ...

The malicious third party will then usurp the user identity to access to company data. Various techniques allow protecting against this type of threats: use information filtering functions to replace the special html language characters (in particular « < » and « > ») by their encoded equivalents, or install firewall applications detecting, in the http flow, suspicious queries and delete them.

Phishing is, for a malicious third party, to pretend to be a trusted company contact to obtain sensitive informations (passwords) allowing accessing the infrastructures. Most common communication means include e-mail and messages on social networks. In addition to phishing targeting the company and aiming to obtain the access to its data managed by the storage provider and pretending to be this latter, cloud storage data also expose their owner to phishing targeting the storage provider employees. Such an attempt on Salesforce.com allowed the phishers obtaining a list of service user accounts and access to their informations.

Furthermore, other threats which are not specific to cloud computing exist.

Specific Threats to Cloud Computing

The first attack target affects virtualized infrastructures. When a company externalizes its servers, virtual machines manage services executed by the servers. These virtual machines run in virtualization environments such as Xen or VMware. In the hypervisors, security flaws can be used to obtain company data access. These flaws are especially easy to find since hypervisors usually use Linux kernels (VMware) and even also an open source (Xen).

Cloud service provider strategy is to protect their infrastructures with firewalls. However, this does not prevent a malicious third party to subscribe to provider services to bypass the cloud external security strategy. It is difficult to overcome this type of threat: it should be possible to isolate the virtual machines but this cannot be done effectively without relying on material resources.

Another issue concerns user identification and authentication. Indeed, the company security infrastructure remains usually local and its extension to services provided by the cloud does not come without implementation difficulty. Attack exposure by identity theft is thus much higher.

Finally, while the trust in service provider can not be absolute, information protection solutions must be implemented for infrastructure managers, and controls must be provided to service users.

Existing Solutions to Improve Cloud Storage Security

Some requirements are needed to implement cloud storage security. First, data must be available. Classical techniques to implement this availability are based on redundancy storage. Secondly, the data integrity must be guaranteed. Indeed, the user must be able to check whenever he wants that neither deletion nor alteration happened. Lastly, the confidentiality of data is crucial as they are no longer managed by their owner.

Solutions for Better Data Availability

The first category of solutions relates to data availability. A data is said unavailable if a request sent by a user receives no response. Possible reasons for such a non-response are directly related to the storage architecture typically used in the cloud. Two architectures are in competition: the use of SAN and NAS, or the implementation of storage systems distributed across server clusters. This second solution is preferred to the first one (Ford, 2010), because if the SAN/NAS allow a simple implementation, they are still significantly more expensive and limit the concurrent I/O rate. Therefore we will now consider a storage system composed of several clusters of servers interconnected by a high-speed network. The implementation of a distributed storage solution on such architecture requires a set of software layers allowing:

- A seamless and uniform access for the users, either through a filesystem (POSIX compatible or not), or through a specific programming interface;
- The persistent data storage on the nodes using the appropriate operating system mechanisms acting on these nodes.

Typically, data writing by a user is not done on a single node: data are cut in chunks, and these chunks are spread over the different nodes. This usually results in an intermediate layer (sometimes implemented in the user access layer) which divides the data in blocks and transfers these blocks to the nodes involved.

In such a distributed storage system, data availability is based on redundancy mechanisms: this information redundancy is necessary to compensate the unavailability of one or more storage nodes. Several types of redundancies can be used: data replication or parity-based correcting codes or Reed-Solomon codes for example. In fact, the classical techniques implemented within the RAID are found but at the node layer. There are thus two major solutions: the replication, from one node to another node (the equivalent of RAID 1) and data interlacing with use of error codes (the equivalent of RAID 5).

Data replication is defined by the writing of the same data on at least two different nodes. This solution uses the most space on the drive (since a creation strategy of p replicas of a given size t leads to a waste of $p*t$), but it has two advantages. First, management is easy: data modification leads to the rewriting of this data on all the nodes on which it was present. It is not necessary to implement a complex algorithm or use additional communications to determine the redundant information to write or where to write it. Second, it is favourable to the readings: a read request can be sent simultaneously to different nodes hosting the data, allowing the user to receive the data faster. Disadvantages, in addition to the waste already mentioned, are numerous. First, a significant increase in traffic-related writings is observed: when a data must be written (created or modified) with a strategy with p replicas, these p replicas must be sent to the network to update all the nodes hosting this data. The cost is proportional to the number of replicas used (and thus competes with the guarantee provided by a higher number of replicas) as well as the writing volume. Second, these strategies must cope with parallel accesses (either because data are used by

parallel applications, or accessed by several users). In this context, mechanisms for consistency and concurrency management must be implemented to ensure data integrity. These mechanisms (such as quorums) are complex to implement and can cause a significant overload both on the network and system, penalizing the overall storage system performance.

Data interlacing with error codes is the separation of the objects to write into fixed size blocks, it distributes these blocks on different nodes and writes redundant data calculated through error correction techniques (parity, Reed-Solomon code) on other nodes. The number p of redundant data, calculated and stored as supernumerary on the nodes, induces directly the storage scheme reliability - and its cost in terms of drive space. If these patterns can appear more attractive because they limit drive waste, they have at least a major pitfall: any data change requires $p+1$ additional reading - in addition to writing of data block and p blocks corresponding to the error codes. Indeed, when a data from a block is modified, it is necessary to update the blocks containing the error codes for this data. This means that the previous version of the data block must be read to calculate, compared to the new version of the data block and the current error code block, the new version of the error block - and this for each of the p error blocks. This overload becomes quickly prohibitive and limits the use of such techniques. To overcome this disadvantage, it is possible to manage separately the calculation of the parity. In (Narayan, 2007), an independent thread is responsible for optimizing communications by breaking down parity updating in two steps: the first step is performed on the data storage node by comparing the old and new data, and this intermediate parity is then sent to the parity storage node which, using the old and intermediate parity, updates the parity value stored on the drive. To overcome any failure problem during this process, recovery informations are stored temporarily on the user drive. Results show a significant impact on performances compared to a traditional parity management, but a lower performance is still noticeable compared to a solution with no parity management.

Note that Sobe (Sobe, 2006) defines a general framework for studying redundancy patterns in which replication (such as data interlacing) is only a particular example of a more general theoretical structure. Thus, he defines the concepts of simple unidimensional parity, multiple unidimensional parity and multidimensional parity. He shows that Reed-Solomon error code-based schemes are less efficient. However, it is shown in (Ford, 2010) that these codes guarantee a better data availability.

Other types of schemes exist, such as threshold schemes used in the PASIS architecture (Ganger, 2001). A p-m-n threshold scheme (Wylie, 2000) is defined by information division in n pieces, these different pieces being stored in separate locations with the following constraints:

- Any group of m pieces allows recovering the original information.
- At least p pieces are necessary to retrace the original information.

This theoretical framework includes, again, simplest strategies, such as methods based on shared secret, replication, interlacing...

Independently of the strategy chosen for the implementation of the redundancy, the choice of the node that must host a data is essential. Several techniques have been suggested. In (Kermarrec, 2010), availability vectors are defined for each node. These vectors depict, at regular time intervals, the status of a node (available or not). The concept of correlation is then defined, to determine whether two vectors (and thus the availability of the corresponding nodes) are complementary. The correlation Θ of two vectors A and B is defined by the arc cosine of the ratio of the vector product of these vectors by the product of the norm of these vectors. When Θ equals 0, the two vectors are perfectly correlated, meaning that the corresponding nodes have the same availability ranges. When Θ equals $\pi/2$, the two vectors are not correlated (the operating node ranges have no similarity). Finally, when Θ equals π, the two vectors are perfectly anti-correlated. This means that the corresponding nodes have a complementary availability (when a node is available, the other is not, and vice versa) and are candidates to host the same replica. However, this strategy is not applicable to cloud storage, in which by definition, all nodes (dedicated servers) have a high availability.

The concept of node availability is pivotal in the data placement scheme in (Ford, 2010), but directed to cloud constraints. The concept of burst failure is defined, allowing the combination of the nodes for which failures are closely related in time. These concomitant unavailability is due to the presence of nodes within a same rack (with a failure), or to the application of patch or service packs simultaneously (due to system policies). Based on these burst failures, the concept of domain is defined to guide replica or error code storage methodology - for example by avoiding the storage of two replicas on nodes belonging to the same rack.

All these techniques aim improving data availability if one component (or more depending on the redundancy degree) of the storage infrastructure fails. These data being available, it is now necessary to ensure their integrity.

Data Integrity Check

As already mentioned above, cloud storage points the issue of data integrity checking for data stored in a provider infrastructure. This checking can be done either by the user himself or entrusted to a third party auditor (TPA) by the user. The simplest strategy for checking file data integrity is to store a copy and compare it with the file stored by the provider. Obviously this has no interest. Then, a problematic arises: how to check that a storage provider really keeps the data stored by a user unless the user himself has to own a copy of these data? This problematic is even more difficult since multiple parameters have to be considered.

Firstly, the solution must be efficient both at the user and server levels. For example, at the server level, a checking of the overall file blocks is not conceivable, because the bandwidth necessary for such an operation would compete with that required by the input/output operations requested by the users Therefore, various existing solutions use a block list randomly selected for performing integrity checking, making them non-deterministic.

Secondly, the number of checking requests must not be limited. Some systems, easier to implement, only guarantee a limited number of checking which needs to be fixed. To be really usable in a production environment, no limit must be imposed.

Thirdly, the user can want, for the same reasons justifying the externalization of his data storage, to externalize the check process. A TPA must thus be able to proceed to user data integrity check, while these data remain confidential, even for him. These checks must not represent an overload and the TPA should conduct validations for a large number of users. This concept of burden is defined at both the execution (CPU and memory resources) and static levels (the process must be with no status in order that the TPA has only to store a significant data volume for each user file).

Finally, data integrity checking process must support dynamic data updates done by their owners; these updates can be block insertions, updates or deletions. This constraint is harder than it seems since the number of blocks in the file is usually used as an index in the checking strategy.

Various solutions have been proposed to solve this problem. There are two main types of patterns: POR (Proof of Retrievalibity) and PDP (Proof of Possession Data). POR-type methods are used to detect file integrity damage and allow, under certain conditions, recovering corrupted or lost data. PDP-type methods provide only a checking tool

for file integrity. However, it is possible to switch from a PDP- to a POR-type method by adding error codes to the first method (Curtmola, 2008).

The concept of POR is defined in (Juels, 2007). They suggest to split the file in blocks, include error codes to enable data recovery when a failure (voluntary or not) of some storage nodes occurs, and add special blocks, called sentinels, whose purpose is to allow detecting alterations. These blocks are indistinguishable from the other blocks, since all blocks are encrypted before being sent to the provider. Thus, this latter can not focus on the storage of these checking blocks to the detriment of others. The checking is not deterministic but probabilistic (it does not affect all blocks but only the sentinels, so a correct answer does not guarantee that all blocks are present). For example, add 1% of sentinel blocks to a file and use 1/1000 of these blocks for each checking allows detecting file integrity damage with a probability of about 75%.

This method has two pitfalls: the limited number of requests, which is a priori fixed, and the presence of these sentinels which is a significant barrier to the file update management. This principle is extended in (Shacham, 2008) to support a TPA checking through the use of homomorphisms to generate the evidence of the existence. It is no longer based on the presence of sentinels in the file, but on the use of signatures similar to those defined in (Ateniese, 2007). However, their solution does not support dynamic updates.

The general framework for PDP-type methods (Ateniese, 2007) is to compute a signature for each block forming the file, and check (or have it checked by a TPA) that the provider really stores the blocks by regularly asking his signature for a set of blocks randomly selected. The various existing solutions are mainly based on mathematical structures such as Galois fields. The interested reader will find in (Ireland, 1990; Lidl, 1984) the elements necessary for a clear understanding of the field.

Concretely, integrity checking protocols are conducted in two steps: the initialization and checking. The initialization is to split a file into blocks, compute tags for each block, encrypt these tags with a private key and send file and tags to the provider. The checking is initiated by the user (or a person authorized by him). A block reference list (typically, these references are block index) is sent to the provider. This latter computes the tags for these blocks, encrypts them, and returns this tag list with the tag list initially provided for the blocks involved in the checking. The user (or his agent) can then, by decrypting the original and generated tags, compare them one by one. If the comparison succeeded, the provider really owns the data for the blocks tested. If the comparison fails, there is a data management failure.

It is clear here that check is not deterministic: it concerns only a subset of blocks forming the file. The probability that a block alteration/deletion done by the provider is detected by the user depends on the file size, number of blocks requested and number of destroyed or altered blocks. For example, for a 10000-block file, less than 500 blocks are required to detect any change with a probability greater than 99%.

In this context, dynamic operation support is difficult. Operations are only partially supported in (Ateniese, 2008), and require a limited number of checking. This scheme is extended in (Erway, 2009). They replace the block index used in the method describe by Ateniese (Ateniese, 2007) by a list, but this operation is more complex (the proof is in 0(log n) instead of 0(1)).

None of these methods brings, for now, the answer to all the constraints issued: efficiency, unlimited number of requests, possible checking by a TPA and support for file changes. Note that none of these techniques raises the problem of security, this latter being orthogonal to the integrity issue.

Data Confidentiality

Data confidentiality is a central issue associated with storage externalization. The problem is different depending on whether we consider a simple storage file service, the storage of data used on a SaaS platform or data managed by virtual machines (Kamara, 2010).

Securing data from data storage service relies on encryption techniques applied to distributed file systems. These techniques implement data encryption at the user level and encrypted data are then sent to the provider who ensures their retention. Several points should be detailed regarding this process.

Firstly, to hide data to the provider, standard encryption methods such as symmetrical or asymmetrical methods can be used. Symmetrical methods, such as AES (Daemen, 2000), are quite effective but require a private encryption key which is shared between all readers/writers. Asymmetric methods, such as RSA (Rivest, 1978), require a high performance. However, they allow differentiating readers (who need the private key) from writers (who must have the public key). However, these two method types are deterministic: a same data block will always identically be encrypted, leading to a higher vulnerability to attacks. Therefore, probabilistic encryptions, such as ElGamal (ElGamal, 1985) or OAEP (Bellare, 1994), are usually preferred. A random vector is added to the encryption and two identical blocks can be undetectable but here, key generation and maintenance are more complex.

Secondly, key management can quickly become problematic if the informations stored must be shared. The user can share the keys (Kallahalla, 2003) but management becomes quickly a major contention issue. It is then possible to use a re-encryption proxy (Ateniese, 2006) to transform a decipherable text with a key in a decipherable text with another key and here, the re-encryption process will never access to the content.

Thirdly, block locking management is complex and sensitive. Complex because if changes are frequent, the allowance of simultaneous updates on different blocks will be of interest (No, 2009). It is also sensitive because locking management by the provider may be biased to artificially maintain quality of service at a required level, by grouping both reading and writing accesses (Tan, 2011).

Finally, the user is not ensured that his data will effectively be removed. Key manager mechanisms can be implemented to ensure key storage removal either on a timestamp basis or during a deletion request (Tang, 2010).

In the SaaS context, data management raises different problems. Indeed, data locking and sharing is meaningless here, since everything is managed by a centralized service in the provider infrastructure. However, information research raises significant difficulties. Indeed, it is unthinkable that the user recovers all the encrypted informations available on the server to decrypt and search required decrypted informations. Not to mention the load required to decrypt large data volume, their simple transfer between provider and user over the network can not be implemented. Therefore, the search on the server itself must be allowed, without giving access to the underlying information. Methods for such mechanisms are called encryption methods with keyword search. They derive from the private search methods (Chor, 1998; Kushilevitz, 1997).

Private search methods were designed to allow highly structured data storage by a provider, without allowing the latter to determine the nature of requests sent by users to be executed on the server. The first works focused on a multi-server environment, in which query result is obtained but no server knows, individually, the exact nature of the information sought. The problem is formalized as follows: multiple servers store identical copies of a database, this latter being a series of bits. The user wants to obtain the value of one of these bits from his index, but this latter must remain unknown for servers. The simplest

method (Chor, 1998) is to query two different servers. The first server receives a bit index list (including those of interest for the user), and answers by the exclusive or of these bit values. The second server receives the same list without the index in the query. A simple exclusive or between the two results allows then finding the required value. More sophisticated methods have been introduced to allow private search on a single server (Kushilevitz, 1997), and are based on the quadratic residue method. These methods allow, from a random vector provided by the user, the server to calculate a set of unique values from which the user will recover the desired information. These methods have several disadvantages. First, the query-induced treatment is not negligible both at the server and user levels. Second, these methods hide user queries but do not protect data confidentiality itself.

To compensate these pitfalls, encryption with keyword search methods have been introduced (Song, 2000). They encrypt the information twice. The first encryption phase uses a deterministic algorithm (each word W_i is encrypted in an identical word X_i, regardless its position in the text). The second phase encrypts the flow derived from the first phase (succession of encrypted words X_i) with a succession of keys generated from the word X_i to be encrypted, using a random encryption process. When searching for occurrences of a word W, it is sufficient to communicate this word in its encrypted form X and the corresponding key. The search process on the server will then resend the corresponding elements. Among all these elements, wrong answers may occur, depending on the type of random encryption flow used. The number of false results can be fixed by choosing a flow long enough, and their probability of occurrence remains low even for low flow lengths. Main disadvantage of this symmetric encryption scheme-based method is related to the balance between search performance and load necessary to update indexes. Moreover, these methods do not allow composed searches (conjunctive or disjunctive searches for several keywords), or very inefficiently (Golle, 2004).

Other methods have been developed and are based on different encryption schemes. Ciriani (Ciriani, 2011) proposes for example the use of fragmentation- dissemination techniques to protect data confidentiality. The use of asymmetric encryption solutions has also been considered (Boneh, 2004), but these schemes provide a lower security level while having a greater performance impact.

Finally, data security used by virtual machines requires other protection mechanisms. Here, the data possession proofs or the hidden searches are useless. The assurance of data confidentiality is the only one to consider. Due to the nature of the problem, the provider can not do this encryption at the file storage layer which corresponds to user virtual machines drives. Virtual machines themselves must encrypt data from their virtual drives. This involves all data, including system files, files used by applications and user data files.

Many studies have been conducted in this field. For a complete and detailed analysis, see (Kher, 2005). Note that because the protection is internal to the virtual machine, encryption techniques that are applicable here are not specific of the distributed storage. However, strict decisions must be taken to ensure proper virtual machine isolation at the host level. Otherwise, dump memory may reveal sensitive informations or even user passwords for these virtual machines. Hardware tools, such as trusted platform modules, may allow the isolation, both at the memory and processor and at the network communication layers.

Implementation of these Solutions

All the solutions described above are purely theoretical and have not been implemented in real systems. Indeed, no solution can implement all together data integrity, redundancy and confidentiality. The most complete works are functionally

so complex that they are not applicable when the only aim is data encryption.

To be usable, storage solution should allow adapting the nature of the security supported at a logical volume layer intended to receive data and to the needs of software using these data. Thus, integrity checking may be implemented if the storage volume is adapted to externalized data backups, while encryption solutions with keyword search will be preferred for volumes adapted to SaaS applications.

This adaptation requires storage virtualization and the definition of different qualities of service for virtual storage volumes which are thus managed. Storage virtualization middleware can then, depending on the selected quality of service, set the appropriate security strategy and thus, underlying security algorithms to use.

STORAGE VIRTUALIZATION APPLIED TO CLOUD COMPUTING

Virtualization is fundamental in cloud computing. It enables a seamless access to heterogeneous and distributed resources and has already solved computing resource management issues.

Virtualization must help to create a single virtual storage component from a set of independent and distributed physical resources within the cloud. This solution can offer a more efficient use of storage resources across the associated services. However, constraints abound: data security, performance improvement...

ViSaGe is a data management middleware developed within the IRIT laboratory. It allows virtualizing heterogeneous and distributed storage resources, with uniform and seamless access. ViSaGe aligns user needs and system availabilities through qualities of service defined on virtual volumes. Originally developed for grids, it has been adapted to cloud computing specific constraints.

Cloud computing has some specificities. First, the hierarchical structure is currently less complex than usual. Indeed, in the grids, resources usually belong to disjointed administrative domains. This involves developing front-end components responsible for inter-site communication and implementing encryption procedures on communications and storage to ensure grid sealing to the external environment. This protection involves both inter-site communication through open networks (Internet type) and communication and storage within a site (handled information within the grid on a site that must not be visible to their users with no access to the grid). Although the InterCloud concept is now appearing (which would tend hierarchically to what is already known in the grid), it remains strictly theoretical.

However, users do not trust cloud managers while they usually trust grid managers. Regarding data security protection, requirements are thus higher for other users of the infrastructure in general, and administrators in particular.

We will first present ViSaGe software architecture. Then, we will see how the initial tests validate the architecture of the solution chosen.

Storage Organization within Visage

Visage is a middleware to install on linux servers. It enables the aggregation of storage resources distributed on the different nodes to provide a seamless access to virtualized storage spaces and ensure defined qualities of service.

For ViSaGe, the higher abstraction layer is the virtual space. A virtual space is a set of virtual storage resources. For the cloud storage provider, a virtual space can, for example, correspond to a particular user.

In each virtual space, several logical volumes can be created. These logical volumes will allow data reading and writing through a specific filesystem (VisageFS). Logical volumes, once created, must be formatted before being installed on different nodes intending to use them.

To ensure data persistence, logical volumes are based on physical storage resources shared at each node. Thus, the storage provider can, at each node of its different clusters, specify the percentage of drive space to be granted for each logical volume of each virtual space. The definition of physical resources forming a logical volume by the cloud storage provider can integrate the nature of the underlying drives (speed, wear) according to user requirements.

Thus, the use of a logical volume requires the following steps:

1. Creation of a virtual space;
2. Creation of a logical volume in this virtual space;
3. Division of storage resources and assignment to the logical volume;
4. Formatting of the logical volume;
5. Installation of the filesystem VisageFS on the nodes that must read and/or write in the logical volume.

In ViSaGe, there is an additional layer in the storage hierarchy, hidden from the user: the containers. The filesystem uses these containers to implement particular qualities of service. These qualities of service allow implementing the security policies mentioned above. A logical volume is thus composed of several containers, each with specific characteristics according to storage requests conducted by the filesystem.

Quality of service definition is thus done through the filesystem using extended attributes. These attributes, applied to a folder or a file, will be used to determine the container adapted to store data.

Note that a POSIX semantic, using conventional open/read/write/close primitives, is used to access the filesystem. The choice of this semantic ensures that most written applications do not require the execution of rewriting/recompiling on our platform.

This storage structure is supported by the different components of Visage that must be deployed on the nodes involved in the infrastructure. It includes both nodes sharing physical storage resources and nodes using logical virtual volumes to read and write data. There are five components:

- **Vcom:** communication service controlling messages and data transfers;
- **Vrt:** virtualization service achieving the logical aggregations of physical storage resources;
- **VisageFS:** specific filesystem for accessing logical volumes;
- **Vccc:** extensible Concurrency and Consistency Controller;
- **Admon:** administration and monitoring service controlling and managing the whole.

All ViSaGe software component functionalities are described below.

Communication Service (Vcom)

ViSaGe communication service is called "ViSaGe communication" and has Vcom for acronym. It is a communication abstraction layer. This is a safe, efficient and adaptable way to communicate between ViSaGe components without being concerned by underlying infrastructure details. Vcom allows message exchange between two ViSaGe components located on the same node or on remote nodes.

Vcom provides two types of communication: asynchronous (message sent through the mailbox) or synchronous (message sending implemented through a communication tunnel).

To enable asynchronous exchanges, each ViSaGe component has a mailbox. This mailbox, used to receive messages, indirectly represents the component. It should be noted that mailbox use is exclusively dedicated for message exchange controlling, and is never used for transferring data between nodes.

For data transfer, a synchronous communication is necessary and therefore, communication

tunnels must be used. These tunnels provide a connected communication through an API-like read/write.

Various performance, communication or security needs can be implemented using Vcom. For example, communications are typically encrypted by SSL, but this function can be disabled if not useful. In addition, different transfer qualities can be added. For example, it is thus possible to choose between UDP and TCP, or use a low-grade interface if data transfers are only done on a set with a broadband network (such as Myrinet for example).

In conclusion, Vcom service design offers a flexible API communication for transferring data between ViSaGe components or sending control messages.

Storage Virtualization Resources (Vrt)

A storage resource can be a raw partition, formatted partition with a local file system, FTP server, storage array... These heterogeneity and dispersion are two major cloud infrastructure characteristics, and the challenge of such a system is to manage effectively storage and resource accesses. These storage resources will be designated by the cloud manager as having to be integrated in the infrastructure, so the Vrt will be integrated in the virtual space representing the ViSaGe storage pool.

The Vrt is distributed on storage and compute nodes. Following the logical aggregation of storage resources, it allows adding virtual storage spaces to VisageFS filesystem. These virtual spaces are divided into logical volumes that are then split into placement objects. These components are the abstraction of the physical data placement on storage resources. A placement object is associated with data placement policy suited to the information semantic stored there. For example, according to data access needs, the policy will favor storage resources with a large bandwidth network/drive, some degree of replication or a consistency management protocol adapted to read/write rates and to the level of data sharing between readers and writers. A consistency management protocol is then chosen within a protocol pool provided by ViSaGe component library called Vccc: "ViSaGe Concurrency and Consistency Controller".

Data related to data semantic and effective placement on storage resources are progressively collected during data exploitation and processing. This information is transmitted to the Vrt to implement an appropriate placement policy on the placement object. During data exploitation, if the placement policy chosen can no longer meet the quality of service recommended by the application, the Admon service will inform the Vrt to start actions to adapt the placement policy. These actions can be, for example, consistency protocol change, new replica creation...

Filesystem (VisageFS)

VisageFS provides a file-like interface for data access to cloud users (both physical and application users). It provides basic traditional filesystem functionalities in a large-scale distributed environment. It is represented by a user module, installed with fuse15, allowing access to files through POSIX interface. A fuse library has been chosen to allow a fast integration to Linux virtual file system switch while developing VisageFS in user space. With this interface, a user can access the filesystem from a mounting point on his device. VisageFS uses the Vrt library to store distributed data on different nodes with some quality of service. This library (see next section) is based on ViSaGe Vccc component. This latter allows, among other, file metadata competition management to be ensured.

Concurrency and Consistency Controller in ViSaGe (Vccc)

In ViSaGe, concurrency access and redundant data consistency managements are ensured by the Vccc component. The use of a single component for these two tasks is not accidental; in fact, it has been shown the effectiveness of some consistency management protocols ensuring also concurrency access management.

Here, Vccc provides a set of concurrency and consistency management protocols. While various data access models can be encountered in existing applications, Vccc has been developed to withstand protocol adding through plugins. The administration and monitoring service Admon will help choosing between these different protocols.

Administration and Monitoring in ViSaGe (Admon)

In ViSaGe, Admon is the administration and monitoring component. It owns an administration module and a monitoring module and each module has three components.

The monitoring module collects relevant information on different nodes. This information is used to do statistics on the use of system resources (CPU, drive, networks) and accesses to the various data stored by ViSaGe. It is thereby possible to inform the Vrt for adapting the positioning policy.

The administration module administrates ViSaGe components installed on the different nodes. For example, a webmaster can list a new computing and storage data resource that will therefore be used for storage virtualization. ViSaGe administration tasks are accessible by this module that disseminates actions towards other ViSaGe components distributed within the infrastructure.

Admon architecture allows both disseminating collected data and, when necessary, intervening to improve storage management and data access based on these collected information. Vcom ensures communications between administration and monitoring components. A web service has been developed to allow communication between a physical user and ViSaGe. This service is only a communication interface including virtualization management and node status virtualization methods.

Interaction between ViSaGe Components

The various applications using ViSaGe will conduct reading and writing operations. These operations will be processed by VisageFS that will contact the Vrt for accessing the corresponding storage components, for example, the searched files. Through the Vccc library, VisageFS will also manage access concurrency. In turn, the Vrt is responsible for virtualization; therefore it will handle the aggregation of physical storage resources distributed on different nodes in a single logical storage resource, provided to VisageFS. Virtualization lifecycle, as resource sharing, management of various positioning and data migration policies rely on Admon, the administration and monitoring component of ViSaGe. Admon is central in ViSaGe and used by all the other components and infrastructure manager. It aims to exploit data collected by its monitoring module to help improving data access performances through the administration module.

Data Security Implementation within Visage Middleware

This software architecture is well suited to implement security in cloud storage. We are going to review the three main issues in cloud storage security and show how they are handled with a storage virtualization middleware.

Implementation of Data Availability

As explained in section 2, data availability is implemented by the redundant storage of data on appropriate nodes. Thus, when a write operation is performed, our middleware must ensure:

- Data splitting into blocks;
- Error code computation and aggregation if appropriate;

- Blocks placement on nodes using an adequate policy.

Data writes in ViSaGe are done seamlessly using VisageFS, since the latter offers a POSIX like API. VisageFS then transfers the data to the virtualizer. The splitting into blocks is done at this stage, as well as the computation and aggregation of error codes - if required by the selected quality of service defined on the logical volume in which the write is performed. According to the placement policy (which is also defined by the quality of service) the blocks are sent to the virtualizer of the selected nodes. These ones store the received blocks locally to their disks.

Similarly, when a read is performed, Visage must:

- Retrieve the required blocks on the nodes;
- Verify (and correct if necessary) the blocks retrieved;
- Reconstruct the data and send it back to the user.

The read operation is performed seamlessly by using VisageFS. The request is given by VisageFS to the local virtualizer. The latter sends requests to the virtualizer on the nodes where the blocks are stored. Each of them replies to the local virtualizer. When all (no redundancy) or enough (redundancy storage) response blocks are received, and after error check if appropriate, the original data is reconstructed and given back to VisageFS.

We have done some experimentation with replication in ViSaGe, which validated the relevance of our solution to address this issue. However, it must be extended to improve the guarantee of data availability. Thus, data distribution within servers belonging to different clusters in different racks is a first improvement to be made (Ford, 2010). This feature can be supported by the virtualizer, based upon information from the administration and monitoring tool. This tool can thus list burst failures and define node groups involved in the formation of container physical storage support according to overlaps on the simultaneity of node unavailability.

Implementation of Data Integrity

The implementation of data integrity check is also fairly simple on such a software infrastructure. To check data integrity, a special shell command must be invoked which performs an IOCTL call to VisageFS. When invoking this command on a file, the filesystem uses the local virtualizer services to proceed to the required checks. The local virtualizer calls the virtualizers on the nodes involved on the file storage (according to the placement policy defined), each of them providing the proof of storage and integrity. The local virtualizer synthetize these proofs and send the result back to the user through the filesystem.

To validate file integrity, the virtualizer can use any method presented above: either Proofs of Data Possession or Proofs of Retrievalibity algorithms can be implemented at the virtualizer level and distributed among nodes.

Data Security and Virtualization

Fragmentation-redundancy-dissemination techniques (Fabre, 1994) have recently been updated (Ciriani, 2011) for highly structured data. The use of a virtualizer layer makes it possible to implement it for weakly structured data, stored through a filesystem.

To implement data security this way, the user first creates a key (if he does not yet has one) and stores it on his device local folder. This key, which must remain confidential, will be used for encryption/decryption. It can be a symmetric key because it needs not to be disclosed.

The user creates a logical volume and formats it and then, associates an extended « FRS »-like attribute to a folder that he associates with the key created. The cloud manager cannot reach this key since it is located on a local volume of the user

device. The filesystem creates then a new container with the physical storage resources shared within this logical volume.

During a write operation, the virtualizer present on the user device will receive the data to write from ViSaGe filesystem. It will fragment these data into blocks and send the encoded blocks to the dedicated virtualizers for which storage resources have been shared for the affected storage volume. The sequence in which blocks are sent to the storage nodes may depend on the key. Thus, the distribution of encoded information on the different nodes is non-deterministic.

During a reading operation, the local virtualizer receives the query from VisageFS. It then contacts virtualizers involved in the storage for this logical volume, recovers data blocks, decrypts them with the local key, retraces the information and, finally, sends it to the user.

When the key is locally stored within the user device, data security is maintained. This method is well suited to solve cloud storage externalization issue: seamless user access and guaranteed data security.

These encryption mechanisms can be implemented to manage a virtualized infrastructure. Then, there is no guarantee that the data will not be accessible by the cloud manager and the user must thus anticipate by encrypting his data on virtual drives. However, for the provider, this solution allows managing easily and seamlessly all his storage resources.

The implementation of a Saas-like solution on a virtualized storage infrastructure has all the advantages of storage virtualization (transparency of both accesses and implementation for the provider) and allows the easy implementation of search mechanisms. Indeed, like what is offered to check data integrity, the use of an IOCTL command with the filesystem allows communicating the data required to proceed to the searches on encrypted contents with the virtualizer. Thus, the local user can invoke a search command on the encrypted documents stored in ViSaGe. This command induces an IOCTL call with keys to use as parameter, as seen previously. Then, the local virtualizer recovers these information and transfers them to the different nodes involved by data physical storage for which performing the search. Search processes can thus, on each node impacted by the storage, proceeds to the calculation of the necessary algorithms with the required information.

In all cases, the virtualization component is the cornerstone of the implementation of security policies within the storage virtualization architecture for cloud computing.

CONCLUSION

In this chapter, we presented the issue of data security for cloud computing. We saw that this security relies on three axes: data availability, integrity and privacy. This concept of security, multi facet by nature, is easy to implement in the context of storage virtualization. The definition of quality of service within the filesystem allows adapting subtly the type of security process to use according to storage containers.

The availability allows guaranteeing that data will be provided when it will be asked by the user. Information redundancy techniques allow ensuring, with a sufficient probability, that a default from one or more nodes will not interfere with the supply of this service. With the information provided by monitoring tools, the virtualizer can evaluate the most appropriate physical resources to ensure data persistence.

Data integrity allows ensuring that the storage provider still owns the assigned data and that no alteration – voluntary or not – damaged them or rendered them definitively unreachable. Again, the virtualizer can implement the controls necessary to ensure the user that all his data are really there with a guarantee proportional to the load generated.

Finally, privacy is necessary to protect sensitive data against the other users of the provider, but also against the provider himself. We can rely on the virtualizer services to encrypt data. This component can also be requested to implement the search mechanisms on encrypted data.

Whatever the axis considered, storage virtualization offers the abstraction level required for implementing the various security policies adapted to each case.

REFERENCES

Ateniese, G., Burns, R., Curtmola, R., Herring, J., Kissner, L., Peterson, Z., & Song, D. (2007). Provable data possession at untrusted stores. *CCS'07, 14th ACM Conference on Computer and Communication Security*, (pp. 598-609).

Ateniese, G., Di Pietro, R., Mancini, L., & Tsudik, G. (2008). Scalable and efficient provable data possession. *SecureComm, 2008*, 1–10. doi:10.1145/1460877.1460889

Ateniese, G., Fu, K., Green, M., & Hohenberger, S. (2006). Improved proxy re-encryption schemes with applications to secure distributed storage. *ACM Transactions on Information and System Security, 9*(1), 1–30. doi:10.1145/1127345.1127346

Bellare, M., & Rogaway, P. (1994). Optimal asymmetric encryption – How to encrypt with RSA. *Advances in Cryptology (Eurocrypt'94). Lecture Notes in Computer Science, 950*, 92–111. doi:10.1007/BFb0053428

Boneh, D., Di Crescenzo, G., Ostrovsky, R., & Persiano, G. (2004). *Public key encryption with keyword search*. Eurocrypt 2004.

Chor, B., Kushilevitz, E., Goldreich, O., & Sudan, M. (1998). Private information retrieval. *Journal of the ACM, 45*(6), 965–981. doi:10.1145/293347.293350

Ciriani, V., De Capitani, S., Foresti, S., Jajodia, S., Paraboschi, S., & Samarati, P. (2011). Combining fragmentation and encryption to protect privacy in data storage. *ACM Transactions on Information and System Security, 13*(3), 1–33. doi:10.1145/1805974.1805978

Curtmola, R., Khan, O., & Burns, R. (2008). Robust remote data checking. *4th ACM Workshop on Storage Security and Survivability*, (pp. 63-68).

Daemen, J., & Rijmen, V. (2000). The block cipher RIJNDAEL. *(Cardis '98). Lecture Notes in Computer Science, 1820*, 247–256. doi:10.1007/10721064_26

ElGamal, T. (1985). A public key cryptosystem and a signature scheme based on discrete logarithms. *IEEE Transactions on Information Theory, 31*(4), 469–472. doi:10.1109/TIT.1985.1057074

Erway, C., Küpçü, A., Papamanthou, C., & Tamassia, R. (2009). Dynamic provable data possession. *CCS'09, 16th ACM Conference on Computer and Communication Security*, (pp. 213-222).

Fabre, J.-C., Deswarte, Y., & Randell, B. (1994). Designing secure and reliable applications using fragmentation-redundancy-scattering: An object-oriented approach. *(EDCC-1: 1st European Dependable Computing Conference) Lecture Notes in Computer Science, vol. 852*, (pp. 21-38).

Ford, D., Labelle, F., Popovici, F. I., Stokely, M., Truong, V.-A., & Barroso, L. … Quinlan, S. (2010). Availability in globally distributed storage systems. *9th USENIX Symposium on Operating Systems Designs and Implementation*, (pp. 61-74).

Ganger, G. R., Khosla, P. K., Bakkaloglu, M., Bigrigg, M. W., Goodson, G. R., & Oguz, S. … Wylie, J. J., (2001). Survivable storage systems. *2001 DARPA Information Survivability Conference and Exposition*, Vol. 2 (pp. 184-195).

Golle, P., Staddon, J., & Waters, B. (2004). Secure conjunctive keyword search over encrypted data. *Applied Cryptography and Network Security Conference (ACNS'04)*, (pp. 31-45).

Ireland, K., & Rosen, M. (1990). *A classical introduction to modern number theory* (2nd ed.). New York, NY: Springer-Verlag.

Juels, A., & Kaliski, B. S., Jr. (2007). PORs: Proofs of retrievability for large files. *CCS'07, 14th ACM Conference on Computer and Communication Security*, (pp. 584-597)

Kallahalla, M., Riedel, E., Swaminathan, R., Wang, Q., & Fu, K. (2003). Plutus: Scalable secure file sharing on untrusted storage. *FAST '03 Proceedings of the 2nd USENIX Conference on File and Storage Technologies*, (pp. 29-42).

Kamara, S., & Lauter, K. (2010). Cryptographic cloud storage. *FC'10 Proceedings of the 14th International Conference on Financial Cryptography and Data Security*, (pp. 136-149).

Kermarrec, A.-M., Le Merrer, E., Straub, G., & Van Kempen, A. (2010). Availability-based methods for distributed storage systems. *HAL-Inria Open Archive*. Retrieved from http://hal.inria.fr/hal-00521034/en

Kher, V., & Kim, Y. (2005). Securing distributed storage: Challenges, techniques, and systems. *StorageSS '05 Proceedings of the 2005 ACM Workshop on Storage Security and Survivability*, (pp. 9-25).

Kushilevitz, E., & Ostrovsky, R. (1997). Replication is not needed: Single database, computationally-private information retrieval. *38th Annual Symposium on Foundation of Computer Science*, (pp. 364-373).

Lidl, R., & Niederreiter, H. (1984). *Finite fields*. Cambridge, UK: Cambridge University Press.

Narayan, S., & Chandy, J. A. (2007). Parity redundancy in a clustered storage system. *SNAPI '07 Proceedings of the Fourth International Workshop on Storage Network Architecture and Parallel I/Os*, (pp.17-24).

No, J. (2009). Data consistency protocol for distributed file systems. *IDAACS 2009, IEEE International Workshop on Intelligent Data Acquisition and Advanced Computing Systems: Technology and Applications, 2009*, (pp. 253-258).

Ristenpart, T., Tromer, E., Shacham, H., & Savage, S. (2009). Hey, you, get off of my cloud: Exploring information leakage in third-party compute clouds. *CCS '09, 16th ACM Conference on Computer and Communication Security*, (pp. 199-212)

Rivest, R., Shamir, A., & Adleman, L. (1978). A method for obtaining digital signatures and public-key cryptosystems. *Communications of the ACM, 21*(2), 120–126. doi:10.1145/359340.359342

Shacham, H., & Waters, B. (2008). Compact proofs of retrievability. *ASIACRYPT, 08*, 90–107.

Sobe, P., & Peter, K. (2006). Comparison of redundancy schemes for distributed storage systems. *5th IEEE International Symposium on Network Computing and Applications*, (pp. 196-203).

Song, D., Wagner, D., & Perrig, A. (2000). Practical techniques for searches on encrypted data. *IEEE Symposium on Security and Privacy 2000*, (pp. 44-55).

Tan, C., Liu, Q., & Wu, J. (2011). *Secure locking for untrusted clouds*. 4th IEEE International Conference on Cloud Computing (CLOUD 2011).

Tang, Y., Lee, P., Lui, J., & Perlman, R. (2010). *FADE: Secure overlay cloud storage with file assured deletion*. Securecomm 2010.

Wylie, J. J., Bigrigg, M. W., Strunk, J. D., Ganger, G. R., Kilite, H., & Khosla, P. K. (2000). Survivable information storage systems. *IEEE Computer, 33*(8), 61–68. doi:10.1109/2.863969

ADDITIONAL READING

Bowers, K., Juels, A., & Oprea, A. (2009). HAIL: A high-availability and integrity layer for cloud storage. *(CCS '09) 16th ACM Conference on Computer and Communications Security*, (pp. 187-198).

Chandy, J. (2004). *Parity redundancy strategies in a large scale distributed storage system*. 21st IEEE Conference on Mass Storage Systems and Technologies.

Chen, Y., & Sion, R. (2010). On securing untrusted clouds with cryptography. *9th Annual ACM Workshop on Privacy in the Electronic Society*, (pp. 109-114).

Cheng, G., & Ohoussou, A. (2010). Sealed storage for trusted cloud computing. *(ICCDA), 2010 International Conference on Computer Design and Applications*, (pp. 335-339).

Chow, R., Golle, P., Jakobsson, M., Shi, E., Staddon, J., Masuoka, R., & Molina, J. (2009). Controlling data in the cloud: Outsourcing computation without outsourcing control. *(CCSW '09) 2009 ACM Workshop on Cloud Computing Security*, (pp. 85-90).

Deswarte, Y., Quisquater, J.-J., & Saïdane, A. (2003). Remote integrity checking — How to trust files stored on untrusted servers. *(IICIS 2003) 6th IFIP Working Conference on Integrity and Internal Control in Information Systems*, (pp. 1-11).

Feng, J., Chen, Y., Ku, W.-S., & Su, Z. (2010). *D-DOG: Securing sensitive data in distributed storage space by data division and out-of-order keystream generation*. 2010 IEEE International Conference on Communications - Communication and Information System Security Symposium (ICC'10 CISS).

Fontaine, C., & Galand, F. (2007). A survey of homomorphic encryption for nonspecialists. *EURASIP Journal on Information Security Archive, January 2007.*

Gao, X., Ma, Y., Pierce, M., Lowe, M., & Fox, G. (2010). Building a distributed block storage system for cloud infrastructure. *(CloudCom) Second IEEE International Conference on Cloud Computing Technology and Science*, (pp. 312-318).

Hu, J., & Klein, A. (2009). A benchmark of transparent data encryption for migration of Web applications in the cloud. *(DASC'09) 2009 Eighth IEEE International Conference on Dependable, Autonomic and Secure Computing*, (pp. 735-740).

Lan, T., Lee, R., & Chiang, M. (2010). *Secure and reliable distributed storage without secret keys.* Technical report. Retrieved from http://www.seas.gwu.edu/~tlan/paper/storage_complete_v3.pdf

Litwin, W., & Schwarz, T. (2004). Algebraic signatures for scalable distributed data structures. *(ICDE '04) 20th International Conference on Data Engineering*, (pp. 412-423).

Pletka, R., & Cachin, C. (2007). Cryptographic security for a high-performance distributed file system. *MSST '07 Proceedings of the 24th IEEE Conference on Mass Storage Systems and Technologies*, (pp. 227-232).

Rabin, M. (1989). Efficient dispersal of information for security, load balancing, and fault tolerance. *Journal of the ACM, 36*(2), 335–358. doi:10.1145/62044.62050

Schwarz, T., & Miller, E. (2006). *Store, forget, and check: Using algebraic signatures to check remotely administered storage.* (ICDCS '06) 26th IEEE International Conference on Distributed Computing Systems.

Sebé, F., Domingo-Ferrer, J., Martinez-Ballasté, A., Deswarte, Y., & Quiquater, J.-J. (2008). Efficient remote data possession checking in critical information infrastructures. *IEEE Transactions on Knowledge and Data Engineering, 20*(8), 1034–1038. doi:10.1109/TKDE.2007.190647

Shaer, A., Cachin, C., Cidon, A., Keidar, I., Michalevsky, Y., & Shaket, D. (2010). Venus: Verification for untrusted cloud storage. *(CCSW '10) 2010 ACM Workshop on Cloud Computing Security Workshop*, (pp. 19-30).

Shamir, A. (1979). How to share a secret. *Communications of the ACM, 22*(11), 612–613. doi:10.1145/359168.359176

Soa, C., Sutton, B., & Huang, H. (2010). PicFS: The privacy-enhancing image-based collaborative file system. *16th IEEE International Conference on Parallel and Distributed Systems*, (pp. 99-106).

Subbiah, A., & Blough, D. (2005). An approach for fault tolerant and secure data storage in collaborative work environments. *(StorageSS '05) 2005 ACM Workshop on Storage Security and Survivability*, (pp. 84-93).

Wang, C., Wang, Q., Ren, K., Cao, N., & Lou, W. (2011). Towards secure and dependable storage services in cloud computing. *IEEE Transactions on Services Computing, 5*(2).

Wang, Q., Wang, C., Ren, K., Lou, W., & Li, J. (2011). Enabling public auditability and data dynamics for storage security in cloud computing. *IEEE Transactions on Parallel and Distributed Systems, 22*(5), 847–859. doi:10.1109/TPDS.2010.183

Wei, L., Zhu, H., Cao, Z., Jia, W., & Vasilakos, A. (2010). SecCloud: Bridging secure storage and computation in cloud. *(ICDCSW'10), 30th IEEE International Conference on Distributed Computing Systems Workshops*, (pp. 52-61).

KEY TERMS AND DEFINITIONS

Data Availability: Guarantee that data requests (both read and write) will be satisfied.

Data Confidentiality: Guarantee of the limitation of accesses and disclosure to authorized people only.

Data Integrity: Guarantee that data have not been changed inappropriately.

Distributed Storage System: Storage system distributed among numerous nodes (usually, tens, hundreds or even thousands nodes). A special access mechanism is needed to access data stored in a distributed storage system, such as storage virtualization.

Storage as a Service (StaaS): Simple file storage service. The user buy a storage space hosted and managed by a third party (the provider).

Storage Virtualization: Creation of a virtual storage device using numerous physical storage devices. The virtual device is seen as a physical one by the users.

Chapter 10

Policy Management in Cloud:
Challenges and Approaches

Hassan Takabi
University of Pittsburgh, USA

James B. D. Joshi
University of Pittsburgh, USA

ABSTRACT

Cloud computing paradigm is still an evolving paradigm but has recently gained tremendous momentum due to its potential for significant cost reduction and increased operating efficiencies in computing. However, its unique aspects exacerbate security and privacy challenges that pose as the key roadblock to its fast adoption. Cloud computing has already become very popular, and practitioners need to provide security mechanisms to ensure its secure adoption. In this chapter, the authors discuss access control systems and policy management in cloud computing environments. The cloud computing environments may not allow use of a single access control system, single policy language, or single management tool for the various cloud services that it offers. Currently, users must use diverse access control solutions available for each cloud service provider to secure data. Access control policies may be composed in incompatible ways because of diverse policy languages that are maintained separately at every cloud provider. Heterogeneity and distribution of these policies pose problems in managing access policy rules for a cloud environment. In this chapter, the authors discuss challenges of policy management and introduce a cloud based policy management framework that is designed to give users a unified control point for managing access policies to control access to their resources no matter where they are stored.

INTRODUCTION

Cloud computing has recently generated intensive interest within computing research communities. It essentially tries to consolidate the economic utility model with the evolutionary development

of many existing computing approaches and technologies such as distributed services, applications, information and infrastructure consisting of pools of computers, networks, information and storage resources (Cloud Security Alliance, 2011), Catteddu & Hogben, 2009). Cloud computing has shown tremendous potential to enhance collaboration, agility, scale, and availability (Takabi,

DOI: 10.4018/978-1-4666-2125-1.ch010

Joshi, & Ahn, 2010). Its definitions, attributes, characteristics, issues, underlying technologies, risks, and values have been evolving and change over time. Confusion still exists about how a cloud is different from existing models and how these differences might affect its adoption. Some see a cloud as a novel technical revolution while others consider it a natural evolution of technology, economy and culture (Takabi, Joshi, & Ahn, 2010).

So far, no single, agreed upon definition of cloud computing exists. The US National Institute of Standards and Technology (NIST) defines cloud as follows: "Cloud computing is a model for enabling ubiquitous, convenient, on-demand network access to a shared pool of configurable computing resources (e.g., networks, servers, storage, applications, and services) that can be rapidly provisioned and released with minimal management effort or service provider interaction. This cloud model promotes availability and is composed of five essential characteristics, three service models, and four deployment models." (Mell & Grance, 2011). The five key characteristics of cloud computing include on demand self-service, ubiquitous network access, location independent resource pooling, rapid elasticity, and measured service, all of which are geared toward using clouds seamlessly and transparently (Mell & Grance, 2011). The three key cloud delivery models are software as a service (SaaS), platform as a service (PaaS), and infrastructure as a service (IaaS) (Mell & Grance, 2011).

In IaaS, the cloud provider provides a set of virtualized infrastructural components such as virtual machines and storage on which the customers can build and run applications. The most basic component is a virtual machine (VM) and the virtual operating system (OS) where the application will eventually reside. Issues such as trusting the virtual machine image, hardening hosts, and securing inter-host communication are critical areas in IaaS. PaaS enables the programming environments to access and utilize the additional application building blocks. Such programming environments have a visible impact on the application architecture. One such impact would be that of the constraints on what services the application can request from an OS. For example, a PaaS environment may limit access to well-defined parts of the file system, thus requiring a fine-grained authorization service. In SaaS, the cloud providers enable and provide application software enabled as on-demand-services. As clients acquire and use software components from different providers, securely composing them and ensuring that information handled by these composed services are well protected become crucial issues.

Various cloud deployment models include public cloud, private cloud, community cloud, and hybrid cloud composed of multiple clouds (Mell & Grance, 2011). A public cloud refers to an external or publicly available cloud environment that is accessible to multiple tenants, while a private cloud is typically a tailored environment with dedicated virtualized resources for a particular organization. Similarly, community cloud is tailored for a particular group of customers.

As more and more consumers start using cloud services, Service Level Agreement (SLA) is becoming a key aspect of immigrating to the cloud. The SLA is used to describe the relationship between cloud providers and consumers and is fundamental of consumers' trust in cloud service providers. An SLA should clearly address several factors like a list of services the provider delivers along with a specific definition of these services, the responsibilities of both parties, a set of metrics to ensure the provider is delivering the services as stated, an auditing mechanism to monitor the quality of services, business continuity and disaster recovery plan, location of data, seizure of data, how to address failures of the provider and disputes between the provider and consumer, the available options when the terms of the SLA are not met, system redundancy and maintenance, jurisdiction, and how the SLA term can be modified over time. Some of the other requirements that need to be taken in account in SLAs are security, privacy, data encryption, transparency, data retention and deletion, hardware erasure and destruction, monitoring, auditing, metrics used for monitoring and auditing, regulatory compliance, and machine-readable SLAs.

The complex and dynamic nature of the cloud requires a sophisticated approach to managing SLAs. A continuous monitoring of quality of service (QoS) attributes and measuring the performance of the service is necessary. The service level management gathers the performance information and ensures that terms of the SLA are being met. The current market offers two types of SLAs: Off-the-shelf non-negotiable SLAs and negotiated SLAs for consumer's specific requirements. A non-negotiable SLA is far less expensive than a negotiated one but is not acceptable for consumers with mission-critical data and applications. However, most public cloud service providers do not offer negotiated SLAs and if the consumers' needs aren't met, they can either receive a credit towards next month's bill or stop using the service.

Moreover, cloud computing increases legal risks and issues like liability, data protection, compliance, data portability, and copyright should be addressed when moving data to the cloud. There has been a lot of debate on the legal landscape of the cloud but many issues are not yet resolved. For example, it is not clear who has control over the data in cloud, what happens to the data when it's transferred across various jurisdictions, and which laws are applicable to the cloud.

In EU, the Data Protection Directive 95/46 is most relevant regulation to the cloud computing. It can be applied to cloud service providers where they process personal data within the EU jurisdiction. Although the principles of this legal framework can be applied in the cloud computing environment, in practice, things are more complicated and there are a lot of challenges when trying to apply these principles. This is because

the data protections laws are outdated and are not able to deal with the legal problems raised by cloud computing environment. In USA, some of the existing regulations are applicable to cloud and perhaps the most controversial one is Patriot Act under which the government can demand access to consumers' data and the cloud service providers are bound to provide that data without consumers' consent. In general, EU regulations are more restrictive than regulations of other countries like USA. However, it is not clear how different regulations from various jurisdictions (EU and USA for example) are applied to the data stored and processed in the cloud and whether they are compatible. Perhaps, we need some kind of international legislation to deal with this issue.

Nevertheless cloud computing is being pursued as a very important paradigm and its architectural features allow users to achieve better operating costs and be very agile by facilitating fast acquisition of services and infrastructural resources as and when needed. However, these unique features also give rise to various security and privacy concerns (Takabi, Joshi & Ahn, 2010). Without appropriate security and privacy solutions designed for clouds this potentially revolutionizing computing paradigm could become a huge failure. Several surveys of potential cloud adopters indicate that security and privacy is a number one concern hindering its adoption (Catteddu & Hogben, 2009; Bruening & Treacy, 2009). However, cloud computing is here to stay because of its potential benefits and hence, understanding the security and privacy risks and developing effective solutions are critical to the success of this new computing paradigm (Takabi, Joshi & Ahn, 2010).

In this chapter, we focus on access control and policy management. The cloud environment does not allow use of a single authorization mechanism, single policy language or single management tool for various cloud service providers. Each cloud service provider has its own access control solution. Authorization component is often tightly bound to cloud service provider. This approach is not user-centric and hence, can be a significant bottleneck to its widespread adoption. The definition of access control policies clearly is the business of the organization/users deploying the cloud service. However, not only the cloud service providers themselves are dictating how these policies should be defined but also each of them does it in its own way. An ideal access control scheme must be able to work with all types of content regardless of where they are stored. Users should be able to manage policies to govern access to their information and resources from a central location.

Currently, users must use different access control mechanisms available for each cloud service provider to secure their data and control its dissemination. Access control policies to protect users' resources may be specified in incompatible policy languages and maintained separately at every cloud service provider (Takabi, Joshi & Ahn, 2010). When such mechanisms are used on a daily basis, they add considerable overhead. This may frustrate users and make them feel that they have given up all control of where their data ends up and how it is used. The challenge here is to design an integrated access control framework that can be used across services from different providers. Security solutions delivered as cloud-based services will have a dramatic impact on the industry. Cloud computing will enable security controls and functions to be delivered in new ways and by new types of service providers. It will also enable customers to use security technologies and techniques that are not otherwise cost-effective. Enterprises that use cloud-based security services to reduce the cost of security controls and address the new security challenges that cloud based computing will bring are most likely to prosper.

In this chapter, we describe a cloud based policy management framework that puts users in full control of their resources which may be scattered across multiple cloud service provid-

ers. It is designed to give cloud users a unified control point for specifying authorization policies, no matter where all the data is stored and distributed on the cloud. It facilitates the ability of users to manage access policies using a centralized policy manager which provides usable interfaces for specifying access policies and exporting them to the cloud service providers on behalf of the user.

BACKGROUND

In this section, we briefly discuss unique features of cloud computing and their security and privacy implications. We also indicate most important security and privacy challenges in cloud computing environment and propose some approaches to deal with these challenges.

Cloud Features and Security and Privacy Challenges

The architectural features of the cloud allow users to achieve better operating costs and be very agile by facilitating fast acquisition of services and infrastructural resources as and when needed. However, these unique features also give rise to various security concerns. Table 1 summarizes these unique features with corresponding security implications; more detailed information can be found in (Takabi, Joshi & Ahn, 2010).

Cloud computing environments can be considered as an instance of the multi-domain environment where each domain has its own security, privacy and trust requirements and potentially employ various mechanisms. The existing research on multi-domain policy integration and the secure service composition can be leveraged to build a comprehensive policy based management framework in the cloud computing environments (Takabi, Joshi & Ahn, 2010). In Table 2, we list the key security and privacy challenges that cloud computing raises.

Table 1. Security and privacy implications

Feature	Security Implication
Outsourcing	Users may lose control of their data. Appropriate mechanisms needed to prevent cloud providers from using customers' data in a way that has not been agreed upon in the past.
Extensibility	There is a tradeoff between extensibility and security responsibility for customers in different delivery models.
Multi-tenancy	Issues like access policies, application deployment, and data access and protection should be taken into account to provide a secure multi-tenant environment.
Service Level Agreement	The main goal is to build a new layer to create a negotiation mechanism for the contract between providers and consumers of services as well as the monitoring of its fulfillment at run-time. Also, ensuring that cloud providers and clients comply with established SLAs.
Virtualization	There needs to be mechanisms to ensure strong isolation, mediated sharing and communications between virtual machines. This could be done using a flexible access control system to enforce access policies that govern the control and sharing capabilities of VMs within a cloud host.
Heterogeneity	Different cloud providers may have different approaches to provide security and privacy mechanisms, thus generating integration challenges.
Compliance & Legal Issues	Cloud computing raises legal issues like liability, data protection, compliance, and data portability. There needs to be mechanisms to ensure that cloud providers and clients comply with existing regulatory requirements.

POLICY MANAGEMENT IN CLOUD

In this section, we discuss policy management in cloud. First, we show how policy management systems in the cloud are heterogeneous using an example. Then, we describe the problem of policy management and its requirements in cloud computing environment. Finally, we present a cloud based policy management framework.

Use Case Scenario

In this section, we present a use case scenario to show heterogeneity of policy management systems and discuss how individual users and organizations that use cloud services can benefit from the policy management framework we propose.

Alice is a PhD student who uses multiple cloud services from different service providers for various purposes. She is working on a research project and wants to have access to the project files from anywhere. Sometimes she works at her office using her PC and other times she works at home or a coffee shop and uses her laptop. For synchronizing the project files, she uses *Dropbox*, a file hosting service which uses cloud computing to enable

users to store and share files and folders with others across the Internet using file synchronization (http://www.dropbox.com). Sometimes she needs to share some of the project files she stores at *Dropbox* with her colleagues or her advisor.

She has accounts in *Facebook*, a social networking site that allows users to create a personal profile, add other users as friends and share information, to communicate with her friends and family (http://www.facebook.com). She has also a professional account in *LinkedIn*, a business-oriented social networking site with the purpose of maintaining a list of contact details of people users know and trust in business, to be in touch with professionals in her field (http://www.linkedin.com).

Alice may also have other documents and spreadsheets that include important content like financial data and she uses *Google Docs*, a service to create and share various types of files online and access them from anywhere (http://docs.google.com). Moreover, she stores some of her older files at *Amazon S3*, an online storage service that provides unlimited storage through a simple web services interface (http://aws.amazon.com/s3). She occasionally shares some of these files

Table 2. Security and privacy challenges

Challenge	Issues raised
Authentication and Identity Management	• Interoperability issues resulting from using different identity tokens and different identity negotiation protocols. • Privacy concerns related to protection of private and sensitive information associated with users and processes • The effect of multi tenancy on the privacy of identity information
Access control	• Domains' diverse access requirements • enough flexibility to capture dynamic, context or attribute/credential based access requirements • integrate privacy protection requirements derived from complex rules • generic access control interfaces for proper interoperability, which demands for a policy neutral access control specification and enforcement framework
Policy Integration	• Issues such as semantic heterogeneity, secure interoperability, and policy evolution management • policy engineering mechanisms are needed to integrate access policies of different cloud service providers and define global access policies to accommodate all collaborators' requirements • semantic conflicts and/or inconsistencies among their policies
Trust Management	• very dynamic/transient and intensive interactions • Capture a generic set of parameters required for establishing trust and to manage evolving trust and interaction/sharing requirements. • support the establishment, negotiation and maintenance of trust to adaptively support policy integration
Service Management	• the traditional WSDL cannot fully meet the requirements of cloud computing services description • issues like QoS, service price, and SLAs are critical in service search and service composition
Privacy and Data Protection	• By migrating workloads to a shared infrastructure, customers' private information is on increased risk of potential unauthorized access and exposure. • Provide a high degree of transparency into operations and privacy assurance. • Privacy protection mechanisms need to be potentially embedded in all the security solutions • Balancing between data provenance and privacy is a significant challenge in clouds where physical perimeter is abandoned
Organizational Security Management	• Shared governance can become a significant issue if not properly addressed • Dependence on the external entities can also raise fears about timely response to security incidents, and implementing systematic business continuity and disaster recovery plans. • newer risks introduced by a perimeter-less environment, possible data leakage within multi-tenant clouds, and resiliency issues such as local disasters and economic instability of the providers • Existing life cycle models, risk analysis and management processes, penetration testing and service attestation need to be critically re-evaluated to ensure that the potential benefits of clouds can be enjoyed by cloud clients. • Insider attack surface is significantly extended when outsourcing data and processes to clouds.
Compliance & Legal Issues	• Although some of the existing regulations can be applied to the cloud, the data protections laws are outdated and are not able to deal with all the legal problems raised in cloud landscape. • Many laws in different countries restrict the transfer of data out of the country. Mechanisms are needed to deal with these situations and ensure compliance with the regulation. • It is not clear what regulations are applicable when data is transferred across various jurisdictions in regional, national or international levels.

with family members. Furthermore, she uses *Mint*, an online personal finance service, to manage her financial and budget planning (http://www.mint.com). Sometimes she may want to share some of these files with a family member or a close friend.

Some of the above mentioned services are used for convenience and others for sharing and collaboration purposes. With the increasing amount of data that Alice puts online, managing access

control for her resources becomes difficult and time consuming. Each of these applications has its own access policy mechanism forcing users to specify separate access control policies for each service. However, with resources being scattered across multiple service providers, it is difficult to manage access to them. Alice needs to understand the service providers' policy mechanisms and specify access policies in their specific policy languages which are challenging tasks for her and most users like her. Moreover, introducing new access policy rules or modifying existing ones is problematic due to heterogeneity of these access policy mechanisms. Suppose Alice wants to modify an access policy rule to a resource or a set of resources, or a new colleague is added to her current project and she needs to share some resources with him. In order to do this, she needs to scan all her applications and services to modify access policy rules. In order to better manage security, Alice needs a centralized policy management system to have a better view on access policies applied to her resources. Cloud based policy management service not only allows Alice to centralize management of her access control policies but also enables her to find errors or inconsistencies in the specified access policies very quickly. The access control policies can be applied to a distributed set of resources hosted on various cloud service providers. It gathers information from all of the services Alice uses and provides her with an interface to centrally manage access to her resources regardless of where they are stored at and what cloud service provider they belong to.

Limitations of the Existing Policy Management Systems

In this section, we analyze the scenario described previously in order to identify limitations of existing access control mechanisms for the cloud and determine requirements that an access control mechanism should have to be able to address those limitations and be an appropriate candidate for the cloud environment. Some of the limitations of the existing policy management mechanisms are as follows.

- **Authorization mechanisms are bound to service providers:** each cloud service provider employs its own authorization model where access control mechanism is bound to the service and application. In some cases these access control mechanisms can only address simple scenarios where data is either made public or accessible only by a predefined set of users of the application. This limits the configuration of the application and it cannot be easily adapted to particular user's security requirements. Alice, for example, must use the mechanisms provided by *Dropbox*, *Facebook*, *LinkedIn*, *Google-Docs*, *Amazon S3*, and *Mint* which may not necessarily meet all her security requirements. These mechanisms may not allow Alice to group users and assign access rights to such groups or may not support fine-grained access control policy rules. Most security novice users probably choose their preferred services based on their functionality rather than based on their security features. However, security conscious users may decide to leave cloud service providers which do not support particular security features.

- **There is no unified policy management system:** There is no unified policy management system used among different cloud service providers. Cloud services are controlled by different authorities and often use different policy specification mechanisms. This leads to access control policies that are composed using diverse and possibly incompatible policy languages. For example, Dropbox uses a simple access control model while Facebook supports a more flexible and expressive access control language. Therefore, Alice is unable to define access control rules only once and apply these rules to her various resources such as photos, video clips and documents which are spread across different cloud Services. Moreover, if Alice decides to move some of her resources from one cloud service provider to another, for example from Dropbox to Amazon S3, then she may not be able to reuse already defined policies and may need to define these policies again.

- **There is no unified policy management tool:** There is no unified policy management tool used by all cloud service providers. Various cloud service providers deploy different access control solutions and may force users to use their specific policy management tools. This may result in an inconvenient and inconsistent user experience. For example, Alice, to be able to share her resources efficiently and securely, must learn how to use interfaces and management tools at all her cloud services which may differ significantly from one service provider to another. Underlying mechanisms used by these services often are different and incompatible with each other, thus cannot be easily reused for distributed resources hosted at various cloud service providers. Some of these tools are not usable which defeats the purpose of access control system and negatively impacts the intended use of the tool.

- **The access control policies are heterogeneous:** The access control policies in existing solutions are distributed and heterogeneous. As a result, users cannot have a consolidated view of the access control policies applied to their resources over the cloud. In our scenario, Alice does not have a holistic view of the access control policies applied to her information and resources at *Dropbox, Facebook, LinkedIn, Google-Docs, Amazon S3,* and *Mint.* Furthermore, with the increasing amount of resources that Alice may store on the various cloud service providers, another challenge is how to manage relations between access policies and resources. Additionally, with the heterogeneity of access policies, in order to introduce new access control policies or modify existing ones, users need to go over all cloud service providers and con-

figure access control policies appropriately which is s challenging task.

Based on the discussion about the aforementioned shortcomings, we believe that approaches to access control for cloud computing environment should enable users to control how their information is shared and with whom. The users should be a core part of access control system and should be able to easily determine how the shared information will be used, and what the consequences of sharing this information are.

However, it appears that existing authorization mechanisms do not support these properties. We need to come up with a usable policy management solution that addresses challenges of the cloud environments and the limitations of existing access policy management systems. The access control solution should provide the granularity, simplicity and usability required to respond to security and privacy challenges in the highly collaborative user-centered cloud environment. The proposed framework should be user centric enabling users to set their access control policies for resources with the use of their preferred policy management system in a centralized location. It should also provide users with usable and unified policy management interfaces and tools and allow them to have a consolidated view of the policies being applied to their resources. At the same time, it should preserve privacy of the users and their access policies and offer a representation-agnostic policy management.

The Cloud Based Policy Management Framework

We next present a cloud-based framework that efficiently delivers policy management services. It is built on the concept of centrally expressing user's security requirements that are applied to a user's resources scattered across the cloud. Such security requirements are expressed in the form of access control policies to protect users' resources distributed across multiple cloud service providers. The framework provides the capabilities to the customers to manage access policies for services and products running on a cloud infrastructure which are accessible through usable interfaces. The customers do not manage or control the underlying cloud infrastructure, network, servers, operating systems, storage, or even individual application capabilities. Figure 1 shows a high level view of the framework which includes four main components: *cloud user*, *policy management service provider*, *cloud service provider*, and *requester*. In the following, we provide a brief overview of each of these components.

- **Cloud User:** A cloud user uses different cloud service providers for various purposes. The cloud user is in charge of managing access policies on the policy management service provider which in turn will be used by cloud service providers to control access to the protected resources when a requester attempts to access them. The cloud user is also responsible for registering the cloud service providers at the policy man-

agement service provider so they can communicate the specified access policies.

- **Policy Management Service Provider (PMSP):** A policy management service provider enables the cloud users to define, edit and manage their access policies. The cloud users can specify their policies in natural language which in turn are translated by the policy management service provider into a machine readable policy language. It also conducts a conflict resolution on the policies to find and resolve possible conflicts and finally exports the policies into target cloud service providers. Therefore, a policy management service provider acts as a policy administration point (PAP) and a policy information point (PIP).

- **Cloud Service Provider (CSP):** A cloud service provider offers one or more cloud services that are used by cloud users. A cloud service provider controls access to the protected resources based on the policies specified by the cloud users. It evaluates access requests made by a requester against applicable policies and is in charge of making access decisions and enforc-

Figure 1. The high level overview of the proposed framework

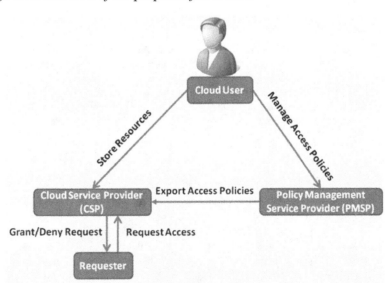

ing those decisions when a requester attempts to access the protected resources. Therefore, a cloud service provider acts as a policy decision point (PDP) and policy enforcement point (PEP).

- **Requester:** A requester is an application controlled by a person or a company that interacts with a cloud service provider in order to get access to a protected resource belonging to the specific cloud user. It can be a cloud service provider that accesses resources stored in another cloud service provider.

The Cloud Service Provider (CSP)

As shown in Figure 2, each cloud service provider keeps a repository of all the resources that cloud users store and has its own access control system that makes decisions and enforces them based on input from the policy management service provider. The policy framework does not impose any restrictions on what access control model the cloud service providers use and how they make

decisions to whether grant an access request or deny it, and enforce those decisions. It means that each service provider has its own policy engine and may use a simple access control matrix or a complex flexible policy engine. Each cloud service provider has also a local policy base to store policies and an authorization API that is used by the policy management service provider to export access policies into the cloud service providers.

The Policy Management Service Provider (PMSP)

The policy management service provider (PMSP) is the most important part of the framework and as shown in Figure 2, has two main components, the *policy editor* and the *policy server* as explained next.

- The policy editor acts as policy administration point (PAP) and provides interfaces for cloud users to manage access policies in a single centralized location. It facilitates the policy management process for cloud us-

Figure 2. The proposed framework

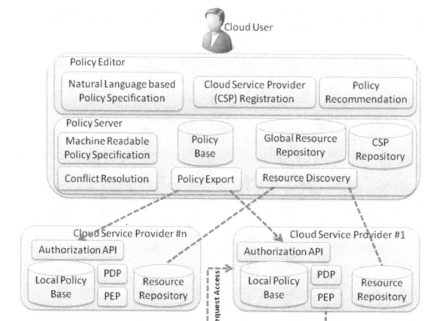

ers by allowing them to specify their policies in natural language. It also handles the cloud service provider registration process which will be explained later. Moreover, it includes a policy recommendation unit that uses information related to the cloud user and its resources to recommend some policies; needless to say that the cloud user can accept these recommended policies, modify them or ignore them.

- The policy server acts as policy information point (PIP) and is responsible for interacting with the policy editor and the cloud service providers as well as translating the policies specified by the cloud user into a machine readable policy language. It keeps a repository of registered cloud service providers associated with each cloud user. It is also responsible for the resource discovery process which we will explain later. After the cloud user registers its cloud service providers at the PMSP, the PMSP communicates with each cloud service provider to find resources and stores them in a global resource repository which contains all resources and their association with cloud users and cloud service providers. These resources are presented in policy editor interface to the cloud user to help him/her in specifying policies. Moreover, it receives the policies specified by cloud user in policy editor, parses them, transfers them into machine readable policy language and stores them at a policy base. The output policy language could be XACML (http://www.oasis-open.org/committees/xacml/) or an OWL-based policy language such as Rei (http://rei.umbc.edu). Since there is no one agreed-upon policy language that all cloud service providers use, the framework should have capability to provide the output policies in multiple languages to support as many cloud service providers as possible. Next, the policy server detects

and resolves possible conflicts among access policies. And the final step is to export policies into the cloud service providers; the policy server first separates the policies related to each cloud service provider based on the resource-provider association and then exports them into the associated cloud service provider using its authorization API.

The Policy Management Process

At a high level, interactions among components of the proposed framework include the following steps: *registering cloud service providers, resource discovery, specifying policies,* and *exporting policies* which are discussed below.

Step 1: Registration of CSPs at PMSP

In this step a cloud user registers all cloud service providers he/she uses at the policy management service provider. This can be achieved by providing the location of the cloud service provider to PMSP. For example, a resource owner may provide the URL of their host application to PMSP by typing it into a text field on a Web page. When the location of the cloud service provider is provisioned to the PMSP, it uses the host-meta discovery mechanism (http://tools.ietf.org/html/draft-hammer-hostmeta-13) to obtain a host-meta document from the cloud service provider. Such a document defines the location of a user authorization URL among other items. The PMSP then uses the user authorization URL to initiate the process of acquiring authorization to communicate with particular cloud service provider. When a PMSP receives the host-meta document from the cloud service provider, it obtains the cloud user's authorization information to communicate with this cloud service provider. This is achieved by receiving a verification code authorized by resource owner from the cloud service provider. At the end of this step, a PMSP is able to communicate with the cloud service provider to discover resources and also export access policies specified by the cloud user.

Step 2: Resource Discovery by PMSP

After a cloud user registers cloud service providers at the PMSP, we have a repository of all cloud service providers at the PMSP. Next, the PMSP communicates with each of the cloud service providers to discover the resources stored in them. We recommend using of POWDER-S or Semantic POWDER (http://www.w3.org/2007/05/powder-s) for resource description. The Protocol for Web Description Resources (POWDER) facilitates the publication of descriptions of multiple resources such as all those available from a Web site (http://www.w3.org/TR/powder-dr). These descriptions are always attributed to a named individual, organization or entity that may or may not be the creator of the described resources. Its main unit of information is the Description Resource (DR), one or more of which are contained in a POWDER document. Processing such a document yields RDF triples describing the resources that are within the scope of the DRs. POWDER documents are written in XML and have relatively loose semantics, however, POWDER-S is developed to support Semantic POWDER of Description Resources.

For the cloud service providers that do not support/use POWDER-S, the host-meta discovery mechanism can be used for resource discovery. It contains information about individual resources controlled by the cloud service provider.

Step 3: Specification of Access Policies at PMSP

There have been some efforts to allow users to specify policies in controlled natural language. IBM's SPARCLE tool aims to enable users to enter policy rules in natural language (http://www.research.ibm.com/sparcle). The same system can be adopted to be used in our framework for policy specification. However, it uses structured entry methods and guided natural language which is a kind of controlled natural language for policy specification. The goal here is to allow cloud users to specify their policies in natural language without any restriction. Our framework does not impose any constraints on how cloud users specify access policies.

Step 4: Translation of Access Policies by PMSP and Exporting them into CSPs

After the access policies are specified in natural language, the PMSP parses the policy, identifies policy elements, and transforms the policy into machine readable language. Next, a conflict detection and resolution is done on the policies to remove potential conflicts. Then, using the association between resources and cloud service providers, the policies are separated based on target cloud service provider. Finally, the access policies are exported into their related cloud service provider using an authorization API. In order to export policies into the host applications, we use the W3C Rule Interchange Format (RIF) which is a format to exchange rules between rule engines that operate over both XML and RDF data (http://www.w3.org/TR/rif-overview). RIF is a standard for exchanging rules among rule systems, in particular among Web rule engines. Although it provides more than just a format, the concept of format is essential to the way it is intended to be used. The ultimate medium of exchange between different rule systems is XML and central idea behind the rule exchange through RIF is that different systems will provide syntactic mappings from their native languages to RIF dialects and back. The systems can talk through a suitable dialect, which they both support. In order to be able to communicate rule sets from one system to another, the mappings should be semantics-preserving. Due to its extension mechanisms, RIF is an ideal language to investigate machine-readable first-order logic rules.

The Framework Deployment

In general, for the PMSP to be able to export policies into the cloud service providers, it should be able to exchange data with the CSPs. The ideal situation for PMSP is that cloud service provider supports well known policy languages such as XACML and provides required APIs to exchange data with the PMSP. However, some cloud service providers may not be willing to do any changes and do not support well known policy languages. In this case, it is the responsibility of the PMSP to generate policies in a format that the cloud service provider understands. It is clear that the more machine readable formats the PMSP provides and the more CSPs offer APIs, the more PMaaS would be deployed. The requester sends access requests to the CSP, and the CSP handles them locally. Our proposed framework does not impose any limitations on the requester and the CSP's decision making functionality. The requester can send a request to access protected resources similar to every other system. The CSP, checks the request against its policy base; makes decision, and grants or denies the access to the requester based on access policies defined by the cloud user.

One approach to implement the authorization API is to use RESTful Web service technology, which enables the remote invocation of the methods for the different parties involved. A RESTful Web service is implemented in the MPSP side and the CSPs are implemented as RESTful clients. The authorization API establishes a secure channel to the PMSP using SSL. Authentication of the provider and server is done using OAuth (http://www.oauth.net) which is an open protocol to allow secure API authorization in a simple and standard method from web applications and a simple way to publish and interact with protected data. The authorization API provides methods to *insert*, *remove*, *update*, *access,* and *search* information in the policy base.

Whenever cloud user changes his policies, the PMSP applies the required updates and communi-

cates them with the target cloud service providers. This could be done by push and pull strategy. In push strategy, whenever there is a change, the PMSP updates the policies and exports them to target CSPs while in pull strategy, the CSP initiates the communication and checks for possible policy changes/updates in certain time periods. However, we believe that push strategy is more efficient in this situation. Since the associations between policies, resources, and cloud service providers have been already identified, the PMSP only needs to relate the changes to target cloud service providers and export them. Similarly, whenever cloud users add/remove resources to/from cloud service providers, appropriate updates need to be done. However, in this case we believe that pull strategy is better because resources are stored in cloud service providers and whenever there is a change; CSPs can inform the PMSP to get updated policies.

Advantages and Disadvantages of the Proposed Framework

In the following, we discuss some of the advantages the cloud based policy management service has over existing systems.

- Access policy specification functionality is externalized from cloud service providers and can be done in a centralized location for all cloud providers. Decisions about who has access to what resources are made locally and enforced by each cloud service provider. However, the specification of policies for all resources and services is done centrally in a single location.
- Cloud users use a unified policy management system to control access to all their resources scattered over the cloud. They do not need to deal with various policy management systems bound to each cloud service provider.

- Cloud users compose access control policies using natural language and do not need to use various policy specification languages. They do not need to learn different policy languages employed by various cloud service providers and can simply specify policies using natural language.

- Cloud users use a single management tool to compose access policies which allows them to have a consistent user experience when managing these policies. They do not need to learn to work with different interfaces and tools that may even not be usable.

- Since access policies are composed using a single policy management tool and hosted in a single location, cloud users have a consolidated view of the access policies applied to their resources.

- If cloud users move their resources from one cloud service provider to another for any reason, they do not need to redefine all the policies again. For example, if Alice moves one document from *GoogleDocs* to *Amazon S3*, she does not need to redefine the policies associated with that document in *Amazon S3*.

- It is easier for users to introduce new access control policies and modify existing ones when needed.

- With existing systems, the cloud user is limited to the functionality provided by the cloud service providers' policy engine. However, our proposed framework may be able to apply extra policies by transforming them into the provider's policies. For instance, in *Facebook* Alice can share her location but she is not able to define any temporal constraint on that. If she wants to share her location at some specific times, she cannot do it in *Facebook* but she can do it using our proposed framework. She can specify a policy that her location should be private between 8 am and 5 pm

everyday otherwise it can be shared with friends. Our system exports a policy into the *Facebook* at 8 am that makes Alice's location private and when the time is 5 pm, it exports another policy into the *Facebook* to share her location with friends.

Despite all the advantages the proposed framework provides, it has some drawbacks.

- The question may arise regarding privacy of cloud user's identity and privacy of his policies and the concern is that cloud users have to trust PMaaS provider to provide their identifications in different cloud service providers and specify their access policies using the PMaaS. We assume that there is enough level of trust between cloud user and PMaaS provider to deploy the service. However, the PMaaS could be deployed as private cloud within an organization's premise or fully controlled by an individual user to avoid privacy concerns.

- In order to successfully deploy the framework, the cloud service provider should provide some kind of APIs to exchange data with the PMSP and support output languages of the PMSP. In real world, however, some cloud service providers may not be willing to do any changes and the PMSP is responsible to generate policies in a format that the cloud service providers understand. In order to increase its deployment, the PMSP should provide more machine readable formats and we need to incentivize the CSPs to offer APIs for interaction with the PMaaS.

FUTURE RESEARCH DIRECTIONS

The issue of integrating policies has been addressed to ensure secure interoperation and policy engineering mechanisms are provided to integrate access policies of different policy domains and define global access policies. Secure interoperation can be achieved in centralized or decentralized fashion. In a centralized approach, a global policy is created that mediates all accesses and is appropriate for a cloud application that is composed of various services with different requirements and is more or less fixed. In a more dynamic environment, the domains are transient and may need to interact for a very specific purpose and centralized approaches are not appropriate in such cases. Decentralized approaches are needed in such cases.

One key aspect of the complex cloud computing environments is the semantic heterogeneity among policies. There needs to be ways for automatic detection of semantic conflicts among different service providers' policies. Use of ontology is the most promising approach to address the semantic heterogeneity issue. Combination of OWL 2 and SWRL for policy management has the following advantages:

- It offers high expressiveness by providing a wide variety of constructors to describe knowledge.
- Its reasoning could be implemented using rule-based engines which offer good performance.
- It provides scalable reasoning without sacrificing too much expressive power.
- It provides separation between domain description and policy description.
- It provides heterogeneity management and interoperability among different cloud service providers.

An OWL based framework is desirable to support semantic heterogeneity management across multiple service providers. For such a framework, a system-driven policy framework to facilitate the management of security policies in heterogeneous environments and policy enforcement architecture are essential.

CONCLUSION

The key features of the cloud, among many, that exacerbates the security and privacy issues include outsourcing of data and applications which generate significant concerns related to trust, multi-tenancy, heterogeneity of services, and compliance. Cloud computing is still in its infancy and although security issues are delaying its adoption, it is growing and we need to provide security mechanisms to ensure that cloud computing benefits are fully realized.

We have proposed a cloud based policy management framework that puts users in full control of their resources which may be scattered across multiple cloud service providers. It is designed to give cloud users a unified control point for specifying authorization policies, who and what can get access to their data, content, and services, no matter where all those things live on the cloud. It relies on a user's centrally located policy manager of those resources and enables users to manage access policies using a centralized policy manager which provides usable interfaces for specifying access policies and exporting them to the cloud service providers on behalf of the user.

We described various components of the framework in detail and explained how these components interact with each other to provide the desired service to customers. We also discussed how to deploy the proposed framework and what are the challenges we face when trying to use the framework with real world applications and services. Furthermore, we have discussed advantages that the proposed framework has over existing systems. There are some privacy concerns that need to be taken into account for its successful deployment. However, with some efforts to incentivize the CSPs to offer appropriate APIs and establishing enough trust for customers, the proposed framework can be deployed and used in real world.

REFERENCES

Ahn, G. J., Hu, H., & Jin, J. (2009). Security-enhanced OSGi Service Environments. *IEEE Transactions on Systems, Man and Cybernetics. Part C, Applications and Reviews, 39*(5), 562–571. doi:10.1109/TSMCC.2009.2020437

Bertino, E., Paci, F., & Ferrini, R. (2009). Privacy-preserving digital identity management for cloud computing. *IEEE Computer Society Data Engineering Bulletin, 1*(32), 1–4.

Bhatti, R., Joshi, J. B. D., Bertino, E., & Ghafoor, A. (2003). Access control in dynamic XML-based Web-services with X-RBAC. In L. J. Zhang (Ed.), *First International Conference in Web Services* (pp. 243-249). Las Vegas, USA.

Bhatti, R., Joshi, J. B. D., Bertino, E., & Ghafoor, A. (2005). X-GTRBAC: An XML-based policy specification framework and architecture for enterprise-wide access control. *ACM Transactions on Information and System Security, 8*(2), 187–227. doi:10.1145/1065545.1065547

Blaze, M., Kannan, S., Lee, I., Sokolsky, O., Smith, J. M., Keromytis, A. D., & Lee, W. (2009). Dynamic trust management. *IEEE Computer, 42*(2), 44–51. doi:10.1109/MC.2009.51

Bruening, P. J., & Treacy, B. C. (2009). *Cloud computing: Privacy, security challenges*. Privacy & Security Law Report, the Bureau of National Affairs, Inc.

Catteddu, D., & Hogben, G. (2009). *Cloud computing: Benefits, risks and recommendations for information security*. European Network and Information Security Agency (ENISA) Report. Retrieved August 10, 2011, from http://www.enisa.europa.eu/act/rm/files/deliverables/cloud-computing-risk-assessment/at_download/fullReport

Chakraborty, S., & Ray, I. (2006). TrustBAC: Integrating trust relationships into the RBAC model for access control in open systems. In I. Ray (Ed.), *11th ACM Symposium on Access Control Models and Technologies (SACMAT06)* (pp. 49-58). Tahoe City, CA: ACM Press.

Chen, Y., Paxson, V., & Katz, R. H. (2010). *What's new about cloud computing security?* (Technical Report No. UCB/EECS-2010-5). EECS Department, University of California at Berkeley. Retrieved August 10, 2011, from http://www.eecs.berkeley.edu/Pubs/TechRpts/2010/EECS-2010-5.html

Cloud Computing Use Case Discussion Group. (2010). *Cloud Computing Use Cases white paper*, version 4.0. Retrieved December 10, 2011, from http://opencloudmanifesto.org/Cloud_Computing_Use_Cases_Whitepaper-4_0.pdf

Cloud Security Alliance. (2011). *Security guidance for critical areas of focus in cloud computing* V3.0. Retrieved December 10, 2011, from https://cloudsecurityalliance.org/guidance/csaguide.v3.0.pdf

Joshi, J. B. D., Bertino, E., Latif, U., & Ghafoor, A. (2005). A generalized temporal role-based access control model. *IEEE Transactions on Knowledge and Data Engineering, 17*(1), 4–23. doi:10.1109/TKDE.2005.1

Joshi, J. B. D., Bhatti, R., & Bertino, E., & Ghafoor. (2004). Access control language for multi domain environments. *IEEE Internet Computing, 8*(6), 40–50. doi:10.1109/MIC.2004.53

Kim, M., Joshi, J. B. D., & Kim, M. (2008). Access control for cooperation systems based on group situation. In E. Bertino & J. B. D. Joshi (Eds.), *4th International Conference on Collaborative Computing: Networking, Applications and Worksharing (CollaborateCom2008)* (pp. 11-23). Berlin, Germany: Springer.

Ko, M., Ahn, G. J., & Shehab, M. (2009). Privacy enhanced user-centric identity management. In G. Fettweis (Ed.), *IEEE International Conference on Communications* (pp. 1-5). Dresden, Germany: IEEE Press.

Kodali, N. B., Farkas, C., & Wijesekera, D. (2004). Specifying multimedia access control using RDF. *Journal of Computer Systems, Science and Engineering, 19*(3).

Mell, P., & Grance, T. (2011). *The NIST definition of cloud computing*. NIST Special Publication 800-145 (Draft). Retrieved August 10, 2011, from http://csrc.nist.gov/publications/drafts/800-145/Draft-SP-800-145_cloud-definition.pdf

Shin, D., & Ahn, G. J. (2005). Role-based privilege and trust management. *Computer Systems Science & Engineering Journal, 20*(6).

Takabi, H., & Joshi, J. B. D. (2010). StateMiner: An efficient similarity-based approach for optimal mining of role hierarchy. In B. Carminati (Ed.), *15th ACM Symposium on Access Control Models and Technologies* (pp. 55-64), Pittsburgh, PA: ACM Press.

Takabi, H., & Joshi, J. B. D. (2012). *Policy management as a service: An approach to manage policy heterogeneity in cloud computing environment.* In 45th Hawaii International Conference on System Sciences (HICSS), Hawaii, USA.

Takabi, H., & Joshi, J. B. D. (2012). Semantic based policy management for cloud computing environment. *International Journal of Cloud Computing, 1*(2-3), 119–144. doi:10.1504/IJCC.2012.046717

Takabi, H., Joshi, J. B. D., & Ahn, G. J. (2010). SecureCloud: Towards a comprehensive security framework for cloud computing environments. In S. I. Ahamed, D. H. Bae, S. Cha, C. K. Chang, R. Subramanyan, E. Wong, & H. I. Yang (Eds.), *34th Annual IEEE Computer Software and Applications Conference Workshops (COMPSACW 2010)* (pp. 393-398), Seoul, South Korea: IEEE Press.

Takabi, H., Joshi, J. B. D., & Ahn, G. J. (2010). Security and privacy challenges in cloud computing environments. *IEEE Security and Privacy, 8*(6), 24–31. doi:10.1109/MSP.2010.186

Takabi, II., Kim, M., Joshi, J. B. D., & Spring, M. B. (2009). An architecture for specification and enforcement of temporal access control constraints using OWL. In E. Damiani, S. Proctor, & A. Singal (Eds.), *2009 ACM Workshop on Secure Web Services* (pp. 21-28). Chicago, IL: ACM Press.

Teo, L., & Ahn, G. J. (2007). Managing heterogeneous network environments using an extensible policy framework. In R. Deng & P. Samarati (Eds.), *2nd ACM Symposium on Information, Computer and Communications Security* (pp. 362-364). Singapore: ACM Press.

Zhang, Y., & Joshi, J. B. D. (2009). Access control and trust management for emerging multidomain environments. In Upadhyaya, S., & Rao, R. O. (Eds.), *Annals of emerging research in information assurance, security and privacy services.* Emerald Group Publishing Limited.

ADDITIONAL READING

Ahmed, M., Yang, X., & Ali, S. (2010). Above the trust and security in cloud computing: A notion towards innovation. *2010 IEEE/IFIP 8th International Conference on Embedded and Ubiquitous Computing* (EUC), (pp. 723–730).

Almorsy, M., Grundy, J., & Ibrahim, A. S. (2011). *Collaboration-based cloud computing security management framework.* IEEE International Conference on Cloud Computing (CLOUD).

Basescu, C., Carpen-Amarie, A., Leordeanu, C., Costan, A., & Antoniu, G. (2011). Managing data access on clouds: A generic framework for enforcing security policies. *AINA '11: Proceedings of the 2011 IEEE International Conference on Advanced Information Networking and Applications.*

Bernstein, D., & Vij, D. (2010). Intercloud security considerations. *2010 IEEE Second International Conference on Cloud Computing Technology and Science* (CloudCom), (pp. 537-544).

Celesti, A., Tusa, F., Villari, M., & Puliafito, A. (2010). Security and cloud computing: inter-cloud identity management infrastructure. *2010 19th IEEE International Workshop on Enabling Technologies: Infrastructures for Collaborative Enterprises* (WETICE), (pp. 263-265).

Christodorescu, M., Sailer, R., Schales, D. L., Sgandurra, D., & Zamboni, D. (2009). Cloud security is not (just) virtualization security. *CCSW '09: Proceedings of the 2009 ACM Workshop on Cloud Computing Security.*

Deng, M., Petkovic, M., Nalin, M., & Baroni, I. (2011). A home healthcare system in the cloud- -Addressing security and privacy challenges. *2011 IEEE International Conference on Cloud Computing* (CLOUD), (pp. 549-556).

Di Modica, G., & Tomarchio, O. (2011). Semantic security policy matching in service oriented architectures. In D. S. Milojicic & M. Kirchburg (Eds.), *2011 IEEE World Congress on Services* (pp. 399-405), Washington, DC: IEEE Press.

Dowell, S., Barreto, A., Michael, J. B., & Man-Tak, S. (2011). Cloud to cloud interoperability. In I. Ray (Ed.), 6*th International Conference On System of Systems Engineering (SoSE)* (pp. 49-58). Tahoe City, CA: ACM Press.

Echeverria, V., Liebrock, L. M., & Shin, D. (2010). Permission management system: Permission as a service in cloud computing. In S. I. Ahamed, D. H. Bae, S. Cha, C. K. Chang, R. Subramanyan, E. Wong, & H. I. Yang (Eds.), *34th Annual Computer Software and Applications Conference Workshops (COMPSACW '10)* (pp. 371-375). Seoul, Korea: IEEE Press.

Grobauer, B., Walloschek, T., & Stocker, E. (2011). Understanding cloud computing vulner-abilities. *IEEE Security & Privacy, 9*(2), 50–57. doi:10.1109/MSP.2010.115

Gruschka, N., & Jensen, M. (2010). Attack surfaces: A taxonomy for attacks on cloud services. *2010 IEEE 3rd International Conference on Cloud Computing* (CLOUD), (pp. 276-279).

Guojun, W., Liu, Q., & Wu, J. (2010). Hierarchical attribute-based encryption for fine-grained access control in cloud storage services. *CCS '10: Proceedings of the 17th ACM Conference on Computer and Communications Security.*

Hu, Y. J., Wu, W. N., & Yang, J. J. (2011). Semantics-enabled policies for information sharing and protection in the cloud. In A. Datta, R. Rogers, & S. Shulman (Eds.), *3rd International Conference on Social Informatics (SocInfo'11)* (pp. 49-58). Singapore.

Itani, W., Kayssi, A., & Chehab, A. (2009). Privacy as a service: Privacy-aware data storage and processing in cloud computing architectures. Eighth IEEE International Conference on Dependable, Autonomic and Secure Computing, DASC '09, (pp. 711–716).

Jaeger, T., & Schiffman, J. (2011). Outlook: Cloudy with a chance of security challenges and improvements. *IEEE Security & Privacy, 8*(1), 77–80.

Jansen, W. A. (2011). Cloud hooks: Security and privacy issues in cloud computing. 2011 44th Hawaii International Conference on System Sciences (HICSS), (pp. 1-10).

Jasti, A., Shah, P., Nagaraj, R., & Pendse, R. (2010). Security in multi-tenancy cloud. *2010 IEEE International Carnahan Conference on Security Technology* (ICCST), (pp. 35-41).

Jensen, M., Schäge, S., & Schwenk, J. (2010). Towards an anonymous access control and accountability scheme for cloud computing. In W. Chou & A. M. Goscinski (Eds.), *3rd International Conference on Cloud Computing (Cloud '10)* (pp. 540-541). Miami, FL: IEEE Press.

Jensen, M., Schwenk, J., Bohli, J.-M., Gruschka, N., & Iacono, L. L. (2011). Security prospects through cloud computing by adopting multiple clouds. *2011 IEEE International Conference on Cloud Computing* (CLOUD), (pp. 565-572).

Kim, A., McDermott, J., & Myong, K. (2010). Security and architectural issues for national security cloud computing. *2010 IEEE 30th International Conference on Distributed Computing Systems Workshops* (ICDCSW), (pp. 21-25).

Kretzschmar, M., Golling, M., & Hanigk, S. (2011). Security management areas in the intercloud. *2011 IEEE International Conference on Cloud Computing* (CLOUD), (pp. 762-763).

Li, J., Zhao, G., Chen, X., Xie, D., Rong, C., & Li, W. … Tang, Y. (2010). Fine-grained data access control systems with user accountability in cloud computing. In G. Zhao & J. Qiu (Eds.), *Second International Conference on Cloud Computing Technology and Science (CloudCom '10)* (pp. 89-96), Indianapolis, IN: IEEE Press.

Li, Y., Shi, Y., Guo, Y., & Ma, W. (2010). Multitenancy based access control in cloud. In Y. He (Ed.), *2010 International Conference on Computational Intelligence and Software Engineering (CiSE)* (pp. 1-4). Wuhan, China: IEEE Press.

Liu, J., Wan, Z., & Gu, M. (2011). Hierarchical attribute-set based encryption for scalable, flexible and fine-grained access control in cloud computing. In F. Bao & J. Weng (Eds.), *7th International Conference on Information Security Practice and Experience (SPEC'11)* (pp. 98-107). China: Springer.

Lv, H., & Hu, Y. (2011). Analysis and research about cloud computing security protect policy. *2011 International Conference on Intelligence Science and Information Engineering* (ISIE), (pp. 214-216).

Nguyen, T. D., Gondree, M. A., Shifflett, D. J., Khosalim, J., Levin, T. E., & Irvine, C. E. (2010). A cloud-oriented cross-domain security architecture. *Military Communications Conference, MILCOM 2010*, (pp. 441-447).

Pearson, S., & Benameur, A. (2010). Privacy, security and trust issues arising from cloud computing. *2010 IEEE Second International Conference on Cloud Computing Technology and Science (CloudCom)*, (pp. 693-702).

Popa, L., Yu, M., & Ko, S. Y. (2010). *CloudPolice: Taking access control out of the network.* Hotnets '10.

Prasad, P., Ojha, B., Shahi, R. R., Lal, R., Vaish, A., & Goel, U. (2011). 3 dimensional security in cloud computing. *2011 3rd International Conference on Computer Research and Development (ICCRD)*, (pp. 198-201).

Prasadreddy, P. V. G. D., Rao, T., Srinivasa, V., & Phani, S. (2011). A threat free architecture for privacy assurance in cloud computing. *2011 IEEE World Congress on Services* (SERVICES), (pp. 564-568).

Preiya, V. S., Pavithra, R., & Joshi. (2011). Secure role based data access control in cloud computing. *International Journal of Computer Trends and Technology, May/June.*

Ruoyu, W., Ahn, G.-J., Hu, H., & Singhal, M. (2010). Information flow control in cloud computing. *2010 6th International Conference on Collaborative Computing: Networking, Applications and Worksharing* (CollaborateCom), (pp. 1-7).

Sabahi, F. (2011). Cloud computing security threats and responses. *2011 IEEE 3rd International Conference on Communication Software and Networks (ICCSN),* (pp. 245-249).

Sandhu, R., Boppana, R., Krishnan, R., Reich, J., Wolff, T., & Zachry, J. (2010). Towards a discipline of mission-aware cloud computing. *CCSW '10: Proceedings of the 2010 ACM Workshop on Cloud Computing Security Workshop.*

Sang-Ho, N., Park, J.-Y., & Huh, E.-N. (2010). *Personal cloud computing security framework. 2010 IEEE Asia-Pacific Publication Services Computing Conference* (pp. 671–675). APSCC.

Santos, N., Gummadi, K. P., & Rodrigues, R. (2011). *Towards trusted cloud computing.*

Sasaki, T., Nakae, M., & Ogawa, R. (2010). Content oriented virtual domains for secure information sharing across organizations. *CCSW '10: Proceedings of the 2010 ACM Workshop on Cloud Computing Security Workshop.*

Sengupta, S., Kaulgud, V., & Sharma, V. S. (2011). Cloud computing security--Trends and research directions. In Y. He (Ed.), *2011 IEEE World Congress on Services* (pp. 524-531), Washington, DC: IEEE Press.

Srivastava, P., Singh, S., Pinto, A. A., Verma, S., Chaurasiya, V. K., & Gupta, R. (2011). An architecture based on proactive model for security in cloud computing. *2011 International Conference on Recent Trends in Information Technology (ICRTIT),* (pp. 661-666).

Tchifilionova, V. (2010). Security and privacy implications of cloud computing: Lost in the cloud. *iNetSec'10: Proceedings of the 2010 IFIP WG 11.4 International Conference on Open Research Problems in Network Security.*

Verma, A., & Kaushal, S. (2011). Cloud computing security issues and challenges: A survey. *ACM Transactions on Information and System Security, 193*(4), 445–454.

Wei-Tek, T., & Qihong, S. (2011). Role-based access-control using reference ontology in clouds. 2011 *10th International Symposium on Autonomous Decentralized Systems (ISADS),* (pp. 121-128).

Weiwei, J., Haojin, Z., Zhenfu, C., Lifei, W., & Xiaodong, L. (2011). SDSM: A secure data service mechanism in mobile cloud computing. *2011 IEEE Conference on Computer Communications Workshops (INFOCOM WKSHPS),* (pp. 1060-1065).

Xue, J., & Jian-jun, Z. (2010). A brief survey on the security model of cloud computing. *DCABES '10: Proceedings of the 2010 Ninth International Symposium on Distributed Computing and Applications to Business, Engineering and Science.*

Yildiz, M., Abawajy, J., Ercan, T., & Bernoth, A. (2009). A layered security approach for cloud computing infrastructure. 2009 10th International Symposium on Pervasive Systems, Algorithms, and Networks (ISPAN), (pp. 763-767).

Youngmin, J., & Mokdong, C. (2010). Adaptive security management model in the cloud computing environment. *2010 The 12th International Conference on Advanced Communication Technology (ICACT)*, Vol. 2, (pp. 1664-1669).

Youngmin, J., & Mokdong, C. (2010). Adaptive security management model in the cloud computing environment. *2010 The 12th International Conference on Advanced Communication Technology* (ICACT), Vol. 2, (pp. 1664–1669).

Yu, S., Wang, C., Ren, K., & Lou, W. (2010). Achieving secure, scalable, and fine-grained data access control in cloud computing. In M. C. Chuah, R. Cohen, & G. Xue (Ed.), *29th Conference on Information Communications (Infocom'10)* (pp. 1-9). San Diego, CA: IEEE Press.

Zhao, G., Rong, C., Jaatun, M. G., & Sandnes, F. E. (2010). Deployment models: Towards eliminating security concerns from cloud computing. *2010 International Conference on High Performance Computing and Simulation (HPCS),* (pp. 189-195).

KEY TERMS AND DEFINITIONS

Access Control: Access control systems provide the essential services of authorization that determines what actions a subject is allowed to do on an object. In access control systems, subjects are the entities that perform actions and objects are the entities representing resources on which the action is performed.

Cloud Computing: Cloud computing is a model for enabling ubiquitous, convenient, on-demand network access to a shared pool of configurable computing resources (e.g., networks, servers, storage, applications, and services) that can be rapidly provisioned and released with minimal management effort or service provider interaction.

Cloud Service Provider: A cloud service provider is an entity that offers one or more cloud based services that are used by cloud users.

Interoperability: Interoperability refers to the ability of systems to work together, exchange information, and use the exchanged information without any restricted access or implementation.

Policy Management: The process of defining, modifying and managing access control policies in a system is called policy management.

Semantic Heterogeneity: Semantic heterogeneity means that different entities in a system have differences in interpretation of the meaning of data are source of semantic heterogeneity.

Semantic Interoperability: Semantic interoperability is the ability of computer systems to communicate information in a way that the exchanged information can be automatically and meaningfully interpreted by the receiving system the same as the transmitting system intended. In order to achieve semantic interoperability, both systems should use a common information exchange reference model and they should derive the same inferences from the same information.

Semantic Web: The Semantic Web is a web of data that can be processed directly and indirectly by machines. It is a system that enables machines to understand and respond to complex human requests based on their meaning. The Semantic Web is not a separate Web but an extension of the current one, in which information is given well-defined meaning, better enabling computers and people to work in cooperation.

Compilation of References

Ahn, G. J., Hu, H., & Jin, J. (2009). Security-enhanced OSGi Service Environments. *IEEE Transactions on Systems, Man and Cybernetics. Part C, Applications and Reviews*, *39*(5), 562–571. doi:10.1109/TSMCC.2009.2020437

Alhazmi, O. H., Woo, S. W., & Malaiya, Y. K. (2006). Security vulnerability categories in major software systems. In *Proceedings of the Third IASTED International Conference on Communication, Network, and Information Security* (pp. 138-143). Cambridge, MA: IASTED/ACTA Press.

Almorsy, M., Grundy, J., & Ibrahim, A. S. (2011). Collaboration-based cloud computing security management framework. *2011 IEEE International Conference on Cloud Computing (CLOUD)*, (pp. 364–371). Washington, DC: IEEE. Retrieved from http://ieeexplore.ieee.org/xpls/abs_all.jsp?arnumber=6008731

Anderson, R. (2008). *Security engineering. A guide to building dependable distributed systems* (2nd ed.). Indianapolis, IN: Wiley Publishing, Inc.

Anderson, R., Bond, M., Clulow, J., & Skorobogatov, S. (2006). Cryptographic processors-a survey. *Proceedings of the IEEE*, *94*(2), 357–369. doi:10.1109/JPROC.2005.862423

Annas, G. J. (2003). HIPAA regulations—A new era of medical-record privacy? *The New England Journal of Medicine*, *348*(15), 1486–1490. doi:10.1056/NEJMlim035027

Arnold, T. W., & Van Doorn, L. P. (2004). The IBM PCIXCC: A new cryptographic coprocessor for the IBM eServer. *IBM Journal of Research and Development*, *48*(3-4), 475–487. doi:10.1147/rd.483.0475

Arora, A., Krishnan, R., Telang, R., & Yang, Y. (2004). *Impact of vulnerability disclosure and patch availability - An empirical analysis.* Third Workshop on the Economics of Information Security.

Asadoorian, P. (2007). Escaping from the virtualization cave. *PaulDotCom*. Retrieved July 12, 2011, from http://www.pauldotcom.com/2007/07/31/escaping_from_the_virtualizati.html

Ateniese, G., Burns, R., Curtmola, R., Herring, J., Kissner, L., Peterson, Z., & Song, D. (2007). Provable data possession at untrusted stores. *CCS'07, 14th ACM Conference on Computer and Communication Security*, (pp. 598-609).

Ateniese, G., Di Pietro, R., Mancini, L., & Tsudik, G. (2008). Scalable and efficient provable data possession. *SecureComm*, *2008*, 1–10. doi:10.1145/1460877.1460889

Ateniese, G., Fu, K., Green, M., & Hohenberger, S. (2006). Improved proxy re-encryption schemes with applications to secure distributed storage. *ACM Transactions on Information and System Security*, *9*(1), 1–30. doi:10.1145/1127345.1127346

Aviram, A., Hu, S., Ford, B., & Gummadi, R. (2010). Determinating timing channels in compute clouds. *Proceedings of the 2010 ACM Workshop on Cloud Computing Security Workshop*, Chicago, Illinois, USA.

Avizienis, A., Larpie, J. C., & Randell, B. (2000). *Fundamental concepts of dependability*. In Information Survavility Workshop.

Avizienis, A., Laprie, J., Randell, B., & Landwehr, C. (2004). Basic concepts and taxonomy of dependable and secure computing. *IEEE Transactions on Dependable and Secure Computing*, *1*(1), 11–33. doi:10.1109/TDSC.2004.2

Bajikar, S. (2002). *Trusted platform module (tpm) based security on notebook pcs-white paper*. Mobile Platforms Group, Intel Corporation (June 20, 2002).

Baker, T., Taleb-Bendiab, A., & Al-Jumeily, D. (2009). Process-oriented e-government application development. *UKSim 2009: 11th International Conference on Computer Modelling and Simulation*, (pp. 634-639). Cambridge, UK: IEEE Computer Society. ISBN: 978-0-7695-3593-7

Baker, T., Taleb-Bendiab, A., & Al-Jumeily, D. (2010). Assurance support for full adaptive service based applications. *12th International Conference on Computer Modelling and Simulation* (UKSim), (pp. 179 – 185).

Baker, T., Taleb-Bendiab, A., & Randles, M. (2009). Auditable intention-oriented Web applications using PAA auditing/accounting paradigm. *Proceeding of the 2009 Conference on Techniques and Applications for Mobile Commerce*, (pp. 61–70).

Bannerman, P. L. (2008). Risk and risk management in software projects: A reassessment. *Journal of Systems and Software*, *81*(12), 2118–2133. doi:10.1016/j.jss.2008.03.059

Baresi, L., & Guinea, S. (2005). Towards dynamic monitoring of WS-BPEL processes. In *Conference on Service-Oriented Computing* (ICSOC-05), (pp. 269-282).

Barham, P., Dragovic, B., Fraser, K., Hand, S., Harris, T., Ho, A., et al. (2003). Xen and the art of virtualization. *Proceedings of the nineteenth ACM symposium on Operating systems principles*, Bolton Landing, NY, USA.

Barnett, M., & Schulte, W. (2001). Spying on components: A runtime verification technique. In *Proceedings of OOPSLA 2001 Workshop on Specification and Verification of Component Based Systems*, Tampa, FL, USA.

Barry, B. W. (1991). Software risk management: Principles and practices. *IEEE Software*, *8*(1), 32–41. doi:10.1109/52.62930

Bellare, M., & Rogaway, P. (1994). Optimal asymmetric encryption – How to encrypt with RSA. *Advances in Cryptology (Eurocrypt'94). Lecture Notes in Computer Science*, *950*, 92–111. doi:10.1007/BFb0053428

Benson, T., Sahu, S., Akella, A., & Shaikh, A. (2010). A first look at problems in the cloud. *Proceedings of the 2nd USENIX Conference on Hot Topics in Cloud Computing* (pp. 1-7). Boston, MA: USENIX Association. doi:10.1.1.150.2883

Beran, M. J., Couchman, J., Coutinho, M., Boomer, J., & Smith, J. D. (2010). Metacognition in nonhumans: Methodological and theoretical issues in uncertainty monitoring. In A. Efklides & M. Plousia (Eds.), *Trends and prospects in metacognition research* (pp. 21-35). Springer Science +Business Media, LLC 2010.

Berger, S., Aceres, R. C., et al. (2006). vTPM: Virtualizing the trusted platform module. In *USENIX-SS'06: Proceedings of the 15th Conference on USENIX Security Symposium*.

Bertino, E., Paci, F., & Ferrini, R. (2009). Privacy-preserving digital identity management for cloud computing. *IEEE Computer Society Data Engineering Bulletin*, *1*(32), 1–4.

Best, R. M. (1980). Preventing software piracy with crypto-microprocessors. *Proceedings of IEEE Spring COMPCON*, *80*, 466–469.

Bhattacharjee, B., Abe, N., Goldman, K., Zadrozny, B., Chillakuru, V. R., del Carpio, M., et al. (2006). Using secure coprocessors for privacy preserving collaborative data mining and analysis. *Proceedings of the 2nd International Workshop on Data Management on New Hardware*.

Bhatti, R., Joshi, J. B. D., Bertino, E., & Ghafoor, A. (2003). Access control in dynamic XML-based Web-services with X-RBAC. In L. J. Zhang (Ed.), *First International Conference in Web Services* (pp. 243-249). Las Vegas, USA.

Bhatti, R., Joshi, J. B. D., Bertino, E., & Ghafoor, A. (2005). X-GTRBAC: An XML-based policy specification framework and architecture for enterprise-wide access control. *ACM Transactions on Information and System Security*, *8*(2), 187–227. doi:10.1145/1065545.1065547

Blaze, M., Kannan, S., Lee, I., Sokolsky, O., Smith, J. M., Keromytis, A. D., & Lee, W. (2009). Dynamic trust management. *IEEE Computer*, *42*(2), 44–51. doi:10.1109/MC.2009.51

Boneh, D., Di Crescenzo, G., Ostrovsky, R., & Persiano, G. (2004). *Public key encryption with keyword search*. Eurocrypt 2004.

Braz, F. A., Fernandez, E. B., & VanHilst, M. (2008, September). Eliciting security requirements through misuse activities. *Proceedings of the 2nd Int. Workshop on Secure Systems Methodologies using Patterns (SPattern '08)- in conjunction with the 4th International Conference on Trust, Privacy & Security in Digital Busines (TrustBus '08)* (pp. 328-333). Turin, Italy.

British Standards. (2006). Information security management systems. *British Standards, BS, 7799*, 2006.

Broda, M., Buttyan, L., Clemo, G., Kijewski, P., Merle, A., Mitrokotsa, K., & Munro, A. (2010). *Priorities for research on current and emerging network trends*. ENISA.

Bruening, P. J., & Treacy, B. C. (2009). *Cloud computing: Privacy, security challenges*. Privacy & Security Law Report, the Bureau of National Affairs, Inc.

Brunette, G., & Mogull, R. (2009). *Security guidance for critical areas of focus in cloud computing V2.1*. Cloud Security Alliance.

Bugiel, S., Nürnberger, S., Pöppelmann, T., Sadeghi, A. R., & Schneider, T. (2011). AmazonIA: When elasticity snaps back. In *Proceedings of the 18th ACM Conference on Computer and Communications Security*, (pp 389-400). New York, NY: ACM.

Catteddu, D., & Hogben, G. (2009). *Cloud computing: Benefits, risks and recommendations for information security*. European Network and Information Security Agency (ENISA) Report. Retrieved August 10, 2011, from http://www.enisa.europa.eu/act/rm/files/deliverables/cloud-computing-risk-assessment/at_download/fullReport

Catteddu, D., & Hogben, G. (2009). *Cloud computing: Benifits, risks and recommendations for information security. European Network and Information Security Agency*. ENISA.

Cellan-Jones, R. (2009). The sidekick cloud disaster. *BBC News*. Retrieved January 14, 2012, from http://www.bbc.co.uk/blogs/technology/2009/10/the_sidekick_cloud_disaster.html

Chakraborty, S., & Ray, I. (2006). TrustBAC: Integrating trust relationships into the RBAC model for access control in open systems. In I. Ray (Ed.), *11th ACM Symposium on Access Control Models and Technologies (SACMAT06)* (pp. 49-58). Tahoe City, CA: ACM Press.

Charette, R. N. (1999). The competitive edge of risk entrepreneurs. *IT Professional, 1*(4), 69–73. doi:10.1109/6294.781627

Chen, Y., Paxson, V., & Katz, R. H. (2010). *What's new about cloud computing security*. University of California, Berkeley Report No. UCB/EECS-2010-5 January (Vol. 20). Berkeley, CA. Retrieved from http://www.eecs.berkeley.edu/Pubs/TechRpts/2010/EECS-2010-5.pdf

Chen, F., & Rosu, G. (2003). Towards monitoring-oriented programming: A paradigm combining specification and implementation. *Electronic Notes in Theoretical Computer Science, 89*(2).

Choo, K. R. (2010). *Cloud computing: Challenges and future directions, Trends & issues in crime and criminal justice*. Australian Institute of Criminology, No. 400.

Chorafas, D. (2011). *Cloud computing strategies*. Boca Raton, FL: CRC Press.

Chor, B., Kushilevitz, E., Goldreich, O., & Sudan, M. (1998). Private information retrieval. *Journal of the ACM, 45*(6), 965–981. doi:10.1145/293347.293350

Chowdhury, A., & Meyers, S. (1993). *Facilitating software maintenance by automated detection of constraint violations*. Tech. Rep. CS-93-37 Brown Univ.

Christodorescu, M., Sailer, R., Schales, D. L., Sgandurra, D., & Zamboni, D. (2009). Cloud security is not (just) virtualization security. *Proceedings of the 2009 ACM Workshop on Cloud Computing Security - CCSW '09* (p. 97). New York, NY: ACM Press. doi:10.1145/1655008.1655022

Chuang, I., Li, S. H., Huang, K. C., & Kuo, Y. H. (2011). An effective privacy protection scheme for cloud computing. *2011 13th International Conference on Advanced Communication Technology (ICACT)*, (pp. 260-265).

Ciriani, V., De Capitani, S., Foresti, S., Jajodia, S., Paraboschi, S., & Samarati, P. (2011). Combining fragmentation and encryption to protect privacy in data storage. *ACM Transactions on Information and System Security, 13*(3), 1–33. doi:10.1145/1805974.1805978

Cloud Computing Use Case Discussion Group. (2010). *Cloud Computing Use Cases white paper*, version 4.0. Retrieved December 10, 2011, from http://opencloudmanifesto.org/Cloud_Computing_Use_Cases_Whitepaper-4_0.pdf

Cloud Security Alliance. (2010). *Guidance for identity & access management* v2.1. Retrieved from https://cloudsecurityalliance.org/guidance/csaguide-dom12-v2.10.pdf

Cloud Security Alliance. (2010). *Top threats to cloud computing* v1.0. Retrieved January 14, 2012, from https://cloudsecurityalliance.org/topthreats/csathreats.v1.0.pdf

Cloud Security Alliance. (2011). *Security guidance for critical areas of focus in cloud computing* V3.0. Retrieved December 10, 2011, from https://cloudsecurityalliance.org/guidance/csaguide.v3.0.pdf

Cloud Survey. (2008). *IT cloud services user survey (2008), pt. 2: Top benefits & challenges*. Retrieved from www.blogs.idc.com

Corritore, L. (2003). On-line trust: Concepts, evolving themes, a model. *International Journal of Human-Computer Studies, 58*(6), 737–758. doi:10.1016/S1071-5819(03)00041-7

Curtmola, R., Khan, O., & Burns, R. (2008). Robust remote data checking. *4th ACM Workshop on Storage Security and Survivability*, (pp. 63-68).

D'Amorim, M., & Havelund, K. (2005). Event-based runtime verification of Java programs. In *Proceedings of the Third International Workshop on Dynamic Analysis*, St. Louis, Missourim, May 17 -17, 2005), WODA '05 (pp. 1-7). New York, NY: ACM Press.

Daemen, J., & Rijmen, V. (2000). The block cipher RIJNDAEL. *(Cardis '98). Lecture Notes in Computer Science, 1820*, 247–256. doi:10.1007/10721064_26

Dahbur, K., Mohammad, B., & Tarakji, A. B. (2011). *A survey of risks, threats and vulnerabilities in cloud computing*. International Conference on Intelligent Semantic Web-Services and Applications 2011 (ISWSA '11). ACM, April 2011.

Dalkey, N., & Helmer, O. (1963). An experimental application of the DELPHI method to the use of experts. *Management Science, 9*(3), 458-467. JSTOR. doi:10.1287/mnsc.9.3.458

Dardenne, A., van Lamsweerde, A., & Fickas, S. (1993). Goal-directed requirements acquisition. *Science of Computer Programming, 20*, 3–50. doi:10.1016/0167-6423(93)90021-G

Das, A. S., & Srinathan, K. (2007). Privacy preserving cooperative clustering service. *15th International Conference on Advanced Computing and Communications (ADCOM 2007)* (pp. 435-440). Guwahati, India: IEEE. doi:10.1109/ADCOM.2007.52

Desai, N. (2003). *Intrusion prevention systems: The next step in the evolution of IDS*. SecurityFocus. Retrieved from http://www.securityfocus.com/infocus/1670

Doelitzscher, F., Reich, C., & Sulistio, A. (2010). Designing cloud services adhering to government privacy laws. *2010 10th IEEE International Conference on Computer and Information Technology (CIT 2010)*, (pp. 930-935).

Dropbox. (2011). Retrieved June 16, 2011, from https://www.dropbox.com

Dunn, J. (2011). DDoS attack sends Hong Kong stock exchange back to paper. *Techworld,* Aug 2011. Retrieved September 08, 2011, from http://bit.ly/nSAb84

Dyer, J. G., Lindemann, M., Perez, R., Sailer, R., Van Doorn, L., & Smith, S. W. (2001). Building the IBM 4758 secure coprocessor. *Computer, 34*(10), 57–66. doi:10.1109/2.955100

ElGamal, T. (1985). A public key cryptosystem and a signature scheme based on discrete logarithms. *IEEE Transactions on Information Theory, 31*(4), 469–472. doi:10.1109/TIT.1985.1057074

Erway, C., Küpçü, A., Papamanthou, C., & Tamassia, R. (2009). Dynamic provable data possession. *CCS'09, 16th ACM Conference on Computer and Communication Security*, (pp. 213-222).

European Network and Information Security Agency (ENISA). (2009). *Cloud computing. Benefits, risks and recommendations for information security*. Retrieved August 4, 2011, from http://bit.ly/CLeIX

Fabre, J.-C., Deswarte, Y., & Randell, B. (1994). Designing secure and reliable applications using fragmentation-redundancy-scattering: An object-oriented approach. *(EDCC-1: 1st European Dependable Computing Conference) Lecture Notes in Computer Science, vol. 852*, (pp. 21-38).

Feigenbaum, J., Pinkas, B., Ryger, R. S., & Saint Jean, F. (2004). Secure computation of surveys. *EU Workshop on Secure* (pp. 1-6). Retrieved from http://citeseerx.ist. psu.edu/viewdoc/download?doi=10.1.1.100.3258&amp ;rep=rep1&type=pdf

Feng, J., Chen, Y., Ku, W. S., & Liu, P. (2010). Analysis of integrity vulnerabilities and a non-repudiation protocol for cloud data storage platforms. In *39th International Conference on Parallel Processing Workshops* (pp. 251-258). Washington, DC: IEEE Computer Society.

Fengzhe, Z., Yijian, H., Huihong, W., Haibo, C., & Binyu, Z. (2008, October). PALM: Security preserving VM live migration for systems with VMM-enforced protection. *Third Asia-Pacific Trusted Infrastructure Technologies Conference, APTC '08* (pp. 9-18).

Ferguson, T. (2009). Salesforce.com outage hits thousands of businesses. *CNET News.* Retrieved January 14, 2012, from http://news.cnet.com/8301-1001_3-10136540-92. html

Fernandez, E. B., & Sorgente, T. (2005, August). A pattern language for secure operating system architectures. *Proceedings of the 5th Latin American Conference on Pattern Languages of Programs* (pp. 68-88). Campos do Jordao, Brazil.

Fernandez, E. B., Yoshioka, N., & Washizaki, H. (2009, March). Modeling misuse patterns. *Proceedings of the 4th International Workshop on Dependability Aspects of Data Warehousing and Mining Applications* (DAWAM 2009), in conjunction with the 4th International Conference on Availability, Reliability, and Security (ARES 2009) (pp. 566-571). Fukuoka, Japan.

Firesmith, D. (2003). Engineering security requirements. *Journal of Object Technology*, *2*(1), 53–68. Retrieved from http://www.jot.fm/issues/issue_2003_01/column-6doi:10.5381/jot.2003.2.1.c6

Ford, D., Labelle, F., Popovici, F. I., Stokely, M., Truong, V.-A., & Barroso, L. ... Quinlan, S. (2010). Availability in globally distributed storage systems. *9th USENIX Symposium on Operating Systems Designs and Implementation*, (pp. 61-74).

Forum, J. (2009). *Cloud cube model: Selecting cloud formations for secure collaboration.* Retrieved from http://www.opengroup.org/jericho/cloud_cube_model_v1.0.pdf

Foster, I., Zhao, Y., Raicu, I., & Lu, S. (2008). *Cloud computing and grid computing 360-degree compared. 2008 Grid Computing Environments Workshop* (pp. 1–10). Austin, TX: IEEE.

Frei, S., May, M., Fiedler, U., & Plattner, B. (2006). Large-scale vulnerability analysis. In *Proceedings of the 2006 SIGCOMM Workshop on Large-Scale Attack Defense* (pp. 131-138). New York, NY, USA: ACM.

Ganger, G. R., Khosla, P. K., Bakkaloglu, M., Bigrigg, M. W., Goodson, G. R., & Oguz, S. ... Wylie, J. J., (2001). Survivable storage systems. *2001 DARPA Information Survivability Conference and Exposition*, Vol. 2 (pp. 184-195).

Garfinkel, T., & Rosenblum, M. (2005). When *virtual is harder than real: Security challenges in virtual machine based computing environments. Proceedings of the 10th conference on Hot Topics in Operating Systems*, Santa Fe, NM.

Garfinkel, T., Pfaff, B., Chow, J., Rosenblum, M., & Boneh, D. (2003). Terra: A virtual machine-based platform for trusted computing. *ACM SIGOPS Operating Systems Review*, *37*(5), 193–206. doi:10.1145/1165389.945464

Gellman, R. (2009). *Privacy in the clouds: Risks to privacy and confidentiality from cloud computing.* Retrieved from http://www.worldprivacyforum.org/pdf/WPFCloud_Privacy_Report.pdf.

Gellman, R. (2009). *WPF REPORT: Privacy in the clouds: Risks to privacy and confidentiality from cloud computing.*

Gentry, C. (2009). Fully homomorphic encryption using ideal lattices. *Proceedings of the 41st Annual ACM Symposium on Theory of Computing*, (pp. 169-178).

Gentry, C. (2011). *Fully homomorphic encryption without bootstrapping*, Gutmann, P. (2000). An open-source cryptographic coprocessor. *Proceedings of the 9th Conference on USENIX Security Symposium*, Vol. 9, (p. 8).

Ghemawat, S., Gobioff, H., & Leung, S. (2003). The Google file system. *19th ACM Symposium on Operating Systems Principles* (SOSP '03), Vol. 37, (pp. 29-43). ACM, October 2003.

Ghinste, B. V. (2010). Gartner: Private cloud computing plans from conference polls. *MSDN Blogs*. Retrieved June 27, 2011, from http://blogs.msdn.com/b/architectsrule/archive/2010/05/07/gartner-private-cloud-computing-plans-from-conference-polls.aspx

Girouard, D. (2010). *Keeping your data safe*. Official Google Enterprise Blog. Jan 2010. Retrieved August 10, 2011, from http://bit.ly/7SabbN

Goldreich, O. (2000). *Secure multi-party computation*. Working Draft.

Golle, P., Staddon, J., & Waters, B. (2004). Secure conjunctive keyword search over encrypted data. *Applied Cryptography and Network Security Conference (ACNS'04)*, (pp. 31-45).

Gong, C., Liu, J., Zhang, Q., Chen, H., & Gong, Z. (2010). The characteristics of cloud computing. *Proceedings of the 2010 39th International Conference on Parallel Processing Workshops*. Washington, DC: IEEE Computer Society, USA.

Gresty, D. W., Shi, Q., & Merabti, M. (2001). Requirements for a general framework for response to distributed denial-of-service. *IEEE ACSAC, 2001*, 422–429.

Grobauer, B., Walloschek, T., & Stocker, E. (2011). Understanding cloud computing vulnerabilities. *IEEE Security & Privacy Magazine, 9*(2), 50–57. doi:10.1109/MSP.2010.115

Gurav, U., & Shaikh, R. (2010). Virtualization: A key feature of cloud computing. *Proceedings of the International Conference and Workshop on Emerging Trends in Technology* (pp. 227-229). Mumbai, Maharashtra, India.

Hao, F., Lakshman, T., Mukherjee, S., & Song, H. (2010). Secure cloud computing with a virtualized network infrastructure. *Proceedings of the 2nd USENIX Conference on Hot Topics in Cloud Computing* (pp. 16–16). Boston, MA: USENIX Association. doi:10.1234/12345678

Hardesty, L. (2009). *Secure computers aren't so secure*. MIT Press. Retrieved from www.physorg.com/news176107396.html

Härtig, H., Roitzsch, M., Lackorzynski, A., Döbel, B., & Böttcher, A. (2008). *L4 – Virtualization and beyond*. Korean Information Science Society Review.

Havelund, K., & Rosu, G. (2001A). Monitoring Java programs with Java PathExplorer. In *Proceedings of the 1st International Workshop on Runtime Verification (RV'01)*, (pp. 97-114).

Havelund, K., & Rosu, G. (2001B). Monitoring programs using rewriting. In *Proceedings of International Conference on Automated Software Engineering (ASE'01)*, (pp. 135-143). Coronado Island, CA: Institute of Electrical and Electronics Engineers.

Havelung, K., & Rosu, G. (2002). Sinthezising monitors for safety properties. In *Tools and Algorithms for Constrction and Analysis of Systems (TACAS '02), LNCS 2280*, (pp. 342-356). Springer.

Houmb, S. H. (2007). *Decision support for choice of security solution- The aspect-oriented risk driven development (AORDD) framework*. PhD thesis, Department of Computer and Information Science, Norwegian University of Science and Technology.

Hu, H., & Xu, J. (2009). Non-exposure location anonymity. *2009 IEEE 25th International Conference on Data Engineering* (pp. 1120-1131). Shanghai, China: IEEE. doi:10.1109/ICDE.2009.106

Huynh, T., & Miller, J. (2010). An empirical investigation into open source web applications' implementation vulnerabilities. *Empirical Software Engineering, 15*(5), 556–576. doi:10.1007/s10664-010-9131-y

Hwang, K., Kulkareni, S., & Hu, Y. (2009). Cloud security with virtualized defense and reputation-based trust management. In *Eighth IEEE International Conference on Dependable, Autonomic and Secure Computing* (pp. 717-722). Washington, DC: IEEE Computer Society.

Idziorek, J., Tannian, M., & Jacobson, D. (2011). Detecting fraudulent use of cloud resources. In *Proceedings of the 3rd ACM Workshop on Cloud Computing Security Workshop* (pp. 61-72). New York, NY: ACM.

Intel Corporation. (2009). The dark cloud: Understanding and defending against botnets and stealthy malware. *Intel Technology Journal, 13*(02). Retrieved from http://www.intel.com/technology/itj/2009/v13i2/ITJ9.2.9-Cloud.htm

Ireland, K., & Rosen, M. (1990). *A classical introduction to modern number theory* (2nd ed.). New York, NY: Springer-Verlag.

Islam, S. (2009). Software development risk management model: A goal driven approach. In *Proceedings of the Doctoral Symposium for ESEC/FSE on Doctoral Symposium*, The Netherlands.

Islam, S., & Dong, W. (2008). Human factors in software security risk management. In *LMSA '08: Proceedings of the First International Workshop on Leadership and Management in Software Architecture*, (pp. 13–16). New York, NY: ACM.

Islam, S., & Houmb, S. H. (2010). Integrating risk management activities into requirements engineering. In *Proceedings of the 4th IEEE Research International Conference on Research Challenges in IS*, Nice, France.

Islam, S., & Houmb, S. H. (2011a). Towards a framework for offshore outsource software development risk management model. *Journal of Software, 6*(1), 38–47. doi:10.4304/jsw.6.1.38-47

Islam, S., Mouratidis, H., & Jürjens, J. (2011b). A framework to support alignment of secure software engineering with legal regulations. *Journal of Software and Systems Modelling (SoSyM). Theme Section on Non-Functional System Properties in Domain-Specific Modelling Languages, 10*(3), 369–394.

Itani, W., Kayssi, A., & Chehab, A. (2005). Short paper: PATRIOT-a policy-based, multi-level security protocol for safekeeping audit logs on wireless devices. *First International Conference on Security and Privacy for Emerging Areas in Communications Networks, SecureComm 2005* (pp. 240-242).

Itani, W., Kayssi, A., & Chehab, A. (2009). Privacy as a service: Privacy-aware data storage and processing in cloud computing architectures. *2009 Eighth IEEE International Conference on Dependable, Autonomic and Secure Computing,* (pp. 711-716).

Itani, W., Kayssi, A., & Chehab, A. (2008). Policy-based security for M-commerce networks. In Huang, W. W., Wang, Y., & Day, J. (Eds.), *Global mobile commerce: Strategies, implementation and case studies* (p. 53).

Janger, E. J., & Schwartz, P. M. (2001). Gramm-Leach-Bliley Act, information privacy, and the limits of default rules. *Minnesota Law Review, 86*, 1219.

Jeffery, K., & Neidecker-Kutz, B. (2010). *The future of cloud computing opportunities for European cloud computing beyond 2010.* European Commission: CORDIS: FP7.

Jeng, J.-J., Schiefer, J., & Chang, H. (2003). An agent-based architecture for analyzing business processes of real-time enterprises. *Proceedings of EDOC, 2003, 86*–97.

Jensen, M., Schwenk, J., Gruschka, N., & Iacono, L. L. (2009). On technical security issues in cloud computing. *2009 IEEE International Conference on Cloud Computing* (pp. 109-116). Bangalore, India: IEEE. doi:10.1109/CLOUD.2009.60

Jøsang, A. (2007). Trust and reputation systems. In *Foundations of Security Analysis and Design IV, FOSAD 2006/2007 Tutorial Lectures, LNCS 4677.* Springer.

Joshi, J. B. D., Bertino, E., Latif, U., & Ghafoor, A. (2005). A generalized temporal role-based access control model. *IEEE Transactions on Knowledge and Data Engineering, 17*(1), 4–23. doi:10.1109/TKDE.2005.1

Joshi, J. B. D., Bhatti, R., & Bertino, E., & Ghafoor. (2004). Access control language for multi domain environments. *IEEE Internet Computing, 8*(6), 40–50. doi:10.1109/MIC.2004.53

Joshua, L., Hassen, S., & Tomas, U. (2002). Combining monitors for run-time system verification. In Havelund, K., & Rosu, G. (Eds.), *Electronic Notes in Theoretical Computer Science, 70(4).* Elsevier Science.

Juels, A., & Kaliski, B. S., Jr. (2007). PORs: Proofs of retrievability for large files. *CCS'07, 14ᵗʰ ACM Conference on Computer and Communication Security,* (pp. 584-597)

Kagono, T. (2006). Cognitive theories and knowledge management: A review of recent studies. In *The Annual Bulletin of Knowledge Management Society of Japan* (Eds.), *The Knowledge Forum 2005: Japanese Chi: Edge of Evolution*: Nº 7. Track A-1. Knowledge Management Society of Japan. Japan.

Kaliski, B. S., Jr., & Pauley, W. (2010). Toward risk assessment as a service in cloud environments. *Proceedings of the 2nd USENIX Conference on Hot Topics in Cloud Computing* (pp. 13–13). Boston, MA: USENIX Association. Retrieved from http://portal.acm.org/citation.cfm?id=1863116

Kallahalla, M., Riedel, E., Swaminathan, R., Wang, Q., & Fu, K. (2003). Plutus: Scalable secure file sharing on untrusted storage. *FAST '03 Proceedings of the 2nd USENIX Conference on File and Storage Technologies*, (pp. 29-42).

Kamara, S., & Lauter, K. (2010). Cryptographic cloud storage. *FC'10 Proceedings of the 14th International Conference on Financial Cryptography and Data Security*, (pp. 136-149).

Karolak, D. (1996). *Software engineering risk management*. CA, USA: IEEE Computer Society Press.

Kelsey, J., Schneier, B., & Hall, C. (1996). An authenticated camera. *12th Annual Computer Security Applications Conference, 1996* (pp. 24-30).

Kermarrec, A.-M., Le Merrer, E., Straub, G., & Van Kempen, A. (2010). Availability-based methods for distributed storage systems. *HAL-Inria Open Archive*. Retrieved from http://hal.inria.fr/hal-00521034/en

Kher, V., & Kim, Y. (2005). Securing distributed storage: Challenges, techniques, and systems. *StorageSS '05 Proceedings of the 2005 ACM Workshop on Storage Security and Survivability*, (pp. 9-25).

Kiczales, G., Hilsdale, E., Hugunin, J., Kersten, M., Palm, J., & Griswold, W. G. (2001). An overview of AspectJ. In *Proceedings of the 15th European Conference on Object-Oriented Programming*, (pp. 327-353). Springer-Verlag.

Kifayat, K., Merabti, M., & Shi, Q. (2010). Future security challenges of cloud computing. *International Journal of Multimedia Intelligence and Security, 1*(4). doi:10.1504/IJMIS.2010.039241

Kim, M., Joshi, J. B. D., & Kim, M. (2008). Access control for cooperation systems based on group situation. In E. Bertino & J. B. D. Joshi (Eds.), *4th International Conference on Collaborative Computing: Networking, Applications and Worksharing (CollaborateCom2008)* (pp. 11-23). Berlin, Germany: Springer.

Ko, M., Ahn, G. J., & Shehab, M. (2009). Privacy enhanced user-centric identity management. In G. Fettweis (Ed.), *IEEE International Conference on Communications* (pp. 1-5). Dresden, Germany: IEEE Press.

Ko, S. Y., Jeon, K., & Morales, R. (2011). The HybrEx model for confidentiality and privacy in cloud computing. *Proceedings of the 2011 conference on Hot topics in cloud computing*, Portland, OR. Retrieved from http://www.usenix.org/event/hotcloud11/tech/final_files/Ko.pdf

Kodali, N. B., Farkas, C., & Wijesekera, D. (2004). Specifying multimedia access control using RDF. *Journal of Computer Systems, Science and Engineering, 19*(3).

Kontio, J. (2001). *Software engineering risk management: A Method, improvement framework and empirical evaluation*. PhD thesis, Helsinki University of Technology.

Koriat, A. (2004). Metacognition research: An interim report. In Perfect, T., & Schwartz, B. L. (Eds.), *Applied metacognition* (pp. 261–286). Cambridge, UK: Cambridge University Press.

Krautheim, F. J. (2009). Private virtual infrastructure for cloud computing. *Proceedings of the 2009 Conference on Hot Topics in Cloud Computing* (pp. 5–5). San Diego, CA: USENIX Association. Retrieved from http://portal.acm.org/citation.cfm?id=1855538

Krutz, R., & Vines, R. (2010). *Cloud security. A comprehensive guide to secure cloud computing* (p. 61). Indianapolis, IN: John Wiley & Sons, Inc.

Kushilevitz, E., & Ostrovsky, R. (1997). Replication is not needed: Single database, computationally-private information retrieval. *38th Annual Symposium on Foundation of Computer Science*, (pp. 364-373).

Lamsweerde, van A. (2009). *Requirements engineering: From system goals to UML models to software specifications*. Wiley.

Lawson, N. (2009). Side-channel attacks on cryptographic software. *IEEE Security and Privacy, November/December*, 65-68.

Lazovik, A., Aiello, M., & Papazoglou, M. (2004). Associating assertions with business processes and monitoring their execution. In *Conference on Service-Oriented Computing* (ICSOC-04), (pp. 94-104). Lee, H. L., & Whang, S. (2000). Information sharing in a supply chain. *International Journal of Manufacturing Technology and Management, 1*(1), 79.

Lee, I., Kannan, S., Kim, K., Sokolsky, O., & Viswanahtan, M. (1999). Runtime assurance based on formal specifications. In *Proceedings of the International Conference on Parallel and Distributed Processing Techniques and Applications.*

Leymann, F., & Roller, D. (1997). Workflow-based applications. *IBM Systems Journal, 36*(1), 102–123. doi:10.1147/sj.361.0102

Li, A., Yang, X., Kandula, S., & Zhang, M. (2010). CloudCmp: shopping for a cloud made easy. *Proceedings of the 2nd USENIX Conference on Hot Topics in Cloud Computing* (pp. 5–5). Boston, MA: USENIX Association. Retrieved from http://portal.acm.org/citation.cfm?id=1863108

Li, C., Raghunathan, A., & Jha, N. K. (2010). Secure virtual machine execution under an untrusted management OS. *2010 IEEE 3rd International Conference on Cloud Computing,* (pp. 172-179).

Li, H. C., Liang, P. H., Yang, J. M., & Chen, S. J. (2010). Analysis on cloud-based security vulnerability assessment. In *International Conference on E-Business Engineering* (pp. 490-494). Washington, DC: IEEE Computer Society.

Li, J., Shaw, M. J., Sikora, R. T., Tan, G. W., & Yang, R. (2001). *The effects of information sharing strategies on supply chain performance.* College of Commerce and Business Administration, University of Illinois, Urbana-Champaign, IL. Retrieved September 9, 2011, from http://citebm.cba.uiuc.edu/B2Bresearch/ieee_em.pdf

Lidl, R., & Niederreiter, H. (1984). *Finite fields.* Cambridge, UK: Cambridge University Press.

Li, J., Li, B., Wo, T., Hu, C., Huai, J., Liu, L., & Lam, K. P. (2012). CyberGuarder: A virtualization security assurance architecture for green cloud computing. *Future Generation Computer Systems, 28*(2), 379–390. doi:10.1016/j.future.2011.04.012

Lillard, T. V., Garrison, C. P., Schiller, C. A., & Steele, J. (2010). The future of cloud computing. In *Digital Forensics for Network, Internet, and Cloud Computing* (pp. 319-339). Syngress.

Lombardi, F., & Di Pietro, R. (2011). Secure virtualization for cloud computing. *Journal of Network and Computer Applications, 34*(4), 1113–1122. doi:10.1016/j.jnca.2010.06.008

Lowe, S. (2009). *Mastering VMware vSphere 4.* Sybex.

Mahbub, K., & Spanoudakis, G. (2004). A framework for requirements monitoring of service based systems. In *Proceedings of the 2ⁿᵈ Internatonal Conference on Service Oriented Computing,* NY, USA

Mayer, N., Heymans, P., & Matulevicius, R. (2007). Design of a modelling language for information system security risk management. In *Proceedings of the 1st InternationalConference on Research Challenges in Information Science* (RCIS 2007), (pp. 121–131).

Mcfredries, P. (2008). The cloud is the computer. *IEEE Spectrum,* (August): 2008. Retrieved July 24, 2011 from http://www.spectrum.ieee.org/computing/hardware/the-cloud-is-the-computer

McGregor, C., & Kumaran, S. (2002). An agent-based system for trading partner management in B2B e-commerce. In *Proceedings of RIDE 2002,* (p. 84).

McGregor, C., & Schiefer, J. (2003). A framework for analyzing and measuring business performance with web services. In *Proceeding of CEC 2003,* (p. 405).

McKnight, D. H., & Chervany, N. L. (1996). *The meanings of trust.* Technical Report MISRC Working Paper Series 96-04, University of Minnesota.

MediaWiki.Org. (n.d.). Retrieved September 9, 2011, from http://www.mediawiki.org/wiki/MediaWiki

Mehta, N., & Smith, R. (2007). *VMWare DHCP server remote code execution vulnerabilities.* IBM Internal Security Systems. Retrieved July 12, 2011, from http://www.iss.net/threats/275.html

Mell, P., & Grance, T. (2011). *The NIST definition of cloud computing.* NIST Special Publication 800-145 (Draft). Retrieved August 10, 2011, from http://csrc.nist.gov/publications/drafts/800-145/Draft-SP-800-145_cloud-definition.pdf

Meyer, B. (2000). *Object-oriented software construction* (2nd ed.). Upper Saddle River, NJ: Prenctice Hall.

Miseldine, P., & Taleb-Bendiab, A. (2005). A programmatic approach to applying sympathetic and parasympathetic autonomic systems to software design. In H. Czap, R. Unland, C. Branki, & H. Tianfield (Eds.), Self-organisation and autonomic informatics (pp. 293-303). Amsterdam, The Netherlands: IOS Press. ISBN I-58603-577-0

Miseldine, P., & Taleb-Bendiab, A. (2007). *Neptune: Supporting semantics-based runtime software refactoring to achieved assured system autonomy.* Technical report, DASEL Technical Report 2007/07/PM01, LJMU. Retrieved September 5, 2011, from http://www.cms.livjm.ac.uk/taleb/Publications/07/TR-2007.07.PM01.pdf

MITRE. (2011). *Common vulnerabilities and exposures: Terminology.* Retrieved January 14, 2012, from http://cve.mitre.org/about/terminology.html

Mouratidis, H. (2004). *A security oriented approach in the development of multiagent systems: Applied to the management of the health and social care needs of older people in England.* PhD thesis, University of Sheffield, U.K., 2004.

Mouratidis, H., & Giorgini, P. (2007). Security attack testing (SAT) - Testing the security of information systems at design time. *Information Systems, 32*(8), 1166–1183. doi:10.1016/j.is.2007.03.002

Mouratidis, H., & Giorgini, P. (2009). Secure Tropos: A security-oriented extension of the Tropos methodology. *International Journal of Software Engineering and Knowledge Engineering, 17*(2).

Mowbray, M., & Pearson, S. (2009). A client-based privacy manager for cloud computing. *Proceedings of the Fourth International ICST Conference on COMmunication System softWAre and middlewaRE - COMSWARE '09* (p. 1). Dublin, Ireland: ACM Press. doi:10.1145/1621890.1621897

Mulazzani, M., Schrittwieser, S., Leithner, M., Huber, M., & Weippl, E. (2011). Dark clouds on the horizon: Using cloud storage as attack vector and online slack space. *Proceedings of Usenix Security.*

Mulholland, A., Pyke, J., & Fingar, P. (2010). *Enterprise cloud computing.* Tampa, FL: Meghan-Kiffer Press.

Naglieri, J. A. (2011). The discrepancy/consitency approach to SLD identification using the PASS theory. In Flanagan, D. P., & Alfonso, V. C. (Eds.), *Essentials of specific learning disability identification* (pp. 147–148). Hoboken, NJ: Wiley.

Narayan, S., & Chandy, J. A. (2007). Parity redundancy in a clustered storage system. *SNAPI '07 Proceedings of the Fourth International Workshop on Storage Network Architecture and Parallel I/Os,* (pp.17-24).

No, J. (2009). Data consistency protocol for distributed file systems. *IDAACS 2009, IEEE International Workshop on Intelligent Data Acquisition and Advanced Computing Systems: Technology and Applications, 2009,* (pp. 253-258).

Ormandy, T. (2007). An empirical study into the security exposure to host of hostile virtualized environments. *Proceedings of CanSecWest Applied Security Conference,* Vancouver, Canada. doi:10.1.1.105.6943

Pearson, S. (2009). Taking account of privacy when designing cloud computing services. *Proceedings of the 2009 ICSE Workshop on Software Engineering Challenges of Cloud Computing,* (pp. 44-52).

Pearson, S., & Charlesworth, A. (2009). Accountability as a way forward for privacy protection in the cloud. *Proceedings of the 1st International Conference on Cloud Computing,* (pp. 131-144).

Peterson, Z., & Gondree, M. (2011). A position paper on data sovereignty: The importance of geolocating data in the cloud. *Proceedings of the 2011 Conference on Hot Topics in Cloud Computing.* Portland, OR. Retrieved from http://www.usenix.org/event/hotcloud11/tech/final_files/Peterson.pdf

Pnueli, A. (1977). The temporal logic of programs. In *Proceedings of the 18th IEEE Symposium on Foundations of Computer Science,* (pp. 46-77).

Popa, L., Yu, M., Ko, S. Y., Ratnasamy, S., & Stoica, I. (2010). CloudPolice: Taking access control out of the network. *Proceedings of the Ninth ACM SIGCOMM Workshop on Hot Topics in Networks* (p. 7). Monterey, CA: ACM. Retrieved from http://portal.acm.org/citation.cfm?id=1868454

Pras, A., et al. (2010). *Attacks by anonymous WikiLeaks proponents not anonymous.* CIIT Technical Report, December 2010. Retrieved September 9, 2011, from http://www.ctit.utwente.nl/news/archive/2010/dec10/Attacks%20-anonymous.docx/

Pressley, M. (2000). Development of grounded theories of complex cognitive processing: Exhaustive withing- and between study analyses of thinking-aloud data. In Schraw, G., & Impara, J. C. (Eds.), *Issues in the measurement of metacognition* (pp. 262–269). Lincoln, NE: Buros Institute of Mental Measurements.

Proofpoint. (2009). Outbound email and data loss prevention in today's enterprise. Sunnyvale.

Resnick, P. (2000). Reputation systems. *Communications of the ACM, 43*(12), 45–48. doi:10.1145/355112.355122

Richter, W., Ammons, G., Harkes, J., Goode, A., Bila, N., de Lara, E., et al. (2011). Privacy-sensitive VM retrospection. *Proceedings of the 2011 Conference on Hot Topics in Cloud Computing* (pp. 1-6). Portland, OR. Retrieved from http://www.usenix.org/events/hotcloud11/tech/final_files/Richter.pdf

Ristenpart, T., Tromer, E., Shacham, H., & Savage, S. (2009). Hey, you, get off of my cloud: Exploring information leakage in third-party compute clouds. *Proceedings of the 16th ACM Conference on Computer and Communications Security* (pp. 199-212). Chicago, Illinois, USA.

Rivest, R., Shamir, A., & Adleman, L. (1978). A method for obtaining digital signatures and public-key cryptosystems. *Communications of the ACM, 21*(2), 120–126. doi:10.1145/359340.359342

Robinson, W. (2002). Monitoring software requirements unsing intrumentation code. In *Proceedings of the Hawaii International Conference on Systems Sciences.*

Rodrıguez-Silva, D., González-Castano, F., Adkinson-Orellana, L., Fernández-Cordeiro, A., Troncoso-Pastoriza, J., & González-Martınez, D. (2011). *Encrypted domain processing for cloud privacy.*

Roy, G. (2004). A risk management framework for software engineering practice. In *Proceedings of the 2004 Australian Software Engineering Conference*, IEEE Computer Society.

Sadeghi, A., Stüble, C., & Winandy, M. (2008). Property-based TPM virtualization. In Wu, T.-C., Lei, C.-L., Rijmen, V., & Lee, D.-T. (Eds.), *Information Security* (*Vol. 5222*, pp. 1–16). Lecture Notes in Computer ScienceBerlin, Germany: Springer. doi:10.1007/978-3-540-85886-7_1

Santos, N., Gummadi, K. P., & Rodrigues, R. (2009). Towards trusted cloud computing *Proceedings of the 2009 Conference on Hot Topics in Cloud Computing.* San Diego, CA: USENIX Association.

Saripalli, P., & Walters, B. (2010). *QUIRC: A quantitative impact and risk assessment framework for cloud security.* IEEE 3rd International Conference on Cloud Computing.

SBA. (2011). Secure Business Austria. Retrieved November 15, 2011, from http://www.sba-research.org/research/

Schneier, B. (2009). *People understand risks - But do security staff understand people?* Retrieved September 1, 2011, from https://www.schneier.com/essay-282.html

Schneier, B. (2009). *Schnier on security.* Retrieved from Http://www.schneier.com/blog/archives/2009/07/homomorphic_enc.html

Schneier, B. (2000). *Secrets and lies. Digital security in a networked world* (p. xii). New York, NY: John Wiley & Sons, Inc.doi:10.1108/146366903322008296

Schneier, B., & Kelsey, J. (1997). Remote auditing of software outputs using a trusted coprocessor. *Future Generation Computer Systems, 13*(1), 9–18. doi:10.1016/S0167-739X(97)00004-6

Schneier, B., & Kelsey, J. (1999). Secure audit logs to support computer forensics. *ACM Transactions on Information and System Security, 2*(2), 159–176. doi:10.1145/317087.317089

School, W. B. (2005). Delphi decision aid. Retrieved October 5, 2010, from http://armstrong.wharton.upenn.edu/delphi2/

Seixas, N., Fonseca, J., Vieira, M., & Madeira, H. (2009). Looking at Web security vulnerabilities from the programming language perspective: A field study. In *International Symposium on Software Reliability Engineering,* (pp. 129-135). Washington, DC: IEEE Computer Society.

Sellink, A., & Verhoef, C. (1999). An architecture for automated software maintenance. In *Proceedings of the 7th Intl. Workshop on Program Comprehension.*

Sen, K., & Rosu, G. (2003). Generating optimal monitors for extended regular expressions. In *Proceedings of the 3rd International Workshop on Runtime Verification* (RV'03), (pp. 162-181).

SERENITY. (n.d.). *System engineering for security and dependability.* SERENITY, EU-funded project. Retrieved from http://www.serenity-project.org/

Serrano, D., Ruiz, J. F., Armenteros, A., Gallego-Nicasio, B., Muñoz, A., & Maña, A. (2009). *Development of applications based on security patterns.* Second International Conference on Dependability (DEPEND2009): IEEE Computer Society.

Shacham, H., & Waters, B. (2008). Compact proofs of retrievability. *ASIACRYPT, 08*, 90–107.

Shanahan, M. (1999). The event calculus explained. In *Artificial Intelligence Today, LNAI 1600*, (pp. 409-430).

Shanahan, M. (1999). The event calculus planner. *The Journal of Logic Programming, 44*, 207–239. doi:10.1016/S0743-1066(99)00077-1

Shen, Z., & Tong, Q. (2010). The security of cloud computing system enabled by trusted computing technology. *2nd International Conference on Signal Processing Systems* (ICSPS), Vol. 2 (pp. 11-15). July 2010.

Shin, D., & Ahn, G. J. (2005). Role-based privilege and trust management. *Computer Systems Science & Engineering Journal, 20*(6).

Siebenhaar, M., Tsai, H. Y., Lampe, U., & Steinmetz, R. (2011). Analyzing and modeling security aspects of cloud-based systems. *GI/ITG KuVS Fachgespräch "Sicherheit für Cloud Computing"*, (April). Retrieved from ftp://ftp.kom.e-technik.tu-darmstadt.de/papers/STLS11.pdf

Skulmoski, G. J., Hartman, F. T., & Krahn, J. (2007). The Delphi method for graduate research. *Journal of Information Technology Education, 6*, 1-21. doi:10.1.1.151.8144

Sobe, P., & Peter, K. (2006). Comparison of redundancy schemes for distributed storage systems. *5th IEEE International Symposium on Network Computing and Applications*, (pp. 196-203).

Somorovsky, J., Heiderich, M., Jensen, M., Schwenk, J., Gruschka, N., & Iacono, L. L. (2011). All your clouds are belong to us: Security analysis of cloud management interfaces. In *Proceedings of the 3rd ACM Workshop on Cloud Computing Security Workshop* (pp. 3-14). New York, NY: ACM.

Song, D., Wagner, D., & Perrig, A. (2000). Practical techniques for searches on encrypted data. *IEEE Symposium on Security and Privacy 2000*, (pp. 44-55).

Spanoudakis, G. (2007). Dynamic trust assessment of software services. *Proceedings of 2nd International Workshop on Service Oriented Software Engineering.*

Stickel, M. (1998). A Prolog-like inference system for computing minimun-cost abductive explanaitions in natural-language interpretation. In *International Computer Science Conference*, Hong Kong, (pp. 343-350).

Stolen, K., den Braber, F., Fredriksen, R., Gran, B. A., & Houmb, S. H. Stama- tiou, Y. C., & Aagedal, J. Â. (2007). Model-based risk assessment in a component-based software engineering process - Using the CORAS approach to identify security risks. In F. Barbier (Ed.), *Business component-based software engineering.* Kluwer Academic Publishers.

Subashini, S., & Kavitha, V. (2011). A survey on security issues in service delivery models of cloud computing. *Journal of Network and Computer Applications, 34*(1), 1-11. Elsevier. doi:10.1016/j.jnca.2010.07.006

Subashini, S., & Kavitha, V. (2011). A survey on security issues in service delivery models of cloud computing. *Journal of Network and Computer Applications, 34*(1), 1–11. doi:10.1016/j.jnca.2010.07.006

Swiderski, F., & Snyder, W. (2004). *Threat modeling.* Redmond, WA: Microsoft Press.

Takabi, H., & Joshi, J. B. D. (2010). StateMiner: An efficient similarity-based approach for optimal mining of role hierarchy. In B. Carminati (Ed.), *15th ACM Symposium on Access Control Models and Technologies* (pp. 55-64), Pittsburgh, PA: ACM Press.

Takabi, H., & Joshi, J. B. D. (2012). *Policy management as a service: An approach to manage policy heterogeneity in cloud computing environment.* In 45th Hawaii International Conference on System Sciences (HICSS), Hawaii, USA.

Takabi, H., Joshi, J. B. D., & Ahn, G. J. (2010). SecureCloud: Towards a comprehensive security framework for cloud computing environments. In S. I. Ahamed, D. H. Bae, S. Cha, C. K. Chang, R. Subramanyan, E. Wong, & H. I. Yang (Eds.), *34th Annual IEEE Computer Software and Applications Conference Workshops (COMPSACW 2010)* (pp. 393-398), Seoul, South Korea: IEEE Press.

Takabi, H., Kim, M., Joshi, J. B. D., & Spring, M. B. (2009). An architecture for specification and enforcement of temporal access control constraints using OWL. In E. Damiani, S. Proctor, & A. Singal (Eds.), *2009 ACM Workshop on Secure Web Services* (pp. 21-28). Chicago, IL: ACM Press.

Takabi, H., & Joshi, J. B. D. (2012). Semantic based policy management for cloud computing environment. *International Journal of Cloud Computing, 1*(2-3), 119–144. doi:10.1504/IJCC.2012.046717

Takabi, H., Joshi, J. B. D., & Ahn, G. J. (2010). Security and privacy challenges in cloud computing environments. *IEEE Security and Privacy, 8*(6), 24–31. doi:10.1109/MSP.2010.186

Tan, C., Liu, Q., & Wu, J. (2011). *Secure locking for untrusted clouds.* 4th IEEE International Conference on Cloud Computing (CLOUD 2011).

Tang, Y., Lee, P., Lui, J., & Perlman, R. (2010). *FADE: Secure overlay cloud storage with file assured deletion.* Securecomm 2010.

Teo, L., & Ahn, G. J. (2007). Managing heterogeneous network environments using an extensible policy framework. In R. Deng & P. Samarati (Eds.), *2nd ACM Symposium on Information, Computer and Communications Security* (pp. 362-364). Singapore: ACM Press.

Theodoropoulos, D., Papaefstathiou, I., & Pnevmatikatos, D. (2008). *Cproc: An efficient cryptographic coprocessor.* 16th IFIP/IEEE International Conference on very Large Scale Integration.

TippingPoint. (2009). *The top cyber security risks.*

Tiwana, B., Balakrishnan, M., Aguilera, M. K., Ballani, H., & Mao, Z. M. (2010). Location, location, location! Modeling data proximity in the cloud. *Proceedings of the Ninth ACM SIGCOMM Workshop on Hot Topics in Networks* (p. 15). Monterey, CA: ACM. doi:10.1145/1868447.1868462

Troncoso-Pastoriza, J. R., & Pérez-González, F. (2010). CryptoDSPs for cloud privacy. *Workshop on Cloud Information System Engineering (CISE'10)* (pp. 1-12). Hong Kong, China. doi:10.1.1.185.429

Trusted Computing Group home page. (n.d.). Retrieved from http://www.trustedcomputinggroup.org/

Tygar, J., & Yee, B. (1993). Dyad: A system for using physically secure coprocessors. *Proceedings of the Joint Harvard-MIT Workshop on Technological Strategies for the Protection of Intellectual Property in the Network Multimedia Environment,* (p. 87).

Vache, G. (2009). Vulnerability analysis for a quantitative security evaluation. In *Proceedings of the 3rd International Symposium on Empirical Software Engineering and Measurement* (pp. 526-534). Washington, DC: IEEE Computer Society.

van den Brand, M. G. J., Sellink, M. P. A., & Verhoef, C. (1999). Control flow normalization for COBOL/CICS legacy system. In *Proceedings of the 2nd Euromicro Conference on Maintenance and Reengineering.*

Van Dijk, M., Gentry, C., Halevi, S., & Vaikuntanathan, V. (2010). Fully homomorphic encryption over the integers. *Advances in Cryptology–EUROCRYPT, 2010,* 24–43.

Veenman, M. V. J., Van Hout-Wolters, B., & Afflerbach, P. (2006). Metacognition and learning: Conceptual and methodological considerations. *Metacognition and Learning, 1,* 3–14. doi:10.1007/s11409-006-6893-0

Verhoef, C. (2000). Towards automated modification of legacy assets. *Annals of Software Engineering, 9*(1-4), 315–336. doi:10.1023/A:1018941228255

Viega, J. (2009). Cloud computing and the common man. *Computer, 42*(8), 106–108. doi:10.1109/MC.2009.252

Vieira, K., Schulter, A., Westphall, C. B., & Westphall, C. M. (2010). Intrusion detection for grid and cloud computing. *IT Professional,* 38–43. doi:10.1109/MITP.2009.89

Vigfusson, Y., & Chockler, G. (2010). Clouds at the crossroads. *Crossroads, 16*(3), 10–13. doi:10.1145/1734160.1734165

VMware. (n.d.). *VMware vMotion – Migrate virtual machine with zero downtime.* Retrieved from http://www.vmware.com/products/vmotion/

Volkel, M., Krotzsch, M., Vrandecic, D., Haller, H., & Studer, R. (2006). Semantic Wikipedia. *Proceedings of the 15th International Conference on World Wide Web,* May 23-26, Edinburgh, Scotland, 2006.

Wang, C., & Zhou, Y. (2010). A collaborative monitoring mechanism for making a multitenant platform accountable. *Proceedings of the 2nd USENIX Conference on Hot Topics in Cloud Computing* (pp. 18-25). Boston, MA: ACM. Retrieved from http://www.usenix.org/event/hotcloud10/tech/full_papers/WangC.pdf

Wang, Q. Luo, Y., & Huang, L. (2008). Privacy-preserving protocols for finding the convex hulls. *2008 Third International Conference on Availability, Reliability and Security*, (070412043), 727-732. IEEE. doi:10.1109/ARES.2008.11

Wang, Q. Wang, C., Li, J., Ren, K., & Lou, W. (2009). Enabling public verifiability and data dynamics for storage security in cloud computing. In M. Backes & P. Ning (Eds.), *LNCS, Vol. 5789, ESORICS 2009* (pp. 355-370). Berlin, Germany: Springer. doi:doi:10.1007/978-3-642-04444-1

Wang, Z., & Jiang, X. (2010). HyperSafe: A lightweight approach to provide lifetime hypervisor control-flow integrity. In *Proceedings of the 31st IEEE Symposium on Security & Privacy* (pp. 380-395). Washington, DC: IEEE Computer Society.

Wang, Z., & Lee, R. B. (2006). Covert and side channels due to processor architecture. *Proceedings of the 22nd Annual Computer Security Applications Conference.*

Wei, J., Zhang, X., Ammons, G., Bala, V., & Ning, P. (2009). Managing security of virtual machine images in a cloud environment. *Proceedings of the 2009 ACM Workshop on Cloud Computing Security* (pp. 91-96).

Weingart, S. H. (1987). Physical security for the mABYSS system. *System, 1*(2), 3.

Wheeler, E. (2011). *Security risk management. Building an information security risk management program for the ground up.* Syngress, MA: Elsevier Inc.

White, S. R., Weingart, S. H., Arnold, W. C., & Palmer, E. R. (1991). *Introduction to the Citadel architecture: Security in physically exposed environments.*

White, S. R., & Comerford, L. (1990). ABYSS: An architecture for software protection. *IEEE Transactions on Software Engineering, 16*(6), 619–629. doi:10.1109/32.55090

Wiki Call for Papers. (n.d.). Retrieved March 9, 2011, from http://www.wikicfp.com/cfp/

Wolfgang Kandek, CTO & Qualys, Inc. (2009). *The laws of vulnerabilities 2.0.* Retrieved January 14, 2012, from http://www.qualys.com/docs/Laws_2.0.pdf

Wood, T., Gerber, A., Ramakrishnan, K., Shenoy, P., & Van der Merwe, J. (2009). The case for enterprise-ready virtual private clouds. *Proceedings of the 2009 Conference on Hot Topics in Cloud Computing* (pp. 4–9). Monterey, CA: USENIX Association. Retrieved from http://portal.acm.org/citation.cfm?id=1855537

Wylie, J. J., Bigrigg, M. W., Strunk, J. D., Ganger, G. R., Kilite, H., & Khosla, P. K. (2000). Survivable information storage systems. *IEEE Computer, 33*(8), 61–68. doi:10.1109/2.863969

Yao, A. C. (1982). Protocols for secure computations. *23rd Annual Symposium on Foundations of Computer Science* (pp. 160-164). Chicago, IL: IEEE. doi:10.1109/SFCS.1982.38

Yee, B., & Tygar, J. (1995). Secure coprocessors in electronic commerce applications. *Proceedings of the 1st Conference on USENIX Workshop on Electronic Commerce,* Vol. 1, (p. 14).

Zhang, S., Zhang, S., Chen, X., & Huo, X. (2010). Cloud computing research and development trend. *Second International Conference on Future Networks* (pp. 93-97). Sanya, Hainan, China.

Zhang, X., Wuwong, N., Li, H., & Zhang, X. (2010). HHH. Information security risk management framework for the cloud computing environments. *10th IEEE International Conference on Computer and Information Technology (CIT 2010),* (pp. 1328-1334). July 2010.

Zhang, Y., & Joshi, J. B. D. (2009). Access control and trust management for emerging multidomain environments. In Upadhyaya, S., & Rao, R. O. (Eds.), *Annals of emerging research in information assurance, security and privacy services.* Emerald Group Publishing Limited.

Zunnurhain, K., & Vrbsky, S. (2010). *Security attacks in solutions in clouds.* 2nd IEEE Conference on Cloud Computing Technology and Science (CloudCom), Poster, November 2010.

zur Muehlen, M. (2004). *Workflow-based process controlling: Foundation, design and application of workflow-driven process information systems.* Berlin, Germany: Logos.

About the Contributors

David G. Rosado has an MSc and PhD. in Computer Science from the University of Málaga (Spain) and from the University of Castilla-La Mancha (Spain), respectively. His research activities are focused on security for Information Systems and Cloud Computing. He has published several papers in national and international conferences on these subjects, and he is co-editor of a book and chapter books. Author of several manuscripts in national and international journals (*Information Software Technology, System Architecture, Network and Computer Applications*, etc.), He is a member of the GSyA research group of the Information Systems and Technologies Department at the University of Castilla-La Mancha, in Ciudad Real, Spain.

Daniel Mellado holds a PhD and MSc in Computer Science from the Castilla- La Mancha University (Spain) and holds a degree in Computer Science from the Autonomous University of Madrid (Spain), and he is Certified Information System Auditor by ISACA (Information System Audit and Control Association). He is Assistant Professor of the Department of Information Technologies and Systems at the Rey Juan Carlos University (Spain). He participates at the GSyA research group of the Department of Information Technologies and Systems at the Castilla- La Mancha University. He is civil servant at the Spanish Tax Agency (in Madrid, Spain), where he works as IT Auditor Manager. His research activities are security governance, security requirements engineering, security in cloud computing, security in information systems, secure software process improvement and auditory, quality and product lines. He has several dozens of papers in national and international conferences, journals and magazines on these subjects and co-author of several chapter books. He belongs to various professional and research associations (ASIA, ISACA, ASTIC, ACTICA, etc).

Eduardo Fernández-Medina holds a PhD and an MSc in Computer Science from the University of Sevilla. He is Associate Professor at the Escuela Superior de Informática of the University of Castilla-La Mancha at Ciudad Real (Spain), his research activity being in the field of security in databases, datawarehouses, web services and information systems, and also in security metrics. Fernández-Medina is co-editor of several books and chapter books on these subjects, and has several dozens of papers in national and international conferences (DEXA, CAISE, UML, ER, etc.). Author of several manuscripts in national and international journals (*Information Software Technology, Computers And Security, Information Systems Security*, etc.), he is Director of the GSyA research group of the Information Systems and Technologies Department at the University of Castilla-La Mancha, in Ciudad Real, Spain. He belongs to various professional and research associations (ATI, AEC, ISO, IFIP WG11.3 etc.).

Mario Piattini is MSc and PhD in Computer Science from the Politechnical University of Madrid. He is certified information system auditor by ISACA (Information System Audit and Control Association). He is Associate Professor at the Escuela Superior de Informática of the Castilla- La Mancha University (Spain). He is author of several books and papers on databases, security, software engineering, and information systems. He leads the ALARCOS research group of the Department of Information Technologies and Systems at the University of Castilla- La Mancha, in Ciudad Real (Spain). His research interests are: advanced database design, database quality, software metrics, object-oriented metrics, and software maintenance.

***

José Luis Fernández Alemán is a Ph.D. Associate Professor of Programming and Software Quality in the Department of Computer Science and Systems at the University of Murcia, Spain. He received the B.Sc. (Hons.) degree in 1994 and the Ph.D. degree in 2002, both in Computer Science from the University of Murcia. Currently, he is individual responsible for a joint doctoral programme in computer science between the University of Murcia and the University Mohammed V Souissi, awarded the excellence label by the Mediterranean Office for Youth. He has published several papers in the areas of e-learning and software engineering. Publications include journal articles in *Software and System Modeling, IEEE Software, IEEE Transactions on Education, Nursing Education Today,* and *Transactions on Edutainment*. Currently, his main research interest is in computer-based learning, software quality, requirements engineering and medical informatics. He has contributed to many Spanish-funded research projects whose topics were related to software engineering.

Thijs Baars, born in Arnhem, now living in Utrecht, The Netherlands, got an interest for Cloud Computing while pursuing his degree in Information Science at the Department of Information and Computing Science at Utrecht University, The Netherlands. His research revolves around information security, online reverse auctions, knowledge networks, social networks, business intelligence, intellectual property, and cloud computing. In his research, he attempts to make thorough usage of diverse range of both qualitative and quantitative methods. He loves to tinker about the ways information systems will change human life now and in the near future, which is reflected in his research: it will always pertain to clear business goals. Please visit http://www.thijsbaars.nl for more information.

Thar Baker has a B.Sc. degree in Computer Science in 1999, a H.Dip. degree in Data Security in 2001, and M.Sc. degree in High Complex Distributed Systems in 2005. In 2010, he finished his PhD in Cloud Computing Systems from Liverpool John Moores University, UK, where he worked thereafter as a Post-Doctoral Research Associate in the School of Computing and Mathematical Sciences. Currently, Thar is a Lecturer of Future Networks and Distributed Systems in the School of Computing, Mathematics and Digital technology @ Manchester Metropolitan University, UK, and a member of Future Networks and Distributed Systems group. The main topics of his research are Distributed Computing (Grid, Cluster, Cloud, Data-Intensive Computing, Utility). He is also the author of many research papers. He is been a track chair and a PCM of leading conferences in Cloud Computing and has served as a referee for a number of scientific journals and conferences.

José Campos is a Statistics Professor at Simon Bolivar University, Coastal Campus and at the Computer Engineering Faculty, Andrés Bello Catholic University. He got a Statistics Science Bachelor from Universidad Central de Venezuela (2000). His current research interests include applied statistics to environment, health, computer engineering and blended learning.

Ali Chehab received his Bachelor degree in EE from the American University of Beirut (AUB) in 1987, the Master's degree in EE from Syracuse University, and the PhD degree in ECE from the University of North Carolina at Charlotte, in 2002. From 1989 to 1998, he was a Lecturer in the ECE Department at AUB. He rejoined the ECE Department at AUB as an Assistant Professor in 2002 and became an Associate Professor in 2008. His research interests are VLSI Testing and Information Security and Trust.

Eduardo B. Fernandez (http://www.cse.fau.edu/~ed) is a professor in the Department of Computer Science and Engineering at Florida Atlantic University in Boca Raton, Florida. He has published numerous papers as well as several books on computer security and software architecture. His current interests include security patterns and cloud computing security. He holds a MS degree in Electrical Engineering from Purdue University and a Ph.D. in Computer Science from UCLA.

Javier Gonzalez is a Researcher at the Proteus laboratory of the GISUM group in the University of Malaga. Currently, he is working on the FP7 European Project PASSIVE and more specifically on its monitoring infrastructure. He has published international peer-reviewed publications related to the project. His research interests are mainly (although not limited to) security related topics such as monitoring in the Cloud Computing field.

Keiko Hashizume is a PhD student of the Department of Computer Science and Engineering at Florida Atlantic University (FAU). She received a Master of Science degree in Computer Engineering from Florida Atlantic University. She received her Bachelor's degree in System Engineering from University of Lima, Peru. For her Master's thesis, she worked on cryptographic patterns for web services under the direction of Dr. Eduardo B. Fernandez. She is a member of the Security Group at FAU, which is led by Dr. Fernandez. Currently she is working on security research in Cloud Computing.

Shareeful Islam is currently working at school of ACE, University of East London, UK. He received the PhD Technische Universität München, Germany. He received M.Sc. in Information Communication System Security from Royal Institute of Technology (KTH), Sweden and M.Sc. in Computer Science and B.Sc. (Hon's) in Applied Physics and Electronics (APE) from the University of Dhaka, Bangladesh. He is a Fellow of the British Higher Education Academy (HEA). He worked as an Assistant Professor, Institute of Information Technology, University of Dhaka. He has published more than 30 referred papers in high quality journals and international conferences. He participated in EU, industry, and KTP projects. His research interest and expertise is risk management, requirements engineering, security, privacy, and trust.

Wassim Itani was born in Beirut, Lebanon. He received his BE in Electrical Engineering, with distinction, from Beirut Arab University in 2001 and his ME in Computer and Communications Engineering from the American University of Beirut in 2003. Currently he is a PhD candidate in the Department of

Electrical and Computer Engineering at the American University of Beirut. Wassim's research interests include wireless and body sensor networks security and privacy, cloud computing trust and security protocols, and cryptographic protocols performance evaluation.

J. Jorda received a Master of Science in 1993 and a PhD in computer science in 1996. Since 2001, he is associate professor at the Paul Sabatier University (Toulouse, France). He has worked on memory organization of supercomputers (memory architecture of high performance computers, data placement in memory) and resource virtualization on distributed systems. His current research themes concern efficient memory accesses on GPU (code optimization, data placement and memory architecture) and storage virtualization on grid and cloud computing. He was involved in the ViSaGe project (Storage Virtualization applied to Computer grids) funded by the ANR (French National Research Agency), and is technical leader of the SVC project (Secure Virtual Cloud project, funded by the French government) for the secure virtualized storage implementation.

James B.D. Joshi is an Associate Professor and the Director of the Laboratory for Education and Research on Security Assured Information Systems (LERSAIS) in the School of Information Sciences at the University of Pittsburgh. His research interests include role-based access control, trust management, and secure interoperability. Joshi has a PhD in computer engineering from Purdue University. He is a member of IEEE and the ACM.

Ayman Kayssi was born in Lebanon. He studied electrical engineering and received the BE degree, with distinction, in 1987 from the American University of Beirut (AUB), and the MSE and PhD degrees from the University of Michigan, Ann Arbor, in 1989 and 1993, respectively. In 1993, he joined the Department of Electrical and Computer Engineering (ECE) at AUB, where he is currently a Full Professor. His research interests are in information security and in integrated circuit design and test. He is a senior member of IEEE and a member of ACM.

Kashif Kifayat received his PhD in Computer Science from Liverpool John Moores University. He worked as a research fellow in network security for two years in the School of Computing & Mathematical Science at Liverpool John Moores University, and he is currently working as a Lecturer. His research interests include network security, security of complex and scaleable systems and security in wireless sensor networks.

Michael Mackay is a Lecturer in the School of Computing and Mathematics at Liverpool John Moores University where his research specialises in network protocols and internetworking. He completed his PhD at Lancaster University in 2005 focussing on IPv6 transitioning and early 2006 he was also involved in the IST 6NET Project. From September 2006 he worked on the IST ENTHRONE 2 Project where his research focussed on Caching and CDNs. Throughout this time, he was also involved in the JANET QoS Development project studying the deployment of QoS on the UK academic network. Finally, until early 2010 he was working on the IST EC-GIN Project looking at the networking aspects of Grid computing. More recently his research has focussed on Cloud Computing, applications of the Internet of Things, and critical infrastructures and security.

Antonio Maña received his PhD degrees in Computer Engineering from the University of Malaga. In 1995 he joined the Department of Computer Science of the University of Malaga where he is currently Professor. His research activities include security and software engineering, information and network security, smart cards, software protection, etc. He has more than 100 peer-reviewed publications. He participated in several EU projects and is the Principal Investigator of the UMA in SecFutur and AS-SERT4SOA projects. He is member of the Editorial Board of the *International Journal of Electronic Security and Digital Forensics* and reviewer of other international journals.

Madjid Merabti is Director of the School of Computing and Mathematical Sciences, Liverpool John Moores University, UK. He is a graduate of Lancaster University and has over 20 years experience in conducting research and teaching in Distributed Multimedia Systems (Networks, Operating Systems and Computer Security). Professor Merabti leads the Distributed Multimedia Systems and Security Research Group, which has a number of government and industry supported research projects. He is an Associate Editor of *IEEE Transactions on Multimedia* and *IEEE Computer Communications*, a Co-Editor in Chief of *Pervasive Computing and Communications*, and a member of the editorial board for the *Computer Communications Journal.* He is a member and chair of a number of conference TPCs and is the chair of the PostGraduate Networking Symposium series (PGNet) for UK PhD students.

Marina Meza graduated as a Doctor in Education from Universidad Pedagógica Experimental Libertador (UPEL) in 2007. She is a university Lecturer in the Language Department at Simon Bolivar University. Her current interests include cloud computing, use of cloud applications for learning languages, and ICTs for teaching English. She is currently working in a multidisciplinary team at Simon Bolivar University.

Mireya Morales graduated as MSc in Computer Science from Universidad Central de Venezuela (UCV) in 2004. She is a university Lecturer in Computer Engineering at Simon Bolivar University. Her current interests include computer and network security. She has also worked in a research in progress about a security method for a public health information system in Venezuela.

Haralambos Mouratidis is Reader at the School of Architecture, Computing and Engineering (ACE) at the University of East London (UEL). He holds a B.Eng. (Hons) from the University of Wales, Swansea (UK), and a M.Sc. and PhD from the University of Sheffield (UK). He is also a Fellow of the Higher Education Academy (HEA) and a Professional Member of the British Computer Society (BCS). His research interests lie in the area of secure software systems engineering, requirements engineering, information systems development and agent oriented software engineering. He has published more than 100 papers and he has secured funding as Principal Investigator from national – Engineering and Physical Sciences Research Council, Royal Academy of Engineering, Technology Strategy Board (TSB) - and international – European Union- funding bodies as well as industrial funding -British Telecom, ELC, Powerchex - towards his research.

Antonio Muñoz is a postdoc researcher in the GISUM group at the University of Malaga. He holds his PhD an MSc degree in Computer Science and a Postgraduate Master degree in Software Engineer and Artificial Intelligence, both of them from the University of Malaga. His principal research interests are in the area of agent technology, digital content protection, cryptographic hardware based systems, security patterns, and security engineering. Antonio was involved in the EU Sixth Framework Programme project within the projects Ubisec, Serenity, and is currently in the EU Seventh Framework Programme projects OKKAM, ASSERT4SOA and PASSIVE.

Abdelaziz M'zoughi received the Diploma in Electronic engineering from the Ecole Nationale de l'Aviation Civile, Toulouse, France, in 1978, and PhD degrees in Computer Science from the University Paul Sabatier of Toulouse, in 1982. Currently, he is professor in the Department of Computer Science at the University Paul Sabatier. His research interests include high performance computing systems and architectures, in particular multiprocessor architecture design, data access and memory management, and storage virtualization in grid and cloud environment. He was leader of the ViSaGe project (Storage Virtualization applied to Computer grids) funded by the ANR and is involved in the SVC project (Secure Virtual Cloud project) for the secure virtualized storage implementation.

Qi Shi received his PhD in Computing from Dalian University of Technology, P.R.C. He worked as a Research Associate for the Department of Computer Science at the University of York in the UK. He then joined the School of Computing and Mathematical Sciences at Liverpool John Moores University in the UK, and is currently a Professor in Computer Security and Head of Research in the School. His research interests include network security, security protocol design, formal security models, intrusion detection, and ubiquitous computing security. He is supervising a number of research projects in these research areas.

Marco Spruit is an Assistant Professor at the Department of Information and Computing Science at Utrecht University, The Netherlands. He received his PhD from the University of Amsterdam, The Netherlands. His research revolves around knowledge discovery processes to help achieve organizational goals through data mining techniques, business intelligence methods, linguistic engineering techniques and social web technologies. Additionally, he investigates information security models and cloud computing frameworks as infrastructural safeguards and enablers for knowledge discovery processes, respectively. His strategic research objective is to realise and valorise a multi-domain knowledge discovery platform. Please visit http://m.spru.it for more information.

Hassan Takabi is a PhD student in the School of Information Sciences and a member of the Laboratory of Education and Research on Security Assured Information Systems (LERSAIS) at the University of Pittsburgh. His research interests include access control models; trust management; privacy and Web security; usable privacy and security; and security, privacy, and trust issues in cloud computing environments. Takabi has an MS in information technology from Sharif University of Technology, Iran. He is student member of IEEE and the ACM.

Miguel Torrealba graduated as MSc in Computer Science from Universidad Central de Venezuela (UCV) in 2003. He is a university Lecturer in Computer Engineering at Simon Bolivar University and a member of CRIPTORED, a thematic network for information security. His current interests include computer and network security. Since 2005, he has been a consultant in IT security and management.

Edgar R. Weippl (CISSP, CISA, CISM, CRISC, CSSLP, CMC) is Research Director of SBA Research and Associate Professor (Privatdozent) at the Vienna University of Technology. His research focuses on applied concepts of IT-security and e-learning. Edgar is member of the editorial board of *Computers & Security* (COSE) and he organizes the ARES conference. After graduating with a Ph.D. from the Vienna University of Technology, Edgar worked for two years in a research startup. He then spent one year teaching as an Assistant Professor at Beloit College, WI. From 2002 to 2004, while with the software vendor, he worked as a consultant in New York, NY and Albany, NY, and in Frankfurt, Germany. In 2004, he joined the Vienna University of Technology and founded together with A Min Tjoa and Markus Klemen the research center SBA Research.

Nobukazu Yoshioka is a Researcher at the National Institute of Informatics, Japan. Dr. Nobukazu Yoshioka received his B.E degree in Electronic and Information Engineering from Toyama University in 1993. He received his M.E. and Ph.D. degrees in School of Information Science from Japan Advanced Institute of Science and Technology in 1995 and 1998, respectively. From 1998 to 2002, he was with Toshiba Corporation, Japan. From 2002 to 2004 he was a researcher, and since August 2004, he has been an Associate Professor, in National Institute of Informatics, Japan. His research interests include cloud computing, security software engineering, agent technology, object-oriented methodology, software engineering, and software evolution. He is a member of the Information Processing Society of Japan (IPSJ), the Institute of Electronics, information and Communication Engineers (IEICE) and Japan Society for Software Science and Technology (JSSST). He has been a board member of JSSST since 2012.

Belén Cruz Zapata is a Ph. D. student in Computer Science at the University of Murcia, Spain. She received the B.Sc. degree in 2010 in Computer Science from the University of Murcia. She was awarded an honorable mention for academic excellence in 2011 for the B.Sc. In 2011 she finished a Master's degree in New Technologies in Computer Science with specialization in software technologies from the University of Murcia. She is currently collaborating with the Software Engineering Research Group from University of Murcia on topics related to software security, Cloud Computing, and model driven development.

Index